RUPERT HUGHES

RUPERT HUGHES

A HOLLYWOOD LEGEND

BY

JAMES O. KEMM

POMEGRANATE PRESS
BEVERLY HILLS, CA

This is a Pomogranate Press, Ltd. book.

RUPERT HUGHES
A HOLLYWOOD LEGEND

Copyright 1997 James O. Kemm

Library of Congress Catalog Card Number 97-0607155

Hardcover Edition ISBN: 0-938817-49-3

First Printing September 1997

10 9 8 7 6 5 4 3 2 1

For Pomegranate Press, Ltd.

Cover & Interior Design: Cheryl Carrington
Editor: Robyn M. Weaver

Printed and bound in USA

POMEGRANATE PRESS, LTD.
P.O. Box 17217
Beverly Hills, CA 90209-3217

CONTENTS

INTRODUCTION vii

1 THE FAMILY HERITAGE 1
2 FROM ST. CHARLES TO NEW YORK 11
3 A WHIRLWIND IN MOTION 25
4 BOOKS, PLAYS, REAL-LIFE DRAMA 33
5 ALL FOR A GIRL 41
6 NEWFOUND SUCCESS 51
7 A NEW HOME, A NEW STYLE 63
8 AND THEN THE WAR 71
9 A MILITARY CENSOR 85
10 AN EMINENT AUTHOR 93
11 ON TO HOLLYWOOD 103
12 AND NOW A DIRECTOR 119
13 AT SUNDAY BRUNCH 131
14 OF HAPPINESS AND GRIEF 141
15 THE MID-TWENTIES 161
16 THE GEORGE WASHINGTON FUROR 171
17 AN ARABIAN NIGHTS MANSION 181
18 WAR FILMS AND STORIES 193
19 THE EARLY THIRTIES 209
20 GOING LIKE SIXTY 219
21 A SPECIAL FRIEND 231
22 RECOGNITION AND CONTROVERSY 241
23 AN EPIC NOVEL 255
24 BACK IN UNIFORM 267
25 THE DIFFICULT YEARS 277
26 A MENACE PERCEIVED 287
27 "LONG OVERDUE" 297
28 IN HIS EIGHTIES 311
29 THE ESTATE BATTLE 345
30 A LIFE IN PERSPECTIVE 321

   ENDNOTES 333
   INDEX 361

INTRODUCTION

In July, 1938, a shy, lanky aviator—well-known as a wealthy motion picture producer—piloted an experimental plane to an around-the-world speed record. But to a petite woman of seventy-two years in Springfield, Missouri, the historic flight by young Howard Hughes was not entirely unexpected.

"He's Rupert's nephew, you know," Katherine Baldridge reminded her grandchildren, of whom I was one. She often measured the accomplishments of Hughes family members against those of the multi-talented Rupert Hughes, who was known primarily as an author but was also a screen director, composer, lecturer, soldier, and radio commentator. He and his brothers and sister, each of whom became successful, were her first cousins, born of her mother's sister, Jean Amelia Summerlin Hughes.

While a college freshman—having edited the Springfield (Missouri) high school newspaper—I wrote to Rupert, inquiring with the eagerness of youth about the job outlook for a beginning writer at a movie studio. To my surprise, he responded promptly with a warm letter, without glossing over the facts of movie-making during the turbulent world of 1940 when jobs were scarce.

More than four decades later, my daughter Kathy, a librarian, brought me several pages of notes jotted down from references to Rupert Hughes in the Reader's Guide to Periodical Literature. I then began reading magazine articles and stories he had written, collecting his books, and copying passages about him from other publications. In the process, I was hooked, wanting to learn more about this man who often said he wanted to live a thousand years and a thousand lives.

This book is the outgrowth of that quest for Rupert Hughes— the story of his life and untiring work. The search led me to libraries throughout the United States, to towns where he lived, and to interviews and correspondence with persons who knew him.

Although acknowledgments of source material are indicated in endnotes, certain persons and institutions deserve special mention.

My heartfelt appreciation goes to Barbara Cameron for her hospitality and for providing family photographs and information about her grandfather, Rupert Hughes, with whom she lived for more than two years. Likewise, the cooperation of her sister, Elspeth (Beth) De Pould, is gratefully acknowledged. The reminiscences provided by these granddaughters have been extremely helpful.

Especially deserving of thanks is Kimberley Cameron of the Reece Halsey North literary agency in Tiburon, California. A great-granddaughter of Rupert, she became aware of this biography when it was near completion and agreed to act as my literary representative. Her encouragement, as well as her cooperation in supplying me with copies of some of Rupert's personal letters, will always be remembered. I also extend my appreciation to Kathryn Leigh Scott, publisher of Pomagranate Press, Ltd., for her willingness to publish this book.

Ruby H. Hughes (Mrs. Felix Hughes), who donated the papers of her brother-in-law Rupert to the University of Southern California, provided much material and an insight into many facets of Rupert's life and career. For her assistance prior to her death in 1992, I am grateful.

The hospitality extended by Colleen Moore (Mrs. Paul Maginot), star of several Hughes silent motion pictures, will never be forgotten; she shared memories of the author/director who helped boost her career. Similar details were provided by the lovely actress Eleanor Boardman (the Countess d'Arrast). Both are now deceased.

Many university, public, and private libraries have made it possible to study Hughes correspondence and manuscripts. Especially appreciated is the cooperation of Leona L. Wise, Gifts and Exchange Librarian for the University Libraries at the University of Southern California, who provided access to the Rupert Hughes papers in the Doheny Memorial Library there. Likewise, the helpfulness of Frank Paluka, then head of Special Collections at the University Libraries, University of Iowa, is acknowledged. Debts of gratitude are also owed to the Beinecke Rare Book & Manuscript Library at Yale University; the Princeton University

Library; Honnold Library for the Claremont Colleges; the Archives and the Library at Case Western Reserve University; the Margaret Herrick Library at the Academy of Motion Picture Arts and Sciences; the State Historical Society of Missouri; the Archives of the St. Charles (Mo.) County Historical Society; and the Will Rogers Memorial in Claremore, Oklahoma. Library and administrative personnel at these institutions have been exceedingly cooperative, as have staff members of the Tulsa City-County Library System.

Valuable information has been obtained at the Film Study Center, Museum of Modern Art, in New York, where Charles Silver, Supervisor, made it possible to view Rupert Hughes silent films.

Through tours provided by Scott Lichtig, Los Angeles attorney who owns the Arabian Nights home Hughes built, and Brother Stephen, Manager of the St. John of God Retirement and Care Center, which includes a mansion Hughes leased, it was possible to see the surroundings in which the subject lived and worked.

Many references to Rupert Hughes in books and magazines have been brought to my attention by my good friend Jack Spears of Tulsa, author of *Hollywood: The Golden Era* and other books and a long-time contributor to *Films in Review*, who has provided much encouragement as well as information from his extensive collection of Hollywood books and other materials. His help is deeply appreciated. I am also indebted to Paul L. Freese, of the Los Angeles law firm of Kindel & Anderson, who permitted me to examine Hughes family documents and letters he accumulated in connection with the Howard Hughes estate case.

Throughout my journey of rediscovering Rupert, I have had the cooperation and patient understanding of my wife, Betty Ann, who has traveled with me to libraries and other reference sources and has assisted in taking notes. Her enthusiasm for this project has been shared by my other family members—daughters Nancy Pomerantz, Kathy Doss, and Martha Barrett; and by my sister, Esther Hollender, and brothers Johnny and Richard Kemm, the latter three of whom are now deceased.

In presenting what is intended to be an objective treatment of the life and career of a gifted man, I dedicate this book to the memory of my grandmother, Katherine Baldridge, and my mother, Vivian Kemm, my family links to Rupert Hughes.

CHAPTER ONE

THE FAMILY HERITAGE

"You have made a loathsome failure of your first experience of independence."

t was advice and criticism that could have benefited the rich young heir. Unfortunately, Howard Hughes, Jr., paid no heed to the lengthy letter from Uncle Rupert.

The object of much sympathy after the recent death of his father, eighteen-year-old Howard had deeply disappointed his paternal grandparents and infuriated two uncles, Rupert and Felix Hughes.

Rupert, a highly successful novelist, screenwriter and director, was especially indignant over Howard's behavior. The lovingly crafted but bluntly critical letter he wrote revealed as much about his own character as that of his nephew who eventually would become one of the world's richest men.

"This letter may not be easy to read; it is certainly hard to write," Rupert began the letter, dated April 19, 1924. "You may think it an impertinence from the start to finish, but I feel that I must say what I say out of love for your father and out of my desire to be the best possible friend to you."

Young Howard, or "Son" as the family called him, was the privileged son of an overly protective mother, who died when he was sixteen, and a father who had great hopes for his only offspring and wanted him to have a good education.

But now Son was an orphan and the heir to three-fourths of the Houston-based Hughes Tool Company founded by Howard Robard Hughes, Sr. The remaining one-quarter of the prosperous drill bit manufacturing company was left to Felix Turner and Jean Amelia Hughes, parents of the deceased, and to Felix, his brother. Nothing went to Rupert, who was already well-off financially.

Young Howard wasted little time before finagling his way into buying the portion of Hughes Tool left to his grandparents and Uncle Felix, paying them much less than the shares were worth.

To think the young heir would treat his relatives in that way was anathema to Rupert. While directing movies, he had introduced his nephew to film-making during the teenager's visits to the sets. Rupert had also written popular stories and films based upon family love, reflecting his own feelings about his parents and siblings.

Rupert wrote that he had studied Howard's character for some time, and "though you have not invited me to do so, I will give you the results of it." And he did, for eight single-spaced, typed pages.

> You have good looks, wit and much magnetism. You had as a child and as a younger boy an extraordinary intelligence and imagination and ingenuity. Those last three qualities I have not found so marked in recent years.
>
> Two faults you seem to have which are splendid in moderation but dangerous in excess: selfishness, and a sense of thrift which tends to run almost to miserliness, with occasional outbursts of such recklessness as is common to people who are not inclined to be over-economical.
>
> You were a most lovable child and still have very lovable qualities, but then, as now, you have showed a tendency to give the least possible and take the maximum.

Rupert reminded Howard, "I have always endeavored to treat you with extravagant affection and cordiality. My house has been at your disposal and you have used it when it was convenient and left it when it was convenient." But Howard never acknowledged the hospitality.

After Howard, Sr., died, Rupert said, "My heart ached for you." When he learned Son would like to visit him, he telegraphed an invitation. Young Howard's grandparents, then staying in Rupert's home, were "weeping their hearts out in pity for you and were overjoyed to think that you actually longed to be with them in an hour of tragedy." But since then, wrote Rupert:

To my horror I have never seen an indication that the hour was tragic or in the least important to you. Since your father's death I have never heard you say one word in his praise, make one suggestion of a memorial to him or show any desire to emphasize his greatness or the importance of his splendid achievements. You referred to him a few times the first night you were here, but always in a joking, almost contemptuous and patronizing manner . . .

My father wept like a baby when I had to break to him the news of Howard's death. His first thought was that he must go to you at once and protect you from the possibility of robbery by people who might take advantage of your youth and inexperience.

To his stupefaction and mine it soon became evident that your trip to Los Angeles had nothing to do with a desire for consolation . . . Your very efforts at cleverness made it especially emphatic that you came out here on a business trip to make the best possible settlement of your father's will. You were unable to conceal your purpose, determination or your absolute grimness of intention.

After enumerating Howard's specific actions that had so disappointed his relatives, Rupert continued:

Dishonesty on your part in carrying out your father's expressed wishes, grasping determination to wrest from other people money that belongs to them, and a terrible reluctance to be generous can only result in robbing your life of friendship, love, and passion and all the things that make life beautiful and worth while . . .

For your own sake, consider what I have written very earnestly . . . . The prosperity of your soul and of your whole lifetime will hinge largely upon your actions in the next few years. If you have any real love of yourself, ponder these things seriously.

And realize that there are few things on earth that would give me more pleasure that to be devotedly and affectionately yours.

(Signed) Rupert Hughes.[1]

Legendary film producer Samuel Goldwyn lured him to Hollywood as one of the seven original "Eminent Authors" assigned to turn their novels and stories into screenplays. Unlike the others, Rupert Hughes adapted his talents to movie-making, became a successful writer and director, then stayed on as a leading figure in the West Coast film community.

However, screenwriting was only one facet of the Missouri-born author's productive career—a career he wished he could enjoy through a thousand lives in a thousand years.

His ancestors on both sides had come from Wales, England, and Scotland, landing in Virginia and North Carolina in the 17th and 18th centuries. Later generations moved westward to Kentucky and eventually to Iowa and Missouri.[2] From his forebears who served in the Revolutionary War, Blackhawk War, and the Civil War, Rupert inherited a patriotism and a willingness to enter the military service.

His own father, while teaching school, enlisted in the Missouri Militia, on the Union side, in the Civil War. But his mother, whose father had kept slaves, had one brother in the Union Army and another who was a Confederate soldier; she sympathized with the South. As a result, Rupert later wrote, he grew up thinking "both the North and South were infallibly right."[3]

Shortly after the Civil War ended, Felix Turner Hughes took Jean Amelia Summerlin as his bride in the little northeast Missouri town of Memphis. Jean, more than other girls he had known, loved beauty, literature and art. She wrote poetry and was a talented musician and omnivorous reader. Felix, at 26, was three and a half years older, tall and strong, with a keen mind and amiable disposition. Although his financial prospects appeared dim, Felix and Jean were married August 1, 1865, by Josiah Hildebrand, a Methodist minister.[4]

Within the next year, Felix fulfilled his boyhood dream when he was admitted to the bar in the state of Missouri. Soon after, the couple moved to Lancaster, the county seat of neighboring Schuyler County, where he set up his law practice.[5]

Their house was unpretentious, but attractive—a frame structure, with a white picket fence and a garden of modest size. Although Lancaster, a town of 500 in the gently rolling hills of northeastern Missouri, was outwardly calm, the Civil War's harsh realities had left an undercurrent of divided loyalties. Arguments sometimes erupted into gunfire, and it was not unusual for lawyers and judges to take pistols to court.[6]

In this setting, Jean and Felix began a family. Their first child was a daughter, Greta, born June 4, 1866.[7] By then Felix had been elected Superintendent of Schools for Schuyler County.[8] A second child, born September 9, 1869 was a boy. His parents named him Howard Robard Hughes [9]—a name both he and his son would carry.

This was a time of change, with railroads advancing from the East to the Middle West. Every town wanted to be on or near a railroad line. Rival railroad companies tried to enlist public support in areas where they hoped to gain rights of way. At a Lancaster town meeting, when supporters of one company threatened those favoring the other, Felix Hughes, taking the side of the second line, won the crowd over to his views. In appreciation, the Missouri, Iowa and Nebraska Railway Company hired him as its attorney to handle cases in the area.[10]

It was a joyous occasion when on May 14, 1872, the construction train for the Missouri, Iowa and Nebraska Railway entered Lancaster. As a historian wrote, "a great rally was held and a public dinner given." [11]

Just a few months before the railroad reached Lancaster, another important event occurred in the Hughes household. A third child, Rupert, was born on January 31, 1872. Many years later, Rupert described his arrival: "I was that great rarity, an eleven months' child, and I was born with a complete suit of hair." [12]

Within two years, another son arrived. Jean insisted the newcomer be named for his father, and so the baby, born October 1, 1874 became known as "young Felix." In 1876, a fifth child, Reginald, was born.[13]

Meanwhile, along with the railroad lawsuits, Felix the father continued practicing civil and criminal law, but despite the work and travel involved, he did not neglect his family.

One of the most exciting aspects of the Hughes children's early lives was accompanying their father on train trips to such places as Peoria or Keokuk, where they would watch the courtroom proceedings.[14] Such learning experiences were matched by the attention paid them by their mother.

At age five, Rupert learned to read from a first reader, following her around to ask what some of the words were.[15] Within two years of learning to read, his habit had him thinking about becoming a writer. His earliest attempts were at poetry, and when only seven, his first poem was published. It displayed the imaginative use of words that would characterize his later poetry and prose:

BE KIND

Be kind to the butterfly
That flutters harmlessly by.
Be kind to the dog —
Be kind to the frog
That sits and croaks on the log.
Be kind, be kind to everything
That walks on foot, or soars on wing.[16]

In 1879, the same year he wrote this poem, the Missouri, Iowa & Nebraska Railway rewarded his father for successfully handling court battles by naming him its solicitor general. Soon after, the family moved to Keokuk, Iowa, an important railroad center, where Felix established a law firm.[17]

After a short time, the family purchased a new red brick house, the appearance of which contrasted sharply with that of their modest home in Lancaster. There were bay windows on the front and side of the first floor, with railings above them on the second floor. A square tower on the roof, complete with gables, was topped by a widow's walk. Although the house was far from showy, its overall effect boasted that a family of substantial means lived there.[18]

One advantage of the house was its convenient location—less than two blocks from the First Ward School at Fifth and Fulton, which the Hughes children attended, and just a few blocks from the Mississippi River. The neighborhood was built high above the river, a magnet for youngsters, including Rupert. He later recalled that he spent "a large part of my boyhood" in the Mississippi.[19]

But the household happiness was marred considerably in 1880, when a sixth child, Jean, died a few months after her birth. Before the family could recover from this loss, the youngest boy, Reginald, died the same year at age five.[20]

Rupert later wrote about seeing his father, usually in command of his emotions, weeping uncontrollably after the baby's death. And Jean was nearly devastated by the loss of each beloved child. Years later she said she had neglected the surviving children after Reginald's death, but Rupert assured her this was untrue. If anything, she became overly concerned about their health, trying to protect them from normal diseases—mumps, measles, and typhoid fever. Rupert was sick from the latter for several months and accepted many financial bribes for taking medicine. He offered his mother a refund, but when she refused it, he "bought her a velocipede"—a popular term for a tricycle—"and rode it for her."[21]

Young Felix took bribes as well. His superb singing voice amazed everyone, but when he sang on the porch at sunrise, a neighbor paid him a penny a day to postpone his vocalizing until a later hour.[22]

At about this time, Rupert began writing plays, produced in the living room for the family and neighbors to view. The first of these, when he was nine, was titled "Little by Little," and Rupert played the lead "wonderfully badly," he recalled.[23]

The young producer not only devised plots for action-filled dramatic ventures, but wrote the scripts, designed costumes, and cast himself as the hero. He usually selected his brothers as villains, while neighborhood chums played lesser roles.[24]

In Jean's eyes, each of her children was the best at whatever talent he or she had. One day, after reading a newspaper article saying it was about time for another Shakespeare to appear, she told Rupert, "He may be at this moment a young lad standing at his mother's knee." She then hugged him and added, "Here he is now." [25]

The walls of their home were adorned with reproductions of great paintings; the family library contained a large number of books; and each child took piano and voice lessons. Rupert later called his mother "one of the most artistic souls I ever met, with as great a love for art and romance as my father for law. I was brought up on Greek sculpture and Italian art at her knee." [26]

This parental encouragement and education had a profound influence upon the Hughes children. In addition, the experiences Rupert had in Keokuk and the people he knew there shaped the plots and characterizations of some of his best short stories and novels.

As a schoolboy, he so enjoyed reading that whenever his mother offered to bring him something when she took out-of-town trips, he would ask for a biography of a famous person. A somewhat chubby lad, he looked so bookish and studious that his schoolmates nicknamed him "History" [27]—a label that stuck and became the name of a character in his first published book, a collection of stories about boys titled *The Lakerim Athletic Club*.

At ten, Rupert decided he needed a middle name, and chose to become the namesake of one of his favorite characters in history: Sir Walter Raleigh. He became known as Rupert Raleigh Hughes, signed his name that way, and so it stands in the records of schools he attended. It appeared on a diploma when he was awarded an honorary doctorate more than a half century later, even though he had dropped the middle name six years after first using it.[28]

When Rupert was eleven, another boy born to Jean and Felix—their seventh and last child—died before being named and is identified on a gravestone in Keokuk as Baby Hughes.[29] The parents made up for their grief by lavishing attention upon the surviving four, determined to provide for them the best educational opportunities affordable.

In Rupert's case, one of the joys of growing up in Keokuk was his friendship with Ed Brownell, a boy who lived across the street. Ed was the namesake of an uncle who was a close friend of Samuel Clemens, better known as Mark Twain. Clemens had lived in Keokuk in 1855 while working as a printer in his brother Orion's shop. He had then set out for South America, but, getting sidetracked in New Orleans, had become a Mississippi River pilot.[30]

Rupert devoured Mark Twain's books about the river and felt a kinship with him. Both had been born in Missouri, had lived in Keokuk, had pals by the same name, and knew the attraction of the mighty Mississippi. Once, when Twain visited in Keokuk, Rupert obtained his autograph and heard him tell about some of his experiences.[31] There is no doubt that this influenced the ambitions of young Rupert, who later would write and speak about his admiration for the famous author.

Meanwhile, Rupert was a good student, learning to speak Latin by the time he was a teenager, all the while showing promise of becoming a writer. It has been said that when he was only twelve, he sought a publisher for a collection of his poems.[32] Whether his work was accepted is not known.

In educating their children, Jean and Felix did not neglect their religious training. Rupert attended Sunday School regularly, said his daily prayers, and at age thirteen joined the Congregational Church. He had become well versed in the Scriptures by the time he entered college.[33]

In 1885, Rupert's father's career took a significant step forward when financier Jay Gould broke up the Wabash system. With the dismantlement, the Missouri, Iowa & Nebraska, which had merged into the Wabash, was reorganized as the Keokuk & Western Railroad and Felix became its president and general counsel. He proved such a good administrator that the railroad paid a dividend the first year.

He also continued to practice law and was active in civic affairs, becoming recognized as an outstanding community leader. His work schedule was arduous, but brought increasing financial rewards. The career progress was fortuitous, for the children were developing interests and ambitions that would require substantial amounts of money.

As Rupert put it, "My mother instilled the ambitions, and my father found the funds." [34]

Billie Burke

MISS BILLIE BURKE, the fascinating screen favorite, is starring in "Gloria's Romance," the new George Kleine motion picture novel from the pen of Mr. and Mrs. Rupert Hughes, through special arrangement with F. Ziegfeld, Jr. In her mighty conquest for supremacy she has risen to stellar heights in filmdom. Her mastery of technique in a new art, the radiant sparkle of her eyes, and a smile of cheerful vivacity, proclaim her an apostle of happiness.

CHAPTER TWO

FROM ST. CHARLES TO NEW YORK

"I had an awfully good time, studied hard,
played hard, rushed the girls hard, and joined
in all deviltry that was afoot."

W hen fourteen-year-old Rupert went away to boarding school in 1886, he entered an environment vastly different from the towns in which he had lived. About the only similarity between St. Charles, Missouri, and Keokuk, Iowa, was that both were important river centers.

St. Charles also had a reputation as a city of learning. In the mid-1830s a local woman and her son organized and endowed St. Charles College as a school for boys "of all ages." Although it became the first chartered Methodist college west of the Mississippi River, it was run as a nonsectarian boarding school and provided a classical education and military training until the federal government took over the building during the Civil War to serve as a prison and hospital. After the war, it returned to its original purpose, again offering instruction and boarding facilities, along with optional military training.[1]

When Rupert and his brother Howard enrolled there for preparatory courses, the place had an atmosphere of strict discipline. But there were also games and recreation, parties, and church social events.

A military flavor prevailed, with students wearing uniforms. Rupert was chosen drum major of a band consisting of three drums and two fifes. He was, he later said, "a veritable peacock." [2] Already instilled with a deep sense of patriotism, he enjoyed parading on the drill field and took naturally to military life.

His interests ranged in other directions, too, such as writing more substantial plays than those produced in the living room back home. Recognized by his teachers as a bright youngster with exceptional talent, he was allowed to produce his plays in the Opera House on St. Charles's Main Street. Constructed in 1880, this unusual building had a dry goods store on the first floor, with a separate Main Street entrance leading to the Opera House upstairs. [3]

In later years, local historians would point with pride to the fact that the first public performance of a play by Rupert Hughes, whom they referred to as the college's "most famous scholar," occurred in the Opera House.

On January 22, 1887, at the Annual Entertainment given by St. Charles College, Rupert acted in two one-act plays, each time in a female role—as Ruth Lawrence in *The California Jungle* and as Kitty in *Barr's Borders: or, That Pesky Widow*. It was traditional for boys to play the female roles in plays put on by a school for boys; and in *Barr's Borders*, five of the seven cast members played such parts. One of the two in male roles was Howard Hughes, as Mr. Algernon Smythe. Rupert has been credited with *Barr's Borders* as his first play. One historian said he also wrote *Tit for Tat*, which led off the evening program, as his first musical. [4]

Rupert was also treasurer of the Agassiz Society, a literary club, and played shortstop on the baseball team, while Howard won honors at the annual field day exercises. [5]

Although it was an all-male school, there were opportunities to meet local girls at church and other gatherings. Church attendance was mandatory for the boys, and early in the school year Rupert carried on a glowing romance with a freckle-faced lass he met at one of the services.

Finally, it was June and time for year-end activities, including a week-long encampment of military cadets at Creve Coeur Lake. Commencement Week included contests of oratory, declamation, and essays, all before a full crowd assembled at the Opera House. Along with a sermon by a Presbyterian minister, there were musical numbers, such as a rendition of "Sunrise" by a singing quartet that included Rupert.

Then came the essay contest, with two boys preceding Rupert's reading of his essay. His title was by far the longest: "Love, the Most Complex and the Most Simple, the Gentlest and the Harshest, the Newest and the Oldest Passion that Has Ever Influenced Mankind." Perhaps he was thinking of his infatuation with the freckle-faced lass. In any event, when judges announced the results, they awarded first honors and the silver medal to "Rupert R. Hughes of Keokuk, Iowa." It was the first of many words of praise Rupert would receive for his writings about love and its complexities. Rupert also won the silver medal for highest scholarship. [6]

Later that night, he worked up enough nerve to put his arm around the girl who had been the object of his affection all year, but she gently put a halt to the only physical contact he ever had with her. Soon their love was only a memory, and when he next saw her, she was married with children. [7]

Before long Rupert's mind was on other matters, including plans to attend Western Reserve Academy in Hudson, Ohio, to prepare for undergraduate study at Yale University. When he entered the academy in the fall of 1887, fifteen-year-old Rupert was about two years younger than the average age of the other students. Despite his precocious appearance and small stature—about five feet five—he was a sturdy lad who enjoyed athletics. He soon became involved in activities of all sorts, often playing a leadership role. [8]

Times were difficult at what he later called little "Hardscrabble Academy." The school in Hudson, a small town between Akron and Cleveland, was barely able to meet its financial obligations and certainly unable to afford a new tennis court, which students wanted. That did not stop Rupert and his classmates, who raised the necessary amount by obtaining donations.

As at St. Charles College, Rupert and the other students attended church regularly in the village—which most of them enjoyed because they could meet Hudson girls. Although Rupert was an ardent student of the Bible and firm in his Christian beliefs, when it came time for his first appearance as a chapel speaker, he was so terrified he could hardly say anything.

Surely it never occurred to him that one day he would appear before audiences large and small, be paid handsomely for doing so, and become one of America's foremost after-dinner speakers and masters of ceremonies.

As for now, he involved himself in student activities, including the tennis team, dramatics, and glee club. He told an interviewer decades later, he "had an awfully good time, studied hard, played hard, rushed the girls hard, and joined in all deviltry that was afoot." [9]

Ambitious and anxious to get on with his education, Rupert intended to go to Yale as soon as possible after finishing at the academy. But his plans changed when a friend, Fred Ashley, persuaded him to pursue his undergraduate studies at Adelbert College, a liberal arts college that had recently moved from Hudson to Cleveland. Ashley, who later became chief assistant librarian at the Library of Congress, convinced him that Adelbert could prepare him for graduate or professional study at Yale.[10] Rupert opted for Adelbert and enrolled as a freshman in the fall of 1888.

The enrollment at Adelbert College consisted of about 100 males. With the exception of those from Cleveland, they lived in Adelbert Hall, a rambling brick structure referred to as having "the romantic aroma of an Oxford Quad." Despite the outward dignity of the place, the atmosphere in the rooms was one of frivolity. One member of the 1894 class, two years behind Rupert, recalled that the young Hughes spent most of his time writing. "He was that peculiar creature who LIKES to write. When one went to see him, he would usually want to consult about a story, a poem, a play, or an editorial for *The Adelbert*, of which he was editor. Or maybe it was an overture or the score of an opera he was composing. He was a fine piano player."

Rupert did not play just any piano; he had his own piano in his room, a sure indication that he was more affluent than most of the students. But his playing did not make him popular with everyone. Having acquired the habit of getting by on little sleep, he would study until midnight, and then—as classmate Frederick Waite would recall—start playing the piano while another student played the flute, just after Waite had returned from working off-campus and wanted to get some sleep. The sound would go right through the ceiling. [11]

But the piano was just one of Rupert's interests at Adelbert. If something was going on, he was usually in the middle of it, or in charge. He still enjoyed baseball, playing left field on the class team; but with only ten members in his class, it would have been surprising if he had not participated. He also played left tackle on the class football team.

A bigger achievement was winning the bicycle race, doing a mile in two minutes and eight-and-a-half seconds during Field Day in his junior year. He became vice president of the lawn tennis team and organized the college's second annual Junior Prom. [12]

Active in the Dramatic Club, he appeared as a footman in a farce called *Hearing and Believing,* and a year later as a fortune hunter in a one-act farce, *Suspended Animation.* He was treasurer in his freshman year, Class Poet in his sophomore and junior years, and Senior Class Captain. He also served as marshal and recording secretary of the Philozetian literary society. [13]

Other activities were precursors of the direction his career would take. His first published short story appeared in *The Adelbert,* the college newspaper, while he was a freshman. He became assistant editor while a junior, and editor in his senior year. [14] Meanwhile, he wrote for and was illustrator for *The Reserve,* the yearbook, as a sophomore and junior, drawing "pictures of young men in swallowtail suits and girls with bustles and bangs," and became an editor of *The Reserve '92.*

While in college, he also made his first sale to *Life* magazine—not for a story or article, but for a drawing. His skills as a public speaker were also being honed. He entered oratory contests and won honorable mention as a sophomore with his declamation of Cassius's Address to Brutus from Shakespeare's *Julius Caesar.* During the Junior Exhibition in April, 1891, he gave the honor oration on "Culture for Its Own Sake." [15]

He was elected president of the Delta Upsilon fraternity chapter,[16] and his comradeship with members provided lasting memories of good times at Adelbert. Throughout his life he would prize his affiliation with the fraternal organization.

While at Adelbert he took private music lessons from 1890 to 1892 with Wilson G. Smith, a performance, voice, and composition teacher who had studied in Europe and composed numerous songs and performance pieces. [17]

In Adelbert College records, the Hughes name is always listed as Rupert Raleigh Hughes. The alliterative double R initials inspired innovative classmates to call him "Railroad" (no doubt because of his father's position) or "Romulus Remus" Hughes.[18] To others, however, he remained known as "History."

In the 1892 *Reserve,* the year he was editor, there is a quotation for each of the young men. The one for Hughes was: "He capers, he dances, he has the eyes of youth, he writes verses, and speaks out of the common style." [19]

Classmate Clarence Bill recalled in 1936 that Rupert had been "preeminent for something better and rarer than money. Young as he was, he had the most exquisite manners, quiet, gentle ways and he knew what to say and how to say it. And how the girls did like him! I remember to this day when I introduced him to Mrs. Bill, a young girl then, and what a delightful fellow she thought him." [20]

As his senior year ended, Rupert was selected to give the Latin Salutatory Commencement address and was chosen for membership in Phi Beta Kappa. Armed with the prestigious key that went with that honor, along with a Bachelor of Arts degree and a mustache he sported in the class graduation picture,[21] he was ready to move on again, this time to become a graduate student at Yale University.

Rupert settled into a rigorous schedule in New Haven, Connecticut: mainly one of serious study to broaden his knowledge of literature, while doing some writing. Knowing his father had hoped he would prepare for a law career, Rupert dreaded telling him that he had decided to concentrate on English literature. He aimed for a doctorate and then a teaching position at a college or university. But to his relief, Felix Hughes assured him that it was entirely up to him to choose his own career. "Go ahead on your own lines," urged the father, "and I will back you to my last dollar."[22]

While at Yale, Rupert spent daytime hours in the library, then loaded up on books to take to his room, where he would spend most of the night reading. He would sleep until mid-morning and start out again on the same schedule.[23]

His studies included research on satires by Bishop Joseph Hall, first published in the late 1500s. Unable to find the earliest editions in the Yale Library, he obtained information he needed from the library at Harvard University. When Rupert wrote to thank the librarian for his help, he apologized for not doing so earlier, explaining he had been seriously ill for a month.[24] The nature of his illness is not known, but it was an unusual occurrence, for he was in good health throughout most of his life. It is doubtful that a month's illness interrupted to any great extent his studying, writing, or composing.

He was already a published composer, having had two songs, "Tears, Idle Tears" and "In a Gondola," published in 1892.[25] While at Yale, he also wrote most of an epic poem published later.

Despite his enjoyment of graduate study, Rupert was restless as he approached the end of the school year. More and more, he wanted to get on with his career, and after weighing the pros and cons of continuing to study toward a Doctor of Philosophy degree in literature, by May he settled on a Master of Arts degree, having completed most of the requirements, and set out on a career of "creative work."[26] He packed his bags and headed for New York City.

The telegram Felix Turner Hughes read in Keokuk, Iowa, brought startling news from his son who had moved to New York only a few months earlier. It announced the twenty-one-year-old Rupert's intention to take a bride. The betrothed young lady, with whom he had carried on a whirlwind courtship that began while he was at Yale, was Agnes Wheeler Hedge, daughter of Charles L. and Julia Hedge of Syracuse, New York.[27]

A graduate of the Keble School in Syracuse in 1892, Agnes had toured Europe with friends before enrolling that fall at Evelyn College. During her second year there she met Rupert while on a visit to New York. At the time of her marriage she was nineteen.[28]

In keeping with Felix's tradition of permitting his sons and daughter to make their own decisions, he wired Rupert his blessings, wished the couple happiness, and sent a gift of five hundred dollars. But knowing the problems encountered in establishing a home while embarking on a new career, the devoted father—undoubtedly with Jean's concurrence—also began to provide a monthly allowance for Rupert and Agnes that would continue for years.

This financial subsidy was no more than the parents had provided and would continue to provide for their other children. Greta, who had married James Frederick Howell in Milwaukee in 1889, was receiving every opportunity to develop her singing voice, including lessons in Chicago, New York, and then Paris. Howard had enrolled at Harvard a few months before Rupert's wedding, and Felix would benefit from the best music education possible in Europe after going there to join his sister.[29]

The wedding of Rupert and Agnes took place at 7:30 p.m., December 12, 1893, at St. George's Episcopal Church in New York City. The Reverend John Lewis, Jr., served as officiating clergyman, and witnesses were Charles L. Ailen and Greta Hughes Howell, Rupert's sister.[30]

As with his romance, Rupert needed little time to become part of the literary scene in New York. His first job, as a reporter for the *New York Journal*, enabled him to become acquainted with the city as he attended banquets and meetings, listened to speeches, and wrote about them for the paper.

His first assignment was a dream come true: covering a speech by Mark Twain, the Missouri author whose work he so admired. Rupert took great pride in writing a detailed report of the humorist's remarks, but was disappointed when the *Journal* published not a word of his account.[31]

In his free-lance writing sideline, he turned from one subject or medium to another, sending essays, poetry, and fiction to some of the most highly regarded publishers. Among markets he tried to crack in 1893 was *Scribner's,* to which he sent the lengthy poem, "Gyges' Ring," that he had started while at Yale and had finished shortly afterward. The publisher rejected it and also a novel submitted the same year; called *John Muth,* the latter was based in part on a Mississippi River background.[32]

Along with the discouragement and some success that he encountered as a writer, he found life in the city was much different from the Midwest and college. He had also undergone changes in long-cherished convictions. College had provided him with a new awareness and understanding of many subjects, but it had shaken his religious beliefs that had once been so firm.

In recalling this period, Rupert later said, "My college studies taught me that the Bible was absolutely unbelievable as a book of fact." But this revelation left him with no alternative steadying influence in his life. As he put it, "When I left college I was in a state of collapse as a Christian. I did not know what to believe." [33] He had taken literally the advice of a philosophy professor who had told his class that the most important lesson in life could be summed up in two words: "Question everything." Rupert thought it was unnecessary advice in his case, because he was already naturally "skeptical in every direction." [34]

It was also during this period, when he was twenty-one, that he took up smoking for the first time—the beginning of a lifetime cigar-smoking habit.[35] Only rarely would he smoke cigarettes, but many of his posed photographs throughout his career would show him with a cigar in hand.

His stay on the *Journal* lasted only about six months. He preferred writing on subjects of his own choosing, but doubted that he could support himself and Agnes in that manner, even with the allowance his father provided. So, in 1894, when he had a chance to buy into a promising literary publication called *Storiettes,* he again wired his father for help, was provided the $500 needed, and became the magazine's editor as well as an owner.[36]

In the same year, Adelbert College awarded him a Master of Arts degree for the completion of work he had started there earlier. Soon he also began to make headway as a free-lancer, with three articles appearing within a six-month period in 1894 in *Munsey's Magazine*, a popular monthly that published a potpourri of material, much of it by well-known writers. His pieces included one about American composers, a subject of special and long-lasting interest to him; another about a sculptor; and the third on the intriguing topic of "Secret Societies at Yale."

In the latter, Hughes described the influence of the secret organizations, including Skull and Bones, Yale's oldest and wealthiest. He wrote that "he is not a Yale man that would prefer any scholarship honors or prizes to membership in old 'Bonesy'." He added, "The chief arguments against these organizations come from men who have failed of admission to them." [37]

After a year with *Storiettes* it became obvious that the magazine was not a success and that it was, in fact, going downhill. As Rupert later recalled, it cost his father another $2,000 to bail him out of the magazine "when it died under my skillful editorship." [38]

From there he moved to two jobs he held at the same time with leading magazines. *Godey's Magazine*, formerly *Godey's Lady's Book*, featured illustrated articles about art, music, and fashions; and *Current Literature*, a beautiful and bright magazine edited by George W. Cable, dealt mainly with current events and comment. Rupert handled his responsibilities as assistant editor of each publication by working for *Godey's* in the mornings and *Current Literature* in the afternoons. With *Godey's* he was also the book reviewer, a job once held by Edgar Allan Poe. In these positions, he became acquainted with leading editors and numerous other writers. Meanwhile, the prodigious output of his own writings continued, and he often submitted articles and stories under as many as five bylines, in addition to his own name.[39]

Of all his accomplishments in the mid-1890s, the one that seemed to offer the most promise was the staging of a musical comedy, *The Bathing Girl*, for which he had begun writing the libretto while at Yale. When he and his collaborator, Robert Coverly, first considered producing the musical in New York, there was one major problem—the $2,500 that Rupert would need for his share of production costs. But that did not stop him for long. Although he was only twenty-three years old and had no experience with Broadway or other big-time productions, he had been successful with shows at the Opera House in St. Charles, Missouri. He also had a father with deep pockets.

Not knowing whether there might be a limit to the backing he could obtain from Felix, Rupert thought he would give it a try.[40] And, as was usually the case, Felix came through with the necessary amount, and Rupert was on his way to what he hoped would be his first New York stage triumph.

On September 2, 1895, the day before *The Bathing Girl* opened at the Fifth Avenue Theater, the Sunday *New York Times* provided an advance description:

> The piece is offered as a satire on fashionable society, and is in three acts . . .
>
> The libretto deals with the experiences of Lord Fitzpoodle, who has brought over a yacht to race for the America's Cup, and who aspires to the hand of Miss Terriberry, a Boston heiress. The heiress, however, is rescued from drowning by J. Kingsbury Botts, who pretends to be a Wall Street millionaire, but is really a drygoods clerk on his vacation, and he carries off the prize. Bicyclists, bathing girls, and Summer visitors are introduced, and there will be plenty of dancing . . .[41]

An advertisement in the same issue announced that the "comedy opera" by Coverly & Hughes, with F. C. Whitney's Company, would open the preliminary season and was scheduled to run "Two Weeks Only." Two days later the *Times* review did not mention Hughes's partner, who had composed the music; instead, it praised some cast members and described in detail—in mostly unflattering terms—the plot and stage settings, saying:

> Mr. Rupert Hughes has written what he calls a satirical comedy opera. It was produced last night at the Fifth Avenue under the misleading title of "The Bathing Girl." A name suggestive of dervishes howling outside the gates of Mecca would have been equally appropriate.
>
> It is supposed that Miss Grace Golden, who is known in the production as Miss Terriberry of Boston, is the bathing girl referred to. But she doesn't bathe. She falls overboard, or gets out into the surf, or meets with some sort of watery mishap which takes place out of sight of the audience.

Although the review indicated that the musical comedy met with audience approval, the September 2 performance proved to be its first and last. Rupert's initial effort at a New York stage production made history, but not as he had hoped. In *A History of The New York Stage*, T. Allston Brown wrote, "The play was so bad that it was given but one performance." [42]

The editors of *The Best Plays of 1894-1899* observed that the season of 1895-96 "was not particularly impressive for its immortal works," adding that "The greatest failure, perhaps, was the single performance achieved by *The Bathing Girl*. . . A clue to the failure might be found in a sample of the dialogue: Q.—Where is your Yacht? A.—Why, she's in the water, where she yacht to be." [43]

The author of those less than immortal lines never attempted to conceal his failure. In a brief autobiographical account he put the experience in perspective:

"My first theatrical production was a terrific failure . . .," he wrote. "Besides being amateurishly written, and outrageously produced, it was counted a silly dream because it tried to put contemporary costumes on the stage in comic opera . . . . It is a fact that most of the managers refused to consider the work on the ground of its modernity and Americanism." [44]

A lesser man would have been shattered by the failure, perhaps vowing never to attempt another New York play, but in the opinion of drama critic Burns Mantle, the experience worked otherwise for Rupert. The failure of *The Bathing Girl*, Mantle recalled in 1929, was "probably as helpful an experience as Mr. Hughes could possibly have had. It gave him training in accepting defeat early in his career which is always an asset to a dramatist." [45]

In 1898 Hughes moved to a new job with *The Criterion*, a highly respected literary journal that had started as a society publication called *St. Louis Life*. Its owner, Mrs. Grace L. Davidson, had changed its name and hired French-born Henri Dumay to join the staff, then moved it from St. Louis to New York after Dumay promised to help make literary history by lining up brilliant contributors. He lived up to his promise, publishing essays, poetry, criticisms, and satire by top new writers, plus work by leading illustrators. Dumay was editor, and Hughes was hired as one of two associate editors, along with George Henry Payne. In addition, Hughes was the music critic.

The Criterion became a "highbrow literary magazine" with a circulation of about 10,000, but much of its content was too sophisticated for some readers and considered improper for many libraries. In 1898 one of Dumay's articles so shocked Mrs. Davidson that she fired him and put Rupert in charge for a few weeks until Irish poet and journalist Joseph I. C. Clarke was hired as editor.[46]

While working for *The Criterion*, Rupert's own writing—essays, sonnets, and musical and art criticism—appeared frequently in *Century* and other magazines, although he had trouble selling short stories. He found a market for drawings and verse at *Scribner's*, which, at twenty-five cents a copy, was the lowest-priced "quality magazine." And *Everybody's Magazine* published his "potboilers," a term also applied by a journalism historian to the work of Theodore Dreiser in the same magazine.[47] Rupert also corresponded with other writers and critics, sometimes in friendly debate about current trends in literature, music, art, and music composition.

It was against this background of sophistication, so far removed from his earlier life in Midwestern towns, that Rupert's thoughts often returned to his boyhood, and he began to spend time on a series of stories, aimed at young readers, about his chums of years gone by.

The tales are peopled with a dozen high school age boys from a town called Lakerim, who form the Lakerim Athletic Club in order to compete in football and other sports against their arch rivals from neighboring Greenville, who attend a military academy.

The Lakerim boys have nicknames, ranging from "Jumbo" to "Sleepy" to "Sawed-off." One main character, "History," bears a distinct resemblance to the author as a boy. As to their actual names, Rupert wrote: "I believe their fathers and mothers nicknamed them 'Robert Williams' and 'Clement Robinson' and 'Thorndyke Pendleton' and such ridiculous things; but their real names were, of course, just what their chums chose to call them." As for "History," he said, "History's schoolbooks had 'Willis Campbell' written in them, though I can't imagine why." He added, "He knew many big words by name, but his spelling was a bit shaky." [48]

The Lakerim Athletic Club stories were published in serial form in *St. Nicholas* magazine in 1897—the first of many serials he would write—and proved popular with boy readers. Their publication was a breakthrough for Hughes, who had enjoyed only a modicum of success with fiction until then. Moreover, *St. Nicholas* was a beautifully printed magazine that attracted many well-known authors—Louisa May Alcott, Mark Twain, Rudyard Kipling, Robert Louis Stevenson, and Bret Harte—some of whose best work appeared in serial form. For his first serialized stories, Hughes was in good company.

But an even bigger accomplishment took place when The Century Company, publisher of *St. Nicholas*, decided to publish *The Lakerim Athletic Club* as a separate volume. It appeared in book stores in 1898 as a handsome book, with a lake scene on the front cover, twenty-four illustrations by C. M. Relyea scattered throughout, and gold lettering on the front and spine.

This was the first published book by Rupert Hughes, and he gave credit where it was due. The dedication was: "To my bonny Mother whose devotion has saved my life many's the time; whose comradery [sic] made my boyhood one golden memory."

CHAPTER THREE

A WHIRLWIND IN MOTION

*"The worst crimes in every nation were committed
in the name of religion by religious people."*

Two events made 1897 an important year for Rupert Hughes. One was the
birth of a daughter, and the other was his enlistment in the National Guard.

Elspeth Hedge Hughes, born to Agnes and Rupert on May 23, brought
the usual obligations that come to every couple when a child is born. For the
new father working long hours, the birth of what was to be his only child
brought a need for additional funds. He told R. U. Johnson of *The Century*
three weeks later that Elspeth's arrival had resulted in expenses that were
"sky-high somewhat unexpectedly." [1]

He had signed up on January 23, 1897, as a private in Company F,
Seventh Regiment, of the New York National Guard,[2] carrying on a family
tradition of militia enlistment and beginning what was to become an increasingly important part of his life: service as a citizen soldier. Although he had
attended military school, Guard duties brought him his first taste of the routine chores involved in military service.

At first there seemed a certain amount of glory as well as self-sacrifice to
the idea of serving his country, as evidenced by a brief poem he wrote while
in his twenties:

THUS WOULD I DIE

Leading some fight for liberty,
I'd find my final bed
On a battlefield of victory
Whence all the foe have fled;
And my cheering men charge over me,
Not knowing I am dead.[3]

His early years in the National Guard coincided with concern about growing tension between the United States and Spain over the status of Cuba. Outraged by the Spanish oppression of Cubans, Hughes was among the first to take a stand supporting Cuban patriots by writing several articles on the subject.

In February, 1898, after the U. S. battleship *Maine* was sunk in Havana harbor, resulting in the death of 260 persons, Americans blamed Spain and war fever peaked. With "Remember the *Maine*" resounding as a national slogan, President McKinley demanded full independence for Cuba.

It was at about this time that Felix T. Hughes wrote to Iowa Governor L. M. Shaw, informing him that Rupert would like to enter the volunteer service of Iowa in the event that his help might be needed because of the trouble with Spain. Felix recounted his son's service with the "famous New York Seventh" as well as his writing and editing background, and said it was Rupert's idea to "secure a Captain's commission or something of that kind." [4]

Rupert followed up by telegram, confirming the offer, and the governor promptly acknowledged it. Then, eight days after the U. S. declared a state of war existed with Spain as of April 21, Rupert again expressed the hope to Governor Shaw that "you will indeed call on me, if you need me." [5]

Although Iowa did not call him to service, he was named an acting captain in the 114th New York Regiment. He did not see action during the war,[6] which ended in August with victory for the United States, independence for Cuba, and increasing recognition of the U. S. as a world power. After the war ended, Rupert continued with the Guard in New York and in 1900 was appointed a first lieutenant and battalion adjutant of the Sixty-Ninth Regiment, known as "The Fighting 69th." [7]

In the same year, his patriotic feelings and appreciation of sacrifices by America's soldiers were expressed in what became one of his most frequently published poems, "For Decoration Day," which appeared in *An American Anthology, 1787-1900*. In paying tribute to the dead soldiers of the Civil War and the Spanish-American conflict, it concluded:

> Make sorrow perfect with exultant pride—
> Our vanished armies have not truly died;
> They march today before the heavenly host;
> And history's veterans raise a storm of cheers,
> As the Yankee troops—with glory armed and shod—
> In Grand Review swing past the throne of God.[8]

While continuing with *The Criterion*, Rupert wrote for other publications, including a lively magazine called *M'lle New York*, sometimes using pseudonyms on material he submitted.

Readers shocked by *The Criterion* would have been even more so by *M'lle New York*. Patterned after Parisian weeklies, it was, as co-founder James G. Huneker called it, "audacious, fearing neither man, nor the printer, yet this fortnightly was unlike any publication I have ever seen." Hughes had met Huneker, a famous critic, author, and editor, soon after moving to New York. Before long, Hughes, Huneker, and Vance Thompson, who had worked for *The Musical Courier* and then in France before coming up with the idea of publishing the new magazine, became close friends.

M'lle New York was published in two series, with eleven issues in the first, beginning August, 1895, and only four in the second. In October, 1895, a story Rupert wrote about an aging prostitute, "When Badger Meets Con," appeared in the fifth issue of the first series. By that time he, Huneker, and Thompson were spending so much time together that they were often called the "Three Musketeers." [9]

M'lle New York never broke even financially, even though it was popular with the literati. But after the first series ended, Marc Blumenberg, publisher of the *Musical Courier*, came to its rescue by agreeing to publish it. To publicize the revived magazine, Huneker announced in the October 26, 1898 issue that readers would find in it a "shocking story" written by "a genius discovered by *M'lle New York*."

The genius was identified as Marmaduke Humphrey. Two stories were published under his byline, including "When Pan Moves to Harlem," which Huneker described many years later as a "nocturnal adventure of

Slabsided Sal told in purest Americanese." [10] The yarn caused a stir, and readers long speculated as to the true identity of Marmaduke.

It was not until 1914, when Huneker inadvertently revealed the secret, that the real name of Marmaduke Humphrey would came to light—Rupert Hughes.

According to Huneker's biographer, Arnold T. Schwab, "Hughes made the editors promise not to reveal the real identity of Marmaduke Humphrey . . . for he feared that conventional magazines would reject his other work if it were known that he had written 'off-color' tales . . ." This is understandable, for it was at that time that Hughes's Lakerim Athletic Club stories for boys were enjoying great popularity. Even though his identification as Marmaduke Humphrey did not occur until years later, Hughes protested even then at the revelation.[11]

James Huneker regarded the Marmaduke story "When Pan Moves to Harlem" as Rupert's "most brilliant short story." In his 1920 book, *Steeplejack*, Huneker wrote, "O. Henry is insipid compared with this tale, a forerunner to many." But despite Huneker's best efforts, "neither he nor Marmaduke Humphrey could keep the magazine afloat," according to Schwab, "and after four issues it died." [12]

The writing Hughes did for M'*lle New York* was only a diversion from producing saleable short stories, articles, and books as the twentieth century approached. In this he was increasingly successful, with articles published in 1898 and 1899 in leading magazines. The subject matter showed a wide range, from "The Catacombs" in *Scribner's* to "Art in Portrait Photography" in *The Cosmopolitan*. Another article for the latter, "A Story of the Modern Battleship," was later published in braille by the Institution for the Blind.

Hughes's Lakerim Athletic Club stories had been so popular with *St. Nicholas* readers that he wrote a second series, "The Dozen from Lakerim," published with illustrations by C. M. Relyea in the same magazine starting in May, 1899. After serialization, The Century Company published a book by that name that included the magazine stories, plus others written by Hughes.

Also in 1899 a second Master of Arts degree was bestowed upon Rupert, this one from Yale for his postgraduate work in English, thereby adding prestige to his credentials as a serious writer.

He continued to study music, taking lessons from Edgar Stilman Kelley, a composer and teacher of performance, organ, and composition, who later taught at Yale and in Berlin before heading the composition department at the Cincinnati Conservatory.[13] Meanwhile, Hughes corresponded with various composers, including the esteemed A. M. Foerster, who in the following year dedicated a song to him.[14]

The interest Hughes showed in the works of American composers was based upon his belief that many of their compositions were the equal of music by better-known European composers. He even saw merit in ragtime music, writing an essay about it for *The Musical Record*.[15] Titled "A Eulogy of Ragtime," Hughes's scholarly and prophetic analysis was still being quoted and praised by music historians more than eight decades later.

The pioneering essays and articles about American music he wrote for three magazines in the late 1890s—*Godey's Magazine*, the *Century Magazine*, and the *Criterion*—attracted so much interest that he decided to write a book that would include some of his magazine pieces on the subject. The finished result was published by L. C. Page & Company in 1900 as *Contemporary American Composers*.

In his foreword, the author wrote that "the greater part of the world has stayed aloof" from American music, adding that "aside from occasional attentions evoked by chance performances . . . the growth of our music has been unloved and unheeded by anybody except a few plodding composers, their wives, and a retainer or two." He said he believed "some of the best music in the world is being written here at home and that it only needs the light to win its meed of praise."

In research for the book, Hughes chose composers who showed serious promise, including some whose work had not been published. Reading their manuscripts became a "hideous task which might be substituted for the comparative pastime of breaking rocks, as punishment for misdemeanors."

The book provided a general survey, plus chapters on "The Innovators," "The Academics," "The Colonists," "The Women Composers," and a brief treatment of "The Foreign Composers" who had done much of their work in the United States.

Inclusion of a chapter about women might have surprised some of Rupert's contemporaries, but it was in keeping with his belief that often "the best things done by women equal the best things done by men." [16] He cited examples to prove it.

His book also contended that early Puritans, with a "granite heart, and suspicious eye for music," had hindered the development of American music.[17] In future writings he would be more specific in condemning the narrow-mindedness of Puritans.

Contemporary American Composers, as well as its subsequent editions with slightly different titles, broke ground previously untouched by most critics, and it has stood as a classic throughout the years. Although some of the author's conclusions were challenged by later historians and critics, Edward Jablonski in 1981 stated that Hughes "did not benefit from quite as much hindsight . . . as those historian-musicologists who came after." [18]

He started from scratch in his research, then wrote the book while holding down a full-time job on *The Criterion*, tending to duties as a father and husband, serving in the National Guard, and writing stories, essays, music, and poetry. Despite this whirlwind of activity, his output was not then near its peak, and in years to come he would produce an astounding variety and quantity of materials.

During the early part of the twentieth century, Rupert could be seen most days in a new setting, huddled over ancient books and manuscripts at the British Museum in London, scrutinizing them for their historical impact.

The boy nicknamed "History" had become a scholar who had taken on a monumental project as chief assistant editor of *The Historians' History of the World*, to be published in twenty-five volumes by the prestigious Encyclopedia Britannica. He had left *The Criterion* in 1901 to write advertisements and articles for the encyclopedia company, but soon was given a full-time assignment on the history project, for which his interests and talents were well suited.[19]

The work was not simply editing what others had written, but included researching the history of nations and evaluating the contributions made by their leaders and others in significant roles. In this manner he attempted to establish the relationships of movements and events as they influenced the lives of people throughout the world.

Accompanied by Agnes and Elspeth, Rupert traveled to London in May, 1901. During their stay, lasting until November, 1902, there were frequent trips to Paris, where he studied in the Bibliotheque Nationale.[20] Taking advantage of the opportunity to learn about both cities, he came to appreciate their history, cultural attractions, and literature, while remaining loyal to America. He had expressed some of his intense feelings about the United

States in a poem about the lighting of liberty's torch in New York Bay that was published in London "with great acclaim," as Hughes put it, the year before his arrival there.[21]

Not all of his time was spent on historical research while in Europe—concentration on a single project for so long would have been alien to his nature. For one thing, he studied music with Charles W. Pearce, a noted organist, composer, choirmaster, and professor.[22]

Rupert's interest in music ran primarily toward composition, lyric writing, and history, while his brother and sister, Felix and Greta, concentrated on public performances, and, later on, teaching voice. It is noteworthy that the careers and studies of three of the children of Jean and Felix Turner Hughes had taken them to Europe. Both Greta and Felix had preceded Rupert there to study and sing.

Greta's 1897 debut as a coloratura soprano, singing as Jeanne Greta at St. James Hall in London, had met with critical and popular acclaim, with some reviewers calling her voice one of the most beautiful in the world. A successful tour of England and Scotland brought comparisons of her singing to that of Carlotta Patti and Nellie Melba. Then, just before a command appearance for the Princess of Teck, she caught a severe cold. Ignoring doctors' warnings not to sing, she went on as scheduled, resulting in damage to her vocal cords that forced her into a long retirement. When she eventually resumed her career in New York, it was on a limited basis.[23]

Divorced by her husband, James Frederick Howell, on February 6, 1899, she had a sudden romance later in the year with Herbert Witherspoon, an American bass singer and Yale graduate studying in Europe. They were married on September 25. Later, he would have a successful recital debut in New York and go on to notable acclaim as a Metropolitan Opera soloist.[24]

As for Felix, his music career preparations were extensive. He lived in Paris and studied at the Rudy Institute with some of the world's leading voice teachers, then went on to Germany and London. With a flair for acting, Felix was a natural for operatic roles, and although he was a baritone he could also sing tenor parts. Following a successful singing debut in La Juive, Liege, Belgium, he presented numerous concerts. His stay in Europe lasted ten years before he returned to the United States. He then performed as a soloist with leading symphony orchestras and sang in concerts that included appearances with Madame Schumann-Heink during her United States tour.[25]

Howard was the only one of the Hughes offspring who did not study or work in Europe, although he later traveled there on his honeymoon. He had no special musical talents, but had played the guitar as a youth.[26] Never an outstanding student, he preferred things mechanical and technical to classroom studies. After taking special courses at Harvard from 1893 to 1895 he attended the State University of Iowa at Iowa City, where he studied law for a year but did not graduate. Instead, he went into practice with his father's law firm in Keokuk. But after soon discovering that he had no real interest in legal work, he turned to more exciting enterprises, from prospecting for silver near Denver to looking for lead and zinc in the Tri-State mining area centered around Joplin, Missouri. It has been reported that he took out a marriage license while in Joplin in 1900, but apparently no wedding took place. Before long, after the fabulous Spindletop oil discovery took place near Beaumont, Texas, he rushed there to get in on the action.[27] That proved to be the right decision, and his participation in oil and drilling deals started him on the way to a highly successful and prosperous career.

Meanwhile, Felix Turner Hughes had done well for himself. Elected Keokuk mayor in 1894 and 1896, he then become a judge of the superior court.[28] In the late 1890s, he conceived the idea of a dam, nearly a mile long, across the Mississippi River to Illinois to harness water power and stop flooding of the area. When the dam, with only one lock, was finally completed in 1913, it was called "the engineering marvel of the world." [29]

It was the nature of Hughes family members to think big and to pursue ambitions almost unlimited in scope. Certainly this was true of Rupert, whose involvement with the *Historians' History of the World* seemed almost without end. But it had many benefits for him, including the opportunity to put historical occurrences into perspective.

His research also had a definite influence on his religious thinking. With his faith already shaken by college studies, and despite religious implications of some of his writings (including references to God in his poem "For Decoration Day"), he came to believe that "the worst crimes in every nation were committed in the name of religion by religious people." [30] This concern would plague him throughout much of his life.

BOOKS, PLAYS, REAL-LIFE DRAMA

"There is no deeper mystery about the tools and
the trade of music than about those of any other
carpentry and joinery."

During his stay in Europe, Hughes continued to submit freelance material to publications in the United States, with some success. His tongue-in-cheek essay on "Animal and Vegetable Rights" appeared in the November, 1901, issue of *Harper's*.

At about the same time, the lengthy poem he had completed shortly after leaving Yale was published in book form by R. H. Russell.[1] A dramatic monologue of Greek life, written in blank verse, *Gyges' Ring* was well received by critics. The author later boasted that some "curious people" had considered it to be "the biggest poem written by an American."[2] Nearly three decades after its publication the *National Cyclopedia of American Biography* would state that its "classical theme and a literary quality . . . has placed it among permanent literature."[3]

Hughes himself would recall "one rather remarkable achievement" that could be credited to the poem:

Shortly after its publication in book form, the publisher told me: "Thanks to the very cordial reviews, it is doing very well—for poetry. It has already sold one hundred forty-eight copies!"

But when the royalty statement was sent to me several months later, the total sale was sixty-two copies. I told him of my astonishment at such a paradox—a backward sale. But he stuck to his figures and paid me for sixty-two copies only. Fortunately the sale stopped there. Else, the book might have become entirely unpublished; and the sale gone on and on into algebraic minuses of alarming magnitude.[4]

When he returned to New York in November, 1902, Hughes's work with the Encyclopedia Britannica was far from over. It would continue through much of 1905, during which time he would do intensive research in libraries in New York and Boston and at the Library of Congress in Washington, D. C.[5]

While the world history occupied his attention during the day, he wrote about other subjects during long off-duty hours, resulting in the publication of five non-fiction works and two novels, in addition to the production of several plays, during a four-year period. Also published were a book of music he composed and a volume of songs he edited.

Of the latter two, A Riley Album, published by Edward Schuberth & Company, New York, in 1902, included musical settings Hughes composed for ten James Whitcomb Riley poems. He dedicated the book "in all friendship and homage" to Riley, "whose songs to tell the truth, sing themselves without further music of mine." But he also dedicated some individual arrangements to members of his family, including "For my brother Felix," "To my ain little Mither," and another "To the Elspeth."

Songs by Thirty Americans, which he edited, was published in 1904 in two editions—for high and low voices—as Volume XIII of the Oliver Ditson Company's Musicians Library series. In his foreword, Hughes tells how attitudes had changed since he wrote his first magazine articles about American composers.

"In those days," he said, ". . . the public singer, pianist or conductor who included an American name in his program was looked at with amazement as straining after eccentricity . . . . Today the American composer does not need to be isolated like a pest to a ward of his own. His name is seen on almost every program, mingling with the classics and the European standards in democratic good-fellowship." [6]

Included in the song book was Adolph M. Foerster's "Tristram and Iseult." Highly regarded as a composer and professor of music, Foerster was delighted that his song would be published. He sent Hughes a check in appreciation, but it was returned along with a note that said:

> The spirit which led you to send me a cheque was extremely kind and very pleasant, but it is quite impossible for me to accept any commission from anyone included in the collection.
>
> It is refreshing to find an American composer who gives me credit and I am very grateful for your cordiality. But it is your artistic work that led me to ask you to contribute to this collection, and I should have asked for a song from you had you been as boorish as some of the Americans, instead of as courteous as you have.

Soon after, Hughes apologized to Foerster for not writing when the subject of the check first came up, "but I have so large a correspondence and so much writing, that it slipped my mind until the cheque itself arrived. Hence I had to send it back." [7]

The volume of correspondence mentioned was related to several time-consuming projects in which he was involved, including finishing up on what was to be one of his most lasting accomplishments—an encyclopedia first published in two volumes in 1903 as *The Musical Guide*.

The preparation of this work, suggested by the publisher, McClure, Phillips & Company, would have been a monumental accomplishment for any author or researcher, but it was even more so for Hughes, who still worked a full schedule on world history. Putting together *The Musical Guide* single-handedly—doing research, writing original material, editing chapters by other authorities, proofreading, and handling the correspondence necessary to acquire information—made the achievement even more remarkable.

One of the most interesting and useful features was the opening chapter, "An Introduction to Music for the Uninitiated: A free translation of its technicalities into untechnical language (especially for those who do not read music and do not care to study it)." In it Hughes stated:

> There is almost as much humbug about the mysteries of music as there was about the oracles of Delphi. . .
>
> There is no deeper mystery about the tools and the trade of music than about those of any other carpentry and joinery. It is far easier for some people to write a melody than to drive a nail straight. But anybody who will earnestly try, can learn to do the one as easily as the

other. And there are thousands of professional composers who ought to be earning honest livings driving nails home instead of starving to death dishonestly driving audiences home.[8]

An indication of the success of Hughes's effort to make his two-volume work "the most nearly complete reference work of its kind in existence," is told in the publisher's preface to a revised edition a decade later: "On account of the completeness of its contents and their extremely convenient arrangement, the book at once took its place on the reference shelves of libraries, public and private, large and small; and everywhere the worn condition of its bindings, and the testimony of its readers have proved how invaluable it has been found." [9]

Within a few weeks after publication of the *Musical Guide*, another Hughes book about musicians was published in the L. C. Page & Company's Music Lovers Series. It bore the intriguing title of *The Love Affairs of Great Musicians*. Portions had appeared serially in *The Criterion* and the final chapter had been published in *The Smart Set*.[10]

In addition to the nonfiction books about music and musicians, Rupert reached a career milestone during the early 1900s: publication of his first novel. In *The Whirlwind*, the subject was the Civil War, and the setting was his native Missouri. And, just as he had dedicated his first published book to his mother, he now dedicated his first novel to the other person who had meant so much to his career: "To the noblest man I've ever known: Felix Turner Hughes, my father."

Published by Lothrop Publishing Company of Boston in 1902, *The Whirlwind* brought a highly favorable review, headed "A Romance of the War," in the *New York Times*. Calling the novel "the most exuberant of romances," it added that "Mr. Rupert Hughes possesses strong dramatic powers. The words he uses are chosen with skill and often produce marked effects." [11]

Publication of *The Whirlwind* brought recognition for Hughes from *The Bookman*, a respected magazine that reported on literary happenings. Its April, 1903, issue contained a photographic portrait of a dashing Rupert Hughes with a handlebar mustache, high collar, and wide tie, looking every bit the important figure of a successful novelist.

The Whirlwind was followed by two other Hughes books published while he shepherded the world history through the final stages. One of them must surely have been one of the most unusual guide books ever written; the other was another novel.

The Real New York is an entertaining, heavily illustrated book he wrote to inform readers about places to see while visiting the city. A vast amount of information is included in the fictional account of out-of-towners whose misadventures take them to various areas of New York.

Published by the Smart Set Publishing Company, it was illustrated by Hy. Mayer, with 100 drawings of New York places and people. A *New York Times* reviewer thought Mayer's work was the best part of the "guide story book." As for the story, the *Times* considered the romance too thin and thought there were too many facts, but added that "things may be learned from it which it is quite worth while to know and which are not, so far as we recall, set forth in any more accessible fashion elsewhere." [12]

Though this less than enthusiastic review must have disappointed Hughes, he took delight in advertisements in *The Smart Set*, the sophisticated magazine that H. L. Mencken later would co-edit. Hughes told Arthur Hoffman, a well-known editor and writer:

> I learned only the other evening that you are the man who wrote the extremely clever advertisements, in *The Smart Set* for *The Real New York* . . . Let me thank you now, not only for my own pleasure in hearing someone else blow my horn with such dulcet technic, but also for my delight in them as exhibitions of downright advertising genius of a sort that should bring you all the good luck I wish you. [13]

Hughes's next novel was unlike his previously published fiction. *Zal: An International Romance* tells the story of a young Polish pianist's attempt to win recognition in New York. He falls in love with a wealthy girl whose father wants her to marry an English duke. The sacrifices required of a performing artist are described in detail, and it is obvious the author was well acquainted with the hardships of becoming a professional musician.

The *New York Times* critic wrote, "The book is of value, not only because of its musical quality, but because it enlarges information and intensifies sympathy for what may truly be called the land of genius." A reviewer for *The Outlook* stated, "The contrast between the Polish and American natures is excellently indicated." [14]

In *Zal*, the dramatic quality of writing that a critic had noted in *The Whirlwind* was apparent. This was not unexpected, for Hughes had been honing his skills by writing a number of plays that had public performances during the early 1900s.

While still in London in 1902, he had viewed a stage production of his one-act play *The Wooden Wedding*, inspired by a Mathilde Serao story.[15] In the same year, another play with which he was associated opened at Mrs. Osborn's Playhouse in New York on October 20. A musical comedy called *Tommy Rot*, its music and lyrics were by Safford Waters and dialogue by Hughes, Joseph Herbert, Paul West, and Kirke La Shelle. Unlike Hughes's ill-fated first New York stage venture, this was moderately successful, with thirty-nine performances.[16]

As soon as *Tommy Rot* ended its run, another musical comedy by Waters and Hughes, *Fad and Folly*, opened at the same theater, after being revised by Paul West, the lyricist. A parody of Joseph Herbert's *Iris*, it lasted thirty-four performances.[17] In the same year, *In the Midst of Life*, written by Hughes in collaboration with Dr. Holbrook Curtis, was also produced in New York, but little is known about it.[18]

An ambitious play, *Alexander the Great*, which Rupert wrote with Collin Kemper, toured the United States throughout the 1903-04 season. Produced by Louis James and Frederick Warde, the five-act "tragedy in prose" was cut down from the six acts originally written.[19] While pleased that it had played a season on the road, Hughes later noted that it "never reached New York— thank heaven! This was my last effort at ancient or foreign art." [20]

In the middle of this productive period, a real-life drama unfolded. In late 1903, Rupert filed for divorce from Agnes, naming eight corespondents; but she also sought to divorce him, charging cruelty and adultery. Their marriage had been on the rocks for some time, according to testimony in the case, although it is impossible to know which of the charges, if any, made by Rupert and Agnes were true. New York law limited the grounds for divorce, and in many such disputes phony testimony was introduced to prove that a spouse had been unfaithful.

It is doubtful that anyone in the Hughes case expected the court proceedings to erupt into the public dispute that made headlines in the *New York Times*. A front page story on October 16, 1903, described a fracas that broke out after one day's lengthy testimony and deliberation:

USE VIOLENCE TO
DEFEND HUGHES JURY

Court Officers Rescue Them from
Corespondents and Other Too Eager
Questioners—Lawyer Strikes a Witness

The newspaper reported that five days of testimony had been heard before the jury retired at 5 p. m. to determine whether Rupert (identified as "the author, playwright, and sculptor") was entitled to a divorce. As the jury went out, a scuffle outside the courtroom took place between Lyman Spalding, Agnes's attorney, and Herbert Witherspoon, concert singer and husband of Rupert's sister. Spalding, who claimed that Witherspoon called him "a mud-slinging scoundrel," hit the singer on the jaw, sending him "reeling backward ten or twelve feet." Spectators broke up the fight and Witherspoon left the building.

Among those awaiting the verdict were two of the eight men named as corespondents—Lieutenant Reynolds of the United States Navy and Arthur Vandeveer Conover, a member of the United States Lighthouse Service—and lawyers for the plaintiff and defendant. At midnight, as jury members left for the night, they were nearly mobbed by persons wanting to know what the outcome might be. Court officers intervened, knocking down one or two questioners.

It was a scene that Rupert's imagination could hardly have conceived—one that was surely out of character for Greta's husband, Herbert Witherspoon. And the prominent publicity was not what Hughes had sought in filing for divorce. In fact, his distaste for divorce laws became a subject that he would write and speak about for years to come.

When a settlement was reached in the Hughes case six weeks later, again there was publicity. A page one story in the *New York Times* on November 30, 1903, reported details from the perspective of Agnes's attorney, under the headline: "HUGHES DIVORCE IS SETTLED OUT OF COURT."

Lyman A. Spalding announced that the agreement called for Agnes to receive substantial alimony and that she and Rupert would have joint custody of six-year-old Elspeth. He added, "Judgment was entered in favor of Mrs. Hughes, alimony was granted, and alternate custody of the child was agreed upon as the best solution."

The favorable settlement for Agnes, as announced by her attorney, appears to have been overstated, an examination of the court document reveals. The Separation Consent Judgment, ordered by Justice James Fitzgerald of the New York Supreme Court on November 25, 1903, declared the couple separated and dismissed the counterclaim of the defendant, Rupert Hughes. But it stated that "the custody, control and education of Elspeth Hedge Hughes, the issue of the said parties hereto, be and the same hereby is awarded to the defendant, Rupert Hughes." It also stated that the custody of Elspeth "is awarded to the plaintiff, Agnes Hedge Hughes, during the period of three months in each calendar year beginning in the months of May or June," and that Rupert agreed to pay $100 a month for the support of plaintiff and Elspeth when she was in the plaintiff's custody.[21]

It was obvious that both Rupert and Agnes had a genuine love for Elspeth and that each desired to have custody. This was a matter that would prove important in another legal battle decades later, long after both parents were deceased, when once again their names would be dragged into a bitter courtroom struggle to determine the rightful heirs to the fortune of billionaire Howard Hughes, Jr.

But in the meantime, having no foreknowledge of such events, Rupert and Agnes went on with their separate lives. Their divorce in New York, based upon Agnes's charge that Rupert had committed adultery with an unnamed woman, became final on July 12, 1904.[22]

Four months later, on November 15, Agnes married U. S. Navy Lieutenant William Herbert Reynolds in a New York ceremony presided over by a Navy chaplain.[23] The bridegroom had been one of those Rupert had named as a corespondent when filing for divorce.[24]

CHAPTER FIVE

ALL FOR A GIRL

"Though the notices were excellent and audiences enthusiastic, they were not numerous enough to make the play a success."

G uests roared with laughter at the witticisms of Mark Twain, the featured speaker at a 70th birthday dinner in his honor at Delmonico's in New York City. His remarks ended "on a note of simple pathos that brought new tears to eyes already drenched with the tears of laughter."

The quote came from Rupert Hughes, who was not there to report Twain's remarks as he had done twelve years earlier on a newspaper assignment; this time he was an invited guest in the company of many leading authors and seated at a table of eight under the wing of the esteemed William Dean Howells.

He found Twain's remarks about health especially interesting. The habit of smoking cigars had taken hold of Rupert, and he chuckled when Twain declared, "I never smoke when I am asleep; and I never smoke more than one cigar at a time." It was a quote that Hughes would often use, sometimes in reference to himself. He appreciated the comment that "I never go to bed while there's anybody to sit up with; and I never get up till I have to."[1] Rupert also enjoyed staying up late with friends, but would then remain awake even longer to study or write, regarding sleep a time-waster.

In 1905 his affiliation with the Encyclopedia Britannica ended with the publication of the twenty-five-volume *Historians' History of the World*. With that accomplished, he could devote more time to writing plays. While his intention was to "mirror the ordinary life of his time," [2] not all of his plots were about people of ordinary means; often, with sophisticated humor, he contrasted the backgrounds of those involved in romance. Such was true of *The Triangle*, in which a beautiful young woman of modest circumstances and the high-sounding name of Persis Van Duyn is engaged to a millionaire weakling, Willie Enslee, but really loves Army Lieutenant Harvey Forbes.

The play, with a tragic ending, was produced by Walter N. Lawrence and opened at the Manhattan Theater in New York on February 20, 1906. Charlotte Walker played the role of Persis, William Morris was Harvey Forbes, and Ferdinand Gottschalk was Willie Enslee. Although the *New York Times* gave it a lengthy review, the critic found fault with the author's treatment of the subject matter, saying that if the plot had been developed in another manner, "a very different result might have been achieved." [3]

Hughes had no time to dwell on the lukewarm reception. Less than three weeks after it began its run, he was in St. Louis for the opening of his new comedy *The Richest Girl in the World* at the Olympic Theater.

This time the response was much more favorable. A *New York Times* review, headlined "Miss George's New Play" and subheaded "Audience Enthusiastic Over 'The Richest Girl in the World,'" told of the welcome given Grace George. It reported that "there was prolonged applause at her first performance." [4] A stunning actress with a considerable record of stage successes, she also produced the Hughes play.

Pleased with the reviews, Rupert took time off to spend a week in Houston, Texas, visiting his older brother, Howard, who was now married and the father of a son. From there Rupert would go to New Orleans for the play's next opening. [5]

The Houston visit provided an opportunity for the brothers to catch up on happenings in the Hughes family. The Keokuk and Western Railroad their father had headed had been sold in 1901 to the Burlington system and was now its Keokuk and Western division. Felix had agreed to represent the Burlington as an attorney while continuing his private law practice. [6] Meanwhile, Greta Hughes Witherspoon was helping to advance the career of her husband, Herbert, whose 1902 recital at Mendelssohn Hall in New York had been followed by concerts in the U. S. and England.[7]

Both of Rupert's brothers had taken wives in 1904. Felix, after success as a concert singer in Europe, had returned to the United States and often appeared in concerts and as a soloist with symphony orchestras.[8] He lived in Cleveland, Ohio, where he married Adella Prentiss on October 5; in time he would help her form the Cleveland Orchestra and become a leader in cultural activities in that city.[9] Howard's wedding to Allene Gano had taken place on May 24 in Dallas.[10]

When Rupert visited Howard and Allene at their Houston home in March, 1906, their son, Howard Robard Hughes, Jr., was less than three months old, having been born on Christmas eve in 1905.[11] As things turned out, the boy was one of only two grandchildren—Elspeth, then nine years old, being the other—that Felix and Jean Hughes would have.

Like others in the petroleum industry, Howard Hughes, Sr., had learned that drilling for oil was no sure thing. As Rupert described his brother's situation, "One year he had fifty thousand in the bank. The next he owed the bank fifty thousand."

Howard was successful in many drilling ventures, but in 1907 encountered a flint barrier that caused the fishtail bits used by drillers to snap. His partner, Walter Sharp, knowing Howard's inventive mind, suggested he tackle the problem, so Howard went to visit his parents in Keokuk and began drawing sketches on paper attached to a breadboard. Then, in Rupert's words, "He emerged from the family dining room with an Archimedean cry of 'Eureka!' and the picture of a bit that had no less than 166 cutting edges."

The question was whether such a device would work. A model Howard arranged to have built drilled easily through granite, and in a Texas oil field test it chewed through flint at breakneck speed. After that, Howard and Sharp in 1909 brought in a discovery well for the Goose Creek oil field in Texas, formed the Sharp-Hughes Tool Company, and produced the bits commercially. They wisely decided to rent them on a royalty basis rather than sell them.[12] Several years after Sharp's death, Howard bought full control of the company. Eventually, Hughes Tool Company would become the inheritance of his son, creating the basis for what was to grow into the fabulous fortune of the legendary and mysterious Howard Hughes, Jr.

The significance of the Hughes invention cannot be overstated: it revolutionized drilling for oil and gas. As Hughes Tool Company declared a half-century later: "The true worth of the first Hughes bit can never be known. But at the time when it was most needed, it enabled the rotary to drill through hard rock and tap oil treasures that might otherwise have long remained nature's closely guarded secret." [13]

While Howard, Sr., was heavily involved in oil deals and drilling ventures, no fewer than a half dozen productions of Rupert's plays made it to the stage between 1907 and 1910.

After his responsibilities with Encyclopedia Britannica ended, he worked as assistant editor for *Appleton's Magazine*. Its editor was Trumbull White, who had established an excellent reputation with *Red Book*. He and Hughes developed a lasting friendship and produced a magazine later called "a high-class monthly in both form and content." [14]

The latter part of the century's first decade also saw the publication of several books and a number of short stories by Hughes, as well as poetry. A simple poem called "With a First Reader," first published in *Appleton's* and then in *Current Literature*, expressed the delight of discovery when a child first reads great works of literature. An introduction by the *Current Literature* editor said, "Poetry about books and book-writers is usually of a second-hand quality. First-hand inspirations come from life direct, not through the prisms of another man's genius. But here is a bookish poem that is not open to such an objection." It has been reprinted in anthologies and elsewhere more often than any other that Hughes wrote, and four of its lines were included in a 1952 collection of famous sayings compiled by Franklin P. Adams, called *FPA Book of Quotations*. [15]

The year 1907 was a time of deteriorating economic conditions—a financial panic characterized by uncertainty and financial disaster. It was also the year in which Rupert Hughes lost his job with *Appleton's Magazine*. Despite his free-lance work, the loss was a real hardship, but not for long. He later referred to it as the time when "the panic, to my eventual profit, forced me out." [16]

Another story he wrote for young readers, titled "The Boy Who Mixed His Holidays," ran in a Sunday edition of the *New York Herald*. [17] In the same year, his 1902 London play, *The Wooden Wedding*, was produced in New York as *She Borrowed Her Own Husband*, a one-act comedy. [18]

Meanwhile he had written a play of a different sort, which he called *The Bridge* and sent to Harrison Grey Fiske to read, after checking it with a bridge builder to make sure all technical details were accurate. [19] Knowing Fiske's influence and experience as owner of the *Dramatic Mirror* and drama critic for the *New York Star*, Hughes was anxious for him to produce the play. Fiske liked the script and produced *The Bridge* two years later.

Companies involved in the fledgling motion picture industry, seeking ideas for films, occasionally turned to stories by well-known authors such as Rupert Hughes. One of the first times he received payment from a movie company was when Louella Parsons, story editor for the Essanay Company and later a Hollywood columnist, paid him seventy-five dollars for a story that never reached the screen. Many years later, she told him she had nearly lost her job by being so extravagant.[20]

In the first decade of the 1900s, however, authors interested in drama and comedy were not yet looking toward the screen as an outlet for their work; their goal was still the New York stage. Hughes sometimes wrote to actresses or actors he thought might want to star in his plays. One such letter to Shakespearean actress Julia Marlowe in 1908 requested that she examine a play, the title of which was not indicated. He then made his pitch on behalf of a play that had been printed but not produced: "It has made a great sensation, it seems, among those who have read it, and several stars have declared their intention to produce it if the chance arose. But it requires a special opportunity. You might find it—if the play interests you." [21] Miss Marlowe's opinion of the script is not known, nor is there any available record to indicate whether she ever appeared in a Rupert Hughes play.

Among stage actresses with whom Hughes was well acquainted was Blanche Bates, star of many New York plays including *The Girl of the Golden West*,[22] But it was not for her acting ability alone that he held her in high regard; he felt especially indebted to her for introducing him to a young actress with the stage name of Adelaide Manola.[23]

Her maiden name was Adelaide Mould. She was the daughter of Henry Scrivener Mould of Cleveland and his wife Marion, an actress and star of light opera who had been given the stage name of Manola by her voice teacher. Adelaide had spent her early childhood in Europe, where her parents studied opera.

Her ambition to be on the stage was fortified by the knowledge that she had inherited her mother's beauty. As she matured, she occasionally took over her mother's role on stage without the audience knowing the difference. When Adelaide joined a stock company, using the stage name of Adelaide

Manola, she met another member of the company, Blanche Bates, with whom she developed a lifelong friendship.

The introduction of the twenty-four-year-old Adelaide to Rupert Hughes, twelve years her senior, came while he was writing a play for Blanche. The play was never completed, but the introduction made a lasting impression.[24] Shortly after, on June 22, 1908, Rupert and Adelaide went to Atlantic City, New Jersey, where they were married.

Adelaide, like Rupert, had been married before, having wed George Bissell when she was only sixteen. There were two children from this union: a daughter named Avis, and a son, Rush. The marriage had ended in divorce.[25] When Adelaide and Rupert married, it was decided that Avis, nearly eight years old, would live with them, and Rush, six, with his father. Rupert's eleven-year-old daughter, Elspeth, was then staying with her mother and step-father in Washington, D. C.[26]

Rupert looked upon Adelaide not only as an ideal choice for a wife but an actress with considerable ability, beauty, and stage presence. He wasted no time in casting her in the leading role in his play *All for a Girl*, which opened at the Bijou Theater in New York on Saturday night, August 22, exactly two months after their wedding.

Advertising and publicity played up the name of the male lead, Douglas Fairbanks, emphasizing his "first New York appearance as a star," and noted that "Adelaide Manola will make her first New York appearance as a leading woman . . . playing opposite to the star." [27]

Although advance notices called it a new play, which it was for New York, it was actually a production of what had previously been called *The Richest Girl in the World*, the Grace George vehicle that had been successful in St. Louis and New Orleans. The New York opening night audience also enjoyed the story about the rich heroine posing as a stenographer and escaping fortune-seekers by taking refuge in a New Hampshire farmhouse where she finds true love. The next day's *New York Times* published a lengthy and favorable review, headlined: "A PLEASANT COMEDY BY RUPERT HUGHES," with a subhead adding "In Which Bright Lines Redeem a Theme That Has Grown Threadbare." Complimenting Fairbanks for his natural and breezy manner, with "very agreeable support in Miss Adelaide Manola," the critic noted that Hughes had treated the theme as "nearer farce than comedy" and had brought freshness to its complications. The review also called the dialogue "exceptionally bright and entertaining" and added that "the audience was obviously amused and the laughter frequent and prolonged." [28]

As Rupert later would recall, "Though the notices were excellent and the audiences enthusiastic, they were not numerous enough to make the play a success." [29] But its run of thirty-three performances was sufficient to boost the career of Douglas Fairbanks and provide name recognition for Rupert's bride.

In a somewhat exaggerated account more than a quarter of a century later, Hughes wrote that Fairbanks, by then his close friend, owed some of his later fame in motion pictures to him: "He made his debut in a stellar role in a play of mine, *All for a Girl*, produced by William A. Brady, who kept it on, as a favor to me, for three weeks." After a few other stage ventures, the actor began making movies, Rupert said, but "if my play had been a big success, he might have stuck in the theater." [30]

As for Adelaide's stage career, Rupert later wrote that she appeared in leading roles in two other plays, including one of his, but neither drew good attendance. She revealed in each, as in *All for a Girl*, "a very great dramatic ability" but was so discouraged that she never acted again. [31]

Whether because of his heavy involvement in writing plays, his increased family responsibilities, or some other reason, Rupert decided, in the year of his marriage, to resign as captain of Company D of the 69th Regiment of the National Guard. [32] But this was to be only a temporary interruption of his military career.

Three more of his plays were produced the next year—one in Syracuse, another in Chicago, and the third in New York. The Syracuse offering, *The Transformation*, was an adaptation from T. Cicconi's Italian play; after a tour, it would later become even more successful under another name. Little is known about the Chicago play titled *My Boy*. [33]

The other 1909 production of a Hughes play proved to be his biggest stage success up to that time. It was *The Bridge*, the four-act play that Harrison Grey Fiske now produced at the Majestic Theater in New York with a September 4 opening. It starred seasoned actor Guy Bates Post as the hero, John Stoddard, a bridge builder involved in a struggle between labor and capital; Katherine Emmet was the heroine.

After the New York opening, a *New York Times* review, headed "'The Bridge' Has a Big Scene," called Post's acting "thoroughly delightful" and reported the plot was clever and held the audience's interest until the final curtain. One scene was singled out: "It showed the construction of a huge cantilever bridge with workmen swinging in midair and a real compressed-air riveter making a bedlam of a noise. It is one of the most perfect pieces of stage realism that has been seen in a long time." [34]

The big scene praised so highly prompted a letter to the editor protesting that it subjected the actors to personal danger. Specifically, the letter writer said, "a man is hoisted on a flimsy looking girder....at least sixty feet in the air, hanging by one hand to a frail looking rope. It's thrilling, but far too danger-ous . . . We need a theatrical censor for more reasons than one." [35]

Hughes responded promptly in a published letter stating that "every pre-caution is taken, and the girder is not 'flimsy'." He said the actor "who is hoisted aloft, singing one of his native melodies, would be heartbroken if the incident were omitted" from the play. "Since the incident is necessary in truth, since it seems to thrill the gaping audiences to loud applause, and since the actor is willing to take the risk, I think that your correspondent has no cause for complaint." [36]

The Bridge ran for thirty-three performances in New York before moving to Albany, Rochester, and other cities.[37] But it was the start of something much bigger. When revived in 1910 as *The Man Between*, it toured the nation for three seasons.[38]

During the period of 1908-1910, Hughes found a ready market for arti-cles about music and musicians at such popular magazines as *Smith's*, *Ainslee's*, *Century* and *The Delineator*. Some of the topics covered were "What Everyone Should Know About Music," "Women Composers," and "First Aids to the Unmusical." *The Delineator*, edited by Theodore Dreiser, published Hughes's "Before You Buy Your Piano," an expose of frauds prac-ticed by unscrupulous sellers.[39]

Turning to familiar subjects for his stories, Hughes wrote a tall tale about the oil fields, "Born in Missouri Is Born Into Trouble," that *Pearson's* pub-lished in August, 1908.

Another short story, "The Mouth of the Gift Horse," in the *Saturday Evening Post*, brought unexpected results. Described by the author as "a pic-ture of village ingratitude to a would-be benefactor," it angered some residents of the author's hometown, who thought it was based on what appeared to be their lack of appreciation toward a local citizen, John C. Hubinger, during the time he had lived there. To make amends, Hughes wrote an open letter to

Keokuk residents that read in part: "If I have given pain to anybody in Keokuk, it gives me even greater pain. There is no city without its tragedies and 'The Mouth of the Gift Horse' is simply a fiction based on fact. It is by no means an attack on the beautiful city on the Iowa palisades." [40]

More pleasing than the reaction to the story were reviews of his next book, which also used the word "gift" in its title. Called *The Gift Wife*, it tells the story of a hard-drinking young surgeon—a Yale graduate, no less—who gets drunk while on a train in Europe and wakes up penniless in a Turkish harem, where he falls in love with one of the wives of a wealthy Turk. The sultan offers him a slave girl, and although the American does not want her, he cannot refuse the gift; since her veil has not been lifted, she is known as a "gift-wife."

Smith's Magazine serialized the story in the summer of 1910, and Moffat, Yard and Company published it as a book the same year. Many years later, the International News Bureau would purchase newspaper serial rights.[41]

A reviewer for *The Bookman* congratulated Hughes for his success in "transferring to paper the somewhat elusive feelings and impressions that a foreigner receives upon his first plunge into Turkish environments."

The *New York Times*, in a rave review, pointed out, "If *The Gift Wife* by Rupert Hughes comes perilously close to the fantastic, it is saved first by the excellence of the telling and secondly by the author's knowledge of Turkey and its social life." [42]

The versatility displayed in writing such an imaginative story while turning out plays on a variety of topics, was shown further by two unrelated Hughes books published during this period. One was a new edition of *Contemporary American Composers*, issued in 1908 by L. C. Page & Company as *Famous American Composers*. The other was another volume of Lakerim stories for boys; published by The Century Company in 1910, it bore the title of *The Lakerim Cruise*. A *Literary Digest* reviewer thought the book would interest boys, but he considered it "not above the average." [43]

The year 1910 also brought productions of two Hughes plays in addition to the touring success of *The Man Between*. One was *The Transformation*, the play that had opened a year earlier in Syracuse and now went on tour.[44] Meanwhile, a highly successful production of a revised version of the same play opened under the name of *Two Women*.

The November tryout of the latter, in five acts, took place in Cleve-land for a good reason, as Rupert told a *Cleveland Press* interviewer. "I want to prove to my old schoolmates that after all there WAS something in 'that Hughes kid.' You see, I went to Adelbert and out there I wrote little sketches and appeared in amateur theatricals. Lots of the boys kidded me, but I made up my mind then to show 'em some day, and I hope I will be able to Tuesday night." There were other reasons, too, for launching the play in Cleveland. It was where Rupert's brother Felix lived and the show's star had grown up.

Mrs. Leslie Carter, who played the dual lead, was famous for starring in such plays as David Belasco's *Zaza* and *Madame Du Barry*. But producer John Cort predicted that the Hughes play at Cleveland's Colonial Theater "is so big, so vital that we just cannot help knowing it will be the greatest thing seen in a long while." The actress called her new role bigger than anything she had ever done.[45]

In *Two Women* Mrs. Carter played first the wife of a poor artist who has invented an engraving process. Suffering from tuberculosis, she poses for a portrait but dies before learning that the invention will make him rich. He then persuades a dancer who bears an eerie resemblance to his dead wife to pose in order that he might complete the portrait. At first he does not like the dancer (played by Mrs. Carter), but in time grows to love her.

After the play's New York opening at the Lyric Theater on November 29, 1910, the *Times* reported on a warm welcome for the actress and said that although the drama needed pruning, it provided Mrs. Carter with "such opportunities as she probably likes best and which, also, the audiences that admire her undoubtedly prefer. As a result, her present engagement . . . begun last evening under auspicious circumstances, is likely to prove profitable." [46]

The play continued there for forty-seven performances, then later ran at the Cort Theater in New York, and went on a nationwide tour that lasted three seasons.[47]

Although Rupert in 1910 had two plays touring nationally, it was not until the next year that he would score his biggest hit with an unlikely vehicle, a farce, that would enable him and Adelaide to adopt a much more comfortable life style.

CHAPTER SIX

NEWFOUND SUCCESS

*"Nothing I have ever done has given me the pride
and delight I got from. . .'The Old Nest'"*

Rupert's plays starring some of the brightest names in the theatrical world had met with varying degrees of success. But it was not until *Excuse Me* that he knew he had a real hit. Strangely, it required only a small amount of his time, compared with his other stage efforts.

Soon after it became successful, he told how easy his task had been: "One night I said to my wife, 'I believe I will write a farce. I wish I had a predicament.'" Among his unfinished manuscripts he found a novelette about a railroad journey, changed the characters around, and wrote a brief scenario that he submitted to producer Henry W. Savage, who promptly accepted it. The first draft took only ten days to write, and alterations consisted mainly of additions. After rehearsals, the play opened in January, 1911, at the Lyceum Theater in Allentown, Pennsylvania.

"It is really scandalous how comfortable it was," said Hughes, calling it "an exception that proves a rule."

But it was not without diligent research that he prepared the script about a transcontinental railroad trip. He studied Pullman car pictures so he could arrange the characters' seats to fit the plot, and pored over timetables before choosing the best route.[1]

The problems of a Navy lieutenant and his fiancee, heading west from Chicago on the Overland Limited, were the stuff of which the farce was made. Frustrated in an attempt to marry before the lieutenant's scheduled departure from the west coast for service in the Philippines, they become involved in a series of ludicrous happenings affecting an unusual cast of passengers in the two cars—a Pullman sleeper and a combination car—in which the play takes place.

Apparently unconcerned about superstition, the producer began tryouts on January 13 in Allentown, then took the play to New York for its February 13 opening at the Gaiety Theater at Broadway and 46th Street. Advertisements described the production as "A Pullman Carnival in Three Sections." [2]

On opening night in New York, there seemed no doubt that *Excuse Me* would be a hit. But when artist and illustrator James Montgomery Flagg congratulated the playwright, who was pacing the lobby during intermission, Hughes replied, "After all, I'm only human. Even I can't fail all the time." [3]

Life magazine, in its "Life's Confidential Guide," called the play "Mr. Rupert Hughes's diverting farce of sleeping car travel," and another reviewer reported that the actor playing the part of the sleeping car porter "created a sensation." In keeping with custom, the role had not been assigned to a black actor but to Willis P. Sweatnam, a seasoned performer from the Sweatnam Minstrels, who played the porter in blackface.[4]

Excuse Me was one of three hits Savage produced in 1911. Its 160 performances at the Gaiety made it one of only three plays with more than 150 New York performances that year that did not boast an established star.[5]

Hughes soon wrote a novelized version, and the book publisher, H. K. Fly Company, rushed it into print the same year, with an exclamation mark added to the title. *Excuse Me!* was illustrated by Flagg, who would provide illustrations for many of the author's other novels and become his close friend.

But the success of the farce was just beginning. After its New York run, two companies took it on tour throughout the United States for three years, beginning in 1912; another toured Australia in 1913; and it was produced in London in 1915. Plans were also made for its production in France, Germany, Italy, Russia, and Scandinavian countries.[6] The book would go through various reprints, and two movie versions of the play would be made, including a highly successful one in the mid-twenties. In 1934 Samuel French, Inc., would publish the play script.

As Rupert once said, "*Excuse Me* was my first real success and I worshipped the ground it walked on. It was very good to me."[7]

It was doing so well for him that he and Adelaide were able to move from New York City to a comfortable rural estate in the rolling hills country of Bedford Hills, an upscale area in Westchester County that was attaining a reputation as a literary community.

In addition to Adelaide's daughter, Avis, who lived with them, the couple also took Rush to their new home. After having discovered that the boy's father, George Bissell, had placed him in a Syracuse orphanage, they had managed to win his release. Although Rupert raised Adelaide's children as if they were his own and they became known as Rush and Avis Hughes, he never actually adopted them. It has been reported that Bissell would not permit their adoption, although he apparently had no objection when Hughes provided for their education at private schools, such as the Mercersburg Academy in Pennsylvania for Rush and the Foxcroft School in Middleburg, Virginia, which Avis later attended.[8]

With the success of *Excuse Me* no doubt a factor, Hughes was asked to dramatize Grace Miller White's popular novel about a "girl of the soil," *Tess of the Storm Country*. He took on the task gladly, hoping for another Broadway hit, and after finishing the script he went to Atlanta for the tryout. But the producer, instead of taking it to New York as planned, opened it in Paterson, New Jersey, intending to book it across the nation at inexpensive theaters where stock companies played. The problem with this arrangement was that motion pictures were becoming so popular, at low ticket prices, that many dollar theaters showing stage plays were folding. As a result, the *Tess* company closed after a few weeks, and no stock company wanted the play.[9]

But *Tess of the Storm Country* would be reborn in a few years—thanks to the medium that doomed it in 1911—at great profit to Hughes and Grace Miller White. At the same time, it would play a significant role in advancing the film career of one of America's all-time favorite actresses.

Along with the overwhelming success of *Excuse Me* and the initial disappointment about *Tess*, Rupert had been heartened and amazed by the critical and public response to a story he had written. Called "Miss 318," it depicted the frustrations of overworked shopgirls in dealing with irritable customers, primarily women, who delayed their Christmas gift buying until a few days before the holiday.

The story centers on the sharp-tongued Miss 318, so known by her badge number, who manages to keep her job only because "she sells the stuff." As one department store partner says to the other, "We ain't running a etiquette store. Ladies get mad at her, but they come back when we mark something low. You better give her a call-down, but don't let her get loose."

This is the Miss 318 they know, but she is also a dreamer, longing for the romance with a floorwalker that is never to be; instead, he falls for another shopgirl. It is a poignant story, as simple as the prayer Miss 318 utters upon returning to her flat after working until 2 a. m. on Christmas Day: "Thank God for the takin' off of shoes! Thank God for sleep." [10]

Published in the December 3, 1910, issue of the *Saturday Evening Post*, the imagery and descriptions used provide sharp contrast to the down-to-earth language of Miss 318. Hughes had obtained facts about wages and hours of clerks, and the story was undeniably written for a social purpose—"an attack on the annual shopping orgy because of its cruel follies," as the author put it. [11]

The Fleming H. Revell Company published a book version in 1911, containing a foreword by the author that said, "Many, many people have asked for Miss 318 in book form, so here she stands; begging whoso reads the story of these victims of Christmas as it is, to remember always that this is in no sense at all a protest against the beautiful festival itself, but a plea for Christmas as it ought to be." [12]

Critics joined in praise of *Miss 318*, with *The Independent* declaring that the brief tale had "more genuine human nature in it than most novels of twice the price." The American Library Association *Booklist* called it "interesting, sincere and a powerful plea for early Christmas shopping." The *New York Times* critic reported, "There is much humor, some of it rather riotous, and flashes of real wit." He said the author had depicted the "brutal phases of Christmas with adroitness and cleverness." [13]

Department store owners and managers also took note of the book. As a result, needed reforms took place throughout the country, and a *New York Herald Tribune* writer stated more than two decades later that "Miss 318 probably did more to bring about early Christmas shopping than any other one thing." [14]

The outlook appeared rosy indeed for the Hughes family during this period, until a sudden disaster brought them back to grim reality. On December 3,

1911, a fire destroyed their Bedford Hills home and with it most of the author's cherished library, his published works, and notes. A letter Rupert wrote to Dr. Charles F. Thwing, president of Western Reserve University, with which Adelbert College was affiliated, provided details of the near tragedy:

> The loss of my library, with all its associations and annotations, is indeed irreparable; but Mrs. Hughes had the inspiration to save my manuscripts first of all, and that fact has saved me from despair. Furthermore, the fire was so sudden and so terrific, and our escape so narrow, that this in itself tends to minimize the loss of so many other things that are only less valuable than life itself.

Soon after the embers cooled, Rupert and Adelaide hired an architect and began the tedious task of rebuilding. But the new house was to take a different form from the one destroyed, with extra precautions planned for the preservation of the library Rupert immediately began to reassemble.[15]

He sent his male secretary, named Sweeney, to the *Scribner's Magazine* office to look through files and to copy poems and other Hughes items that the magazine had published. In a letter to Robert Bridges at the magazine, Rupert recalled that his submissions had begun "pretty far back, perhaps with the 'Sonnet to Spring,' which appeared in a driving snow storm, or 'A Prayer for Rain,' which appeared after three weeks of unmitigated downpour." He wondered whether it could be determined which "anonymous publications" were his.[16]

While overseeing construction of the new home, Hughes took comfort in the enthusiastic reception accorded three more of his *Saturday Evening Post* stories when they were published as separate books. One of them was a touching story that brought astounding results.

The Old Nest was inspired by a realization that his mother longed to see her grownup children more often; busy with their own careers, he and his brothers and sister seldom managed to return to Keokuk. He wrote the story, based somewhat on circumstances of the Hughes family, about a fictional Midwestern mother who hopes that she and her husband might be reunited with their family. Things turn out happily when a son, appointed a United States Supreme Court justice, returns home on a surprise visit and invites his parents to a reception the President is planning in his honor. He promises that their other children will be there, too.

Rupert was in Paris when the *Post* published the story in its issue of June 3, 1911, and was amazed when a bundle of letters reached him—all expressing appreciation for the story. One woman told him that her son, who had not written in years, had sent her a lengthy letter with a copy of the Hughes story and a check in four figures. A man who had not seen his mother in months said he had wired her that he was on his way home.[17]

Publication of *The Old Nest* in book form by The Century Company in 1912 brought an even greater response, prompted in large part, no doubt, by the final paragraph:

> That is all. This has not been much of a story to read—not much plot, not much adventure; and yet, if you who read it should be moved to remember piously your mother—if she is dead; or if she lives, if you were impelled to sit down and write her a letter or send her a long telegram saying, "I am well, I am thinking of you and I want you to know how much I love you!" or, above all, if you should be persuaded to go home and see her—why, then, this story would have given more real joy than perhaps any other story ever written.[18]

It was obvious that Hughes had tapped a deep well of emotion that brought forth waves of guilt affecting countless readers. Fifteen years later a columnist for *The Bookman* would recall that in Kansas City alone, young men had lined up for blocks, "waiting to call their mothers on the long distance." Rupert reported an estimated "20,000 young men had returned home, besides those who had telephoned, telegraphed, or worn white carnations." But not all of the messages went to mothers; large numbers of letters, telegrams, and flowers arrived at the Hughes home.[19]

"Nothing I have ever done has given me the pride and delight I got from 'The Old Nest,'" he told a *New York Times* interviewer in 1914. Earlier, the *Times* called the book "a sincere and forceful piece of work" and one whose pages are "full of tender things beautifully imparted." [20]

The popularity of Hughes's *Saturday Evening Post* stories continued, and the one about Miss 318 was followed by a Christmas satire. Called "Mrs. Budlong's Christmas Presents," it—like many of his short stories—has a small-town Midwestern setting, the fictional town of Carthage patterned after the author's memories of Lancaster and Keokuk.

When D. Appleton and Company published *Mrs. Budlong's Christmas*

Presents in book form in 1912, its cover was appropriately decorated with a color picture of lavish Yuletide gifts. The *Springfield Republican* called it "a seasonable and highly-amusing volume in which the lengths and depths to which the habit of present-giving may lead otherwise respectable citizens are deliciously burlesqued." [21]

About six months after the *Post* published the Budlong story, it followed up on "Miss 318" with a sequel, "Miss 318 and Mr. 37," that soon became a book published by Fleming H. Revell and Company. As with the first story about the shopgirl, it had a social theme, depicting the fictional Mammoth store that risks the lives of thousands of employees and shoppers by not providing adequate fire protection. When a fire does occur, Mr. 37— a fireman with whom Miss 318 is in love—proves to be the hero.

The book was commended by the American Library Association *Booklist* as "at once humorous and tragic and a grave warning to those 'whom it may concern.'" *The Nation* gave it a mixed review, saying that Miss 318's "view of life, and the strange lingo through which she utters it, are even more amusing than pathetic. But Mr. Hughes has not brought us into her company a second time for her own sake. He has made her the central figure in a highly-colored tract." [22]

This concern about Hughes's use of a message in his fiction would be echoed many times as he increasingly devoted attention to social concerns and attempted to stir action against wrongs he thought should be righted. As for the "strange lingo," a columnist for *The Bookman* told Hughes years later that his favorites among the author's many books were those about the shopgirl. The reason: "I have always loved Miss 318 for her haughty remark: 'Me woik? Me! Why, I'm a poil diver at Tiffany's.'" [23]

This fictional character, as well as Hughes, came close to winning what could have been an important distinction when Thomas Alva Edison, the famous inventor, decided that *Miss 318 and Mr. 37* would be an appropriate subject for a motion picture. But this would not be just another silent film; his serious intention was to make it the first talking picture! Edison's reasoning was that the drama and excitement of the department store fire, along with the love story, could be woven into an unusual film in which the addition of sound would stimulate audience interest.

After paying Hughes a small amount for the script, however, Edison decided not to film it after all, choosing instead a minstrel show for his first sound movie. But his effort to combine the use of two of his inventions, the kinetoscope and the phonograph, proved a fiasco. At the show's first and only screening, which Hughes attended, he was thankful it was not his story being shown when the audience, realizing something was amiss, first laughed and then was embarrassed at the lack of sound/picture synchronization. As for *Miss 318 and Mr. 37*, the inventor later sold the script to another company, which made a silent film from it and eventually went bankrupt.[24]

In maintaining ties with Western Reserve University, Hughes had hoped to attend the twentieth anniversary reunion of Adelbert College's class of 1892, but a schedule change forced him to cancel. He responded, however, to the university's request for a biographical sketch, stating that he was "now chiefly devoted to the writing of fiction and plays . . ." He also wrote an essay, "How I Write a Play," that the *Cleveland Press* published.[25]

His three books published in 1912 added to his popularity as an author of fiction, while at the same time he began a revision of *Contemporary American Composers*. He also revised his two-volume 1903 encyclopedia, *The Musical Guide*. When published in 1913 as a single volume with a new title, it revealed the extent of his scholarly research. Several thousand additional short biographical sketches were included, as were stories of many operas that had been added to repertoires of opera companies.

Critics hailed the new edition, *Music Lovers' Cyclopedia*, published by Doubleday, Doran & Company, Inc. Excerpts from reviews include: "A compend of just such information about musical terms and musicians as the student of music most often feels the need of."—*The Independent*. "It remains, although even now it has only 960 pages, in some respects the most comprehensive and useful of all musical works of reference."—*The Nation*.[26]

By the time Hughes turned forty in 1912, he was carrying on a wide correspondence with editors and authors about literary matters. One letter to Walter Prichard Eaton of *American Magazine* provided his opinion on what he regarded as stilted and bookish language in the dialogue of many novels and plays:

You will find whole books in which there is nothing to distinguish the conversation of the people from the elaborate syntax of the author except the quotation marks. Seeing how rarely book reviewers observe

58

this vital untruth and how greedily they swallow polysyllables and Johnsonese syntax in the dialogue to be found in novels, it is, perhaps, not strange that they consider a playwright to be good in proportion to the bookishness of his dialogue. As a matter of fact, he is good in the inverse ratio to his bookishness and rotten in direct ratio to it.[27]

In addition to the touring companies of *Excuse Me, The Man Between*, and *Two Women*, the four-act *Sadie*, which Hughes adapted from a novel by Karl Edwin Harriman, was produced in New York in 1911.[28] Two other plays he wrote were staged within the next year, while his dramatization of *Miss 318* became a highly popular vaudeville sketch, touring the nation for four years. Two companies presented it one season, and it was nearly as successful as *Excuse Me*. In creating the sketch, Rupert tried something new; instead of writing everything in longhand, he dictated the script to his secretary. But when he finished it he went back to his old style of scribbling, scratching out, rewriting, pasting pieces together, and then turning over to his secretary an almost indecipherable manuscript to be typed neatly for presentation to a publisher or producer.[29]

The other 1912 Hughes play was an unusual production of what he called a "calisthenic farce," titled *What Ails You?*, that was as far from bookish as an author could get. In fact, the *New York Times* sent a sports reporter, rather than the drama critic, to view what was a sort of three-ring circus with a strange cast, in which nearly everyone suffers from some type of ailment. "But farce, comedy, or anything else supposed to have dramatic form, this piece is not," the *Times* reporter said, "though the friendly first-night audience seemed to find amusement in the exhibition." Produced by Henry W. Savage, *What Ails You?* ran twenty-five performances at the Criterion Theater in New York.[30]

The next play produced from a Hughes script was one of his last, for he was turning to other activities. Called *Uncle Zeb*, about the only reminders left are references in biographical sketches indicating that it was staged in New York in 1913.[31]

That was the year in which Hughes appeared as himself in a short motion picture, *Saved by Parcel Post*, produced by International Motion Picture Company for Universal release.[32] The riotous movie, made for the Dutch Treat Club, of which he was a member, also featured such notables as George Barr McCutcheon, Charles Dana Gibson, John Wolcott Adams, Will Irwin,

James Montgomery Flagg, Julian Street, and Charles Hanson Towne, each playing himself. Two stills from the film, showing Rupert as a cast member, were published in the *Saturday Evening Post* in 1935 to illustrate a series he wrote about silent film days. With the exception of a propaganda film that came along later, this is believed to be the only time that his acting talents were put on screen.

He was, however, becoming increasingly interested in the motion picture industry. At a studio near the Hudson River, he first watched a film in production; its interior scenes were shot outdoors, and the sunlight cast odd shadows on the players.

Soon after, at a movie house in Mount Kisco, he viewed for the first time—much to his surprise—a motion picture made from one of his stories. After the main feature, the two-reel *The Man That Might Have Been* was shown, with a line crediting Rupert Hughes as author of the original story. *Hampton's Magazine* had published it in March, 1910, but the magazine had gone bankrupt and Hughes had turned down a chance to buy back the remaining rights. Now, here it was on the screen in 1914, produced by Vitagraph.

The story is about a small-town bookkeeper whose wife dies in childbirth as does the infant. From then on the despondent widower spends his evenings in front of a stove, imagining the boy growing up and achieving great things—becoming an attorney, going on to the United States Senate, and eventually to the Presidency. Finally, when the imagined son has been inaugurated for a second term, the old bookkeeper dies, sitting in front of the fire.

Hughes was amazed to see many viewers weeping openly, thereby teaching him a lesson that would carry over into his future film work—that sincerity and simplicity would work as well in motion pictures as in other forms of fiction.[33]

Not only was he not paid for the movie, but the story was distributed to newspapers in 1913 by Continental Newspaper Syndicate[34]—presumably at no payment to the author, who had declined to buy back the rights. Later, however, he did include it in a book of short stories about life in small towns.

Although he was writing fewer plays, he continued to work on short stories and novels. *The Standard Index of Short Stories* for 1900-1914 lists forty-one of his stories published in well-known magazines, including twenty-five in the *Saturday Evening Post*.[35] But the list is far from complete, for he wrote for other publications not listed. Meanwhile, two more of his books were published in 1913 and another in 1914 before the publication of a novel that was to signal an entirely new phase of his writing career.

One book, a short story, bore the somewhat shocking title *The Lady Who Smoked Cigars*. Published by D. Fitzgerald, Inc., in 1913, with illustrations by J. C. Chase, it depicted a Death Valley prospector's wife who took up smoking to keep her husband, a smoker, from being lonely. Although women smokers were almost unheard of in those days, Rupert was so fond of cigars that he could see no reason why women should not smoke.

In *The Amiable Crimes of Dirk Memling*, published by D. Appleton & Company, he created a character who is both a burglar and a hero. A reviewer called it a "sort of cross between a novel and a collection of short stories" with a certain amount of "obvious humor" in it.[36]

A much more enthusiastic analysis was given to a slim volume, *The Last Rose of Summer*, published first in *Metropolitan* magazine in March, 1914. The plot focuses on an ordinary and homely woman named Deborah Larrabee who has remained at home with her mother, living off dividends from railroad stock her father left them. When the stock plummets and dividends cease, Debby gets a job as a department store clerk. Surrounded by people, she begins to bloom, eventually finding love with a former Carthage man who has gone to New York to work.

When Harper & Brothers published *The Last Rose of Summer* in the fall of 1914, reviewers called it "a sympathetic little story," "very dainty, very charming," and one that Hughes told "with skill and humor." From this pleasant and inspiring tale, the author became known for one of his most memorable quotations. His description of Debby told it all: "Her face was her chaperone."[37]

A few months earlier, he had begun what would become a longtime relationship with Harper & Brothers when the company published the first of an entirely different series of his novels—a form of social history that would be his hallmark for many years. And along with his often controversial novels would come, within the next decade, some memorable motion pictures.

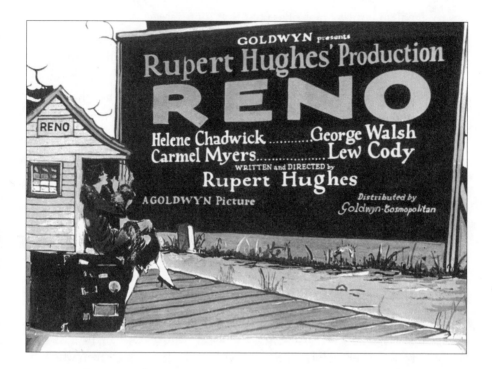

A NEW HOME, A NEW STYLE

"What is the chief need of the American novel? Sanity—a just, fair, reasonable appraisal of life for what it really is."

To replace the home destroyed by fire, a thirteen-room residence in the style of a French villa was built on the Rupert Hughes estate. Known as Whitewood, the house and grounds were patterned after those in a village where he had stayed in the Fontainebleau Forest area near Paris. For fireproofing, architect Aymar Embury II incorporated such features as concrete and tile floors and cork-centered doors.[1]

Nearby neighbors in the Bedford Hills community included literary figures, including Richard Harding Davis and Gouverneur Morris, and the Hugheses often invited other well-known authors and artists as house guests at what they referred to as their farm. One of them, James Montgomery Flagg, drew a cartoon titled "R. Hughes at 'ome" for *The Bookman*, showing Hughes at his desk, surrounded by six dogs of varying descriptions. With his hair awry and a tube from a large coffee dispenser in his mouth, the author is depicted leaning on one hand and writing furiously with the other.[2]

Photos of Hughes and his new showplace illustrated an article about him that filled nearly a full page in the Sunday *New York Times* on May 17, 1914, just as he put final touches on a novel, *What Will People Say?* A photo

63

of the exterior depicted the spacious villa overlooking its mirrored image in a pond complete with rowboat, and an interior picture featured the writer at an ornate, carved desk.

The article, based on an interview, bore a seven-column headline, "SANITY IS THE CHIEF NEED OF THE AMERICAN NOVEL," with a subhead of "So Declares Rupert Hughes, Novelist and Playwright, Who Adds that the Writer in this Country Should Give a Just Appraisal of Life for What It Really Is."

Hughes said that novelists, in a growing market for fiction that fluctuates between "prudery and pruriency," face a dilemma in trying to picture life realistically while maintaining a reputation of respectability. Noting that some people had already denounced *What Will People Say?* as "unpardonably frank," he thought any child could read it without harm.

What Will People Say? was the first of many Hughes novels serialized in *The Red Book* before being published as books. This arrangement came about when Ray Long, the magazine's editor, urged him to rewrite one of his plays as a serialized novel. Hughes was dubious about the idea, but chose his 1906 play *The Triangle*, updating it to emphasize the modern life style of certain New York socialites and using the current dance craze—the tango—to symbolize pleasures of the idle rich.[3]

Red Book published the serial with a certain amount of puffery in 1914. A line above the title in the February issue called it "A 'Vanity Fair' of New York"; the next issue termed it "The Greatest Novel of New York Ever Written." James Montgomery Flagg's illustrations were also played up; one issue contained three—a double-page, a full-page, and an inset.

What Will People Say?, published by Harper & Brothers in 1914, jumped to the top of best seller lists in New York and many cities, remaining there for months. It was ranked second nationally in *The Bookman's* list in April and May, dropped to sixth in June, then rose again to second in July. To the author, such success was astonishing; this had become his biggest seller.[4]

Reviews were mixed, but mostly favorable. It is doubtful, however, if any comment pleased Hughes more than that which came years later from an old friend, critic James Gibbons Huneker, who called the novel "Rupert Hughes at his best." [5]

With the book's popularity, motion picture producers wanted it for a film, but were concerned that the heroine might be too immoral and unrepentant for the screen. Finally Metro offered five hundred dollars and a small royalty, saying it could pay no more because of the heroine's unsavory character and the story's unhappy ending. Although this was a mediocre sum even then, Hughes accepted it, and *What Will People Say?* became the first of his novels to be sold to a motion picture company.

When the film was released in 1915, with Olga Petrova as Persis, the story and characters had undergone drastic changes, to Rupert's distress. The heroine had been sanitized, and wimpish Willie had been made into an unfaithful brute, causing audiences to be pleased when Persis divorced him and married Forbes. Despite the picture's success, Hughes received only ninety dollars in royalties, and although he later sold the remaining rights for $4,000, the story was never again made into a film.[6]

Within a year, his next novel, a mystery, was published by Harper & Brothers after serialization in *The Red Book*. In *Empty Pockets*, Hughes employed a story-telling technique that critics regarded as new. Starting with the discovery of a body, he flashed back to a year earlier, worked forward to the murder, then showed its consequences. He finished the serial at about the time war broke out in Europe and ended it by sending the heroine overseas as a war nurse.

Published in 1915, with illustrations by James Montgomery Flagg, the book brought one reviewer's comment that "it is no more than fair to accredit Mr. Hughes with having succeeded in reducing a typical photoplay melodrama to the more difficult medium of printer's ink."[7] The novel does read like a fast-moving motion picture, with detailed descriptions of New York, from the seamiest side to that of the upper crust.

The rich heroine, in love with a young physician, becomes involved in problems of the poor, helping to improve the lives of immigrant families and seeking a way to provide needed surgery for a crippled newsboy. One critic wrote that while it was a good story it was too long to be read at a single stretch. But another, reviewing it as one of *The Bookman's* Novels of the Month, said that even though he considered it "melodrama running amuck," he had enjoyed it immensely and, in fact, had read it slowly "to make it last the longer."[8]

The *Harper's Bookshelf* praised both author and novel, saying, "Mr. Hughes does with brilliancy, and also with sanity and right feeling, a kind of thing that it is too easy to do sensationally and speciously. For picturing modern metropolitan life . . . he has something like genius." The columnist called him "one of the true magicians of plot, and a master of rapid action." James Huneker also thought *Empty Pockets* was exciting, and he praised Hughes for successfully exploring New York's East Side in fiction.[9]

Although it is not known whether Hughes wrote *Empty Pockets* with the idea that it might be made into a movie, he was becoming increasingly interested in films and the business of making them, while getting acquainted with people in the industry.

One of these was producer David W. Griffith, one of the all-time geniuses of motion pictures who directed some masterpieces, several of which became subjects of great controversy. One that brought both praise and protest was the landmark Civil War story called *The Birth of a Nation*. Based on Thomas Dixon's novel *The Clansman*, it starred Lillian Gish and Mae Marsh and told the story of a family during the war and its aftermath. Battle scenes are startlingly realistic, as are those showing Ku Klux Klan members on night rides. Yet, the film displays much tender emotion.

Before its public release in 1915, Griffith invited Rupert and a few others to view it privately. Hughes's praise of its artistry so pleased Griffith that his press agent offered Hughes $2,000 to put his opinion in writing. As Rupert later recalled, he could have used the money, but "foolish pride, or ostentation, or something compelled me to write the tribute for nothing." [10]

Knowing that a stage play made from *The Clansman* had sparked riots in 1908, Griffith anticipated possible protests when his film was released, even though he had toned down the racism of the play. To avert trouble, he published Hughes's tribute in a program handed out at the high-priced New York opening. In his comments, Hughes pointed out that the film showed both good and bad Negroes as well as whites. He said he had a "great affection and a profound admiration for the Negro," and suggested that "it is to the advantage of the Negro of today to know how some of his ancestors misbehaved and why the prejudices in his path have grown there." Calling *The Birth of a Nation* a thoroughly documented chronicle of human passion, he warned, "The suppression of it would be a dangerous precedent in American dramatic art." [11]

The release of the picture did stir controversy. Some critics—as well as leading citizens who had not seen it—demanded its suppression, while many reviewers called it an extraordinary piece of film art. Griffith then asked Hughes to go with him and several other supporters to see the mayor of New

York, who was under pressure to ban the film. Although Hughes was prepared to speak up at the meeting, Griffith made such an impassioned plea that the mayor agreed to allow the movie to be shown. But some states did ban it, and *The Birth of a Nation* has been the subject of much controversy ever since.[12]

Hughes had not yet written any screenplays, but other things he had written were being brought to the screen. One was the stage play based on Grace Miller White's novel *Tess of the Storm Country*, which Famous Players Company produced in 1914 as a film starring Mary Pickford. The producers paid Hughes and Mrs. White an advance of only $350, and despite the success of the film, directed by the talented director/cameraman Edwin S. Porter, the two authors received royalties of only $84. As Rupert put it, "Bookkeeping has ever been one of the major arts in the movies." [13]

The popularity of *Tess*, however, was to have far-reaching effects. One historian said if any film "made" Mary Pickford, it was Tess, adding, "I can still remember how stock companies used to advertise their stage productions of it as 'MARY PICKFORD'S Great Success'." [14]

Mary Pickford was becoming "America's Sweetheart," and both Hughes and Mrs. White began to reap unanticipated benefits when the film helped revive stock companies' interest in the stage play, for which the authors had retained all rights. It was performed at least three thousand times, not including numerous unauthorized productions and film versions.

When Miss Pickford decided some years later to make another version of the motion picture, she bought the rights for $25,000 from Famous Players, which paid half to Hughes and Mrs. White. The two writers would receive a like amount again in 1933 when Fox purchased the rights for a film starring Janet Gaynor.[15]

But film companies were not paying sums of that magnitude for Hughes's stories during the early years. Although he is credited as author of the original story for the 1914 Vitagraph two-reeler *His Wife and His Work*,[16] he benefited little from it, if at all.

He was paid $1,500, however, for film rights to a 1909 *Saturday Evening Post* short story. After buying "Canavan, the Man Who Had His Way," which may have been patterned after the life of a Tammany Hall boss, George Kleine had his staff adapt it to the screen as *The Danger Signal*, but the results disturbed Hughes. His stirring story was about a hero browbeaten by his wife and destined to spend his life as a street cleaner, until be becomes aware of his potential. After a divorce, he gains a new wife and success. In the movie, he was a blacksmith who was married only once—to a socialite.[17] All was not lost with Canavan, however, for years later another producer made a film that followed the original story much more closely.

Other motion pictures were also made from stories by Hughes in 1915, although he had nothing to do with them. One was the three-reel *Out of the Ruins*, and another, based on Rupert's play *The Bridge*, was released as *The Bigger Man* by Metro Pictures Corporation.[18] In the same year, Henry W. Savage, producer of the stage farce *Excuse Me*, turned out a film version directed by George F. Marion, who played a key role as the porter.[19] But it was not for another decade that a successful movie would be made from the story.

During the years just prior to the United States involvement in World War I, Hughes continued his correspondence with authors and editors, including George Horace Lorimer of the *Saturday Evening Post*. Lorimer published his "The Thumb Twiddlers" as the lead story in the November 13, 1915, issue, with appropriate front-cover publicity.

It was customary for Rupert to compliment and encourage other authors, and he received many such letters in return. Quite often, writers sent him autographed copies of their books, and he responded with comments about the quality of their work. One of these was Sinclair Lewis. He praised Lewis for his novels, and thanked him for writing to him while on his honeymoon and for enclosing a photo of the hotel in which Lewis and his bride had stayed. Hughes invited the Lewises to visit him and Adelaide at Bedford Hills.[20]

Working with other authors on matters of mutual concern provided Hughes with much enjoyment, and he enthusiastically supported organizations that provided writers with economic and fraternal benefits. One such group was the Authors' League of America, made up of "the most distinguished—and delightful—members of our craft," according to Channing Pollock, who joined soon after the League was formed in 1912.[21]

Hughes was a founding member of the League, described by Toast-master Augustus Thomas at its 1915 annual meeting as a "self-confessed trade union, open to any one who ever wrote anything and had it refused." More than 500 writers, both men and women, convened to hear proposals to strengthen the organization and "make the pursuit of literature less of a grind." One speaker, Granville Barker, urged that a fund be established to support talented young writers for a few years in order that they might "follow their literary bent without danger of commercialism."

But Rupert Hughes declared that the writer needing the most help was "the worn-out hack who was struggling along in his 'none-too-ripe old age' to support a family on his literary output." He also spoke for fair treatment from publishers, remarking, "When we get the publishers where we want them we'll own them body and soul." [22]

Despite his tongue-in-cheek comments, Hughes was serious in his support of the organization, writing letters to 100 authors and urging each to contribute $100 toward its goals. He also enjoyed the League's weekly luncheons and conferences at Browne's Chop House, next door to the Empire Theater.[23]

He helped found another group, the Authors' Assurance Association, in 1914, along with Rex Beach, Jack London, and a half-hundred other leading authors, to try to prevent motion picture companies from plagiarizing magazine stories,[24] a common practice then.

A few months later there was an air of excitement in the New York literary and film world when the refurbished Knickerbocker Theater had its grand opening. The plan to show four motion pictures each week was an experiment to see whether movie-goers would pay as much to attend a film showing as they would for a stage play. Ticket prices were as high as three dollars for the opening night program featuring a D. W. Griffith picture, *The Lamb*, starring Douglas Fairbanks in his first movie role.[25] As Fairbanks's biographer reported more than a half-century later, "Sitting down with The Lamb on the night of September 23, 1915, were such lions of New York's artistic circles as Paderewski, painter Howard Chandler Christy, writers Rupert Hughes and Irvin Cobb—and, as it happened, they were moved. So was the press, which proclaimed Fairbanks a very satisfactory hero." [26] For Hughes there was special pleasure in knowing that the actor had first starred in a New York play in *All for a Girl* with the playwright's wife.

Meanwhile, although Rupert Hughes had become recognized as an important literary figure in New York, he had not been forgotten in Iowa, the place that had provided him with much background material for stories of the Midwest that had gained nationwide favor. He was invited to a "Homecoming of Iowa Authors" in Des Moines, sponsored by the Iowa Press and Authors' Club.[27] To the people of Iowa, he was still one of their own.

SHE GOES TO WAR

RUPERT HUGHES

SKRENDA

Illustrated with scenes from the photoplay produced
by HENRY KING for INSPIRATION PICTURES
A UNITED ARTISTS PICTURE

CHAPTER EIGHT

AND THEN THE WAR

*"The characters therefore largely make the story as
the times make them."*

After war in Europe broke out between the Allies and the Central Powers
in 1914, there had been a growing awareness that the United States
might be edging closer to involvement in the fighting.

Always a strong advocate of U. S. preparedness, Rupert Hughes signed up
again for duty with the New York National Guard, and on January 13, 1916,
Governor Whitman appointed him a captain in the Sixty-Ninth Infantry as
requested by the regimental commander. After an absence of eight years,
Hughes plunged immediately into military duties that would occupy much of
his time and require an adjustment in his writing schedule.

The year 1916 also saw the production of another of his plays, *The Vein
of Gold*. Little is known about this, other than that it was based on a novel
and subsequently was renamed *The Lioness*.[1] But if the play brought scant
attention to the author, the same was not true of his two novels published the
same year, including one about the theater and the people involved in it. The
latter, *Clipped Wings*, concerns a young and talented actress from a distinguished stage family who marries a small town manufacturer, agreeing to for-
sake theater life in the city to settle down as a housewife and mother. The
book's title reflects her lot, as her clipped wings keep her from soaring to

heights of which she is capable. Eventually, however, she takes a small part in an amateur performance, thus awakening her husband to a realization that he has kept her from her destined career. He agrees then to let her follow her ambition and divide her time between the stage and home.

Hughes intended the novel to be a "faithful presentation of the life and motives of actors and actresses, not cheap and tawdry mummers, not the usual silly caricatures of the stage, but a just picture of the real status of the better theatres . . . . It was incidentally an enthusiastic brief for a woman's right to a career apart from family ties." [2]

Clipped Wings was based on his story "The Barge of Dreams" that had appeared in *Munsey's* magazine. Shortly after publication of the book by Harper & Brothers, it hit best seller lists, then remained in the top five in many cities for months.[3]

Most reviewers were enthusiastic about the novel, especially the characterization of Sheila Kemble, the actress. *The Nation's* critic said that "Mr. Hughes, from his long experience as a successful playwright, is unsparing in his emphasis upon the toils and troubles of theatrical life. In manner, the book has its traces of the popular playwright and magazine-writer; but it is a book of serious substance." The *New Republic* stated that Hughes's work "places him head and shoulders above the ranks—in the select school of sincere American novelists." [4]

Even before *Clipped Wings* was published in book form, H. W. Boynton sang its praise in a *New York Evening Post* article titled "Rupert Hughes and His Work." He wrote, "I do not recall any novel in which the temper and character of the actor's life have been so credibly upheld. Mr. Hughes does not paint a stage life in which virtue has an easy time, or merit a quick reward. But he does—or his story does, for he is pretty successful in letting it point its own moral—suggest that moral conditions are no worse in the theatre than elsewhere." [5] This latter point was a theme that Hughes would emphasize many times in the future, after becoming heavily involved in another form of play-writing in a city often condemned for what many perceived to be low moral standards.

Numerous actors and actresses told Rupert that *Clipped Wings* was the only "fair portrait" ever written of what they were and did.[6]

Sheila Kemble, the actress heroine of the novel, was an incidental character in his next novel, *The Thirteenth Commandment*, published by Harper &

Brothers in 1916 after serialization in *Red Book*. Hughes dedicated the book "From the Depths of Gratitude and Devotion" to Ray Long, the editor who had proposed the arrangement by which the magazine serialized his novels before they became books. It was, and would continue to be, a happy and profitable publishing relationship for both Hughes and Long.

The central theme of *The Thirteenth Commandment* is extravagance, and the title implies the premise that "Thou shalt not spend all thou earnest"—a lesson eventually learned by Daphne Kip, a young lady who has been pampered by her parents. Engaged to a New Yorker, she is untrained for work and unable to find a job in the city, but she opens a lingerie shop and makes a success of it.

In writing the book, Hughes dramatized the need for every girl to learn a trade in order to support herself if necessary. H. W. Boynton wrote in *The Bookman*, "The author's voice is too insistent from the wings," but the *New York Times* reviewer believed that was the main strength of what he considered a thoughtful and interesting novel that was especially entertaining "when the author lays aside the mask of his characters and speaks out in his own proper person." [7]

Most reviews were favorable, and Hughes was pleased by a letter from William Lyon Phelps, the Yale professor, author, and critic whose opinion he valued highly. In a "Dear Will" response, Hughes thanked him for his comments about the book. He then explained the reasoning behind his current series of novels, in each of which "the story begins as recently as the plot permits, and the conclusion of it is laid in a time future to the beginning, so that by the time I reach it, I am in the midst of conditions unforeseen at the beginning. The characters therefore largely make the story as the times make them." Just as Balzac had included certain characters in more than one book in his *Comedie Humane*, Hughes said he was doing the same with his novels and was, in fact, trying to write a *Comedie Americane*, to present the truth "without regard to prejudice or tradition."

He told Phelps he was not writing for posterity, but was trying to present "an emotional history of my own time, my own country, my own people, in the years from 1913 on to—? I don't know that anybody else has ever laid down for himself just such a program. But it makes 'mighty interesting' writing for me." [8] Novels in the series were also of considerable interest to readers, whose purchases kept the Hughes name on best seller lists and provided him with a popularity he found astounding.

The reference to Balzac was not an isolated comparison; more and more, Hughes was to become regarded by some as "the American Balzac" —a term later included in the publisher's advertising for Hughes books.

While immersed in writing contemporaneous novels, Rupert suffered an intense personal loss early in 1916 with the death of his only sister, Greta Hughes Witherspoon.

Her marriage of more than fifteen years to singer Herbert Witherspoon had ended in divorce nine months earlier, and she had been teaching music since then in New York. After her return to the United States from abroad, she had resumed singing as "Jeanne Greta" for several years, both in New York and in western cities, but after that had not sung professionally for some time. Her death on February 21, 1916, was attributed to tuberculosis of the spine.

Her *New York Times* obituary stated that she was "in her forty-sixth year" when she died, but records indicate that she was at least three years older.[9] She was the first to die of Rupert's siblings who had reached maturity. Griefstricken by her loss, he was moved to write a touching sonnet in her memory:

GRETA

Greta! beautiful my sister, dead!
  Was it yesterday, or years ago you died?
  For grief comes back with the rush of a sudden tide,
Fresh tears, as if my eyes had never bled.
I keep again my vigil by your bed,
  Seeing you suffer again, as when you sighed,
  "Now am I going to die?" I smiled and lied,
You knew—forgave—held up your glorious head.

Against the hideous word my throat was clenched
  My heart denied a fate my love disdains.
  Your wit, your courage are in earth immured;
The flame of your gleaming voice in dust is quenched.
Though like a shackled rebel I fight my chains
  The intolerable truth must be endured.

In another poem, an elegy titled "At Kensico," he wrote again of his love for Greta and of her beauty and her voice, now forever stilled.[10]

74

Although several stories and novels by Rupert had been made into motion pictures, his first opportunity to write specifically for the screen came in 1916. He had wanted to do this for some time, having tried just about every other form of writing; as he once put it, he had an "innate restlessness to have a finger in every pie."

He got his chance with a big assignment for a screen serial that was to take up forty reels of material. Hired by producer George Kleine to write a script for what would become known as *Gloria's Romance*, he was unprepared for problems he would encounter in tailoring a story for the talents of the lovely Billie Burke, wife of famed stage impresario Flo Ziegfeld. Hughes's fee was an "extraordinary" $25,000, but the assignment also included writing a serial for the *Chicago Tribune*, a partner in the film venture; the star, Miss Burke, was paid $150,000.[11]

Rupert turned to Adelaide for help with the script—probably because of his own heavy schedule and to get a woman's viewpoint and provide her with writing experience. Instead of a thriller, typical of serials then prevalent, they would write a story with a high society setting appropriate for Miss Burke's acting style.

At weekly champagne luncheons at Delmonico's, studio executives praised Rupert's work. But he discovered that his high-priced script was being revised by a young man making twenty-five dollars a week, and the filmed scenes bore little resemblance to what Rupert had written. Other problems also caused concern. When *Chicago Tribune* representatives insisted that the story begin with scenes showing the star as a little girl, Hughes had to write six new reels of material.[12]

Gloria's Romance was a costly venture, but the producers had high hopes for its success and publicized Miss Burke as "The Star Supreme." [13]The serial, described as "A Motion Picture Novel by Mr. and Mrs. Rupert Hughes," [13] opened first at the Globe Theater in New York, with the distinction of being the first and probably the only serial formally reviewed in the *New York Times*. The choice of the Globe also marked the first time a serial was shown in a Broadway legitimate theater rather than in a movie theater. This seemed a logical choice, because many of the cast members were known for their stage performances.

Although filming of the final episodes had not been completed, the first two chapters opened on May 22, 1916, for a two-week run; other chapters were scheduled for later showings. Jerome Kern, who composed a score for the serial, conducted the orchestra at the opening. Ticket prices were twenty-five and fifty-cents each.[14]

Rupert attended the gala opening and was not surprised that the audience seemed bored by the chapters that were so unlike what he had written. Although he reported years later that critics panned the show, the *New York Times* review was mixed. Showing the serial at the Globe was an interesting experiment, wrote the reviewer, who said that the Hughes couple had provided a role for Miss Burke as a "young hoyden, whose enthusiasm for excitement gets her into all kinds of scrapes." The review praised Miss Burke and called the casting of stage players in the serial "a relief." [15]

Hopes that *Gloria's Romance* would be a financial success had vanished before its filming was completed, when a nationwide epidemic of infantile paralysis scared people away from public places, and many theaters closed. Hughes, however, had another reason not to go to theaters. He was suddenly called with the Sixty-Ninth Regiment of the New York National Guard to duty near the Mexican border, in response to a raid by Mexican bandit Pancho Villa on Columbus, New Mexico. As a result, Hughes never did see any more episodes of the ill-fated *Gloria's Romance*.[16]

Although the call to serve with one of the units led by General John J. Pershing promised to be exciting, it proved otherwise for Captain Hughes. Seventeen Americans were killed in raids on New Mexico and Texas by the revolutionary Villa and his guerrilla band, but Pershing and the U. S. troops were unsuccessful in their pursuit of Villa into Mexico. The role of Hughes and the troops he commanded soon became boring as they drilled and hiked along the Rio Grande, with the sun almost unbearably hot.[17]

The National Guard troops were ill-equipped for their task, but so were others sent to help out. Captain Hughes later wrote: "A regular army captain with a company of only 35 told me that at night his men had slept with their rifles across their arms and bayonets fixed. They actually had only one cartridge apiece!" [18]

For Hughes, the border experience was more than an inconvenience; it could have wrecked him career-wise. Before being called, he had begun a ten-part serial for *Red Book*, titled *We Can't Have Everything*, and was staying just a little ahead of publication, as with other serials he had written. It is no wonder that the editor was alarmed when the author went into military service.

"I found, however," Rupert said, "that even there in a tent among the cactuses and tarantulas I could write. It was better than sweating in idleness." [19] Up at 5 a.m. each day to drill troops and fulfill other chores, he spent evenings and long hours at night working on the serial. Writing in longhand, without a secretary to type the chapters before sending them to the editor, he never missed a deadline. It is small wonder, with his desire to chronicle current events, that he would arrange for the fictional hero to be called to duty on the Mexican border.

After three months had gone by, with still no military action, he resigned his post with the Sixty-Ninth and went back to New York.[20] But his return to civilian life would be only temporary.

The prodigious output of written materials from his pen, while he juggled other tasks such as the military assignment, often prompted interviewers to ask how he managed to accomplish so many things with such apparent ease. One such request came from Gordon Ray Young of the *Los Angeles Times*. In reply, Hughes told about his activities during early 1917, which included traveling around as the producer of a dramatization of Gertrude Atherton's 1914 novel *Perch of the Devil*. "We played a week in Buffalo and four weeks in Chicago and Mr. George D. Tyler, the manager, says that we have a great piece of property. He intends to open the season with it in New York next fall."

Hughes told Young that he was rushing the letter to him so Young would not think it was intended to influence "your very anxiously awaited verdict on my volume of short stories which is published this week. Of course it is but I do not wish to give that impression." [21]

The volume referred to was *In a Little Town*. Published by Harper & Brothers in March, 1917, it was a compilation of fourteen stories, some of which had appeared in the *Saturday Evening Post* or other magazines, plus a handful published for the first time in the book, for which James Montgomery Flagg had done the frontispiece. Ranging from "The Mouth of the Gift Horse" to "The Man That Might Have Been," they all had one thing in common—each was set in a Midwestern locale, near the Mississippi River.

Of all the reviews, none was more flattering than that in the *New York Times*, which said Hughes's stories were written with a sympathetic understanding. "He finds vices as well as virtues among the people of these village streets, and the stories of their lives show pathos and comedy and tragedy, meanness and nobility, gentleness and aggressiveness. But Mr. Hughes writes about them all with that tenderness of touch that comes of full comprehension." [22]

The demand for Hughes's stories for publication and motion pictures had grown to such an extent by the spring of 1917 that he reluctantly accepted a generous offer from *Hearst's Magazine*. After having rejected previous requests to sell his entire writing output to Hearst publications, he now signed an exclusive contract to sell the magazine all of the short stories in a series he planned to write during the next year.

"They say," he told Gordon Ray Young, "that this is the highest priced contract given to a short story writer. I don't know about that but it is a very pleasant sum for a very interesting program and it leaves me free to write my novel and such articles as I please." [23]

But the time he had available for writing would prove to be less than he had expected, due to the turn of events in connection with the war in Europe. When he wrote to Young on March 11, he was just a few weeks away from being back in uniform.

Following the sinking of the *Lusitania* by a German submarine in 1915, the buildup of United States armed forces had accelerated, and soon the entry of the U. S. into the war seemed almost certain. Finally, after the Germans sank some American merchant ships, President Woodrow Wilson warned in a somber message to Congress, "The world must be made safe for democracy." Two days later, on April 4, 1917—just two days before Congress officially declared the nation at war with Germany—Rupert, who had volunteered his services for any available post, was called to duty in Albany, New York, as assistant to the state's adjutant general, General Louis W. Stotesbury. Although Hughes's new responsibilities were time-consuming and involved much detailed work, he regarded as important the assignment to assist in the buildup of the New York National Guard toward its goal of 30,000 troops. [24]

Events taking place in *We Can't Have Everything*, which he had worked on while on the Mexican border, had their ending at the very time the author finished writing it. He depicted the entry of the United States into the war and showed the excitement at the Metropolitan Opera House in New York when an announcement was made that President Wilson had asked Congress to declare that a state of war existed.

But wartime references were only an incidental part of the book, published by Harper & Brothers in August, 1917. The main theme was discontent, centering on a realistic study of the institution of marriage, with a plea by the author for the changing of laws in order to permit inexpensive and easy divorces. This intrusion of his personal opinions into the story bothered some critics, but Hughes defended it in a lengthy letter to James Huneker, sending along a copy of the novel (which he called his "latest atrocity") and telling him:

> A lawyer has written me that I have done for divorce what Dickens did for his days' evils. It is indeed a very earnest work though the lack of despair about it leads many critics to rate it as mere flippancy. . . . The fact that so far as I know I am the only American who has dared to write truthfully about divorce, attacking both church and state without the cowardly subterfuge of a "Papa Kiss Mamma" ending, does not get many of the critics.
>
> But there are a few enthusiasts whose extravagances of praise make a pleasant pendulum sensation. As you know, I am just a plain feller with nothing unusual except a willingness to work mighty hard and an inexhaustible enthusiasm and affection for nearly everything that is or was or may be. . . .[25]

We Can't Have Everything is the story of Missouri-born Kedzie Thropp, who moves to New York, learns to dance, and becomes a movie star. Hughes intended to show the "amazing possibilities the moving-picture world has opened for the quick ascent of unimportant women to wealth and world-wide fame." [26]

By now many people regarded him as a social crusader, a role that he considered to be important. Many of his appeals were to help bring about the recognition of women's rights.

In We Can't Have Everything Hughes contended, "Marriage is among the last of the institutions to have the daylight let in and the windows thrown open. For the home is no more threatened by liberty than the State is, and that pair which is kept together only by the shackles of the law is already divorced; its cohabitation is a scandal." Pointing to New York state as an example, he said the law there says that "married couples shall not uncouple amicably and intelligently. . . . One of the two must be driven out through the ugly state of adultery. They must part as enemies and they must sacrifice some third person as a blood-offering on the altar." [27]

The crusading Hughes did during the war years was not confined to championing women's rights and attacking divorce laws. He also wrote about the nation's need to be better prepared for war; one way, he emphasized, was through the National Guard, which he called "the protest of American business men against unpreparedness."

The New York Times Magazine carried his portrait (which indicated that he had shaved off his mustache), along with an article about him, in May, 1917. A banner headline stated, "Captain Rupert Hughes Calls Authors to War." Calling it "the duty of every author of proper age to enlist, without waiting for conscription," he lashed out at critics of the National Guard and predicted that the Guard in New York state would be recruited up to its full strength for war readiness.[28] The article followed three earlier pieces he had written for Collier's in 1916, stating the case for the National Guard.[29]

Invited by Western Reserve University to provide information about his military career, he responded with humor, saying that "one of the chief causes of the German indifference to the entry of the United States into the war was the fact that their spies had learned of my contracts to write stories and novels and things and they thought that I could not be persuaded to take active command." He traced his career with the National Guard and told about his work as assistant to the Adjutant General:

Since I got here the Germans have been steadily pressed backward and the submarine campaign much lessened. There have been spasmodic successes on the part of the Germans, but that was because I have to sleep sometime. Also, at nights I do a little second story and short story work so as to get enough to feed a large and hungry family.

The New York National Guard is to mobilize July 15th so that you may look for the end of the war about that time. I regret that I cannot come out to the Commencement and show you what a real warrior looks like. . .

If you want a picture of me to impress the audience with, take one of Von Hindenburg, enlarge it, beautify it and give it a ferocious look. But don't let any young children or nervous women or hyphenated people see it, as they are apt to go into convulsions of terror.[30]

While in Albany, his days were filled with military duties, but he spent nighttime hours working on manuscripts, including a short story with a wartime flavor published in the September-October issue of Hearst's Magazine. In "The Mobilizing of Johanna" a young farm girl is bored with a monotonous life and longs for a beau. When the 69th Regiment sets up camp across from the farm where she lives, she sells sandwiches and soft drinks to soldiers and soon has many admirers. Eventually, she accepts a proposal to marry an officer.[31]

The story came to the attention of Mary Pickford, who thought it could be made into a film to fit the nation's wartime mood; she also wanted to play the starring role. The movie was produced by Artcraft Pictures Corporation under the title of Johanna Enlists and was released in 1918. In making the film, the assistance of an actual regiment from the Regular Army brought reality to the scenes. Film historians have praised Johanna Enlists for its "wry humor" and have called it a "delightful comedy." [32]

Meanwhile, Rupert had been involved in complicated negotiations over film rights to his play Two Women, which he first sold for $1,200 to Sigmund Lubin, who went broke without producing the film. Hughes then had to repay the $1,200 to the bankruptcy receiver and $450 to an agent in order to sell the story to Joseph M. Schenck, who wanted the story for a film to star Norma Talmadge. Schenck paid Hughes an advance of $1,800 and the play became a 1917 film titled Ghosts of Yesterday that was released the following January.

The star's performance was so brilliant and the film so successful that Schenck wanted to produce a new version. Although he never did, he paid Hughes a "pleasantly large" sum for the rights.

Another arrangement involved an earlier movie, The Old Folks at Home, based upon a Hughes short story. Triangle Film Corporation paid Hughes about $100 and cast famous British actor Sir Herbert Beerbohm Tree as a farmer.[33] The 1916 film was reissued in 1921.

The writing Rupert was doing by the latter part of 1917 provided him and Adelaide with an increasingly substantial income, and his stories that were in demand for motion pictures often became the objects of bidding wars. He told an agent that The Thirteenth Commandment had been bought for a much higher fee than that offered by the agent's client. Even his older stories, such as The Gift-Wife, were the subject of negotiations for newspaper syndication.[34]

Having known disappointment so many times in earlier years, Rupert was sensitive to criticism that he was now turning out popular books solely to make money. It bothered him that several literary friends did not find his current work to be worthy. This seemed true of James Huneker, as indicated in their correspondence. Hughes had chided Huneker for not reviewing *Clipped Wings* in a column he wrote for *Puck*, but the critic explained that he had been ill and that the magazine had put a limit on available space. Then, after Hughes's publisher mistakenly released to the press a personal letter Huneker had written to Rupert that praised *Empty Pockets*, the resulting publicity had made Huneker unhappy.[35] It was in this atmosphere of misunderstanding in 1917 that Rupert wrote a wistful letter to his old friend. He invited Huneker to visit him at an apartment he had taken in the Sixty-Seventh Street Studios and inquired about Huneker's health, before expressing some of his frustrations:

It is my tremendous ambition to see things as they are, with sympathy, without prejudice, without pose, eccentricity, dyspepsia, nausea, animosity; with neither hostility nor lust for the unusual, the new, the old, the classic, the cubist, the futurist, the cheerful, the tragic, the aristocratic, the plebeian, anybody, anything.

I am conceited enough to feel that my tireless scholarship in the ancient, the primeval, medieval, coeval, and other evals, and my determination to consecrate it to as true an analysis and synthesis of my own people while they live and move and have their being—will be far more valued by that damned posterity than many a book which gives a distorted, a morbid, or a loathing caricature of our time. . . .

Don't for God's sake take this as a wild plea for a bouquet. I should hurl it back at you if you flang me an orchid. What I meanter say is that I admire you so much, your amazing scholarship, your indefatigable enthusiasms, your mastery of the language and all, that I feel lonesome outside. But I feel none the less sure that I am doing the right thing for me, and that my books are doing for my country what no one else is doing.

Forgive this self-adulation. I started out to pay homage to you. I do pay it—profound reverent homage.

Yours always,

Rupert[36]

The letter was written shortly after his return from Texas, where he had visited his brother Howard and his family. Howard had invented a machine he and

Rupert thought might be useful to the war effort, and Rupert wanted to see it tested. A portable device based somewhat on Howard's conical drill bit invention, it was designed to drill horizontally through the earth to speed up mining and countermining. A test by Howard showed that it could do in two days what normally would take months: bore to an enemy trench a thousand yards away, "deposit explosive under it, blow it up, and withdraw." But red tape proved a hindrance, despite Rupert's efforts to expedite matters by talking with George Creel, one of President Wilson's closest advisors, and various generals. As a result, the invention was never tested on a battlefield before the war ended.

The visit to Houston gave Rupert a chance to become better acquainted with his nephew, Howard, Jr., who at age twelve was showing that he had inherited his father's inventive talents. After his parents turned down his request for a motorcycle, he had attached a junked battery and an automobile starter motor to his bicycle, "and the damned thing ran," Rupert reported.[37]

Perhaps one reason Rupert tried so hard to help obtain military approval for the drilling device was his disappointment in not being able to go to Europe with his beloved 69th regiment. He was, in fact, turned down for overseas service three times—"my only heartbreak"—because of a slight hearing loss,[38] an inherited disability that later would afflict his nephew Howard.

Rupert's desire to do his part in the war effort carried over into the writing of a wartime novel, which in November, 1917, began its serialization in *Red Book*. Called *The Unpardonable Sin*, it dealt with the brutal treatment of Belgian citizens by German soldiers.

Despite his heartbreak over being rejected for overseas duty, his spirits were buoyed when he received word from author Hamlin Garland that he was about to be recommended for a high honor. Rupert's response: "It would give me great pleasure to be nominated for a halo in the National Institute of Arts and Letters and I thank you and Phelps and Williams for being bold enough to stand for me." [39]

Hughes was one of the proposed "desirable" candidates contacted by an Institute committee, consisting of Garland as chairman and William Lyon Phelps and Jesse Lynch Williams as members, to see if they were willing to be considered for election. Ballots were then sent to Institute members, with the committee members listed as proposers for Hughes and some of the other candidates. Hughes and most of the other candidates did not receive enough votes to be elected. The most votes went to women candidates (with Edith

Wharton in the lead), but they were not admitted that year because the organization had not yet opened its membership to women. As it turned out, only two of thirteen candidates on the ballot were elected that year—Frank Henry Giddings, professor of sociology at Columbia University, and Edward Sheldon, a dramatist.[40]

It became apparent to Hughes that something had gone awry, as he indicated to William Lyon Phelps: "Hamlin Garland said that you, he and Jesse Lynch Williams were going to try to immortalize me but as I've heard nothing more I presume St. Peter declined."

If this was much of a disappointment, Rupert gave no such indication. He obviously was pleased that Phelps, whose reputation as a literary oracle was without peer, had nominated him. He also seemed more concerned with just trying to get together with Phelps for a visit, "especially as I may go back soon to Washington with a commission in the Army." [41]

Socializing with other writers was one of the joys of his life. His friendship with Sinclair Lewis continued to be one of mutual admiration, and their letters expressed appreciation for novels they exchanged. In one instance, Hughes wrote, "I was proud and happy to receive from you a copy of *The Job*. While I have been too frantically busy to read it all I am far enough into it to realize that I am still in the presence of a very brilliant observer and recorder of life. You are still the master of the happy phrase and the vivid picture . . ." [42]

Lewis showed his regard for Hughes in a letter expressing amazement at the amount of time Rupert spent in encouraging young writers. He also passed along a compliment from Gordon Ray Young, the *Los Angeles Times* critic, who had told him that he considered Hughes to be the best writer in America.[43] It was a statement that surely must have boosted Rupert's spirits.

A MILITARY CENSOR

*"The Chief Military Censor is having his attention
called daily to books, periodicals, and articles that
should not be published in time of war."*

The U.S. Army commission Hughes hinted at came through on January 5, 1918, when he became a captain in the Infantry, stationed in Washington, D.C. He promptly wrote again to William Lyon Phelps to tell him he was glad to be back in uniform.[1]

Although Captain Hughes's tasks were much different from those he had hoped for, having preferred to have gone overseas, he had the important responsibility of organizing all of the duties of military censorship into one unit of the Military Intelligence branch.[2] In this assignment he reported to the chief military censor, Brigadier General M. Churchill of the General Staff in the War Department, but also worked closely with an old friend, George Creel, a fellow Missourian and a confidant of President Wilson.

In 1912 Creel had married the stunning actress Blanche Bates, who had introduced Rupert to Adelaide.[3] A former newspaper editor in Kansas City and Denver, Creel created a Committee on Public Information to enlist public support for the war effort. His successful work, demonstrating the techniques of mobilizing opinion, was a milestone in the fledgling practice of public relations.[4]

Hughes appealed to the patriotism of newspaper and magazine editors, finding that persuasion worked better than threats or harsh enforcement of rigid regulations. As an author, he strongly resisted the idea of censorship and later would rebel against it as a film writer and director. But having been put in charge of the operational procedures of a wartime censorship effort, he was determined to make it work.

The voluntary nature of the censorship helped bring about cooperation from editors and publishers. An example of appeals made by the office of the chief military censor is one that Hughes signed and sent to publishers:

The Chief Military Censor is having his attention called daily to books, periodicals, and articles that should not be published in time of war . . . . Often such literature reveals military secrets. At other times, however, it proves to be propaganda so cleverly disguised as to have escaped the notice of even the most patriotic publishers.

We write to request your co-operation in keeping such literature at a minimum. You can do this by referring to us for censorship any articles or manuscripts about which you are doubtful . . .[5]

Fourteen years later Hughes's success in handling his responsibilities as a censor was noted by Gove Hambidge in the *New York Herald Tribune*:

Few people had a more delicate task, in those days of spy hunting and hysteria, than the man who could stop any newspaper or magazine in the United States merely by saying so. Major Hughes kept only one object in mind—nothing must be allowed to interfere with operations against the enemy. For the rest, he tried to keep his sense of humor and his perspective in good working order. . . . Some one said he had more common sense than any one in Washington.[6]

Ironically, in September, 1918, a rumor grew that Hughes himself had been the target of censorship. The incident, which became the subject of a *New York Times* editorial, concerned his timely book titled *The Unpardonable Sin.* In the novel, details of the brutality of German soldiers to defenseless women in Belgium shocked some readers, although reviewers acknowledged that the author had handled them tastefully. *The Bookman* included the novel in its "What to Read This Summer" list, and the *Times* reviewer thought the descriptions were "well done," with the "immensity of the tragedy involved

Above left: Felix Turner Hughes, attorney and railroad president, was the father of Rupert and three others who achieved notable success.

Above right: Jean Amelia Summerlin Hughes encouraged Rupert and her other children in the development of their talents.

The Hughes children from left to right: Howard Sr., Greta, Felix and Rupert.

The birthplace in Lancaster, Missouri, of novelist Rupert Hughes, his brother Howard (father of billionaire Howard), and two other prominent members of the Hughes family.

Rupert Hughes in front of the Arabian Nights home that he built in the 1920's in Hollywood, CA.

A young Howard Hughes Jr., nephew of Rupert, beams for the camera.

Howard Hughes Jr., as a teenager. (Note the striking resemblance to Rupert.)

A young Rupert Hughes while a student in Ohio. He later became one of the nation's most famous writers.

Elspeth and her mother
Agnes, Rupert's first wife.

Allene Gano Hughes,
mother to Howard Jr.

Rupert and his third wife, Patterson Dial.

Ladies' Man stars William Powell and Carole Lombard, 1931.

Rupert Hughes with
Linda Darnell and
Preston Sturges.

Rupert and Jimmy Durante at the Brown Derby Restaurant.

W.C. Fields and Rupert at the opening of Grauman's Chinese Theater.

Rupert with Don Ameche in costume for *The Three Musketeers*.
(Compliments of the American Society for the Hard of Hearing.)

Rupert with Robert Taylor and Gladys Swarthout (1936).

having apparently had a subduing effect upon Mr. Hughes's usually rather flamboyant style." [7]

The *Times* later provided high praise for Hughes in an editorial headed "Censorship at Its Very Worst," in which it reported that someone asking to borrow the book at a New York library had been told that "it was not the intention to have the book there or to assist in its circulation." The editorial called for an investigation, pointing out that "of the innumerable books that the war has produced, not half a dozen, if as many, that would be catalogued as fiction better deserve reading by good Americans of every age and both sexes than does *The Unpardonable Sin*, and none better rewards a careful perusal." [8]

German crimes in the novel include the rape of the sister and mother of the heroine, a California girl who goes to Belgium to rescue her kin. With the help of an American man, she finds her mother and sister, both of whom bear German babies. The sister and her infant die in a submarine crash, but the heroine brings her mother back to her father, who accepts the baby that is not his. In turn, the heroine finds true love with her American admirer.

The stir reported in the editorial ended when the New York Library director responded that Hughes's book had been approved for purchase by branches.[9]

There is no doubt that Hughes had carefully documented the brutality he described. Although critics sometimes found fault with his literary style or character development, few would ever quarrel with the authenticity of his factual material.

Hughes took pride in noting that *The Unpardonable Sin* was the last book praised publicly by Theodore Roosevelt before the former President's death in January, 1919.[10]

The financial return from Hughes's novels proved an incentive to keep writing while in military service. He also composed music, compiling a volume of what he referred to as "the new poetry" set to music. He had not written much verse himself for many years, having learned that he could write a novel more quickly and with less difficulty than he could a sonnet; besides, he was paid only fifteen dollars for a sonnet and could make much more than a thousand times that amount from a novel.[11]

While in Washington, his book of short stories called *Long Ever Ago* was published in March, 1918. It included ten stories, most of which were about middle-class Irish-Americans of New York City. All but two had been published previously in magazines, and six were about a family called the Morahans. During the dozen years he had served as an officer in the 69th Regiment, the "Fighting Irish," Hughes had learned much about the soldiers' backgrounds and had picked up their Irish accents. After being rejected for overseas duty with these men, he decided to assemble his Irish-American stories into a single volume, as a tribute to his former regiment. The dedication, appropriately enough, read:

To
The Fighting 69th
Now the 165th Infantry
With Homage and Envy
"The 69th in France and I Not With Them"

The last line of the dedication was a plaintive cry from Thady Murphy, an underage youth in the volume's first story, "The Murphy That Made America," in which he pleads with his mother for permission to volunteer for duty with the regiment.[12] Eventually she gives in and he enlists. But the line had special meaning for Rupert, who bemoaned the hearing problem that had kept him from leading troops into battle and had forced him to serve as part of what he often called "the swivel-chair Army." In later years he would joke about having been a captain in the Fighting 69th "without being Irish or a fighter." [13]

Critical praise of the book was virtually unanimous, with the *New York Times* calling the Morahans a likable lot and the "ten pleasant little sketches" agreeable entertainment. Other critics cited the author's faithful portrayal of Irish traits.[14]

Long Ever Ago was listed by Edward J. O'Brien in *The Best Short Stories of 1918* as one of the year's Ten Best American Books of Short Stories. O'Brien singled out one story, "At the Back of God Speed," for the annual "Roll of Honor," signifying its more or less permanent literary value, and noted the distinction of "The Murphy That Saved America." In commenting further about the author's work, he wrote:

Three years ago Mr. Hughes published in the Metropolitan Magazine two stories which were as fine in their way as the best of Irvin Cobb's humorous stories. In "Michaeleen! Michaelawn!" and "Sent for Out," Mr. Hughes depicted with his wonted kindliness and pathos the first generation of Irish immigrants. "At the Back of God Speed" now completes the series, which form as a whole the most faithful portrait yet drawn of the Americanized Irishman.[15]

At about the time the Irish book was published, a musical version of *Excuse Me* appeared at the Cohan Theater in New York. Jerome Kern wrote the music for *Toot-Toot!* Edgar Allan Woolf wrote the book, and Berton Braley the lyrics. A reviewer called it a lively musical comedy, but *Toot-Toot!* closed after forty performances—far less than the run of *Excuse Me*.[16]

Rupert turned his hand to play-writing again while in Washington, writing a one-act farce called *For She's a Jolly Good Fellow*. It was published in 1918 by the War Department's Commission on Training Camp Activities, Department of Dramatic Activities Among the Soldiers.[17]

He also wrote a thorough and scholarly analysis of propaganda, consisting of 187 pages of text and many additional pages of clipping reproductions. It was published by the Military Intelligence Branch, General Staff, U.S.A.[18]

During the last year of the war, two more Hughes novels were made into motion pictures. One was the murder mystery *Empty Pockets*, which First National purchased and made into a 1918 film. The second was a movie version of the popular *We Can't Have Everything*, produced by Artcraft and released by Paramount the same year. Cecil B. DeMille directed the film and his brother William wrote the script. Warned by producer Jesse Lasky to hold costs down, they agreed reluctantly to eliminate what was to have been the most exciting and expensive scene—a studio fire that had been an integral part of Hughes's novel. But fate intervened when Cecil and cast members, returning from location one day, saw smoke in the distance and realized that the Lasky studio was aflame. Instantly DeMille rushed cast members into costumes and started cameras rolling.

Firemen fighting the blaze, caused by a crossed wire, had never seen victims enjoying a fire so much. "After they had finally put out the blaze, they did not wait around long enough to see me start another little fire in the ruins, in order to get close-ups," DeMille later recalled.[19]

A critic thought the fire scene was the most remarkable thing about *We Can't Have Everything*. Calling the film the most pretentious of the features showing that week, he said the production was above average. He added, "It may be that Rupert Hughes's novel, upon which the play is based, said something with a meaning, but if so the camera failed to catch it, recording simply a rather inconsistent and impossible story." [20]

During his Washington stay, Hughes became well acquainted with the overcrowded city and absorbed the flavor of its wartime excitement. Turning his attention toward the nation's frantic effort to boost its sea power, he chose Washington and the shipyards as the setting for his next novel. Although the time available for writing was limited to evening and late night hours, he wrote *The Cup of Fury*, which was first published in serial form.

The story is primarily about the conflict of capital and labor, with a spy element woven in along with the love interest between the heroine and the shipbuilder hero. The book, published by Harper & Brothers in May, 1919, was illustrated by Henry Raleigh. Although Hughes did not consider the novel one of his best—later calling it "as inchoate and formless as the public mind"—reviews were mixed. The *Springfield Republican* reviewer said the story rambled, but contained thrilling episodes and pictured wartime Washington vividly. *The New Republic* critic complained about the author's "querulous" arguing, saying he appeared to be "haunted by an obsession." [21]

The *New York Times* critic took a decidedly more positive view. A long account headed "War as Rupert Hughes Sees It" said *The Cup of Fury*, a follow-up to the great success of *The Unpardonable Sin*, dealt with a different phase of the war—the struggle between patriotic shipbuilders and the spies and anarchists who tried to aid Germany by blowing up shipyards, planting bombs on ships, or by sabotage. Hughes was commended for providing a "well-drawn and vivid picture of one of the most important and interesting phases of America's war activities, while giving at the same time an opportunity for some very sensible comments concerning the struggle sure to come after the war." [22]

Despite his war censorship responsibilities and heavy writing load, Hughes kept up a correspondence on topics that ranged from discussions of poetry with William Lyon Phelps to the beginning of what would develop years later into a full-fledged controversy with two other authors, James Branch Cabell and Burton Rascoe, who took sides against Hughes on the subject of the merit of Cabell's and Hughes's writings and those of certain other authors.

Promoted to major on September 4, 1918,[23] Hughes eagerly awaited the end of the war, which finally came, heralded by a false report but soon signed into reality by the Armistice agreement on November 11. He stood beside George Creel and other fellow Missourians as they viewed the parade of soldiers led by Missouri-born General John Pershing down New York's Fifth Avenue.[24]

With the fighting over, there seemed no further need for war censorship. On January 15, 1919, slightly more than two months after the war ended, Major Rupert Hughes was honorably discharged from the U. S. Army[25] and resumed his writing in earnest, soon to embark on an entirely different phase of his career that would take him to a new location.

CHAPTER TEN

AN EMINENT AUTHOR

"The author has at last won the franchise, and it carries with it a heavy responsibility, but the opportunity is glorious."

During filming of *The Unpardonable Sin*, which began before the war ended, its story of German atrocities became subject to the same sort of voluntary censorship that Rupert Hughes had requested from others while performing his military duties. In an effort to bring about peace, President Wilson urged movie producers to refrain from attacks on the German people, hoping he might be able to drive a wedge between citizens and rulers of the enemy country.[1]

The Unpardonable Sin was made by an independent production company headed by Harry Garson, who teamed with Marshall Neilan and Albert Kaufman. Hughes was also involved somewhat with the production, as was Blanche Sweet, who starred in the film in a dual role.[2] To comply with the President's request to go easy on the Germans, producers blamed the philosopher Nietzsche, rather than German leaders, as the cause of the war's atrocities.[3]

A problem of censorship came up during filming when an actress said (by means of a title card) that she was going to become a mother. The taboo word "pregnant" was not used, but the censor said any reference to impending motherhood must be cut.[4] This, of course, seemed ridiculous to Rupert.

Financing problems and Neilan's partying sometimes caused production halts, and by the time the film was released the war was over. When it then became difficult to find a distributor because of concern that the public was tired of war movies, Neilan promoted *The Unpardonable Sin* as "not a war picture." [5]

Years later, Hughes recalled that the film drew big crowds, even at the Detroit opening during a blizzard. Trade journals reported that box office receipts set a record for its first week, and advertisements trumpeted the message: "THE BIGGEST OPENING THE WORLD HAS EVER SEEN, BAR NONE."

After showing in several cities, *The Unpardonable Sin* opened in New York on May 2, 1919, at the newly refurbished Broadway Theater at Broadway and 41st Street, which had been converted from a stage playhouse to a motion picture theater. In keeping with the tone of the film, a symphony orchestra played Tchaikovsky's thundering *1812 Overture*.

Newspaper advertisements the next day proclaimed the movie "The most daring picture of all times!! A gigantic drama that tells the truth and drives it home . . . . Major Rupert Hughes' astounding story . . ." One ad, picturing a beautiful young woman cringing from the outreached arms of a vicious thug, claimed that two thousand New Yorkers had cheered the movie and that "10,000 were sorrowfully turned away last night." [6]

Although Hughes had been named a major in the Reserve Corps on April 3, a few months after his Army discharge, [7] he felt self-conscious about publicity referring to him as "Major Rupert Hughes." He preferred to be regarded as a civilian, but the title stuck with him. Many years later he wrote, "This is because so many people do not know me well enough to call me by my first name and think of me as too unimportant to be called 'Mister.'"

He was even more embarrassed by a studio press kit that misstated his war record, claiming he was a hero who had been promoted to major after taking the place of his captain killed in battle. When Hughes demanded the producers set the record straight, they said the press kits had been distributed and it was too late to do anything. [8]

Within a month after the New York opening of *The Unpardonable Sin* the name of Major Rupert Hughes again was publicized when Goldwyn Pictures Corporation announced it had formed a corporation known as Eminent Authors Pictures, Inc., with a capitalization of a million dollars. [9] This was a venture dreamed up by producer Samuel Goldwyn, who asked author Rex Beach to help him persuade the most prominent writers of the day to bring their talents to the screen by adapting their own works for motion pictures.

Goldwyn believed it was the answer to the industry's lack of good stories—one of its biggest problems. He envied producers who had lined up top stars, and he saw an opportunity to put leading authors under contract to supply him with material that was popular with the reading public. He intended to put the authors' names above those of the featured players in his films.[10]

Rex Beach was under contract to Goldwyn and was an appropriate choice to be his partner, having written successful screenplays that included an adaptation of his popular novel *The Spoilers*. A rugged man who had played football before going to Alaska, he had returned without the gold he had hoped to find but with a wealth of adventure stories he put on paper. After selling some novels to the movies, he had been elected president of the Authors' League.[11]

An announcement in *The Moving Picture World* on June 7, 1919, headlined "Eminent Authors Pictures Formed," stated that Beach was president of the new corporation and Goldwyn chairman of the board of directors. It said: "All the works of Gertrude Atherton, Mary Roberts Rinehart, Rupert Hughes, Basil King, Gouverneur Morris and Leroy Scott are under the exclusive control of the new corporation for screen adaptation. Production rights not only to all the works that have been written to date, but all the works that will be written from now on are held for a long term of years."

The intention, said Beach, was "to star the story instead of the actor," as in the legitimate theater where it was the custom to choose an actor to fit a play rather than to alter a script to suit the actor. But the most unique feature of the arrangement was to give the author "the final power of direction and supervision over his picture," the magazine reported. Beach emphasized that all of the Eminent Authors had written stories or books that had been filmed, but they had never been seriously consulted about the best screen treatment for their work.

Publicity photos of the authors included one of Major Hughes in military uniform. But this was just the beginning of a full-fledged hype campaign engineered by publicist Howard Dietz, who proceeded to tell the world about Goldwyn's master stroke in hiring literary talent.[12]

Hughes recalled what it was like to be a member of Goldwyn's group who had been given the "high style and title of 'eminent authors.'" Twenty-four-sheet billboards, each showing the likeness of an actress or actor on one side and an author on the other, were displayed across the nation. "My regrettable features, hugely enlarged, furnished a shocking contrast everywhere to the bright beauty of Madge Kennedy," he said.[13]

Despite being self-conscious about the publicity, he was pleased with the arrangement. He said the art of making films had equaled in just a decade the progress that other arts had taken centuries to achieve. Recalling the plagiarism and inept film treatment of authors' stories and plots, he said he had never regarded his work as sacred; indeed, he considered his lines "blacksmith's text." He had sometimes been paid as much as $10,000 for screen rights to a story, and after it was filmed could not recognize "one entire incident, theme, or characterization."

Now he said, "The author has at last won the franchise, and it carries with it a heavy responsibility; but the opportunity is glorious." [14]

At first he had turned down Beach's invitation to join the fold, concerned that the terms might not be to his advantage even though the Goldwyn company would take all financial risks. Finally, after Sam Goldwyn met with him, he accepted an offer of $50,000 in monthly installments as a "guaranty against a third interest in the profits of five pictures, the losses on no picture to be charged against any of the others." In addition, he could reject changes in scenarios and veto the selection of cast members. To his later regret, he turned down a clause providing repayment of his travel expenses, thinking he would not do any traveling. He had never visited California and had no desire to go there.

After the agreement was finalized, Goldwyn and Beach decided to base the first Eminent Authors film production on Hughes's book *The Cup of Fury*, despite his argument that the public was tired of war pictures. They turned the novel over to a leading scenarist, but when Rupert read the opening scene, he was enraged. Although he had not complained about changes made from other stories, this time he protested. Goldwyn heard his complaint and urged him to go to Hollywood as his guest, select a scenario writer and cast members, and make sure the production met with his approval. As a result, Hughes went to Hollywood and stayed a week. Soon he would return for longer periods.[15]

As with other authors, he was given royal treatment on that first trip. Put up at the Beverly Hills Hotel, he was provided a car to get around and was offered a variety of entertainment. On Sunday, he met famous comedian/

producer Charlie Chaplin, and they went for a ride in the countryside with Rob Wagner, a portrait painter Rupert had known in New York. Hughes recalled later that they spent four hours discussing "the techniques, the mechanics or chemistry of laughter." That evening the three dined together, then talked till midnight.

Chaplin had just finished making *The Kid*, his "first ambitious picture." He doubted its value, but Sam Goldwyn considered it a masterpiece and urged him to try it out on a few guests. Rupert Hughes was in the select audience with Somerset Maugham, Sir Gilbert Parker, Rex Beach, and Gertrude Atherton. A nervous Chaplin sat between Hughes and Goldwyn and could scarcely believe that the audience enjoyed the film so immensely. "We were enthralled," Rupert said.

Hughes would later write about many entertaining evenings and weekend hours he spent during those early days in Hollywood, as he became acquainted with well-known motion picture personalities and other celebrities. Some of the most enjoyable times were parties at Goldwyn's beach cottage, where guests included such people as Chaplin, heavyweight boxing great Jack Dempsey, and actresses Mabel Normand, Bebe Daniels, and Claire Windsor.

Often at these parties Hughes would talk with Chaplin as they sat on the beach. They developed a lasting friendship, and in a later year Hughes would say of Chaplin: "Unlike many great humorists he is an eager listener and easily convulsed. The only time I ever saw him dumb was when I invited him to meet George Ade. I had a crowd to dinner and promised a gorgeous confrontation of two great humorists. They seemed to be mutually scared to death and neither of them even attempted a light remark." [16]

The conversations Hughes and Chaplin engaged in were not always about humor or the making of movies. The two talked about what Goldwyn later referred to as "topics—just topics," give-and-take talk that he regarded as illuminating. "While Hughes conducted his side of the discussion in a spirit of dispassionate inquiry, the less scientifically trained mind of the comedian struck out with a poet's frenzy at everything he did not like," Goldwyn said.[17]

Soon after publication of *The Cup of Fury*, when the novel had seemed timely, Hughes had been offered $25,000 for the motion picture rights, but he had traded them in on the profit-sharing arrangement with Goldwyn and Beach.[18] Released at the end of 1919, the film featured Helene Chadwick in the first of seven motion pictures based on Rupert Hughes stories in which she would appear.

An analysis of the movie in the *Photoplay Plot Encyclopedia* indicated that there were other problems in addition to the public's disdain for war films: The plot development seemed artificial, with too many coincidences and a melodramatic ending irrelevant to the theme. But the reviewer did not blame Rupert, noting instead, "We are commenting here upon the photoplay rather than upon Mr. Hughes' novel. He is a skilled writer and in the novel he developed the action and the characters so carefully that they were convincing, at least for the time being." [19]

Release of the movie proved that Hughes's misgivings had been accurate; attendance was not good. The film's failure by $12,000 to meet production expenses made him appreciate the arrangement he had made whereby the losses on one picture would not be charged against his share of profits on another. As things turned out, all of his films for Goldwyn would be made inexpensively and quickly, and while some would prove profitable, others would not.[20]

It was largely because of his disappointment with *The Cup of Fury* that he decided to spend more time supervising other films to which his name was attached. But in the early days it never occurred to him that he would someday build a house in Hollywood and become the only one of the Eminent Authors to make California his permanent home.[21]

Even while becoming heavily involved in the world of motion pictures in 1919, Hughes continued to write nonfiction, short stories, poetry, and music—as if driven to express his talents and opinions in every direction.

The Rupert Hughes byline appeared frequently during the first year of the postwar period on essays and articles on topics ranging from European and military affairs to the content of motion pictures. Most of his pieces were published in the *New York Times Magazine* under headlines of full-page width. He stressed the importance of military preparedness and emphasized the need to remember the deeds of those who had served during wartime. His article about the First Division of the Regular Army expressed dismay over the change in public attitude during the past year. The idea of universal service was now both "unmentioned and unmentionable," he said, adding that "the U in U. S. stands for Unpreparedness . . ." This had always been true, he pointed out, noting that during a conflict everyone agrees that the country must not be caught again in a similar plight, but as soon as the guns are silenced the pledge is forgotten.[22]

He was also concerned about children suffering in the aftermath of war, both in Europe and in the United States. In support of an effort to provide food and sustenance for the One Hundred Neediest cases, he wrote a piece titled "The Very Blue Book." He declared, "The Christmas list that does not include at least a tithe for charity is cursed with cruelty. The Christmas list that does not withdraw at least a portion from each personal gift, in order to bestow something on the human family, is inhuman, and false to the whole spirit of the occasion." [23]

There were other instances in which Hughes wrote about children or for them. A story, *The Fairy Detective*, serialized in the *New York Herald Tribune* nine years earlier,[24] was published as a Harper & Brothers book in 1919. Illustrated with drawings by Rhoda Chase, it is a fanciful tale about a little girl who goes into the woods to feed the animals and discovers a talking squirrel that proves to be a fairy detective in disguise, later appearing in other animal forms—a mouse, a fish, and finally an eagle.

Newspaper reviews ranged from enthusiastic to merely complimentary, calling it "delightful" and "a delicate, Christmasy little volume." But the *New York Evening Post* critic wrote that it seemed somewhat sophisticated, with words and satirical remarks better understood by parents than by their youngsters.[25]

It is doubtful that Hughes agreed with this assessment of what children could understand and what should be written for them. He also had definite views about whether movies were detrimental to young minds, expressing his opinions in *The Bookman* in response to statements by author Charles Hanson Towne. The Hughes article, "Viewing With Alarm," commented upon Towne's amazement that a friend's children would rather go to the movies than read such books as *Tom Sawyer*, *Huckleberry Finn*, and *Little Women*. Hughes said he would have expected such a preference, adding that he did not agree that films perverted children's tastes. He contended that the movie terrors Towne had warned against did not compare with those in literature and religious stories. Hughes also defended motion pictures against those who considered them inartistic. He said that "the critic with his personal whims on art and the moralist with his personal schemes for keeping the world out of mischief, are like fussy old women chasing children along the beach." [26]

He again protested, in the July 4, 1920, *New York Times Book Review and Magazine* section, against critics who did not recognize motion pictures as art: "It is our little-appreciated privilege to assist at the birth of as new, as great and as lasting an art as the drama." He said movie writers were in the same position as the first playwrights of Greece—"Euripides, Sophocles, Aristophanes and the other gods of the theatre." He noted that such a statement would provoke laughter from those who could not imagine a time when such classics had been scorned. He also decried the condemnation of films that appeal to a mass audience, saying that "the greatest art properly presented will thrill the greatest number." [27]

It was his setting of motion pictures into a historical context that marked Hughes's writings on the subject, and he became one of the earliest chroniclers of the good and the bad of the film industry.

Although now accustomed to being well-paid for novels, short stories, and motion picture rights, Rupert spent much time providing free advice and assistance when requested. Some replies were typewritten by a secretary, but most were handwritten. When a woman wrote regarding a letter she had received from an Army deserter in prison who wanted money, Hughes advised her not to send it and told her he would forward the letter to General Churchill, his former boss in Military Intelligence, assuring her that the general would advise her of the facts in the case.[28]

Hughes wrote to the editor of *Red Book*, praising a manuscript by author John P. Toohey, and told Toohey he would write similar letters to other editors if the magazine turned it down. A few months later, after Toohey sent him a story, he called the tale a "gem" and said it was similar to his own "The Quicksilver Window," a story about an actress whose daughter announces the birth of a baby that makes the actress a grandmother. At the behest of actress Charlotte Walker, Rupert had agreed to write a play for her based upon his story, but he was now convinced that Toohey's tale was "far better, more adaptable and appealing" and would make a better play. He urged Toohey to send the story to Miss Walker and say that Rupert had recommended it over his own. "I mean this," he told the author.[29]

Not always were Hughes's critiques so laudatory; at times they were pointed criticisms. Such was the case when Harold Waldo invited him to comment on a novel he had written. Hughes wrote, "I have never read in anybody's writing more skillful details and I have never read in anybody's ing more bewildering confusion." His three-page, single-spaced letter continued, "The story got the effect of an endless procession of liqueurs, wonderful colors, scents, smacks, intoxications. But I screamed for a glass of water, for a chunk of bread, for some ordinary people doing something ordinary." [30]

The comments, intended to be constructive, could serve as the basis for a short course in fiction writing, but he was concerned that Waldo might be offended. Two years later, when Waldo sent him a copy of the published novel, *Stash*, Rupert replied he was "lifted high with pride at finding my name in the dedication." [31]

In another letter, Hughes wrote to author Walter P. Eaton, urging him to purchase a limited edition set of the works of Charles E. Van Loan, a writer who died from injuries in an auto accident. Proceeds would go to Van Loan's penniless widow. [32]

Later, Rupert was asked to be toastmaster at the fourth annual dinner of the Contriband, a writers' group, scheduled for January 14, 1920, in the Hotel Majestic in New York. The event was to honor F. P. A. (Franklin P. Adams), the noted wit, critic, and writer. Noting that Robert Benchley, a "sterling 22-karat humorist," was scheduled to perform, Rupert invited Walter Eaton and Julian Street to make after-dinner speeches. Hughes composed a brief, humorous scenario, typed on Famous Players-Lasky Corporation memo stationery, in which the Contriband committee chooses "Rupe Hughes, the Infant Prodigy," to preside at the dinner, but later Rupe finds out that his new show will open the same night in a city far away. "All through the day he lies awake, wrestling with the problem of how to make Two Speeches at Once." Then, "in a burst of genius, Rupe evolves the brilliant scheme of putting his Dinner Speech on the Screen and putting on his Show Speech in Person." [33]

His involvement in the Authors' League of America continued, and he served on a committee, headed by Channing Pollock, to write resolutions memorializing Theodore Roosevelt, who had died in January, 1919. That same year, Hughes wrote to Pollock that he was overwhelmed by the honor of being named a member of the Council of the Dramatists' Guild of the Authors' League.

"All unworthy as I feel," he said, "I accept this crushing burden in order that my grandchildren might be able to put it on their crests." [34]

CHAPTER ELEVEN

ON TO HOLLYWOOD

"The censorship law is like an attempt to save souls by preventing them from reading, seeing, or hearing. It can't be done."

As the 1920s began, Rupert Hughes was spending an increasing amount of time on West Coast trips in connection with motion pictures made from his stories and novels. But he always returned as soon as possible to his Bedford Hills farm.

By now his daughter, Elspeth, had grown to womanhood, while Adelaide's children, Avis and Rush, had reached twenty and eighteen respectively. Rupert's younger brother, Felix, having served during the war as a captain in the Army's Military Intelligence Division and as head of an entertainment committee, was again teaching voice in Cleveland, where his wife, Adella, was manager of the Cleveland Orchestra that she had founded, a position she would hold until 1933. Meanwhile, in Houston the inventiveness of Rupert's nephew, Howard, Jr., was apparent again when he designed a new type of automobile shock absorber before he was fifteen.[1]

It was with great delight that Rupert learned that his wife had begun to write poetry. One afternoon at their farm, Adelaide asked shyly if she could read something to him—making him promise to tell her whether it was any good. Then she read the first poem she had ever written, a free verse piece called "Interval." He was impressed, and so were some *Harper's Magazine* editors who came to visit; they agreed to publish it and urged her to write more poetry.

The beautiful Adelaide, who had gone through lean times with Rupert during his struggle to become accepted as a writer, had established a reputation in recent years as a woman of charm and exquisite tastes. With their increased income she could afford fashionable clothing and had been called by many people, with "hyperbole" as Rupert later recalled, "the best-dressed woman in America." Now Rupert saw in her poetic endeavors the same style evidenced by her attire, manner of speaking, and presence.[2] The only thing lacking was self-confidence, and Rupert attempted to bolster it by encouraging her writing.

Adelaide soon began a drama in free verse, working day and night until she completed it. Along with other shorter poems she wrote later, Harper & Brothers published it in April, 1920, as *Diantha Goes the Primrose Way, and Other Verses*. The cover jacket contained lavish tributes from the editor of *The Bookman*, the assistant editor of *Current Opinion*, and the president of the Poetry Society. The main poem, "Diantha Goes the Primrose Way," covers in forty-nine pages the drama of a young woman who turns from her husband to find love elsewhere; when passion fades, she seeks comfort in her work, then turns again to her husband for support. Critics called it a "swift moving narrative" and a "vivid little drama of a woman's soul," and the Poetry Society president praised it as "intense, convincing and realistic in the best sense, full of power and artistic self-restraint."[3]

Several years later, in an evaluation of her work, the *New York Times* would call "Diantha" Adelaide's most memorable achievement and "in its kind a little masterpiece."[4]

When the book came out, Rupert and Adelaide were staying at the Beverly Hills Hotel. They had not yet seen the finished product but were anxiously looking forward to its arrival before returning to their home in New York state.

While in California, Rupert wrote to a young friend, John Monk Saunders, then a Rhodes Scholar at Oxford University in England, complimenting him on an article he had written. Rupert said he was forwarding the piece to *Harper's Magazine* with "high praise."[5] In later years, Saunders would become closely associated with Hughes.

While Adelaide confined her talents mainly to poetry, Rupert led a life of diversity as a writer, and managed to work in some speaking engagements. He returned to Cleveland in May, 1920, to address the Advertising Club on the topic of Spiritualism, a subject he had written about many years earlier. The *Cleveland Topics* applauded his remarks, noting that he included telepathy among fakes he decried. "That is where it belongs, and where scientific people have always placed it," the reviewer said. Hughes reported to his booking agent, James B. Pond, that the speech brought much applause and laughter from an audience that included galleries packed with women, while two hundred were turned away.[6] Such successes made it apparent that Rupert could attract listeners as well as readers.

His output of short stories had declined somewhat as he concentrated on novels, nonfiction, and screenplays. But in 1920 a collection of thirteen stories, *Momma, and Other Unimportant People*, was published by Harper & Brothers; most had appeared previously in magazines. As with some of Hughes's other short story volumes, it included tales of the Midwest, mainly of hard-working, ordinary people in Iowa and Missouri. Edward J. O'Brien thought so highly of one of them, "The Stick-in-the-Muds," published earlier in the year in *Collier's Weekly*, that he republished it in *The Best Short Stories of 1920*.

O'Brien also praised two others in the book: "Momma," the title yarn, and "The Father of Waters," a Mississippi River tale[7] that would win recognition nearly a decade later. Hughes thought it ironic that a critic accused him of writing some stories too hastily, while citing the high quality of "The Father of Waters." "This shows," said the reviewer, "what Mr. Hughes can do when he takes enough time." The fact was, as Hughes later pointed out, it had taken him years to finish the stories he had been accused of writing too quickly, but the one praised so highly "had been written as fast as the pen could fly, on two nights from midnight to broad daylight, and never revised."[8]

While winning plaudits for short stories, Hughes was honored by the inclusion of a novel in a 1920 anthology called *One Hundred Best Novels Condensed*, edited by Edwin A. Grozier, editor of the *Boston Post*. The four-volume collection also included classics by Defoe, Dickens, and Tolstoy, along with novels by other current writers such as Booth Tarkington and Blasco Ibanez.[9]

The same year brought the publication of the latest Hughes novel, *What's the World Coming To?*, by Harper & Brothers. The hero, Bob Taxter, inherits

$10,000 from a relative who leaves $25,000 to the heroine, April Summerlin, and her mother. Too proud to marry someone wealthier than himself, Bob decides to seek his fortune in Texas, but becomes the victim of swindlers. The Summerlins' aged black servant outsmarts the defrauders and helps bring Bob and April together. A reviewer thought the novel was too long, but said it would please admirers of Rupert Hughes.[10]

Continuing to turn out a serial at least once each year, with publication soon after in book form, Hughes next wrote one that some reviewers criticized for descriptions that ran on for pages. This was a strange tale, *Beauty*, published in 1921 as a Harper & Brothers book. It took its name from a young woman, Clelia Blakeney, who personifies the concept of beauty and is worshipped by many men, including Gad Larrick, a newcomer to New York from Texas. During a house party in the Adirondacks, an unseasonable snowstorm causes everyone to head for home. After Clelia becomes lost in the blizzard, Larrick and a search party find her frozen to death in the solid waters of a lake—her hands folded as in prayer. Despite a gash on her head, she is a vision of still beauty, clad in a silk nightgown. Larrick arranges for a plaster cast to be made from her body and has an artist tint the cast, which he encloses in a glass case so it will look like Clelia when her body was covered with ice.

A reviewer for *The Bookman* wrote, "The reader may suffer vicarious shocks" at the thought of Clelia's body, leaning against the side of a house "where all may—and do—look through ice and silk nightgown to worship." But the critic added, "much of the book is devoted to asserting that scant clothing on dance floor and beach is in no way a contributing factor to unconventional behavior." Other critics pointed to Hughes's extraneous material on censorship, prohibition, women's suffrage, and fashions.[11]

The theme he expressed in one of the few autobiographical sketches he ever wrote—a chapter called "An Autobiography by Request" in the 1919 book *The Men Who Make Our Novels*—was one that he would dwell on in many interviews:

> I hate to go to sleep because I miss some of my brief voyage. I wish I could live a hundred lives and write a hundred times as many novels, stories, poems, essays and articles, though I write too much as it is. Being so charitably inclined to other people's faults, I recognize my own countless failures and shortcomings with a tenderly, forgiving

generosity. And so I stumble on, having a mighty good time; altogether glad to be alive in this greatest period of the world's history, and proud to be permitted to act as a sympathetic chronicler of a few phases of its infinite variety.[12]

Upon other occasions, Hughes said there was hardly any subject he found uninteresting, from comic strips to ancient drama, or medical information, military topics, and on and on. He once wrote that "a single-track mind is infinitely better than a mind with no track at all, but there are countless things we can do to while away or enrich the journey." [13]

At times he turned to politics, as in a piece praising the style of Senator Warren G. Harding, the Republican presidential candidate, shortly before the 1920 election. Hughes thought Harding was what the nation needed after the upheavals of war, and apparently voters agreed. The handsome newspaper publisher won by an overwhelming majority. The same article lashed at the literary critics whom the author considered anti-American, saying, "They worship foreign schools and denounce our writers as cheap and provincial." [14]

Ever a champion of America, Rupert had expressed similar concerns earlier in a *Harper's Magazine* essay, "Our Statish Language," which called for a new Declaration of Independence whereby Americans would begin to write "United-statesish" instead of the British language.

"The critics, like awe-inspiring and awe-inspired governesses, take pains to remind their pupils that Americanisms are not nice, and are not written by well-bred little writers," Hughes said. He declared that the United States language was not a vulgar dialect of English, but "a brilliant, growing, glowing, vivacious, elastic language for which we have no specific name. We might call it Statesish, or for euphony condense it to Statish." [15]

There was no narrow nationalism in his views about language or international affairs, nor were his statements based upon an idealistic vision of the world. They came from a studied outlook on history and a keen insight into human nature. This was true of his views about a League of Nations. In a published debate on the question of "Will the League Stop Wars?", the *New York Times* carried the affirmative views of Raymond B. Fosdick and negative opinions written by Hughes.

Fosdick argued that the World War had started in 1914 without a single conference to prevent it, because there was no machinery in place for settlement of disputes. A League of Nations, he said, would make compulsory the factors then lacking: "delay, discussion, arbitration, law." But Hughes argued, "I have yet to see an ardent devotee of universal and eternal peace who was not an ardent disturber of the peace of his neighbors." He said a League supporter had once accused him of lying, cheating, and misrepresenting facts. The reply from Hughes had been that "every time you lose your equanimity and call me harsh names, however justified they may be, the more you destroy your own case. For unless your calm, your divine serenity and beauty of spirit increase as my wickedness increases, you substantiate my claims." [16]

Articles he wrote about peace and international relations in 1920 showed an awareness of problems in Poland and Russia. He praised Polish leaders and their people for helping to win the war and contended that they were justified in later efforts to regain territory taken from them. A month later, he saw hope for world peace stemming from what he called "The Third Russia," which regarded Poland as a friend and fellow nation of sufferers.[17]

In his comments on domestic affairs, Hughes was especially vocal in denouncing censorship of motion pictures. Concerned that some church leaders were mounting a campaign against movies, he joined with others in the film industry in taking the other side. Although the Methodist Episcopal Church had set up a film studio to produce pictures for use in Sunday Schools and by missionaries, and 4,000 Protestant churches had installed movie viewing machines by 1921, religious leaders lobbied for state censorship laws.

After Methodists began listing Hollywood films that they approved while condemning others, the National Association of the Motion Picture Industry produced a 1921 film, Non-Sense of Censorship, which starred Rupert Hughes in a rare motion picture appearance, along with Samuel Merwin, Montague Glass, and Douglas Fairbanks. In the widely circulated film, Hughes and the others ridiculed the public censorship of motion pictures. Whether the movie made much of an impact is not known, but within a few years the Methodists began letting individual members decide whether to attend movies and other entertainment.[18]

In addition to his role in the film, Hughes sounded his views in speeches, debates, and in writing. In April, 1921, he reported that a woman censor in Pennsylvania had deleted a film scene showing a wife holding up a baby dress for her husband, because of a new law that prohibited any mention of approaching maternity. "And do they claim that Pennsylvania with its censored films is more moral than California, more free from the stain of crime? Well, the figures show it isn't," said Hughes.[19]

His opposition to censorship was more extreme than that of film producers who spoke at a meeting of the National Republican Club in New York City in early 1922. One producer opposed censorship by the states, saying that if any was necessary it should be by the federal government, and another thought some supervision was needed but recommended that it be done by federal licensing of film distributors. Hughes told the large audience that censorship was another attempt in the age-old effort to make people good by passing restrictive laws. He warned, "You can't stop clergymen and moralists from coercing politicians. The censorship law is like an attempt to save souls by preventing them from reading, seeing or hearing. It can't be done." [20]

Although his work as an Eminent Author required much of his time, Hughes in 1920 took one last fling at the Broadway stage with a three-act comedy, *The Cat-Bird*, about an ecologist who leaves the woman he loves to pursue scientific interests elsewhere. Upon his return he learns that she has married, but the next time they meet she is a widow with a lovely daughter. Again the scientist falls in love with the mother and their romance turns out happily.

The play starred John Drew, nearing the end of a brilliant career spanning a half century. During rehearsals the rest of the cast reportedly ran into problems caused by Drew's failing eyesight and the deafness of Hughes, who assisted the director. But the Atlantic City tryouts went well, and when the play moved to Wilmington it met with success—popular, critical, and financial. From there it went to Philadelphia, where it was "jammed into a bandbox icebox," to Rupert's displeasure.[21]

In New York, *The Cat-Bird*, produced and directed by Arthur Hopkins, opened at the Maxine Elliott Theater on February 16, 1920. The cast also included Janet Beecher as the widow and Ruth Findlay as her daughter. Reviewer Alexander Woollcott called it a "polite comedy" that was "agreeable and quietly entertaining," and a few days later again commended the comedy by "the tireless Rupert Hughes." [22]

Despite this approval, *The Cat-Bird* ran for just thirty-three performances.[23] After that, with the exception of one-act plays, Rupert turned his attention from the stage in order to meet growing commitments in Hollywood.

At around the time the play was staged, a screen version of Hughes's novel *The Thirteenth Commandment* was released. Ethel Clayton, Charles Meredith, and Monte Blue played leading roles in the Famous Players-Lasky production, directed by Roger G. Vignola and released in 1920 as a Paramount-Artcraft Picture.[24]

This was followed by the first comedy Eminent Authors Pictures, Inc., produced, called *Scratch My Back*, based upon a Rupert Hughes story. Hughes, with E.T. Lowe, Jr., also wrote the screenplay and humorous titles. Again, Helene Chadwick starred, and T. Roy Barnes was introduced to the screen after a successful stage career. The film presented by Samuel Goldwyn and Rex Beach was directed by Sidney Olcott.[25]

Opening night at the newly-remodeled Capitol Theater at Broadway and 51st Street in New York—the "largest, coolest, most beautiful theatre in the world," according to advertising—brought changes in the theater's programming schedule. Under the supervision of S. L. Rothapfel, the stage had been rearranged and the program time shortened from three hours to two. It included an orchestral rendition of a Victor Herbert overture; a dance troupe; a combination of tableaux, recitation, and singing; news pictures; then *Scratch My Back*, the main attraction.[25]

Variety's reviewer, describing the film as a breezy satire on modern film plots, said it "pleased the first-night audience and bids fair to do so with all other spectators." As predicted, *Scratch My Back* proved popular with audiences. A third of the $40,000 profit went to Hughes.[27]

Before the release of his next motion picture, he was spending most of his time in Los Angeles, but returned whenever possible to New York. His work on films caused him to turn down some requests, and he found it difficult to keep up with scheduled appearances on the lecture circuit. On Armistice Day, 1920, he wrote from Bedford Hills to agent James Pond in New York, saying he was leaving soon for California, and, although he had planned to return home after Christmas, "Mr. Goldwyn strongly urged me to stay in California for two or three months," he said.

Later, writing from Los Angeles, he told Pond, "My time out here is free enough for me to accept any interesting proposition not too far from Los Angeles, but I am debarred from the East for some time to come." [28]

Tired of Hollywood hotel life, Rupert and Adelaide rented a house, and they were becoming much involved in the social life of the film colony. Los

Angeles newspapers frequently mentioned one or both of them, along with other celebrities attending events ranging from Thanksgiving Day auto races in Beverly Hills to the formal opening of the opera season. A columnist reported that Rupert was among celebrities pledging to fight an effort by Easterners to seek passage of national Sunday blue-laws that would prohibit movies, newspapers, sports, and motoring on Sundays.[29]

During 1921 seven motion pictures with which he was associated were released for public showing, including the reissue by Fine Arts Pictures of *Old Folks at Home*, the 1916 Sir Beerbohm Tree film originally released by Triangle.

In January Goldwyn Pictures came out with *Hold Your Horses*, based on the 1909 story "Canavan, the Man Who Had His Way." Hughes was paid $7,500 for rights to his story and for writing the shooting script. This tale of Irish immigrant Dan Canavan, a street cleaner who marries a society belle, starred Tom Moore and Sylvia Ashton and was directed by E. Mason Hopper. It was much more true to the original story than the 1915 *Danger Signal* and proved to be a "happy success." [30]

The famous Polish pianist, composer, and statesman Ignace Paderewski called *Hold Your Horses* the best film he had seen in years and said it had helped him in an hour of need. Paderewski, who later became premier of the Polish republic, owned a ranch near Paso Robles, California, and often visited Rupert in Los Angeles.[31]

Hughes wrote the subtitles for another film released a month later. The Goldwyn Pictures screen version of Herman Bahr's play *The Concert* told the story of a pianist adored by many women, including one who lures him away from his wife. A reviewer regarded Hughes's subtitles as clever but not always appropriate. But he thought he knew how Hughes had become involved: "The impression is given that, when the picture was finished, the producers felt that it fell flat, and therefore called in Dr. Hughes to administer first aid. The result may, or may not, have a box office success." [32]

It was true that after Hughes's success in writing titles for some of his own films, especially *Scratch My Back*, producers asked him to handle the same chore for other pictures, some of which he thought were not suited to his talents. For many years he would be called in to help rescue films in trouble.

The Concert provided a mere prelude to the popular success and critical acclaim that greeted the screen version of *The Old Nest*, the short novel that had stirred readers' emotions a decade earlier.

The film repeated the now familiar Hughes tale, but in writing the screenplay for Goldwyn, Rupert changed the story slightly from the original version. Mary Alden starred as the mother in a memorable performance that won worldwide acclaim, and Dwight Crittenden was her husband, Dr. Horace Anthon. Helene Chadwick played her third role in a Hughes story, and Marshall and Lucille Ricksen were cast as two of the children.[33]

In keeping with the simplicity of the story, Hughes made sparing use of subtitles, for which he was applauded by a *New York Times* columnist, who called him "about the most cinematographic of all of the professional writers who have gone to the screen." Saying that Hughes used titles only when needed "to make his pictures fully expressive," the columnist praised *The Old Nest* as a simple story that unfolded naturally and pointed out that during its first thousand feet Hughes used no words at all.[34]

Even before *The Old Nest* had its first public showing, Rupert was enthusiastic about its chances for success. He wrote to his mother ("Beloved Mimi") to tell her that he and Adelaide were moving to a more expensive place at 100 Fremont Place, where they would be for four months. He said his letter "as usual must be a story of excessive toil broken with lots of good luck to brag about." Involvement in plans for a big benefit "has added to our burdens, Adelaide carrying most of them." The event, sponsored by the Actors' Fund of America, with Rupert one of the organizers, was scheduled for June 4 at the Beverly Speedway.

Usually modest about his accomplishments, Rupert wanted his mother to be proud of him, and so he proceeded to tell her about his standing in the industry. He informed her that fifty Goldwyn Company salesmen, brought in from around the country to view the new Goldwyn films, had unanimously agreed that his pictures *The Old Nest* and *Dangerous Curve Ahead* (the latter to be released in the fall) were the only two they liked. They thought *The Old Nest* was the best picture Goldwyn had ever made and predicted that with the proper exploitation it would "make more money than any other picture ever made." Rupert considered this to be a vindication of his theory that "pictures should be simple, sincere, and very true to life." He reported that many of the salesmen went straight to a telegraph office on the lot after seeing *The Old Nest* and wired money and fond messages to their mothers.

The studio planned to spend $75,000 in exploiting *The Old Nest* and a large sum on *Dangerous Curve*, Rupert told his mother. He was being asked to turn out more scripts, even though the studio had cut down on its output. But he had more good news for Mimi:

> A dazzling compliment was the fact that a man was asked to approach me and offer me almost any price to join the United Artists: Charlie Chaplin, Douglas Fairbanks, Mary Pickford and D.W. Griffith, the giants of the screen.
>
> I said my Goldwyn contract had a year or so to run. They said they would sign a contract to begin 18 months from now and make a payment down!
>
> I don't think I'll go in with them as I am so royally treated where I am, but it is wonderfully flattering.[35]

When *The Old Nest* had its premiere at the Astor Theater in New York on June 21, 1921, many film and theatrical people were in the audience. The reaction was so enthusiastic that tickets were being sold the next day for performances four weeks later.[36]

A *Variety* review said the picture was filled with "human, natural touches. There are no villains, no sex problems, no triangle situations—just the life story of any family; not designed to teach anything but merely to remind us not to neglect our parents, especially our mothers." The reviewer praised the film as "classily told without bathos or other mawkish sentimentality, admirably directed without having recourse to tre-mendous scenes or extravagance of production." [37]

A *New York Times* critic raved: "They've done it. Rupert Hughes as author and Reginald Barker as director, with the aid of an evenly excellent cast, have made a mother-love picture that is sentimental without being sloppy . . . their production seems genuine. It's marked sterling in every way . . . . Go to see it." [38]

Although the critical reaction pleased Hughes, it was the public response that overwhelmed him. Western Union had installed booths at some theaters to enable viewers to send telegrams, and thousands of wires went out from the Los Angeles area alone, mostly from men. Rupert later learned that showings at a single theater brought an outpouring of a hundred thousand telegrams to mothers. The mother in the movie, Mary Alden, received four thousand letters of thanks from viewers in England after the film's release abroad. In Los Angeles, Rupert told his mother, the

California Theater was running the film for the third week, despite its rule of changing movies weekly.[39]

When Rupert responded to a request the next year from Arthur B. Maurice, Book Department editor at the *New York Herald*, to tell about letters he had received that most affected him, he naturally mentioned those from readers and viewers of *The Old Nest*:

It affects me deeply and almost unendurably to think that so brief a bit of fiction should have set on foot such a mighty pilgrimage about the world. It was not a fiction like some of the religious fictions which have started great pilgrimages and great persecutions, yet . . . when I read some of the contemptuous references to the story made by people with a ludicrous pretence of superiority to sentiment, or a maudlin assumption that universal emotions are somehow inartistic, I think of these letters and these countless telegrams, and rejoice that I wrote this story and made this picture. It seems to me that if it was not art, it was something far more worthwhile.[40]

With the film's popular success came financial rewards for the producer and the author. It grossed about a million dollars—an unusually high total at a time when ticket prices even at the Astor started at fifty cents, with top-price seats a dollar for a matinee and $1.50 at night.[41]

Of all the motion pictures written by the Eminent Authors, *The Old Nest* proved most successful. Sam Goldwyn was elated by its popularity, feeling redeemed after having heard comments that the Eminent Authors experience had failed. Film historians agree that Rupert Hughes had proved to be the only one of the group—which had grown to include other well-known authors—who had been able to adapt his talents adequately in the writing of motion picture scripts.

In Goldwyn's view, "Mr. Hughes's success in photoplays is to be ascribed to his prompt recognition of the gulf between those two channels of expression, literature and the screen, and to his determination to master both the technicalities and spirit of the latter." [42]

Rupert reported to Mimi in September that Goldwyn had offered him a "gentleman's agreement" for a new contract to follow the present one that would expire on May 1, 1922. "He says he wouldn't make a similar offer to any other author living. It would tie me up for four years more with a far bigger guarantee than I've had up to now and the same share of profits. It looks as if 'The Old Nest' and 'Dangerous Curve' might make me a real fortune, but the profit won't be known or due for some months to come." [43]

Partially because of the elation Hughes and the producer felt over *The Old Nest*, they developed a close friendship, based upon mutual respect, that was to last a lifetime. But for now, there were other motion pictures in the works.

The first of these, released in October, was *Dangerous Curve Ahead*, based on a Hughes story and directed by E. Mason Hopper, the director of *Hold Your Horses*. Again, Helene Chadwick headed the cast, with Richard Dix as her husband, in performances called "worthy of stellar honors." Hughes wrote subtitles for the film about a small-town couple who move to the city where the husband gains success and the wife becomes a social climber.[44]

By the time *Dangerous Curve Ahead* had its New York opening, Hughes had resigned himself to a realization that he would spend most of his time in California for quite awhile. He told Charles F. Thwing, the longtime president of Western Reserve University, that after a year in Los Angeles he had taken a house for a year longer "since I am so deeply absorbed in this new and wonderful art that I am not only writing, but also directing, my own pictures." [45]

He and Adelaide had looked for a suitable home for a year, but there were not many for rent and prices were high. Their four-month lease on the house at 100 Fremont Place was up on October 1, and although it was for sale, the price furnished was $130,000.[46]

The place they finally leased was in truth a structure of mammoth size—one in which they would entertain friends, many of whom were among the most famous names in Hollywood: stars, directors, producers, authors, and other luminaries.

The three-story Tudor mansion, on three shady acres at 2425 South Western Avenue in a fashionable district, had been built in 1908 for a lumberman who had insisted that the best materials be used in construction. It had forty-two rooms, including a spacious ballroom on the top floor, and large separate quarters for servants. The owner and his family had hosted parties, but there were also quarrels, a fatal shooting, and a suicide before they moved out, leaving behind a grand piano in the ballroom.

The place seemed ideal for Rupert and Adelaide, with more than adequate space for books, workrooms, music, and entertaining. The rich mahogany woodwork provided a warmth of hospitality, and the stairway landing upon which light filtered through amber stained-glass windows was especially impressive.[47]

Even while concentrating on film work, Hughes maintained a keen interest in poetry and often composed music to go with it. *The Bookman* in December, 1921, spread the news that "Rupert Hughes still finds the coast and the movies entertaining. Hughes has been busy taking folk poems of Sandburg, Braley, Whittier, etc., and setting them to delightful music. Of such, the pastimes of a popular novelist in Hollywood."[48]

This actually was nothing new for Hughes, who had composed numerous songs published by G. Schirmer in 1920, some issued separately as well as in collections. The front cover of each bore a distinctive RH monogram. *Three Songs of Love*, for high or medium voice with piano accompaniment, included "Had I a Golden Pound," with words by Frances Ledwidge; "Music I Heard with You," with words by Conrad Aiken, and "The Rose That Bleeds," for which Hughes wrote the words and music. Another composition was "Le Souvenir D'Avoir Chante" (The Memory of Having Sung), a reminiscence by Catulle Mendes, to which Hughes wrote the music. He also set to music Grantland Rice's "The Bugle" and Sara Teasdale's "The Sun-Swept Dunes," published with two others as Four Meditations, for voice and piano.[49]

A review in *Musical America*, headlined "Rupert Hughes When Novels Pall," said the author had a creative faculty given to only a few novelists. "When the delights of imaginative word-painting pall, he can always limn his thoughts and fancies in tone . . . . The fact remains that he has achieved distinction in two very different fields of creative effort."[50]

Perhaps the most important of Hughes's compositions was a dramatic monologue, *Cain*, which Schirmer published in 1920. This "Vocal Scena," based upon the Biblical story of Cain and Abel, demonstrated, as one music historian has pointed out, that the composer had become "something of a modernist, showing investigation of dissonance."[51]

Of all the songs Hughes wrote, the one sung in public most often is "The Roustabout," with words by Berton Braley. George H. Doran & Co. had published it five years before G. Schirmer included it in 1920 as one of Hughes's *Five Homely Songs* for high or medium voice with piano accompaniment. Each of the five, including the Ridgely Torrence poem "The Son," was also published separately and in another collection, *A Book of Homely Songs*, which included a sixth dedicatory song called "The Mother-tribute."

A *Book of Homely Songs* was greeted enthusiastically by music critics, with *Musical America* commenting, "One cannot help but like Mr. Hughes's songs—they are singable, narrative, expressive." In *The Musical Courier* a reviewer noted that the poems of Torrence, Sandburg, Berton Braley, and John Greenleaf Whittier, chosen for A *Book of Homely Songs*, were "as original as the music, which is saying a good deal." Pointing out that Hughes's songs showed "a gift of melody and harmony most rare," he commented: "If he can himself play the accompaniments he has written then Mr. Hughes must be a first class pianist." [52]

Six more Hughes songs were published by G. Schirmer in a 1922 collection, *Free Verse Songs*, for low or medium voice with piano accompaniment. Three poems were by Carl Sandburg, one was by John Drury, and another by Amy Lowell. The other—a beautiful verse about the power of listening—was called "Beholden" and was written by Rupert's wife, Adelaide.

In the same year, Schirmer published four Hughes compositions as *Songs of the Aftermath*. He wrote words and music for "The Rose on Her Green Divan," and composed music for Sara Teasdale's "When I Am Dead," Virginia McCormick's "Hold Sorrow Close," and Annette Wynne's translation of the Bohemian poem "There Was Once."

Hughes's musical and literary talents brought recognition in 1921 from *The Etude*, the well-known music magazine. In publishing Hughes's endorsement of the Golden Hour, a plan to present daily cultural programs in schools, *The Etude* called him "America's most successful novelist, also a musician of splendid attainments." Hughes wrote that the proposal would help form character and provide golden memories for young participants.

"Character is so much more than thou-shalt and thou-shalt-notting," he said. "Such pious, harmless people have such empty character and contribute so little beauty, grace or joy to the world, that they are really characterless. By all means let the 'Golden Hour' of music, pictures, poetry and warm praise shine upon the young hearts." [53]

A year earlier *The Etude* had published a lively, two-part interview with Rupert, headed "Will Ragtime Turn to Symphonic Music?", accompanied by a photo of Major Hughes in uniform, with a description of him as "Author, Playwright, Musical Lexicographer and Critic." Again he emphasized a familiar theme: "My faith in coming American composers is limitless. . . . We shall be Americans in music, not Americans trying to be Germans or Frenchmen in music." His comments about ragtime would be quoted by musical historians for many decades, including his view that "Jazz . . . is Ragtime raised to the Nth power." [54]

Before 1921 had ended, another Goldwyn picture he wrote was brought to the screen. Familiar names were associated with *From the Ground Up*: E. Mason Hopper, the director, and Helene Chadwick and Tom Moore in leading roles. Hughes wrote the screen adaptation of his original story with the same title that had appeared two months earlier in *Cosmopolitan*. In the film, Moore, a pick-and-shovel worker, falls for Miss Chadwick, who rejects the man her father wants her to marry. She inspires Moore to become a contractor, and eventually they marry. [55]

Counting the *Non-Sense of Censorship* picture and reissue of *Old Folks at Home*, this made seven films with which Hughes was associated in some way that were shown within a single year. Things were going well for Hughes and Sam Goldwyn, who had found the right combination of plots, players, and directors. But in 1922 their movies would feature a young actress who would go on to top stardom, and for her start toward that accomplishment she would give Rupert Hughes a good portion of the credit.

CHAPTER TWELVE

AND NOW A DIRECTOR

"It went like wildfire."

With her grandmother as chaperone, Kathleen Morrison arrived in Hollywood in 1917, a star-struck fifteen-year-old from Tampa, Florida. Known as Colleen Moore, she signed a fifty-dollar-a-week contract with D. W. Griffith's Fine Arts Company. Wide-eyed and appealing, she immediately went to work in *Bad Boy*. In this and two other Fine Arts pictures she played parts beyond her years.[1]

Marshall (Mickey) Neilan suggested to Rupert Hughes that she would be right for a Goldwyn picture Hughes planned to make, called *The Wall Flower*.[2] The role, in Colleen's opinion, was a "marvelous part," and so she tried out, knowing that many other actresses had been turned down for the role. When Hughes saw her test he said, "That's the girl I wrote it about." He persuaded Goldwyn to sign her to a contract for four films, three of which Hughes would write.

Years later, Colleen recalled that Rupert told her, "'I have a story in the bottom of my trunk that would just be great for you.' It was called *Come on Over*, and I played a little Irish girl; it was a very cute little story," she said—one that became a "very successful" film.

After that Rupert told her, "'I've got another story for you at the bottom of my trunk,'" she recalled. "The heroine was a little ballet dancer, and she ate so much and became so fat. You see, I could do the thin part so well—I was pathetically thin—and they used to pad me all out to make me big and fat. He wrote that (the film called *Look Your Best*) for me, and I owe him a great debt of gratitude because those three pictures did an awful lot to lift me out of the category of a leading lady into what was called a featured player, and I wasn't yet twenty." [3]

Although *The Wall Flower* was produced in the fall of 1921, *Come on Over* was the first Hughes film featuring Colleen Moore to be released, with premieres in Los Angeles, Chicago, and Cleveland in March, 1922. Alfred E. Green directed the delightful story of three generations of Irish in New York, based upon "Sent for Out," a short story in Rupert's *Long Ever Ago*, but rewritten for Colleen. She plays the role of Moyna Killilea, who comes from Ireland to marry Shane O'Mealia, but through a misunderstanding thinks he intends to wed another girl. The film ends happily, with Moyna and Shane reunited.

Several months before the nationwide opening of *Come on Over*, Rupert told his mother, in a letter from New York, that it had made a big hit at a Los Angeles preview but Goldwyn's New York office did not like it. "The publicity men said it was bad. I said they didn't know anything." After that, Hughes said, "Night before last Mr. Goldwyn took us over to Brooklyn to see it in a preview. It was put on without even a title in front of it. It went like wildfire." After that, "Goldwyn said he never saw a picture go so well. Now they are all crazy about it, going to put big exploitation behind it and show it everywhere March 17th (St. Patrick's Day)." [4]

The opening of *Come on Over* at the Capitol Theater in New York brought enthusiastic praise from a *Variety* reviewer, who said the movie packed "heart punch" and that "mother love, love of home and young love all combine to make this feature a real box office attraction." He added that Hughes's telling of the story brought tears and laughter in rapid succession. [5]

While working with Hughes, Miss Moore became impressed by his kindness and sensitivity to the feelings of cast members. She recalled: "We were shooting (*The Wall Flower*), and the scene was outside of a country club and there I was in my ridiculous finery that had been made by my stupid mother. I had no one with whom to dance; I was a wallflower. Very sad. So I was supposed to be sitting outside the club, weeping. We were waiting to get ready for the scene, and I was over by a tree, thinking about this and feeling very sorry for the poor little girl, and I was crying and crying."

Then, said Colleen, Mr. Goldwyn arrived on the set after a dinner party for the Eminent Authors. "He saw me weeping my heart out, and he came over and said, 'What's the matter, little girl? Who hurt your feelings?' I said, 'Well, nobody, Mr. Goldwyn. I'm getting ready for the scene where I have to cry. 'Oh, keep crying, that's what I pay you for!' Well, of course, that was the end. Every time I tried to cry, I thought, 'Keep crying, that's what I'm paying you for.'

"Rupert understood, perfectly, how I just couldn't cry, so the next morning we went back and did it; I wept my heart out.

"He was so kind. That's the thing I remember most about him, and also his sensitivity to the feelings of an actor. And other people on the set thought the same about him," she added.[6]

While involved with the Colleen Moore pictures, Rupert was called upon to perform an unpleasant task when notified of the unexpected death of Allene Hughes, wife of his brother Howard, in Houston on March 29. During the previous year, she and Howard had spent much time in Los Angeles, and Rupert told Mimi that "Howard and Allene are our constant companions and if we had you here we would feel that the Hughes family was coming to its own again."[7]

At the time of Allene's death, Howard, Jr., or "Son" as family members called him, was attending the Thacher School in Ojai, north of Ventura in California, and his father sent a telegram informing him that his mother was ill and asking that he return home, without telling him she had died. The father asked Rupert to meet young Howard upon his arrival in Los Angeles and send him by train to Houston, where the boy would learn the whole story. But knowing his brother's anguish, Rupert reluctantly broke the news to the lad and tried to console him.[8]

The loss of his mother was exceedingly painful to the sixteen-year-old, but he did not talk about his feelings. For Howard, Sr., his wife's death was a blow from which he would never recover, and he began to find excuses to stay away from Houston. Concerned about his son, he persuaded Annette Gano, his wife's sister, to postpone her plans for marriage and take care of "Son." She agreed to do so, but only for a year.

The three then went to California, where the father stayed at the Ambassador Hotel in Los Angeles when not away on business, and his son and the thirty-one-year-old Annette took a cottage in Pasadena.[9]

Howard, Jr., had visited Uncle Rupert occasionally while at the Thacher School, sometimes spending time with him on the set of a motion picture. Now he continued this practice, and on one visit he became acquainted with Colleen Moore. Later she recalled their first meeting:

"I was making a picture for Rupert—I think it was *The Wall Flower*—and he brought this tall, lanky lad on the set. He was wearing knickers," she said, pointing out that such was then the usual attire of boys his age. Apparently Rupert brought Howard to the studio every day. "I was young," she said, "and we became friends; and we'd sit and talk and talk and talk." [10] While there, Howard absorbed considerable information about the film-making process, which would prove invaluable in later years. But in the fall of 1922 he returned to school at Ojai. [11]

The cast of *The Wall Flower* included Richard Dix, Gertrude Astor, Laura La Plante, Tom Gallery, and Fanny Stockbridge. The film also marked the screen acting debut of Rush Hughes, Adelaide's son. Rupert gave him the role of Phil Larrabee and thought the twenty-year-old, who was dark-haired and handsome, did "splendidly." An acting career was open to Rush, Rupert thought, "though he agrees with me that he ought to get an education before he jumps off." [12]

Many decades later, Colleen remembered the time that Rush first appeared on the set and Rupert introduced him: "Rush was going around with my best friend, Carmelita Geraghty, and I said, 'Well, I met Rupert's son.' She said, 'He's his adopted son.' And I said to Rupert, 'I thought he was your real son.' 'No,' he said, 'he's my adopted son.'"

Colleen recalled that silent actress Eleanor Boardman, who later played leading roles in two Rupert Hughes motion pictures, had the same experience. Both remembered that Rupert always called Rush his adopted son, an important distinction that years later would have a bearing upon the outcome of one of the world's most publicized court cases. [13]

Called by *Variety* a "Cinderella type of story with comedy relief," *The Wall Flower*—marking Rupert's debut as a director—opened at the Capitol Theater in New York in June. It brought a mixed review in the *New York Times*, which praised the early scenes and said that although Hughes sometimes gave the impression that words were the main medium of expression on the screen, his pictures "speak for him more clearly than his words."

The reviewer liked the characterization of Idalene Nobbin as an object of sympathy as well as comedy. As played by Miss Moore, this rather unattractive girl, avoided by young men at social events, seemed at first a real person. But then things changed, wrote the reviewer:

"It would seem that, after Mr. Hughes had shown his wall flower as she might conceivably be, some . . . officially officious studio person came to him and said: 'That's all right, what you are doing there, Mr. Hughes, but . . . the picture can't be as simple as that all the way through.'" As a result, the reviewer added, the picture suddenly grew absurd.

Variety's review called *The Wall Flower* an audience pleaser with an ideal cast, good photography, and titling that brought more laughs than did the action. As for Hughes's dual role, "He is very much present in the titles, but there are spots where little can be said for the direction, yet as a whole the picture is fairly well done." [14]

The initial reaction helped bring about an innovative development in the production and release of motion pictures, as Hughes set about correcting flaws in the film. He told an interviewer:

The Wall Flower received a divided welcome. Some critics declared the story to be splendid, but the young lady who played the lead to be awful; others reversed that opinion and exclaimed that the young lady in question had never done better work in her life, but that *The Wall Flower* as a story was frightful . . . I went over it carefully and found what I thought was the trouble. Then I went to Goldwyn and begged that it be withdrawn, turned back to me, and altered. Goldwyn consented, and for the first time to my knowledge, a program picture came back for final alteration and polishing. [15]

Hughes said this idea was not new, having been the practice of writers and producers of stage plays for many years. His recipe: "Give your picture a routine release, then if it does not go, withdraw and re-film until the flaws have been eliminated." With the changes made, *The Wall Flower* became what Colleen Moore described as "a big success."[16]

Before making the last of the three pictures in which Colleen played the lead, Rupert wrote and directed *Remembrance*, a study of the effects of wealth on a family in which the father collapses from overwork. The Goldwyn film featured Patsy Ruth Miller as Mab, the daughter of John P. Grout played by veteran actor Claude Gillingwater. Other cast members were Esther Ralston, Kate Lester, and Cullen Landis.

The *New York Times* critic believed Hughes had tried unsuccessfully to do for men what he had done for women in *The Old Nest.* The review suggested that Hughes had "not yet got his hand in as a director," and thought that while at times the picture came to life, "at most it lives fitfully." [17]

When the Capitol in New York showed the film, newspaper ad-vertising played up the author and director. Names of actors and actresses were not mentioned, but selections by the Capitol Grand Orchestra, with soloists and dancers, were listed. The ad proclaimed that *Remembrance* was "a picture you will remember forever—and forever is a long time!" [18]

For Hughes, there were reasons to remember *Remembrance*, the making of which brought moments of near-disaster and joy. The former occurred when he directed a storm scene in which an airplane propeller stirred up wind—a practice then in vogue among movie-makers. At first, actress Patsy Ruth Miller enjoyed being drenched, but soon tired of it. Moreover, she came close to being seriously injured or killed in an accident involving the propeller.[19]

A few months after the film's October 8 release, Rupert wrote an article for *Arts and Decoration* magazine contending that critics did not recognize movie-making as a new art. He suggested that they treat films as they do other works of art, expecting a "common mediocrity, and eagerly seeking and praising the high moments." He cited a scene in *Remembrance* as one that had been praised for its artistic value.[20]

Esther Ralston later recalled an incident that occurred while Hughes was directing *Remembrance.* When he pointed out that the set was dark during a scene change, she noted that "all the lights were out except for one spotlight that was on my picture on my father's desk. Mr. Hughes said, 'That is a sign if I have ever seen one. Someday you'll be a star.'" Miss Ralston added, "I thought that was a very kind and very loving thing for him to say." [21]

The face of another beautiful actress, Mary Pickford, graced the screen in one more 1922 motion picture with which Hughes was associated. It was the remake of *Tess of the Storm Country*, the Famous Players hit that had helped make her a national phenomenon. The Mary Pickford Company's version of *Tess*—the only film the star remade—proved much superior to the original.[22] John S. Robertson directed it, and the cast included Lloyd Hughes, Gloria Hope, and Jean Hersholt.

It was inevitable that Rupert would turn his attention as a novelist to the Hollywood colony he found so fascinating, just as he had chronicled happenings in New York in earlier stories and books. He had, in fact, already written about the film world, both for publication and the stage. A short story he wrote was one of the earliest dealing with motion pictures—a tale of thieves masquerading as film-makers who rob a mansion they pretend to use as a setting for their picture. A real motion picture company borrowed the story for a film, but Hughes received nothing for it.

He had also written a humorous vaudeville sketch, *Celluloid Sarah*, about silent motion picture actors who were careless about their language. The sketch, showing what they were supposed to have said and revealing what they actually did say, ran for a season, including a Palace Theater booking in New York. A reviewer reported, "The composition of *Celluloid Sarah* could not have been a severe strain on the talents of Mr. Hughes, but it pleased the audience. And it was not intended for critics anyhow. So there is every reason for the author to be satisfied with the result." [23]

Now, years later, Hughes decided to tell the story of the almost unbelievable world in which stars could be created overnight and fortunes built and lost in the rush to produce screen fare that would attract audiences. The novel he wrote to bring this fantasy world to life was *Souls for Sale*. After its magazine serialization, Harper & Brothers published it in 1922, and Goldwyn made it into a movie for release in the spring of 1923.

In battles against film censorship, Hughes had been consistent in his defense of the motion picture industry. He contended that Hollywood's well-publicized scandals were no more prevalent or shocking than those of other towns and cities.

The year 1922 was one in which there had been notorious cases involving well-known Hollywood figures. Roscoe "Fatty" Arbuckle, a popular film comedian, had been charged with assaulting a young woman at a party who later died. Then, on February 2, police investigating what they thought was a routine death found the body of prominent director William Desmond Taylor, the victim of a mysterious slaying that remains unsolved. Those questioned in the killing of Taylor, who had directed Rupert's *Johanna Enlists*, included actresses Mary Miles Minter, with whom the director reportedly had an affair, and Mabel Normand, the queen of comedy. Although Arbuckle was acquitted and Minter and Normand were not charged, their careers were ruined.

Some people thought it too obvious in *Souls for Sale*, which Hughes wrote and directed, that his purpose was to whitewash Hollywood's soiled reputation, and he did not deny that intent. He considered the condemnation of the film industry following the Arbuckle episode to be just as bad as the outlawing of theatrical productions by Puritans long ago. He wrote speeches for the main male character in *Souls for Sale* in which the morality of Hollywood is defended as equal to that of any other place in the world.[24]

Although the author later recalled that book critics were unanimous in considering the novel atrocious,[25] the film version did not bring the same thumbs down; some reviewers called it the best motion picture Hughes had done. Certainly he had tried hard to create a spectacle that would show the excitement and glamour, as well as risks and dangers, of life in the film studios. He chose an outstanding cast of principal actors and actresses and added an amazing array of most of Hollywood's greatest stars and directors to embellish the realistic settings.

Souls for Sale is the story of Remember Steddon, starring Eleanor Boardman, whose face had been plastered on billboards as "Miss Eastman Kodak." She played a preacher's daughter who has doubts about her new husband—and for good reason, as it turns out he is wanted for murder. She escapes from the train upon which they are riding and almost collapses before being rescued by costumed cast members of a movie being filmed in the desert.

Thankful for their kindness, she goes with them to Hollywood, where film director Frank Claymore (played by Richard Dix) hires her and she becomes a star. Her husband, Owen Scudder (Lew Cody) returns to Hollywood to reclaim her, but is killed by a wind machine during the filming of a circus picture. When the tent catches fire, Remember helps rescue a cast member. Spectacular fire scenes are shown, and "Mem" finally decides she loves the director (Dix).

The film featured Mae Busch and Barbara La Marr, and in a lesser role, Rush Hughes as the second cameraman. But it was the array of big name personalities at work on real studio lots that attracted audiences, including Charles Chaplin, Erich von Stroheim, ZaSu Pitts, Blanche Sweet, King Vidor, Florence Vidor, Claire Windsor, Marshall Neilan—plus dozens of others.

Rupert directed the desert scenes while on horseback, and in another locale took delight in seeing Charlie Chaplin "lying on his belly on my lawn directing a scene in his picture *A Woman in Paris* while I directed him for a scene in my picture."[26]

The film opened at the Capitol Theater in New York on March 27, 1923, its arrival having been heralded by Coming Attractions announcing, "Coming soon, Goldwyn's stupendous production of Rupert Hughes' sensational novel, *Souls for Sale*, the story of a Movie Star in Hollywood." As with newspaper ads, the emphasis was on the name of the author and director rather than on star personalities.[27]

The "Gossip Shop" columnist for *The Bookman* took note of Hughes's return to New York for the opening, saying that he was "one of the few authors who not only has made a success of the motion pictures, but has and still is enjoying his contact with them." The columnist called Hughes "as quick in his movements, as brilliant in arranging his always provocative sentences" as ever.

A drawing of Rupert by E. T. Middleditch, a young woman artist, adorned the *Bookman* column, and when the subject saw it he remarked, "Well, you've been kinder to my face than God was."

A review in the same issue declared that few people knew the tricks of continuity writing, and "if *Souls for Sale* is an example, Rupert Hughes does." Hughes was called "a director of something like genius."[28]

Another review said the movie was "the first picture giving a very fair idea of motion picture life in Hollywood."[29]

Variety's critic called it the biggest thing Hughes had done as screenwriter or director. "It is also a remarkable piece of propaganda for Hollywood, the picture industry as a whole, and its clean-living acting people as well." The reviewer predicted that Eleanor Boardman would now be a box office draw. The prediction was accurate, and Miss Boardman acknowledged in later years the debt she owed to Rupert in helping to advance her career.[30]

Unfortunately, the public enthusiasm for *Souls for Sale* was short-lived. The Capitol opening attracted a crowd that spread into Broadway and blocked automobile traffic, but after that the attendance dwindled. The same was true elsewhere: big openings followed by slim crowds. Rupert thought this was because people expected the film to be an exposé of "the terrific wickedness of the modern Gomorrah." Then, "when they found instead a story emphasizing the hard lives of the toilers and the merely human and normal procedures of their love affairs, they warned their friends to stay away."[31]

Even before the release of *Souls for Sale*, Hughes already was in solid with Hollywood—highly respected by actors, other screenwriters and directors, and studio moguls. More than a half century later, Donald L. Barlett and James B. Steele would describe his impact thus: "Since his arrival in Hollywood in 1919, Rupert had taken the budding film capital by storm, and by the early 1920s he was one of the town's most talked-about celebrities, earning upward of $125,000 a year." [32]

In the opinion of Willis Goldbeck, writing for *Motion Picture Magazine*, Hughes had attained this position despite toppling traditions and routing the Old Guard, while setting his own standards. Goldbeck said a Goldwyn staff member had told him that Hughes often astounded the editorial board by suggesting movie ideas and themes that the board unanimously declared to be impossible. But then "Hughes goes out on the set and turns his great idea into a film at once renegade and money-making." Goldbeck's article, "Mr. Hughes and the Photodrama," described him as an apt observer who peopled his stories with individuals whom readers and viewers regarded as old friends.

One photo published with the article was of Rupert in a familiar pose, with cigar in hand. Another showed him and Adelaide in a cozy setting at home, and a third portrayed Colleen Moore, in costume for a movie, and Hughes with hat tipped down and head thrust back, looking the part of a typical Hollywood director.

Goldbeck said that when Hughes entered a room the air was immediately surcharged with an electric bustle and activity. "It is not his appearance," the writer said, describing him as a man of medium stature, rather square of face, whose bearing carried "a suggestion of importance, dominance. A slight difficulty in hearing has lowered his voice so that one must remain constantly alert or lose much of his rapid speech." The interviewer commented on his geniality and "inexhaustible fund of anecdote and opinion and original thought," reminding readers that "he has made success an instinct. He has ceased to strive for it long since. He is it." Calling him "our highest paid author," Goldbeck said the photodrama was bound to profit by the "Hughes leaven," and added, "More power to him." [33]

Thoughts about Hughes's movies were also expressed in a *New York Times* editorial about the implications of the formation of a congress of motion picture arts by the Authors' League and a large movie producing studio. The editorial called for more writers to have a hand in the making of movies:

A few authors, most prominent among them Mr. Rupert Hughes, now not only write but direct their own pictures . . . Mr. Hughes is perhaps not the greatest of living artists, but his pictures are better than the average, and their defects are the defects of his imagination and not of his knowledge. Other authors, however, have found themselves unable to displace the all-powerful director.[34]

During the early part of 1923 two other motion pictures Hughes directed had been brought to the screen before *Souls for Sale*; they were *Gimme* in January, followed by *Look Your Best*. In writing *Gimme*, Hughes had called upon the talents of Adelaide, and the credits list her as a co-author. A publicity handout promised, "You'll say this picture is the funniest and the truest film play you ever saw. No wife can afford to miss it and no husband will want to! Rupert Hughes wrote 'Gimme!' picturing the real joys and monthly bills of wedded bliss." [35]

Reviewers praised Helene Chadwick and Kate Lester for their acting, but one critic thought the authors strayed from the main story, with too many side adventures. Another, who especially liked the direction and titles, described *Gimme* as a light comedy that should please audiences.[36]

In the story about money problems, Miss Chadwick, who weds Gaston Glass, has borrowed trousseau money from her employer. After her marriage she writes a check on her husband's bank account to pay back the loan, but finds that her mother-in-law (Kate Lester) has cut off funds. The convoluted plot eventually works out satisfactorily. Also in the cast is Eleanor Boardman.

Look Your Best was the last of Rupert's movies in which Colleen Moore had the main part. His short story "A Bitterness of Sweets," provided the basis for the screenplay, but there were many changes from the story to the final screenplay. In the story the heroine was Irish-American Mollie Finnerman, nicknamed Sliver, but in the film she was an Italian-American named Perla Quaranta.[38]

Colleen Moore is a dancer who replaces another who has become too fat for a "Butterfly Act" in which she is lifted into the air on a tightrope. But Colleen also shows a fondness for sweets. The wire-man, whose advances she spurns, causes the wire to break, hoping she will be fired by Antonio Moreno, but Moreno beats up on the wire-man and is thrown into jail. After his release, he and Colleen team up for a dance act and decide to marry.

She recalled later that the film contained a scene in which she danced into a pool, for an underwater ballet. Wearing a tight net costume covered with gelatin sequins, she remained in the heated pool while cameramen prepared for a closeup. But the sequins had melted, "leaving me practically in my birthday suit," and could not be replaced, so the number was cut from the film.[38]

While *Look Your Best* was being made, Rupert invited Colleen to a party he was giving at the Cocoanut Grove. She was engaged to marry John McCormick, a handsome press agent, and wanted to wear something elegant because Sam Goldwyn and "all the Hollywood brass" would be there. She persuaded the studio wardrobe lady to let her borrow a beaded dress she had been wearing for the film, but was warned that the beads were irreplaceable. When Goldwyn asked her to dance he complimented her on the gown, not realizing that it belonged to his studio. "Had I torn that dress, thousands and thousands of dollars of retakes would have had to be made of me in another gown," she recalled.

Later, after having her curls cut, Colleen starred in the film titled *Flaming Youth*, thereby launching her career as the first screen flapper and starting a nationwide craze of bobbed hair.[39] Within a few years Colleen Moore would become the number one box office attraction in the United States, causing F. Scott Fitzgerald to remark, "I was the spark that lit up *Flaming Youth*. Colleen Moore was the torch." [40]

CHAPTER THIRTEEN

AT SUNDAY BRUNCH

*"I scoot through life getting out of nearly every day
eighteen hours of excitement and six or less hours
of perfect sleep."*

I t was a Sunday morning, and as guests arrived at the spacious Hughes home at 2425 South Western Avenue in Hollywood, Rupert and Adelaide greeted them warmly. Among those coming for brunch were some of the biggest names in the film business—a select gathering of writers, directors, actresses and actors, and producers.

These Sunday brunches in the early 1920s were legendary occasions, and those invited felt honored to be included. They enjoyed the cordial atmosphere and the opportunity to eat and mingle with other guests. The shady lawns, arbors, and walkways invited casual strolling and conversation that more often than not involved motion pictures.

Producers and directors visiting the home could see its picture possibilities and sometimes arranged to use the grand staircase and panelled rooms as settings for movie weddings and duels. Charlie Chaplin filmed part of one of his motion pictures on the lawn.[1]

Among those who often attended the brunches were Mr. and Mrs. Sam Goldwyn. The producer wrote in his autobiography, "For both Mr. Hughes and his wife I feel a warmth of friendship quite independent of the profitableness of our business association, and some of the happiest hours of my life have been spent in their home." [2]

In early 1922 Rupert and Adelaide were involved in a whirlwind of activity during a visit to New York. A letter to his mother apologized for not writing earlier, but said that he and his wife had been "gadding socially at a mad pace." They had lunched with the Count and Countess Szecheny—"she was Gladys Vanderbilt and he is now Hungarian ambassador here." There had also been lunch with former President Wilson's daughter and her husband, operas to attend, and other social engagements. Felix and Adella had taken Adelaide to a concert on the previous night. "So you see we fly high. But work hard."

"In spite of all this insanity of gadding I keep disgracefully well. My chief agony is the income tax," he said. "I earned $104,000 last year!!! Isn't it hideous . . . that in spite of my heavy expenses I can't take much of it off. A dozen things that are vital to my work are specifically forbidden as deductions. So I shall spend this year's earnings paying last year's taxes."

But, he added that he ought not to complain. "Most of the people in this poor world had no income to tax and I've certainly cut a swathe." [3]

Adelaide, who had gained a reputation as an engaging conversationalist, was learning to express her own style through the written word as well as through her speech and presence. In addition to collaborating with her husband on the Gimme screenplay, she worked on other films for Goldwyn and had continued to write poetry. Despite a lack of self-confidence, revealed in bouts of melancholy, her wit and personality were greatly admired. Rupert wrote, "I have known her to convulse a small group or a large crowd with a delicious humor that made her the most memorable after-dinner speaker I ever listened to." He said that whenever he and Adelaide were asked to speak at the same occasion, she invariably put him to shame by comparison.

But he worried about her when she became depressed. Much of her condition stemmed from acute physical pain, and whether she took too much medicine at such times is a matter of speculation. Eleanor Boardman remembered seeing her frequently going to the water fountain to take pills while visiting the set of a motion picture Rupert was directing. This led Miss Boardman to think there was a possibility that she was addicted to drugs. [4]

Among Adelaide's interests were Oriental art and flower arranging. She also enjoyed travel and wrote a poem, "Cuivre Dore," published in The Bookman in August, 1922, that told of her desire to visit places she had never seen, from China to the Kashmir Mountains, and to seek treasures and see the birds, trees, and flowers of foreign lands. But, said the poem, she must be content instead to read about such places and the things she longed to know about firsthand.[5]

It was not surprising that when Adelaide's doctor informed her she needed surgery, she told Rupert she would like to delay the operation long enough to take a trip to prepare for the ordeal. She suggested a long sea voyage together to China, but since this was out of the question for him because of his involvement in film-making, they finally agreed that she would go without him.[6]

The Bookman carried this news note in November, 1922:

We hear from Los Angeles that Adelaide Manola Hughes, poetess, writer, beauty, and wife of Rupert, has left movieland for a long trip through the Orient. This in spite of the fact that the picture *Gimme*, which she wrote and Mr. Hughes directed, is to have its premiere this fall. Anyone with her feeling for color and atmosphere should bring home some gorgeous material from China and Japan. She is a busy lady with a movie, a new book of poetry, and a seemingly endless journey to cope with all at once.[7]

The trip was, indeed, good for her, and provided her with many experiences to relate to Rupert. Upon her return to California, exhilarated by her voyage, she was in a party mood, and on the night before she entered the hospital she and Rupert entertained with a large dinner party at home. Then, after successful surgery, she felt like celebrating with another dinner party on the evening after she returned home. Rupert described what happened:

"Though she was not permitted to come to the table, she sent down frequent bulletins whose hilarious humor set the tables in a roar. I remember that Charles Chaplin, after making several beginnings at a reply, exclaimed: 'Oh Lord! What's the use? She's the wittiest person on earth. I'll get her to write my future titles for me.'"[8]

In the months after Howard's wife died, he often attended brunches at Rupert's house, frequently bringing young Howard with him. At one such event, the son became infatuated with Eleanor Boardman, who was at least five years older than his seventeen years. She thought him "unattractive, very shy, hard of hearing, difficult." He was also persistent, asking his father to persuade her to have a date with him, but Eleanor was unimpressed when Howard, Sr., told her that his son would be rich someday. Eventually she had a date with the father, and, later on, went out with the younger Howard a time or two.[9] None of these dates meant anything to her, and although she became a friend of Howard, Jr., she married King Vidor, one of Hollywood's leading directors.

Colleen Moore recalled that at one Hughes brunch she went upstairs with Adelaide for some reason, and Adelaide showed her Rupert's bedroom. Miss Moore was surprised that it was painted in a dark, almost midnight blue—ceiling and walls—in order for him to be able to sleep after sunrise, having spent the night writing until early morning hours.[10]

The long hours he spent working were well-known to his friends, who marvelled at how he could accomplish so much. Some people thought he never slept at all and that he worked twenty-four hours a day, but the fact was, he once said, "I scoot through life getting out of nearly every day eighteen or more hours of excitement and six or less hours of perfect sleep." [11]

One who was amazed at his schedule was Sam Goldwyn. "He has a capacity for work which I have never seen excelled," Goldwyn wrote. "Many times I have known him to arrive in the studio early in the morning, direct all day, go home that evening to work on a scenario, and then, after perhaps a dinner or a dance, write several chapters of his new novel." [12]

In the opinion of Eleanor Boardman, living with Rupert must have been difficult for a wife who tried to cope with the schedule of a husband who in later years would have been called a workaholic.

But even the redoubtable Rupert could not keep up with all the demands upon his time, and he had found it necessary since early 1922 to turn down many requests. He declined an invitation to address the Anama Club in Hollywood, explaining, "When I am in town I am so very busy directing pictures that it is almost impossible for me to get away from the studio during the day, and my nights are taken up with preparations for the following day." [13]

Upon an earlier occasion he apologized when asked to write something humorous: "I am humbly sorry but I have not thought of anything funny for weeks. I have tried in vain to oblige you, but the Lord was deaf to my prayers."[14]

At times Hughes seemed an unusual combination of high brow and popular author-director. While devoting most of his time to motion pictures with a popular appeal, he submitted an essay to the *Yale Review* in 1922, saying he had been working on it for a decade.[15] He also wrote a review praising Jim Tully's book *Emmett Lawler*, the story of a prizefighter. He sounded a familiar theme in describing Tully's heartbreaking picture of orphan life. Rupert criticized people who said movies ruined children and that without censorship "children, particularly poor children, may see things that will give them bad ideas!" He said inmates of orphan asylums learn worse things than "the vilest movie ever hinted." [16]

In March, 1922, Rupert welcomed the arrival in Hollywood of Will H. Hays, who had resigned as Postmaster General to accept the presidency of the new Motion Picture Producers and Distributors Association of America, thereby becoming the first "czar" of the motion picture industry. Bad publicity in the wake of scandals such as the "Fatty" Arbuckle case had made it plain that there was a need for industry standards, and Hays seemed right for the job.

Even though Hays opposed censorship, he knew that his name had become a symbol of censorship. It was in that setting, he recalled in his 1955 memoirs, that during his first week in Hollywood he became acquainted with Hughes in a rather unconventional way:

> At the Ince Studio I met Rupert Hughes for the first time. He jumped on the running board of my automobile and introduced himself just as we were swinging into the circular driveway . . . Then Rupert bent over and whispered in my ear:
>
> "I'm supposed to deliver a eulogy about you. What do you know that's good about yourself?"
>
> "Not a thing!" I replied.
>
> That was the beginning of a continuing and very warm friendship. I recall how Rupert broke down the barriers of constraint when introducing me to the crowd by pointing to me, speaking as if none of them had ever heard of me until this moment, and telling them who I was and what I hoped to do. This started everyone laughing and got the group in a receptive mood.[17]

The same week, when Hays was guest of honor at a banquet the studios sponsored at the Hotel Ambassador, he was delighted to find his "newly found friend, Rupert Hughes," was the toastmaster.

A feud with Carl Van Doren, while not long lasting, began when Van Doren's *Contemporary American Novelists* listed what he considered the ten "most distinguished or significant" living novelists. After Rupert wrote an open letter to *The Bookman*, questioning the list, Van Doren replied that he had not attempted to assign to each author his exact place in posterity.

"Can you and I not agree, Mr. Hughes, that both great authors and stupid critics now and then go wrong?" He suggested they leave their controversy to be settled by time, "one critic we both believe in."

Rupert responded from New York, dashing off another letter to Van Doren, accusing him of "a villainous abuse of the sacred but unsportsmanlike trick of turning away wrath with a soft answer." He complained:

I emit a howl of pain and rage and you answer with a noble piece of music. I can complain of only one misstatement and that is your line: "As for you, who are so sure that time will right you." I never said and never thought that time would "right" me or even know me . . . Furthermore, I don't believe in posterity as a superior judge to ourselves. I don't believe that endurance is a proof of superiority; that a marble rose is better or more distinguished than a rose about to pass its meridian and lose its briefly bought petals . . .

In any case, I thank you for your forbearance and compliment you on your beautiful style.[18]

Van Doren answered politely, and Hughes did the same; the gentlemanly sparring continued while they debated the lasting value of certain authors' works. Hughes also told Van Doren about plans for his next novel, the plot of which would involve historic events that took place near his farm in Westchester County, New York.[19]

The name of Rupert Hughes also appeared in other ways in *The Bookman* in 1923, including the ninth installment of a series called "The Parody Outline of Literature," in which prominent authors, by means of well-known stories, apparently attempted to parody themselves. The installment supposedly written by Hughes was a parody of "Circe and Ulysses." The tongue-in-cheek introduction declared that "this greatest of all novels, written, of course by the Balzac of Bedford Hills, the Sophokles of Keokuk, and the La Rochefoucauld of Los Angeles, reaches heights hitherto unattained even by him." It referred to the charms of home and mother which the author had described in "his famous picture 'The Old Vest' and Manattana, the scene of 'What Won't People Say?', 'Empty Plackets,' 'The Eighteenth Commandment,' 'Clipped Winks,' 'Sails for Soles,'" etc.[20]

In the same year Hughes was listed with other well-known authors, including Homer Croy and Fannie Hurst, as an honorary member of the Missouri Writers Guild.[26] He usually sent a copy of each of his published books to the State Historical Society of Missouri for its collection, inscribing one "With the greetings of Rupert Hughes of Missouri," [21] even though he had not lived in the "Show-Me" state since he was seven.

Another *Bookman* piece he wrote, "On a Certain Condescension Toward Serials," took to task a currently big-selling novel that referred to an author who had "waxed fat and popular" because he could turn out "'serials' to order, and of serials to make pictures to order." Believing that the remarks were aimed at him, Rupert replied that a serial writer merely quickens the interest of readers at regular intervals of ten or twelve thousand words. He said that many great works of literature had been written as serials, including those by Tolstoy, Hawthorne, Dickens, Dumas, and others.

He agreed that many bad novels were also written as serials—"having written some of the worst of them as serials myself"—but said they would have been even worse if they had not been serials.[22]

Early in their association, Sam Goldwyn had tried to persuade Hughes to give up all outside writing and concentrate entirely on his work for the Goldwyn studio, but he would not hear of it. He argued that whatever reputation he had was one that he had built bit by bit as a workmanlike writer over a period of many years. He considered the money earned from movies as a bonus above that which came in from novels and short stories. But he put to good use the handsome sums from screenwriting and directing and was able to live in a style that otherwise would have been beyond his means.

He still tried to complete a novel each year, but found it necessary to stop writing short stories for about three years. Although the 1923 edition of the *Index to Short Stories* listed eighty-three Hughes stories, few had appeared in print after 1921.

The novel with a Westchester County setting that he mentioned to Van Doren in the spring of 1923 was published later in the year under the title of *Within These Walls*, and unquestionably it was one of his best. Like so many others, it was serialized before Harper & Brothers brought it out in book form.

Just as he had written about the Midwest while living in the East, he had turned to New York while in Hollywood, telling the story of the construction in the 1830s of the Croton Aqueduct to carry water for New York City's growing needs. Hughes used as background certain events that had occurred in New York, starting with the 1832 cholera epidemic that drove many people from the city.

The story describes the tragedies befalling the family of David RoBards, who opposes the construction project; their struggle is to appear respectable. Instead of a skeleton in their closet, they have the body of a murder victim embedded in the walls of their home, which eventually succumbs to flood waters.

In his research for the novel, Hughes found a seemingly unlikely source of information. "As to the manners and morals of the time," he told Arthur B. Maurice, the New York Herald book editor, "I found the biographies of ministers particularly fruitful. The parsons always berate their own times and are granted a freedom of expression and an unrestrained license of denunciation not permitted to men of other trades." [23]

While in New York for the premiere of Souls for Sale, he had told friends about the novel he was working on, and a columnist for The Bookman thought it seemed interesting. "Also, it sounds like a good moving picture, and Mr. Hughes, by now well ensconced in Hollywood, has already started his plans for producing it." [24]

When the book came out in late May, the New York World's E. W. Osborn called it "Mr. Hughes's most elaborate and considered work in fiction." The New York Times critic thought the author was at his best in tracing the social history of New York. "Since his early novel Zal Mr. Hughes has done nothing more graphic, painstaking or readable than Within These Walls." Among others extending congratulations was poet Carl Sandburg. And in the Literary Digest International Book Review T. L. Masson wrote: "In spite of what Edith Wharton has done, I am inclined to think that this novel . . . is the best American book of its type." [25]

While enjoying such warm approval, Rupert could take pride in a signal honor awarded him in 1923 from a nation he had written about many times. His friendship with the great Paderewski and his admiration for the Polish people had continued, and he had been considered for the important post of America's first ambassador to Poland. But, as he later recalled, he was "neither a Democrat nor a diplomat, and was not appoint-ed."[26] Now, however, came an announcement in the *New York Times* that revealed the high esteem in which he was held by Polish leaders:

POLAND DECORATES RUPERT HUGHES

Los Angeles, July 24—Rupert Hughes, author and motion picture director, has been decorated by the Polish Government with the Order of Polonia Restituta, grade of officer, according to word from Washington to the Goldwyn Studios here. During the World War Mr. Hughes was a Major in the Army Intelligence Service and specialized in Polish affairs.[27]

Hughes had little time to savor the honor bestowed by Poland, for he was now deeply involved in work on his next motion picture. It would be given a limited release late in 1923, with the New York opening early in January.

Produced by Goldwyn Pictures, *Reno* was based upon a story he had written; he directed the movie, for which he and Adelaide wrote the screenplay. The story gave Rupert an opportunity to expound on his views about the unfairness and inconsistency of divorce laws, but some critics thought he overdid it.[28]

Helene Chadwick plays Emily Tappan, wife of Lew Cody (as Roy Tappan), who divorces her to marry another woman. Left with two children, but no money, Emily weds Walter Heath (played by George Walsh), but is not allowed to live with her new husband when returning to her home state. When her ex kidnaps the children, the newlyweds retrieve them and head for Yellowstone Park, where their marriage is legal.

The movie's climax comes with a car chase through Yellowstone, followed by a fight on a cliff overhanging a geyser. In the opinion of *Variety's* critic, it was "great entertainment." A later *Variety* review, after the opening at the Capitol Theater in New York on January 6, 1924, criticized *Reno* as a lecture on divorce laws and said it was not Rupert's best work.[29]

The *New York Times* critic echoed those comments, calling the picture flat, with few, if any, redeeming features. The exciting "Old Faithful" geyser scene was reminiscent of a cheap serial, he thought. In his opinion *Reno* should have been made into a farce with Charlie Chaplin as the star.[30]

Although Chaplin was not in the movie, its cast won good marks from reviewers. *Variety* praised the work of Rush Hughes as the brother of leading lady Helene Chadwick, calling it the equal of that of the other male cast members. The critic added: "A whale of an appearance, supplemented by personality, young Hughes proves of sufficient background to step forth and emphatically cash in on this performance . . ." [31] Hedda Hopper, who later became a famous Hollywood gossip columnist, was also in the cast.

Appearing as Mrs. Hod Stoat was an attractive young woman named Patterson Dial, who would eventually assume a much more important role than the one in which Rupert Hughes cast her in *Reno*.

CHAPTER FOURTEEN

OF HAPPINESS AND GRIEF

"So don't try to persuade me that Son is a sweet child. He is a miser and a selfish little beast and I shall tell him so at the first excuse."

The early years of what would be known as the "Roaring Twenties" brought joy and sadness to members of the extended Hughes family, even while some of them, including Rupert, rang up new achievements.

Twenty-four-year-old Elspeth Hughes, daughter of Rupert and his first wife, Agnes, married Edward John Lapp on March 20, 1922, in the home of her mother, Agnes, and stepfather, Captain William H. Reynolds, in Washington, D.C. Their vows were solemnized in what has been described as "an elaborately reported society wedding." [1]

Elspeth had informed her father more than six months earlier about her engagement, and Rupert told Mimi that "she writes in a wild rapture" about her fiance. Not having met him, Rupert added, in an enigmatic comment, "I hope she has a chance for happiness, poor darling." At Christmas time, 1921, his future son-in-law visited Rupert and Adelaide in New York, and Rupert was extremely pleased, describing him as a "fine, handsome, lovable young man, really splendid. He was in three big battles during the war." Soon after, the Hugheses had tea with Lapp's parents in New York. [2]

Two months before Elspeth's wedding, Avis, who had studied drama in the hope of becoming an actress, took as her husband John Monk Saunders, who at twenty-five was three years her senior. He had completed undergraduate work as a Rhodes Scholar at Oxford in 1921 and had returned to the United States, going to work on the editorial staff of the *Los Angeles Times*.

Rupert told Mimi, "Avis is in a seventh heaven of happiness and her husband is an ideal man. So we are quite lucky—so far. Pardon me while I pause to rap on wood." [3]

After Avis and Saunders married, they moved in with Rupert and Adelaide. It was not exactly a harmonious household, according to a secondhand report. Actress Fay Wray, later famous for her role in the *King Kong* movie, would recall that Saunders told her that Adelaide was a heavy drinker and Rupert tried to restrain her. As Miss Wray put it, relying on comments from Saunders, "If Rupert was gifted as a writer, he also had a talent for diatribe." Whether or not this was exaggerated, Avis and her husband lived with Rupert and Adelaide only until the next year, when Saunders got a job in New York with the *Tribune*.[4]

In 1923, the year after Avis's wedding, her brother, Rush Hughes, married a singer and actress named Mary Ellen (known on the stage as Marion) Harris. It was a marriage that would bring them a son at about the time they separated two years later.[5]

Meanwhile, also in 1923, the marriage of Rupert's younger brother, Felix, to Adella was dissolved.[6] They continued their respective careers in music—she as manager of the Cleveland Orchestra and he as a successful voice teacher in New York.

Among Felix's students was a baritone singer sent his way by Rupert, who recognized the young man's exceptional talent. He was Lawrence Tibbett, who, when Rupert met him, was struggling to support his family by singing in a church choir and at weddings in the Los Angeles area. Years later author Dale Carnegie wrote about Rupert's discovery of Tibbett and how the young singer went on to an amazing career in opera, recitals, and motion pictures.

According to Carnegie, Tibbett had studied for a year but was getting nowhere. "However, he had a friend, Rupert Hughes, who believed in him. Hughes said: 'You have the makings of a great voice. You ought to study in New York.'"

"That little bit of friendly encouragement proved to be the turning point in Tibbett's life, for it caused him to borrow twenty-five hundred dollars and start East . . . He is now selling his services for thousands of dollars a week in Hollywood," Carnegie wrote in 1937.[7]

Although Carnegie did not say so, Rupert provided more than encouragement for Tibbett; he also helped out financially. After Rupert persuaded his brother to take Tibbett on as a student, Felix taught him to correct flaws in his singing and to sustain high notes, while another teacher coached him for operatic roles. That the two succeeded is shown by the short time it took for Tibbett to gain recognition. His 1923 operatic debut at the Metropolitan Opera House in New York made him an overnight sensation.[8] En route to New York on the night of the debut, Rupert bought a New York newspaper during a stopover in Cleveland and was amazed to see front page headlines about the ovation the singer had received—the greatest in the history of the opera house.

Both Rupert and Felix were modest about advancing the career of the famous baritone, but their friendship with him continued. Years later, Rupert would deny being responsible for Tibbett's discovery. "America would have been America if Columbus had never been born. So with a genius like Tibbett," he declared. "His genius would have carried him forward somehow." The singer, in return, thought so highly of Rupert's talents that his concerts included two songs Hughes had composed.[9]

Although it was not unusual for Rupert to travel to the East Coast, there was no way he could find time for a long sea voyage in 1923, even though Adelaide, still convalescing from her operation of a year earlier, expressed a desire to return to China. But he agreed to let her make the trip and hired a trained nurse to accompany her. The two women set sail in August.[10]

When they arrived in China, Adelaide grew tired of hotels, so she rented a palace in Peking, furnished it to her liking, and wrote her husband a letter with such vivid descriptions that he considered it an example of her best writing. Worried about her condition, he became more concerned after she wrote to him about an idea she had for a motion picture about China. When he cabled her that such a movie would be impossible just then because of economic conditions affecting the industry, she became terribly depressed.

As the threat of winter weather approached, Adelaide decided to go to Saigon and from there to the United States, but then changed her plans, electing instead to travel around the world. Rupert was horrified, but her doctor assured him it would be good for her health, so he agreed to the lengthy voyage and told Adelaide he would meet her when she got to France.

By the time Adelaide and the nurse left Peking on a French ship, she was in a dismal mood. Suffering from an acute ear problem, she thought the doctor aboard the ship was not doing her any good, so she got off at Haiphong to see another physician. When she returned to the ship she was so despondent that two passengers became alarmed and stayed with her until midnight, leaving her then only because they believed she had no way to harm herself.

The next morning she was found dead, hanging from a trunk strap that she had swung over an electric fixture. It was, in Rupert's words, "a ghastly and desperate conclusion, like Sappho's leap from the Leukadian cliff." [11]

The New York Times the next day announced the tragic news of the finding of Adelaide's body on the morning of December 14, 1923:

MRS. RUPERT HUGHES
A SUICIDE IN CHINA

Message from Standard Oil Man at
Haiphong Tells Author of Tragedy
(Special to the New York Times)

Los Angeles, Cal., Dec. 14—Adelaide Manola Hughes, 39 years of age, wife of Major Rupert Hughes, author and playwright, committed suicide at Haiphong, China, today, according to a cablegram received by her husband at his residence here.

The message read:

"Haiphong, China, Dec. 14.

"Rupert Hughes,

"Adelaide Hughes committed suicide here today. Telegraph disposition of body. Cremation impossible

"Signed, Kirby, Standard Oil"

Major Hughes said of her:

"My wife was the most beautiful sort I have ever known—a brave, brilliant woman, whose lack of self-confidence alone prevented her from being known to the world as I have known her.

> "I let her go to China because she thought she could regain her health and courage there. I thought that she had regained them until the cable came, announcing her death. It is my greatest agony that after a life of such close and devoted union she should die alone and far away." [12]

The tersely worded cablegram from A. M. Kirby, the Standard Oil Company representative and American vice-consul in Haiphong, was the first of many acts Kirby performed on behalf of the deceased and the grieving husband. Rupert was forever indebted to him and his wife for taking charge of details. [13]

On Sunday, the second day after the suicide, a *Times* story speculated about a possible cause. It said she and a nurse had taken the trip as recommended by her physicians after she had undergone an operation for cancer. "En route to Yokohama she experienced the terrors of a typhoon, and when earth shocks shattered Japan it was feared for a time that she had perished," the report said. " Word that she was safe reached here several days after the quake, but the catastrophe is believed to have left its impression on her already weakened nerves."

Plans were made for the return of her body to the United States for burial, but there were many problems involved. Diplomatic action seemed necessary before her body could be removed from Haiphong, Indo-China, according to C. F. Meyer of New York, vice president of the Standard Oil Company.

Meyer's marshalling of the resources of his company helped in dealing with the strict laws governing French colonies. In addition, Charles Evans Hughes, then Secretary of State, provided cooperation of U. S. government representatives in China, and the editor of the *New York Tribune* arranged for that newspaper's Paris representative to exert influence upon the French President.

It was not until December 19 that the facts about how Adelaide had died came to light in a cablegram: "Mrs. Hughes hanged herself in the steamer cabin in the middle of the night of Dec. 13. Stewardess discovered her body early in morning Dec. 14. Found long, affectionate cable, apparently unsent to Hughes, indicating depression and complaining of ear, but not suggesting suicide."

Eventually the efforts of those who assisted Rupert brought results. As he later wrote in a touching memorial to his beloved wife: "All these great engines finally succeeded in restoring to these shores the lifeless little body whose soul had long since availed itself of its supreme privilege and resigned an existence of torments beyond endurance. At San Francisco the abandoned flesh was reduced to ashes, inurned, and taken to Kensico, New York, for repose by her mother's ashes." [14]

Despite his great loss, Rupert knew he needed to get back to unfinished tasks and concentrate on the planning and details of work yet to be done. This was to be his salvation from grief and a technique that would serve him well in years ahead.

There was, in fact, little time for mourning during the Christmas season and on into the first part of the next year. The business of directing his next movie required attention, and he wasted little time getting back to it. The film was *True as Steel*, a lighthearted tale based on one of his short stories.

But again, a sudden event occurred that interrupted his concentration and caused him immeasurable grief. It was the completely unanticipated death of his elder brother, Howard, in Houston on January 14, 1924—just a month after Rupert had learned about Adelaide's suicide.

Although Howard had avoided Houston most of the time since the loss of his wife, he occasionally returned there for business meetings, such as one in January. While conferring with the Hughes Tool Company sales manager, he suddenly fell dead at the age of fifty-four. The death certificate called it an embolism of a coronary artery. [15]

His son, Howard, Jr., was in Houston at the time, having enrolled for the fall semester at Rice University. Aunt Annette Gano, who had stayed with him in California, had returned earlier to Houston to marry Dr. Frederick Rice Lummis, and the newlyweds had moved into an apartment. But after Howard, Sr., enrolled his son in Rice as a freshman (even without a high school diploma), he had persuaded the Lummis couple to move into his two-story house on Yoakum Boulevard so "Son" could stay there with them. [16]

It was up to Rupert to break the sad news to his own parents about the death of their oldest son. He could do this in person, for they had been staying at his home for awhile to get away from the Iowa winter and to keep him company. Now in their eighties, "Daddy" and "Mimi" were spry for their years, but Howard's death dealt them such an emotional shock that they felt unable to go to Houston for the funeral. But the service at the house on Yoakum attracted civic leaders, including many from the petroleum industry, and one oil publication wrote of Howard that "there is no man in the oil industry who was more endeared." [17]

For Howard's mother, the depth of her sadness was beyond expression. She wore black clothing and told a friend that Howard had meant more to her than anything else, and now "life is dark and cold." [18] It is true that she had seemed to favor him in the days of his youth, when she had found excuses for his failure to live up to the scholastic achievements of Rupert and the others, and she had been proud of his inventive mind and success in business.

Rupert did everything possible to console her and his father, but he was unable to spend all of his time at home. He had scheduled a trip back East, as he indicated in a letter to Carl Sandburg three weeks after Howard died. The letter also revealed his willingness to try to arrange for the filming of some of Sandburg's stories. He told Sandburg, "The motion picture field is in the doldrums and there is very little production. Things will right themselves soon and novelties will be in demand. The time will surely come when the joyous *Rootabaga Stories* will find their place. I should be very proud to be concerned in their production." He hoped to see Sandburg during a stopover in Chicago on his way to New York or on his return trip six weeks later.[19]

Shortly after Howard's death, young Howard accepted an invitation to visit his Uncle Rupert and grandparents, who were overjoyed that he wanted to be with them.

The will of Howard R. Hughes, Sr., dated April 25, 1913, had left one-half of his property to his wife and one-fourth to his son, but because Allene had predeceased him, her share went to the son. The remaining one-fourth was to be divided equally among Howard's parents and brother Felix. Originally, Felix's portion would have gone to Greta, but after her death Howard had amended the will in 1919 to leave her portion to Felix. Rupert was not included as an heir because he already was financially well-off.

Howard had stated in his will that "I desire and request that my son Howard be given as good an education as possible to fit him for such business or profession as he may desire to enter, and particularly request that if possible a part at least of such education be given in the University of the State in which he may expect to make his home." [20]

But when Son arrived at Rupert's home he was in no mood to go to college, despite the concern of his uncle and grandparents, who thought the terms of his father's will should be carried out. Heated arguments broke out between the young heir and his relatives, and it has been speculated that he thought Rupert wanted to gain control of the estate, which consisted of little cash but all of the shares of Hughes Tool Company. It is doubtful that Rupert, whose ambitions had never leaned toward running a business, had any such intention.

Howard also found the atmosphere of the Hughes household depressing. Gone was the conviviality of a year or two earlier, when he had attended festive brunches there with his father. But living there for awhile did give him an opportunity to visit the Goldwyn studio with his uncle and absorb the atmosphere of movie-making. As Rupert later recalled, his nephew "spent hours on the set, in the projection room, in listening to story conferences and studying the entire business with insatiable interest."[21] The experience whetted his appetite to become involved in movie production himself.

The terms of the will of Howard, Sr., had spelled out clearly what should happen to his estate: "Should my death occur before the majority of my son Howard R. Hughes, Jr., I desire that the Houston Land & Trust Company, or some other solvent and conservative trust company, be appointed guardian of his estate to administer same for his benefit until his majority." [22]

His son, however, thought he should be able to do as he pleased without supervision, and he told Rupert and his grandparents that he wanted to take over control of Hughes Tool. Despite their protests at such a ridiculous idea, he was insistent.

He then offered to buy the shares his grandparents and Uncle Felix had inherited, offering them much less than what the shares were worth. They resisted, and properly so, in Rupert's opinion. He was infuriated at the manner in which young Howard treated them. In a long letter to "Blessed Mimi," written from the Biltmore in New York on March 3, Rupert expressed disgust with his nephew:

I am overjoyed to learn that Son is such a comfort. He must have changed amazingly since I saw him at the house . . . . I never saw him show you any special tenderness, and his conduct in general throughout the will, has been an absolutely astounding display of grasping—dishonorable ungenerous selfishness . . . .

I never in my life heard of such bald robbery as he attempted and carried out as far as he could. He actually robbed you and Felix of what Howard actually willed to you. He pretended to be generous to his darling Mimi and offered you as a gift about a quarter of what your own son wished you to have. When he yielded he yielded only to compulsion, yielded with the worst possible grace, lied flatly again and again and altogether behaved outrageously.

Felix has not yet had the cheque due February first and it is now March third. So don't try to persuade me that Son is a sweet child. He is a miser and a selfish little beast and I shall tell him so at the first excuse . . . .

If I had seen Son shed one tear, or heard him say one word of love, sorrow, or admiration for his father, or heard him suggest one desire to build him a fitting monument or pay him any tribute whatsoever I should see some good in him . . . .

But go on and love him. God knows he needs somebody's tenderness, and it may prove a little contagious.[23]

Rupert told his mother that he would return to California in about two weeks. "I'm dying to see you and, if by that time Son has gone home, you may be willing to receive me as a prodigal."

As promised, he did not waste time in rebuking Howard for the shabby manner in which he had dealt with his relatives. In an eight-page, single-spaced typewritten letter, dated April 19, Rupert recounted many instances of Son's selfishness and rudeness. His worst indictment was in regard to Howard's behavior after the death of his father. It had soon become apparent that the purpose of his trip to Los Angeles was not to escape from grief, but to make "the best possible settlement of your father's will," Rupert charged.

He accused his nephew of taking advantage of a legal loophole in reducing the portions of the estate to which his grandparents and Uncle Felix were entitled under terms of the will. After Felix Turner Hughes had "lovingly and kindly" written to Son that he could not accept this arrangement, the youth had treated his grandfather with "such evasion and negligence and insolence" that Rupert threatened to take young Howard by the throat and "hold you until he finished talking to you."

Howard's behavior had also infuriated his Uncle Felix; only Mimi had been unable to see through Son's chicanery, Rupert said.

"When you first came here you said to my mother, 'Mimi, almost the last words of my father were to keep you in luxury, and I am going to. I am going to give you fifty thousand dollars,'" Rupert said. She was dazed by such generosity, he recalled, but Howard had in his pocket the will he was preparing to break which made her "the legal possessor of hundreds of thousands of dollars."

After that, Howard had lived in Rupert's house, permitting Mimi to spend money on him and his chauffeur, and had sold her car. Rupert charged, "When I heard that you had traded off the car to this actor, Ralph Graves, whom you have adopted for your peculiar crony, I sent a telegram of such violence that the Western Union returned it to me, saying that you could sue them for libel if they sent it." Rupert then sent a less vehement telegram urging Mimi to order Howard out of the house.

Howard never gave his grandmother the money he received for her car, Rupert now wrote, saying she wept when he told her that "the more loving she is to you and the more she hates the thought of money, the more horrible she makes you."

Rupert warned that the boy's grandfather, a legal expert, could remove from young Howard's hands the entire property his father had bequeathed. Rupert himself had nothing to win or lose from the battle, he said, having money enough of his own.

Again, he strongly urged Howard to go to college to improve his "very immature brain," and he pointed out that he had never known anyone who had seen Howard read a book or show any interest in anything but playing golf in the day and disappearing mysteriously at night.

"The only precocious thing I have heard of your doing is to live like a dissipated man of twenty-five at least," Rupert told the eighteen-year-old. Warning that the great fortune the deceased Howard had built up could go to pieces quickly "unless genius is shown in its management," he concluded the letter with the hope that his nephew would consider what he had written as "the very serious diagnosis of a family doctor." [24]

Rupert's accusations did not go unanswered. Although no copy of Howard's reply is known to exist, Rupert followed up with another letter that told his nephew:

You write very loftily about what I ought to have done: I should have quoted certain accusations to you and then asked your explanations.

But I did not have to . . . I saw you commit the offences. I saw the will, the correspondence, the figures. I saw you when you were here . . . .

May I ask what sort of monument you are putting on your father's grave? Mimi is longing to go to Houston and pay her tribute of tears. Will she find a tomb there appropriate?

The young Howard signed his letter "Your disappointed nephew," and Rupert signed his "Your father's loving brother." [25] But Rupert's arguments apparently were to no avail, and Howard's grandparents and Uncle Felix agreed reluctantly to accept $325,000 for their one-fourth interest, with the amount to be paid from the company's cash reserves.

Although Howard was now the sole owner of Hughes Tool, he could not hold the stock in his own name or have control because he was a minor. But such an obstacle was no deterrent to Howard, who learned that under Texas law a minor at age nineteen could petition the court to be declared an adult. He then became the golf partner of the judge who would decide this matter, trying to impress him with what he knew about the company's operations. The judge took only two days after Howard became nineteen on December 24, 1924, to declare him of "full age." [26]

Howard, Jr., was now in full control of the company his father had built. He could proceed with his own interests, which included a strong desire to enter the motion picture business as a producer.

Amid all the unhappiness that had occurred in the Hughes family, there was a bright spot early in 1924—the birth of Rupert's first grandchild. Agnes Christine Lapp was born to Elspeth and Edward Lapp in Washington, D. C. on January 18.[27] Although it probably meant nothing to Howard Hughes that he had a new first cousin once removed, the blood relationship he had with Agnes, as well as others in her family yet unborn, someday would become an important issue in one of the most publicized court cases in history.

By now, Rupert's parents had no desire to spend the rest of their lives in Keokuk, far from their surviving sons, and decided to move to Los Angeles to be near Rupert. Although this put them farther away from Felix, still teaching in New York, they hoped that he, too, might move to California—a desire shared by Rupert.

Ever since Felix T. and Jean had first visited their son, they had been sold on the state, so it was not surprising that they moved there. The place they set-tled on was a stately Mediterranean-style mansion at 204 North Rossmore Avenue in the beautiful Hancock Park area. The first thing "Mimi" insisted on was to add a wing next to the two-story living room. In the downstairs of the addition was a room with a piano for Felix, and upstairs was a room for Rupert, thus making certain that there would always be a place for the sons to stay. She also planted Arizona cedars as a backdrop for a backyard garden.[28]

One of the main reasons for Rupert's visit back East early in the year was to complete the work on his next novel, *The Golden Ladder*, published by Harper & Brothers in late spring. The book is an account of the life of Betty Bowen, who rose from a sordid background as a prostitute in Providence, Rhode Island, and climbed "the golden ladder" to riches and fame as Madame Jumel, one of the most fascinating personalities of the period between the American Revolution and the end of the Civil War. She hob-nobbed with royalty and, at age sixty, married Aaron Burr, then seventy-nine; she later divorced him on grounds of infidelity. Included in Hughes's story, which he said was "first and foremost a novel, but I have nowhere intentionally twisted history,"[29] was an account of the ill-fated duel between Burr and Alexander Hamilton. Many famous names parade through the story, which moves at a fast pace in Providence, New York, and Paris, and ends with events taking place at the Jumel Mansion, which later would become a landmark and tourist attraction in New York.

The Golden Ladder is an intriguing story about a woman's search for recognition. As the author put it, "What Betty longed for with a longing aggravating rapidly to a mania was Respectability. She wanted to be a lady and among the ladies sit." [30]

The "Guide to Fiction" column in *The Bookman* called *The Golden Ladder* "history with the Hughes sparkle" and commented that "more vampish than the modern variety was Mme. Jumel whose brazen career makes fascinating reading." Jim Tully, in the *International Book Review*, said, "Written with sym-pathy and understanding, it is a novel combining the glamor of fiction with the accurate knowledge of a social historian," and the *Boston Transcript* reviewer wrote, "It is as an historical novelist that Mr. Hughes is likely to be remembered. He has the grasp of details which makes for realism." [31]

It was indeed a book that would be remembered as a work of historical fiction—one listed among "books of special worth" in the 1929 *A Guide to the Best Historical Novels and Tales*. It was also listed in the 1967 *A Guide to the Best Fiction*, which described what was then regarded as the best English and American fiction.[32]

Shortly after publication of *The Golden Ladder* came the release of *True as Steel*, produced by Goldwyn Pictures. Written and directed by Rupert, the film was based on Rupert's *Cosmopolitan* story with the same title published the previous December.

The cast included Eleanor Boardman, with Huntley Gordon as her father, a successful manufacturer, and Cleo Madison as her mother. The father becomes enamored with cotton mill manager Aileen Pringle, but she turns him down when he suggests they divorce their mates to wed.

The movie delighted the *New York Times* reviewer at its Capitol Theater opening run during the week of June 17. "Rupert Hughes, who writes his own stories and then translates them into pictures," said the critic, "usually salaams to the 'great gawd' hokum, and is a witty defender of his idol at banquets, but in *True as Steel* he has actually neglected hokum, which fact makes this photoplay vastly more entertaining." [33]

The reference to hokum concerned comments Hughes had made in after-dinner speeches and in an essay in the February 24 issue of the *Times*. Titled "Triumphant Hokum," it answered critics who used the word "hokum" as a harpoon against authors and film producers.

"Classic emotion might be defined as hokum that is over a hundred years old. So hokum might be called classic emotion that is less than a hundred years old—of today and now, in fact." He could not understand why an opera about peasants was regarded as artistic, but when an American wrote about common people it was considered "cheap rot and hokum-pokum." He called films the "youngest son" among the arts, adding that when radio hit its stride "the movie will move up among the elder brothers" and be treated with reverence.[34] As a prophet, Rupert was on target.

Felix Turner Hughes, still a practicing attorney in his eighty-sixth year, was called to New York to wrap up a complicated legal case involving a major corporation, with two million dollars at stake. He had exchanged numerous telegrams with other attorneys before he persuaded them to his point of view, thereby saving the expenses of a court battle.

Proud of his father for having won such an important case at his advanced age, Rupert wrote an essay, "My Father," that *American Magazine* published in August, 1924. It was illustrated by a full-page rotogravure picture of Felix T. and Rupert.

"He looks back with gleaming eyes, a wise brain, and a beautiful heart, on a life that has included the fine intellectual conquests of legal problems and of the minds of judges and juries; has mounted up and up and has never been stained with evil," Rupert wrote. "He has fought hard and he has wept over the deathbeds of his beloved; but he has made the grade gloriously . . . . And so I submit the case. If my father is not a great man, who is or has been?"

By the time the essay was published, Felix and Jean were just a year away from their sixtieth wedding anniversary. To have lived so long with one wife, Rupert said, was in itself "proof of a certain greatness"—not only for the husband but for his wife. And so, he followed the tribute to the "Daddy" he always greeted with a kiss[35] by writing a similar adoring essay about his mother for the same magazine. Blessed with the ability to write anywhere and at any time, he began it on a train from Westchester County to New York City, later recalling, "I wrote it on my knee on a pad with a pencil." [36] It appeared in the September issue.

"She sits in her room, reading a Spanish novel in the original—which is more than I can do," Rupert wrote. "She has turned to this book from a volume of French memoirs . . . She took up the study of French at fifty, and of Spanish at sixty.

"She sits straight, with the fine flat back of a woman of thirty, though she is eighty years old. Her hair is not yet white. She still dresses fashionably, with exquisite taste; but in black now, for she is in mourning again for another of her children whom she has outlived." He called her "as passionately devoted and unselfish a mother as ever I heard of," and said that for her reward she has had her children's idolatry.[37]

Rupert's outpouring of affection in 1924 was not limited to his parents, for within the year after Adelaide's death he edited a collection of her poetry. Published by Harper and titled *The Poems of Adelaide Manola, With a Memorial by Rupert Hughes*, it included some rhymes, but mostly free verse.

In the *Memorial*, Rupert's love for Adelaide was shown in eloquently written biographical information, which told how sculptor Gutzon Borglum had been so inspired by her "Diantha" that he had created a marble statue of her. In addition to that monument, wrote Rupert, "this thin volume will serve as another."

Some of the poems had been returned to the United States after Adelaide's death, and although publication had been arranged earlier, Rupert had organized them into groups, followed by poems previously published in the *Diantha* volume.[38]

The *New York Times* critic called free verse Adelaide's "native medium" and said she used it "with such skill, so naturally, so elastically, that, as we read her, she seems hardly to be writing at all." He continued, "We seem instead to be sitting at a play, a play in which we not only watch the characters working out their drama but can see what is going on in their hearts and minds as well." [39]

At around the time that Adelaide's book of poetry was published, Rupert's own poetry was represented in an anthology, *Poems of Today*. There was also recognition for his accomplishments as a composer in Ernst C. Krohn's *A Century of Missouri Music*. Calling "Cain" a "masterpiece of dramatic inspiration" and saying that Hughes's musical works "reek of modernity," the author reported that one authority had listed Rupert as one of the "twelve modernists" along with such well-known composers as Ravel, Debussy, Stravinsky, and Richard Strauss.[40]

Applause for Hughes also came when Edward J. O'Brien's *The Best Short Stories of 1924* again placed him on the Roll of Honor, along with two stories—"Where Are you, Tod Allerton?" and "Grudges." The latter, from the July issue of *Liberty*, was one of twenty stories O'Brien republished as the year's best.[41]

In the sad days following the death of his wife, Hughes's mind had turned again to the apparent meaninglessness of religion that had caused him to abandon the fervent beliefs so deeply instilled in him during his youth. He wrote an essay for the October *Cosmopolitan* titled "Why I Quit Going to Church," with the magazine's warning that "Rupert Hughes is so drastic in this article that, if you've been backsliding, his attack may irritate you into going back to church—just to prove how wrong his viewpoint is . . ."

It was, indeed, an indictment not only of churches and preachers but of fundamental beliefs in a deity. Hughes knew his article would be taken as an affront by many people, and so it was.

He bluntly told readers that he had not quit church because of laziness, frivolity, or to worship outdoors, but he simply had realized that what was being preached was untrue. He questioned whether most churchgoers believed a fourth of what their creeds declared. Hughes told how his belief had turned to disbelief while he was in college. First he had doubted that the *Bible* was the inspired word of God or that it was factual. "Hell went next. I simply could not stomach a God who could devise and conduct such an infamous institution."

He also doubted that whether a person was a believer had anything to do with his character. As for himself, he was content to let the universe run itself "without trying to talk to the Motorman." But, "If it shall prove to be true that my failure to believe is itself a crime against God; if my failure to pay him the kind of worship which I cannot, to save me, make sure He wants, is an offense against Him, as against you, then you can surely leave my punishment to Him." [42]

Although that was his wish, it was not what happened. As soon as the essay appeared, Rupert became the target of an onslaught of harsh comments. Some preachers devoted complete sermons to the article, and religious newspapers and magazines such as *Zion's Herald*, the *Churchman*, and various *Methodist Advocates* published detailed replies to his arguments. [43]

One publication, *Truth Seeker*, defended him—hardly a surprise, coming from the weekly that carried on the tradition of atheist Robert G. Ingersoll. But other periodicals, secular as well as church-related, called the Hughes article "superficial," "shallow," or a "diatribe."

Current Opinion used the heading of "A Diatribe" for the second page of its review ("Rupert Hughes Indicts Religion"). It also carried a photo portrait of Rupert, identified as "THE ICONOCLAST," and said that he "has surprised his friends by the vehemence of his recent onslaught on Christianity," but averred that he had hardly uncovered new ground. [44]

Many responses applauded Rupert's essay. He told an Alabama newspaper editor that the letters of approval he had received outnumbered by at least ten to one those that condemned him. [45]

A later manuscript Hughes wrote took up in a more direct manner the question of "Am I an Atheist?" He declared, "Since I do not believe in any of the thousands of gods imagined or evolved by groping humanity, and since the countless documents alleged to prove their existence only emphasize my suspicions, I suppose I may be called an 'atheist,' though the word has been applied to almost every belief or disbelief by every other." He certainly was not a dogmatic atheist, if any; to the contrary, "I am very meek about my disbelief and do not pretend to explain anything, least of all how the world could be created and run without a deity."[46]

In labeling Hughes "The Iconoclast," *Current Opinion* was not alone. It was a tag that would stick for much of his career. A biographical sketch published decades later referred to his "agnostic" article in *Cosmopolitan* and said, "After his second wife's death, Hughes entered an iconoclastic phase. A writer of farce and light fiction, he now shocked religious conservatives with an indictment of religion."[47] This phase continued for years, some observers thought, as he wrote about another subject that would occupy much attention during the remainder of the 1920s and early 1930s.

By October, Rupert had left the house that he and Adelaide had rented on South Western. There seemed no need for forty-two rooms for just one person, so he moved in temporarily with his parents on North Rossmore.

In late 1924, just a few days more than one year since the suicide of Adelaide was reported, newspapers in New York and Los Angeles published the news of the engagement of Rupert to Elizabeth Patterson Dial, the actress known to the screen as Patterson Dial.

The *Los Angeles Times* reported that Miss Dial had first met Hughes during the filming of his story, *Reno*, a little more than a year ago. The news item also announced that Hughes had been advanced recently from director to production executive at Metro-Goldwyn-Mayer.[48]

Born May 19, 1902, in Madison County, Florida, the daughter of William Henry and Sarah B. Whitman Dial,[49] Elizabeth Patterson Dial—usually called Patty or Pat by Rupert and close friends—began her film career in 1921 at the age of nineteen. The two films she made that year were *Get-Rich-Quick Wallingford* and the classic *Tol'able David*, starring Richard Barthelmess, in which she played a young mountain woman. By the end of 1924 she had been in a dozen motion pictures, including Rupert's *Reno*.

After it had been suggested that she might be the type of actress Rupert was seeking for *Reno*, an appointment was made for an interview; but before it took place he saw her on the studio lot and thought she was too tall. Reluctant to disappoint her, he went ahead with the interview. With a magnetic personality despite an innate shyness, Patterson made an impression on Hughes. She not only got the job, but he said later that it was "the most blessed day" of his life.[50]

After Adelaide's suicide, followed by Howard's death, Patty had provided comfort and sympathy to Rupert and his parents. But in March, while in New York, he was shocked to learn that his mother had rebuffed Patty during his absence. His letter to Mimi, in which he berated young Howard, was untypical in that he complained bitterly about his mother's faults, while praising her virtues:

> Your special delivery letter has just arrived. I am sorry I spoke of Pat, but you seemed to be so fond of her and she was so faithful during the hard bitter weeks. I thought she helped you to get through many a terrible hour, and she loved you dearly, I know.
>
> Suddenly you dropped the mention of her in your telegrams and I learned that you just refused to see her or talk to her on the telephone. I wondered what had happened. I am sorry you have decided that she is a "stranger" and a nuisance, but that is your business and not mine.
>
> When people have been very sympathetic and affectionate with me I cannot slam the door in their faces and lock them out forever without explanation. But you can and do and always have done. So that's that . . . .
>
> As for Patty, she is simply bewildered and baffled. She gave me her society when I needed somebody to talk to. She gave you her love timidly and eagerly. She is motherless and so ill that she may drop dead at any moment. There is no thought of marriage between us, and I hope you will not add that fear to your grudges against her . . . .
>
> It hurts me always to see you capable of such ruthless cruelty toward people who have been tender with you . . . .
>
> It's too bad that I should have caused all this trouble by urging Patty to be near you and even to force herself on your shy nature. I always do the wrong thing when I try to comfort you, but I do adore you with all my soul, such as it is.
>
> Write me again and often. I can't seem to get a line from you except by loud telegrams.
>
> Oceans of love to you forever.[51]

Apparently his frankness cleared the air and caused no hard feelings on the part of his mother, who preserved the letter along with several others he had written her, tied in a pink ribbon. The loving tribute he wrote for *American* magazine later in the year did not hint of any faults that Mimi might have.

Certainly his mother's opinion of Patty, whether bad or good, did not keep him from seeing her. And despite his protestation that he and Patty had no intention of marrying, they had changed their minds by December.

Patty had an unusual beauty, with red hair and nicely sculpted facial features. Taller than Rupert, at the age of twenty-two she was three decades younger than his nearly fifty-three years and five years younger than his daughter, Elspeth, who was expecting a second child. But despite the age difference, Rupert saw that his bride-to-be had many attributes, and she, in return, admired his intellect, was intensely interested in his work, and seemed to understand him. As time went by, she would become increasingly helpful to him, while his descriptions of her would include such terms as "beautiful," "kind," "devoted," "keenly wise," and "truly the artist." [52]

But for now, there was no doubt that they were deeply in love, and so, on New Year's Eve, Rupert and Patterson were married in Los Angeles, and when the year 1925 arrived, they were on a honeymoon trip to New York. [53]

CHAPTER FIFTEEN

THE MID-TWENTIES

*"I am a glutton for praise, though it makes
me very meek, and fills me with a sense of
unworthiness. When I am kicked I am
always kicked upstairs."*

Life with such a young wife undoubtedly took some adjustment on Rupert's part, as it did on hers, but their marriage soon became a partnership in which her talents and discerning mind were helpful in many ways in connection with his writing.

There was one person who was not pleased with his choice of a mate. Shortly before Rupert married Patterson, the two met with Avis in New York. Whether disturbed by the idea of Rupert's marrying just a year after her mother's suicide, or by his taking such a young partner, Avis did not react kindly. The visit proved to be the last time she ever saw Rupert, and although they occasionally wrote to each other, she reportedly never talked with him again.[1]

Not long after the wedding, an incident occurred that showed Patty had a mind of her own. Rupert, who had owned horses, wanted to go horseback riding and offered to teach her to ride. Although she did not enjoy physical activity, she agreed to try, but as soon as she mounted the horse it threw her to the ground. Rupert helped her up, relieved that she was not hurt, and urged her to try it again to prove to the horse that she was not afraid. Her response was, "And what the devil do I care what that horse thinks!" Never again did she get on a horse. Rupert's own interest in horses did not diminish; later he bought another one, but he rarely had time to ride it.[2]

After their marriage, Rupert and Patty lived at 21 Laughlin Park in Los Angeles, but began making plans to build a new home—one that would feature unusual architecture and attract considerable attention. Meanwhile, there were other things on Rupert's mind.

He became involved in a court case in Los Angeles in which it became evident that the bad publicity he had received after telling why he quit church was still having an impact.

The case involved an application by Rupert and screen actor Conrad Nagel to serve as joint guardians for Marshall Ericksen, the eighteen-year-old brother of actress Lucille Ricksen, the "baby star" of film, who had died a few weeks earlier. Before her death, according to Hughes's testimony, she and her brother, both of whom had appeared in *The Old Nest*, had asked that Hughes and Nagel take charge of their affairs to "protect them from their father." Attorneys for the divorced father, Samuel Ericksen, opposing the guardianship application, attacked both Nagel and Hughes. The actor, they said, was too busy to serve, but they saved their diatribes for Hughes, calling him an atheist—citing his highly publicized magazine article as proof—and "unfit to control the education of a minor." The court ruled otherwise, and although it named the father the administrator of Lucille's $50,000 estate, it appointed Hughes and Nagel joint guardians of the youth.[3]

As for the controversial *Cosmopolitan* piece, it did not fade away. In 1925 it was reprinted in book form by The Truth Seeker Company; included in its 158 pages were Hughes's answers to critics regarding issues raised in the article. Years later, the Freethought Press Association would republish the book, and Hughes would inscribe a copy of the 1940 edition "with the affection of a heathen." [4]

Earlier in 1925 there had been considerable publicity for Hughes and Nagel when the Metro-Goldwyn-Mayer movie production of Rupert's 1911 stage farce *Excuse Me* was released.[5] Rupert wrote the screenplay adaptation and was much involved in production, although Alf Goulding directed it. Nagel played the hero, Lt. Harry Mallory; the lovely Norma Shearer was his fiancee, Marjorie Newton; and Renee Adoree played the role of Francine.

The film's basic plot followed that of the stage play and book, but the *New York Times* critic found the result "a pathetic farce" and "a wearying production in which the comedy is so forced that the laughs are lost, and in quite a number of instances, the situations are little more than slapstick." Only a few sketches were genuinely funny, he said.

An advertisement in the same newspaper presented excerpts from a more favorable review calling *Excuse Me* "one of the funniest farces ever presented on Broadway. Gales of laughter swept the Capitol all day yesterday." [6] But regardless of the critics, the motion picture proved popular with the paying public, and its run—like that of the stage play and stock productions years earlier—could be counted a success.

Prior to its release, however, Rupert found that the pressures of moviemaking had grown to such an extent that they had forced him to delay the completion of books and short stories that were underway or planned. He therefore asked Metro-Goldwyn-Mayer to release him from his contract that involved writing, directing, and producing responsibilities. By mutual agreement, this was done. Although the newspaper announcement that he had terminated his contract revealed no plans for his future,[7] there is no doubt that he intended to do some work on additional motion pictures, for he was too heavily entrenched in Hollywood to walk away entirely from film-making.

In the spring of 1925 a novel he had worked on before his marriage was published and met with mixed reviews. Some readers who knew his controversial views on religion must have thought it strange that this novel would have its opening scene in heaven and depend for its plot upon angels transformed into human beings and sent to earth. A *New York Times* critic thought Hughes intended to prove that angels could not do a better job of living on earth than could human beings already here. The title, *Destiny*, reflected the principle upon which two heavenly creatures—the angel of derision, occupying the body of wealthy and spoiled Niobe Fenn, and the angel of scorn, Joel Kimlin—were ultimately defeated. When God told them they could return to heaven, they declined.

The *Times* review, which along with the author's portrait dominated a page, found much to praise in the book published by Harper & Brothers. Its "swift, sure depiction of character, action, suspense, incident: all are molded into a bright, sparkling narrative, which never runs deep, but is never still." The reviewer thought he knew why the author was so popular: "He likes the human race, without reservations, believes in it, sympathizes with it." And that was the theme the newspaper headlined: "Rupert Hughes Flatters the Human Race." [8]

The Bookman's reviewer considered the novel well balanced, "with many poetic touches," if it had not been "stained by unnecessary vulgarities." But G. W. Wynne, critic for the *New York Tribune* proclaimed, "On the whole I should say that *Destiny* is the best novel Rupert Hughes has achieved." [9]

Free of his M-G-M commitments, Hughes devoted more time to short stories. One of the first sold in 1925 was to the *Saturday Evening Post*. Knowing that his work would be published in the magazine again, after a long absence, made him feel "like a Prodigal Son, or something," he told editor George Horace Lorimer. [10]

Earlier that year Hughes had written to Lorimer to endorse a proposal by author Chandler Sprague to write a biographical sketch about movie executive Joseph M. Schenck, husband of actress Norma Talmadge. But Lorimer turned down the proposed piece on grounds that the *Post* had recently published other articles about motion pictures. [11] The attempt by Hughes to promote Sprague's work was typical of his ongoing effort to advance the careers of other writers by bringing their work to the attention of editors.

His correspondence continued to demonstrate an interest in a variety of subjects, including the search for historical accuracy. He told an interviewer that he considered himself "more of a historian than a novelist." [12] He also urged Henry E. Huntington, the Huntington Library founder, to publish what Hughes regarded as one of the library's most important treasures: the diary of Aaron Burr. In Hughes's words, "historical justice demands publication" of the diary in order to right a wrong done to Burr by "slanderous political rivals." If Huntington did not want to publish it, Hughes volunteered to transcribe it, write an introduction, and arrange for publication. Huntington replied that he planned to publish the diary but did not know when. [13]

Also in 1925, Rupert reaffirmed his views about genius, replying to a suggestion made by author and editor George Sylvester Viereck that wealthy patrons provide financial endowments for those with genius. Hughes wrote:

As to your suggestion that men of wealth endow genius instead of institutions, I am afraid I cannot agree with you, since it was tried for many centuries. . . .

There is one further problem: who is to decide who is the genius? Who knows what a genius is? How do we know a genius during his lifetime?

It is my firm conviction that a number of writers and other artists who are most highly rated now by certain of the high-brow critics will be considered very cheap stuff by posterity; and that many who are ignored or despised by these same critics will be held as geniuses. . . . [14]

Apparently the letter did not lessen Viereck's opinion of Hughes. Two months later Rupert thanked him for including him in a symposium and "for your still more rash inclusion of me among the 'immortals.'" He added, "I had my doubts about the immortality of anybody, but I cannot resist an *argumentum ad hominem*." [15]

During the autumn of 1925 Rupert participated in a relatively new form of short story writing when *Collier's* magazine invited him and three other well-known authors—Octavus Roy Cohen, Sophie Kerr, and Zona Gale—to provide stories of only about twelve hundred words in length. Each was published, along with an illustration, on a single page. The stories proved so popular that *Collier's* continued to run "short short stories" from then on. [16]

On the first day of June, 1925, Howard Robard Hughes, Jr., took as his bride the dark-haired Houston socialite Ella Rice, two years older than his nineteen and a half years and the grand-niece of the founder of Rice Institute. They had known each other since childhood but had grown up in different circles; she was a popular socialite, while he was a loner. But after a few dates she agreed to marry him. Two days before the wedding, Howard had a lawyer draw up a will that, in the event of his death, would bequeath a half million dollars in securities to Ella, give his Aunt Annette $100,000 and the home on Yoakum Boulevard, and provide various sums to a friend; to Uncle Chilton Gano; to an aunt, Mrs. James P. Houstoun; and weekly pensions to two household servants. The will also provided for establishment of the Howard R. Hughes Medical Research Laboratories. The Hughes side of the family was notable by its absence from the bequests, although Howard did praise his deceased father and asked that Hughes Tool Company be preserved. [17]

After a garden wedding at the home of Ella's sister in Houston, the newlyweds spent a relaxing summer, with Howard often playing golf. He seemed little interested in the tool company, having decided to go on to something new; Hollywood beckoned. So, late in the year he and Ella boarded a train for Los Angeles, where they checked into the Ambassador Hotel. Its proximity to the motion picture studios was an attraction to Howard, whose interest in making movies had not lessened since the days when Uncle Rupert had introduced him to the screen world.[18]

One evening Colleen Moore's screen director and his wife invited her to dinner with "some young people from Texas who were on their honeymoon." The pair turned out to be Howard and Ella, and Miss Moore later related an amusing conversation that took place when Howard asked Ella where she had been all day. She replied that she had been to the Universal Studio, which she thought was "just great."

"He said he had been to another studio," Miss Moore recalled. "And he said, 'You know, I think I'm going to buy that studio.' She paused and said, 'Well, why don't you buy that one and then why don't I buy Universal, and each of us will have us a movie studio.' And the thing was, she could have bought it—all by her little lonesome self," Miss Moore laughed.[19]

Howard did not purchase a studio just then, but he did get started right away in the motion picture business with actor Ralph Graves, putting up $60,000 of the sum Graves needed to finance a movie from a story titled *Swell Hogan*. But when the film was made it seemed so certain to fail that it was never shown publicly.

Rupert and other family members urged Howard not to waste his inheritance on such a risky business, but he soon became involved with another film. This offered better prospects, for it was brought to his attention by Marshall Neilan, the director who had suggested that Rupert hire Colleen Moore as the heroine of one of his films—a decision Rupert never regretted. Neilan knew the young man had the money to finance the film he wanted to make, a comedy to be called *Everybody's Acting*. Neilan was also persuasive, and Howard agreed to put up all of the money needed for the venture. *Everybody's Acting*, released in 1926, became a financial success, and to Howard's great delight it paid a return of fifty percent on his investment. With such a profit he was hooked, convinced that he would become a movie producer and take a hand in the actual making of films.[20]

While Howard was doing his thing with the Graves and Neilan films, Rupert's name continued to be associated with motion pictures, including

M-G-M's *Don't*, based on his 1914 *Saturday Evening Post* short story called "Don't You Care." Released in November 1925, the movie, directed by Alf Goulding, starred Sally O'Neil as a schoolgirl flapper who wants to marry John Patrick—defying her parents' wish for her to wed another.

Three motion pictures the following year also had a Rupert Hughes connection. One, a comedy called *Money Talks*, produced by Metro-Goldwyn-Mayer Pictures, was based on a Hughes story with the same title. Archie Mayo directed the film, and Owen Moore played a spendthrift whose wife, Claire Windsor, leaves him. He then goes to an island to promote a seedy hotel as a health resort. The cast included Ned Sparks as captain of a bootlegging vessel.

A reviewer called it a hectic comedy, with "more nonsense than any production screened at the Capitol for many moons," but thought it fell "decidedly flat" as entertainment. The audience enjoyed it, however, and the reviewer reported that Owen Moore's appearance in girl's clothing caused "no little merriment" among women viewers.[21]

Rupert was also involved—although not until late stages of production—with *The Sea Beast*, the 1926 film version of Herman Melville's classic novel *Moby Dick*. Produced by Warner Brothers, it starred John Barrymore and Dolores Costello and was directed by Millard Webb. Many years later, producer-director Mervyn LeRoy recalled that producer Jack Warner credited Hughes for saving him from a major disaster after filming was completed. Warner liked the acting and direction but knew something was wrong, so he went to Hughes, whom LeRoy called "one of the great title writers" of silent movies, and asked him to fix the movie. Rupert "took it apart and put it together again with a whole set of new titles and turned a potential disaster into a hit," LeRoy said. Once more, "Dr. Hughes" had cured a sick patient.

Warner had never discussed the matter of payment with Hughes, thinking the fee might be too high, but after Rupert finished his work Warner sent him a $1,500 check as a down payment. To the producer's amazement, Hughes returned it, saying that he had done the work "as a favor to Warner *and* Herman Melville." For some reason, perhaps a prearrangement with Warner, Hughes did not receive screen credit for the titles.[22]

He did receive credit for titles he wrote for the 1926 film *Old Ironsides*, a historical drama about the famous U. S. Navy frigate *Constitution*—better known by the film's title—and its battles with other ships. The cast of the

Paramount production directed by James Cruze included Charles Farrell, Esther Ralston, Wallace Beery, and George Bancroft.

It was a coincidence that all three of the movies with which Hughes was associated that year dealt with water-related subjects—a rumrunning vessel, a whale, and ship battles. Likewise, his next novel, published in the spring by Harper & Brothers, also concerned a body of water, but one with which he was especially familiar. Titled *The Old Home Town*, its locale was Carthage—familiar to readers of his short stories—on the banks of the Mississippi. The story was based upon circumstances surrounding the building of the Keokuk dam as envisioned by his father.

The Old Home Town is interesting mainly for its descriptions of Mississippi River life early in the twentieth century and for its historic account of a monumental engineering feat. But at the time of its publication one critic considered it too long and dull, with unreal characters, except Mrs. Budlong. And the *London Times* reviewer wrote, "This example of American fiction is sufficiently well written to arouse annoyance over the sentimentality and its very ordinary plot." A much more favorable description came from *The Bookman*: "Clever and dramatic story of a town during the strain of sudden growth." [23]

Such diverse views of the same novel, if taken too seriously, might have sent an author on a roller-coaster ride from euphoria to gloom. But Hughes had known criticism from many angles, having himself penned countless critiques of music, art, and literature, and when asked to write his own views of critics he told how he reacted to both adverse and favorable responses from reviewers. In his comments, "Me and the Critics," he wrote to W. Orton Tewson of the Literary Review, *New York Evening Post*, on September 28, 1926:

I would rather be hit by a humble bouquet tossed by the most awkward layman—or laywoman—than be knocked out by a brickbat hurled by the most eminent critic in full uniform. . . .

I long ago gave up all hope of writing successfully for the critics, or of persuading them to write my work for me as they would have it. They do not know what they want till they get it and then they do not want it long.

So I have gone my way, having the most glorious time, writing about anything that interests me and indulging in my own little whims as to what is good art and is true truth. Now and then somebody flings me a posy. Now and then someone casts a bombshell.

I am a glutton for praise, though it makes me very meek, and fills me with a sense of unworthiness. I could get along splendidly without any abuse at all, but when it comes my way, it stirs my pride and fills me with a self-protective sense of the critic's inferiority. When I am kicked I am always kicked upstairs . . . . [24]

Earlier in the year there were brickbats, along with some praise, for a speech he made, and within a month after writing "Me and the Critics" he would face a barrage of criticism after publication of his newest nonfiction book. Strangely enough, he would be attacked over a matter of patriotism—something that seemed almost unthinkable to anyone who knew how diligently he had served in military assignments. Even while the controversy was at a high, he would write an article for *The American Legion* on "Why I Am Still Going to School for My Country," in which he would praise the National Guard and the Reserves and tell about taking a course in Military Intelligence at the Army War College.[25]

But in the midst of the criticism many of his most recent short stories were considered of high quality. Of his fifteen stories listed in the Index of Short Stories in Edward J. O'Brien's *The Best Short Stories of 1926*, seven were indicated to be "of distinction," and three were of "finer distinction." Another, "Michaeleen! Michaelawn!," published earlier in Hughes's *Long Ever Ago*, but now republished by a magazine, was included once again in O'Brien's "Roll of Honor" for the year.

Before the publication date of his controversial book, which would bring more public attention than anything he had ever written, Rupert could boast of two more granddaughters. Elspeth Summerlin Lapp was born to Elspeth and Edward in Washington, D. C., on March 7, 1925. Their third daughter was born September 4, 1926, in Jacksonville, Florida, and given the name Barbara Patterson Lapp.[26]

Meanwhile, Rupert's brother, Felix, was spending much time in Los Angeles, visiting his parents and Rupert, but had not yet moved there permanently.

Although Rupert's *American* magazine article about his father had described how fit and alert the older man was in 1924, that situation had changed by 1926, and on October 20 Felix Turner Hughes, brilliant attorney,

former railroad president, Keokuk mayor, and judge, died of bronchial pneu-
monia just a few weeks shy of his eighty-eighth birthday. His handwritten
will left his entire estate to his wife, Jean, who continued to live in their home
on North Rossmore.[27]

The loss was great to the two sons of the towering figure whom they had
so loved and admired. He had been an inspiration who had shaped their lives
and encouraged them in their careers. They had seen his fighting spirit
demonstrated in the courtroom on many occasions, and much of it had rubbed
off on Rupert, who now was engaged in a controversy of major proportions.

CHAPTER SIXTEEN

THE GEORGE WASHINGTON FUROR

*"I was not seeking sensationalism or raking
up dead scandals with a ghoulish motive of
self-advertisement."*

I t was a significant evening for Sons of the Revolution members who
gathered at the New Willard Hotel in Washington, D. C., to commemo-
rate the birthday of Edmund Burke—the British statesman of the American Revolutionary War period. Speakers at the January 12, 1926, event
included an Ohio senator and a Virginia congressman.

Then it was Rupert Hughes's turn to address the group. But his extemporaneous comments differed from remarks by the others, focusing on George
Washington instead of Burke.

He made a plea for historical accuracy and attempted to dispel some time-
honored myths concerning the fabled "Father of Our Country." According to
newspaper reports, he said he had learned that Washington had never intended to fight for independence and that the Revolution was actually a "civil
war." But the reaction to the speech was not at all what Hughes expected;
the *New York Times* reported that his comments "fell as a bombshell among
the members and guests."

When Rupert finished speaking, Albion Parris, a past president of the society, and others assailed him for accusing Washington of immorality and for

attacking the "spotless saint of school-book tradition." But Hughes denied calling Washington immoral and said he had merely stated facts.[1]

A front page story in the January 14 issue was headlined: "Rupert Hughes Arouses Ire of Patriots by Attacking the Morals of Washington." The article quoted Parris, who charged Hughes with picturing the nation's first president as a "profane, irreligious and pleasure-loving man." Parris also declared that Hughes stated that Washington played cards, distilled whisky, "was a champion curser," danced for three hours with the wife of a general, never prayed, and avoided taking Communion at church.

News of the Hughes speech swept across the nation by wire services, and attacks on his audacity in daring to picture Washington as a "human being" reached a crescendo. There were some, however, who defended Hughes—including eighty-year-old John Washington, a descendant of George Washington's older brother, who said that when he had visited his grandfather in Virginia in 1861 they had drunk madeira from cellars at Mount Vernon. He declared, "Why, certainly George Washington drank," and asked, "Why try to place a halo around George Washington?"[2]

Two days later, when Hughes spoke at Town Hall in New York on another subject—current tendencies in American literature—he tried to explain his earlier remarks. But again he ran into a protest. When he repeated his assertion that Washington enjoyed dancing and once danced all night, an elderly woman spoke up loudly, "Well, why shouldn't he? He was the Father of our country!" She indignantly left the hall, but her action caused only a minor commotion and Rupert continued.

He contended that in his previous talk he had only stated what was revealed by Washington in his diary—that he danced well, distilled whisky, and used profanity—none of which Hughes considered immoral. He compared criticisms he had received to "a sick tomato" thrown at him.[3]

A *Times* editorial, headed "An 'Immoral' Washington," said many Americans would consider Washington immoral if he did, in fact, play cards with comrades of the Revolution, dance with their wives, and occasionally swear. While pointing out that such details were not significant as to Washington's character, the editorial said there was a place for them in a biography.[4]

Even the laconic President Calvin Coolidge commented on the matter. When asked about the controversy, he looked out the window at the Washington Monument. "The monument is still there," he said with a smile.

The President refused comment on the next day's anniversary of the nation's dry law.[5] There is no doubt that the furor over Washington was exacerbated by the mind-set of many Americans during the period of liquor prohibition, some of whom thought Hughes's statement was part of a plot to overturn the law forbidding the sale of alcoholic beverages.

On the first Sunday after Hughes's speech to the Sons of the Revolution, preachers across the nation took him to task. A Presbyterian minister in Brooklyn contended that irreparable harm would come to the ideals of young men and women if they believed Washington was as bad as Hughes had painted him. Another pastor reminded his congregation that Hughes had previously stirred up an earlier storm by making "an ignorant, unbalanced and bitter attack on the Church and the whole Christian system."

Dr. S. Parkes Cadman, a prominent church leader, was even more blunt, calling Hughes's criticism of Washington "a case of the pup that looked at the king—and not like him." [6]

Two Brooklyn residents, in letters to the editor, thought there was nothing new in statements about Washington's social life, which they called typical of the times in which he lived.[7]

It is not surprising that in the midst of the arguments about what Hughes had said and what his intentions had been, the man who had caused the uproar would be heard from again. The editorial page of the *New York Times* on January 21, 1916, contained a lengthy answer by Hughes that attempted to set the record straight:

RUPERT HUGHES REPLIES
Declares His Critics Traduce
Both Him and Washington

To the Editor of The New York Times:
Though I am not foolish enough to stay the avalanche I brought down on poor George Washington, you publish today two letters that especially sting me. One of them ridicules me for my "discoveries" because they are well known, and the other quotes me as stating that "after exhaustive study I found that Washington never meant to fight for independence." One makes me out a conceited fool, and the other a boastful liar. This was one of the times when I was neither. . . .

I was not seeking sensationalism or raking up dead scandals with a ghoulish motive of self-advertisement. I spoke quietly at a private banquet, where no reporters were present. The morning papers did not mention the banquet, and only one afternoon paper carried an account of it, evidently from hearsay, with mis-quotations of what I had really said. Then the editor of that paper, misunderstanding both the spirit and the nature of my remarks, published a violent denunciation of me. And the riot began. . . .

One notorious pulpiteer was so frantic with rage as to shout that he did not like my face! Of course, I could retort that I don't like it either, and no more do I like his face.

But does this quaint parson really mean to argue that because I do not look as noble as Washington I have no right to refer to him, or to quote from his writings? This is a novel embar-go, indeed, to put on the quotation of history. . . .

I did not attack Washington that night, nor ever in my life. In fact I praised him to the skies, and said he was great enough to shine by revelation. . . .

I cannot retract facts, and Washington cannot live his life over again, even to quiet those ferocious people who defame him under the pretense of defending him.

Rupert Hughes—Washington, D. C., Jan. 19, 1926[8]

Although it became obvious that the uproar would not disappear entirely, after a few weeks the published news articles and letters became less frequent. But the speech that had sparked the furor proved to be only the first of many public utterances Hughes made about Washington, and now he would become in-volved in a related project that would occupy most of his time for years to come.

Interested in Revolutionary War history since working on the *Historians' History of the World*, Rupert had intended to write a historical novel dealing with that period. The invitation to address the Sons of the Revolution had come while he was doing research for the novel.

But now, having been the target of so much abuse, he welcomed an invi-tation from William Morrow, head of the newly-formed William Morrow & Company publishing firm in New York, to write a one-volume biography that would provide a true picture of George Washington. Three other publishers asked him to do the same sort of book. The Morrow company had made the first offer, however, and Morrow had a long-established reputation as a leading figure in New York publishing before opening his own firm, so Rupert accepted his proposal and began intensive research into the life of Washington that would lead him to many sources of materials in public and private libraries across the nation. Fortunately, he had access to the extensive collection of Washington material in the Huntington Library, and he spent countless hours there poring over manuscripts and letters.

Meanwhile, his personal library continued to grow as he accumulated vast quantities of books and research materials about George Washington. It would later be described as one of the best private libraries in existence on the Washington period. But he did not confine his collecting to the numerous published volumes, both recent and rare, about the first President; he also sought out originals or copies of obscure documents, letters, journals, and manuscripts. In searching for clues to unknown aspects of the life of his subject, he especially was interested in such mundane things as records of quartermaster stores, expense accounts, and detailed lists that would enable him to provide a sense of reality in writing about the period.[9]

While Hughes worked on the Washington book, Chicago Tribune writer James O'Donnell Bennett wrote an article about Orion Clemens, brother of Mark Twain, and in his discussion of Keokuk, where Orion had lived, he referred to Jean Hughes as the mother of "rampant, romantic, rebel Rupert."[10] To many who had followed Rupert's career and had noted his recent battles, that seemed an accurate description, and some people undoubtedly questioned whether a writer of popular novels could stick to the facts in writing a biography of Washington.

It was against such a background of doubt and suspicion that William Morrow & Company published George Washington: The Human Being and the Hero, 1732-1762, in mid-October, 1926. But what Rupert had intended to be a complete biography in a single volume covered only the first thirty years of Washington's life. In an Afterword, he said he planned to write another volume devoted to "George Washington: the Rebel and the Conservative."

He also noted that of the 502 biographies of Washington that had been written by 1889, "practically every one of them was devoted to celebration rather than revelation." Too often, he said, Washington had been offered to readers as "a kind of angel, and the biographer as his high priest"—a trend that started when the Reverend Mason L. Weems (known as Parson Weems) collected and invented anecdotes that turned Washington's life into "a Sunday-school book." Others had followed, such as the book by the Reverend Jared Sparks, who had deleted remarks by Washington that might seem objectionable to readers.

Such denaturing did Washington a disservice, Hughes contended, saying "as a god, Washington was a woeful failure; as a man he was tremendous." His own book, said Hughes, was a study of the man himself, told, as fully as possible, in Washington's own words and relying heavily upon John C. Fitzpatrick's unexpurgated edition of the Washington diaries.

Illustrated with seventeen portraits and copies of letters, reports, and maps, the 580-page biography was handsomely bound, with an embossed silhouette of Washington on the front cover. To dispel any thought that this was a superficial treatment, Hughes documented all important facts, providing an authority for each and giving the reader "views opposed to mine so that he may hear both sides and judge for himself where there is dispute."

Most of the book covered details of Washington's formative years, with much human interest material not included in other biographies. "His mysterious love for Sally Fairfax, one of the most poignant of romances, finds its proper place in his biography for the first time," the author said. The volume ended with Washington's marriage and retirement into what he thought would be "a future of unbroken domestic felicity." [11]

The intense interest in the book's publication on October 13, 1926, prompted the *New York Times* to publish a review in the form of a news story the next day, rather than to delay it until the Book Review section came out on Sunday. The headline was:

PAINTS WASHINGTON
AS HUMAN, ARDENT

In First Volume of Biography Rupert Hughes Tells of Rum Deals, Land Speculation SAYS HERO WED FOR GAIN Married Martha Custis for Her Acres and Money, Though He Loved Sally Fairfax, Author Asserts

The review stated that Hughes had found evidence in Washington's diary that he was not a regular churchgoer but had "seized every possible pretext to stay at home." It also called attention to Hughes's proof that Washington had made beer and rum deals during a campaign for election to the House of Burgesses, and that part of his success as a land speculator had come from buying up land claims of old soldiers. In spite of these revelations, the portrait drawn by Hughes was highly favorable, the reviewer wrote.

He added that Washington's romances occupied a large part of the book. "His marriage with Martha Custis, as presented by Mr. Hughes, was founded on mutual esteem and sound business considerations—Washington having land that needed capital and Martha having the capital . . . . After his engagement to Martha, Washington wrote ardently, though in ponderous Johnsonian phrases, to Mrs. Sally Fairfax. Mr. Hughes spends many pages on an interpretation of a letter written by Washington to Mrs. Fairfax after his engagement to Martha Custis." [12]

It was the publication of the Sally Fairfax letter and Hughes's view of the relationship Washington had with her that brought on some of the harshest criticism of the book and its author. The barrage came from readers and, more often, from those who did not read the book but heard about some of its comments, as well as from a few biographers who disagreed with Hughes over the authenticity of the letter and whether it deserved a place in history. But there were other concerns, too including those expressed earlier in regard to Hughes's speech. Side by side with its review, the *Times* published a box headlined "Women of Wisconsin Resent Talk of Washington Drinking." It quoted a resolution by the Wisconsin Federation of Women's Clubs—prompted by Rupert's statements that Washington had drunk alcoholic beverages—condemning "expressions of disrespect and disloyalty to the great men in our history." The women blamed anti-prohibition forces for attempting to make people believe that national heroes did not oppose liquor, and warned that the motive was to pave the way for repeal of prohibition. [13]

Ten days after the news story about the book, the *Times Book Review* section devoted its front page and nearly half of another page to an article about "Washington's Enduring Fame." Saying that new biographers had not destroyed the greatness of Washington, it compared Hughes's book with *George Washington: The Image and the Man*, written by W. E. Woodward. The reviewer said they had the same objective—to provide a sense of the "real" Washington—and called Woodward's biography "immensely readable" and Hughes's account "more painstaking and scholarly." He added: "The strength of Mr. Hughes's work lies in the fact that it has arduously brought together and sifted out all the available material on Washington's early career and made of it an entertaining story. He is never dull. His gift for recording the interesting thing is well employed in his quotations from first-hand documents, of which he has made liberal and pointed use." [14]

A succinct commentary was provided by humorist Will Rogers, who by that time was a good friend of Rupert Hughes. His *Daily Telegram*, published prominently in numerous newspapers across the nation, called attention to Hughes's book:

MR. ROGERS DRAWS A MORAL
FROM WASHINGTON'S DIARY

BEVERLY HILLS, Cal., Nov. 21—Say, did you read what Rupert Hughes dug up in George Washington's diary? I was so ashamed I sat up all night reading it.

This should be a lesson to Presidents to either behave themselves or not keep a diary. Can you imagine, 100 years hence, some future Rupert Hughes pouncing on Calvin's diary? What would that generation think of us?

Calvin, burn them papers!

Yours for the suppression of scandal.

Will Rogers. [15]

For the fledgling William Morrow & Company, Rupert's volume was a bonanza. The national controversy the book provoked—including the public burning of copies by self-styled patriots in Chicago—boosted sales figures, and by December the book went into its fourth printing and the company increased its staff size. [16] Meanwhile, tapping the interest of British readers, Hutchinson & Co., Ltd., of London, rushed the Hughes volume into print.

The Bookman in December took note of what "a wealth of Washingtonia" the season had brought forth. In addition to the Hughes and Woodward books, three others had been published. In the opinion of Claude G. Bowers, the rash of Washington books had brought about a worthwhile result: "We are beginning to approach a sane conception of the man who was great in his achievements but by no means sanctified or perfect." He said that it was in Hughes's book that Sally Fairfax looms large and teasingly "as she unquestionably did in our hero's life." [17]

But where Bowers found reason to praise Hughes for his treatment of the

Sally Fairfax matter, a leading historian disagreed. Albert Bushnell Hart, a Harvard professor emeritus and author of many books, challenged Hughes's accuracy in regard to Sally Fairfax and other aspects of his book. Hughes, in reply, asked Hart to list what he considered to be errors. After an exchange of letters, Hughes thought Hart was satisfied, but apparently not, for a month later the Associated Press reported that Hughes told the professor, "There is not a single unsupported statement in the biography." As for Sally Fairfax, Hughes said that the portion of his book dealing with her came from old letters and documents of Washington.[18] But the statement did not end the argument, and at a later time both Hart and Hughes were condemned by another critic.

With publication of the first Washington volume accomplished, Hughes immediately plunged into research for a second one, in which he intended to show "the blind evolution of the most loyal of Englishmen into the leader of insurgents who, seeking only to reclaim their rights as Englishmen, made the surprising discovery that the insurrection was a great civil war, and that the unthinkable try for independence, instead of being impossible and undesirable, was inevitable." He planned to rely upon the scholarly findings and writings of various authorities, but most of all he would treat Washington as the best authority and let him speak for himself.[19]

While working on volume two, Hughes wrote an article about Washington for the February, 1927, issue of *American Legion Weekly*, and again he made news by asserting that Washington had "won his immortal fame by breaking the law and putting his neck in the halter that threatened all our glorious lawdefying forefathers." Hughes recalled the furor of a year earlier and said he had almost despaired of the human race when self-elected moralists had maintained the contradictory creeds that Washington was a sacred figure and that it was sacrilege to tell what he actually said and did. He added:

> The very Congressman who called me a literary cormorant— whatever that may be—for quoting from Washington's own diaries tried to have legal steps taken against certain newspapers for reprinting a recently discovered recipe of Washington for making beer in camp.
>
> In these days of prohibition . . . it infuriates the bigot to have it even mentioned that Washington was a temperate man, but not a teetotaler. They actually try to enlist him as a prohibitionist because he put down the Whisky insurrection, which was a sectional battle against paying an excise tax.[20]

The magazine piece provided fuel for new flames on February 22 during the observance of George Washington's 195th birthday. Newspapers reported that almost without exception, orators in New York City denounced recent biographers Hughes and Woodward. In Albany, an assemblyman charged that Rupert Hughes "seems to have nothing better to do than dig up trash and untruths about the personal affairs of the great General." [21]

It had become fashionable to target Hughes for condemnation, more so than other writers who followed in his footsteps in trying to humanize George Washington. Hughes was better known than the others; among moviegoers and readers of fiction his name had been for years a household word.

In the spring of 1927 he attended a dinner gathering of writers, editors, and publishers who paid tribute to E. W. Howe, the well-known Kansas author and publisher of the Atchison Globe. Humorist Irvin S. Cobb was toastmaster and Senator Arthur Capper of Kansas the main speaker. The New York Times reported that those present "insulted one another with perfect content" before hearing from the honored guest. One example of the kidding:

"Rupert Hughes was introduced as 'one who is now showing that if George Washington was not the father of his country, he tried to be,' and as one 'who spent Feb. 22 in hissing.' The novelist called Mr. Howe a 'Kansas Diogenes,' and somewhat feelingly praised the truth of the sage's writings as opposed to romantic beliefs which are erroneous. 'People do not like to be told the truth,' he said wistfully." [22]

Despite the blasts from preachers, politicians, and pseudo-patriots, the published reviews of Hughes's first Washington book had been favorable: "A wondrous work done in the spirit of today," wrote W. E. Dodd in the New York Herald Tribune. Allan Nevins, in the Saturday Review of Literature, called the Hughes biography "engrossing" and "much more thoroughly and carefully documented" than the one by Woodward; Rupert's book was, in fact, "the fullest collection of facts upon these thirty years which we possess." [23]

In the summer of 1927, the Little Rock, Arkansas, public library asked the most prominent male librarians across the nation—including those who regularly participated in library conventions and often spoke to civic clubs and other groups—to provide lists of recent books that would appeal to men. Among those mentioned was the first volume of Hughes's biography of Washington. [24]

CHAPTER SEVENTEEN

AN ARABIAN NIGHTS MANSION

*"No matter where we live, and believe me,
Hollywood is no worse or better than any other
city or village in the world, there is beauty all
around us. We create it ourselves. And in the
creation lies our happiness."*

The new home of Rupert and Pat, at 4751 Los Feliz Boulevard on a corner lot in Los Feliz Heights, was a place of beauty, designed for their special needs.

A June 14, 1925 building permit indicated it would be a fifteen-room, two-story residence of frame and stucco, sixty-four by one hundred feet in size, with a composition roof. The *Los Angeles Sunday Times* announced on September 20 that the "beautiful mansion" of Persian architecture, with six baths, was being built on a picturesque knoll with a view of the entire city. The architect and contractor for the $100,000 residence was W. F. Olerich of Los Angeles.[1]

Many years had passed since Rupert had worked in an office other than at home, and it was his desire to have a combined study-workroom, or studio, spacious enough for his growing library. Both he and Pat also wanted an enclosed patio with swimming pool, in a style other than Italian or Spanish, but could not decide on something appropriate.

When Rupert mentioned their dilemma to Douglas Fairbanks, the actor suggested patterning the house after illustrations in a four-volume edition of *Arabian Nights*, which he had used in designing sets for *The Thief of Bagdad*, a movie in which he had starred. A look at the books convinced Rupert and Pat that this was the answer—a combination of grace, beauty, and simplicity. They then met with the architect and arranged for many of the details shown in the illustrations to be incorporated into the planning. The resulting mansion became a talked-about showplace and the subject of magazine and newspaper articles for years.

One of those who later marveled at the *Arabian Nights* theme was Margaret McOmie, who visited in preparation for an article she wrote for *Better Homes & Gardens* in 1935. Rupert showed her the home and books that had inspired design details. Impressed by the ageless appearance, she wrote, "I sensed the artistry of a personality able to use such an unusual and romantic background to make a home that is above all—the desired heaven of today's busy life—comfort." [2]

The house was built around an open square—a patio loggia or "outdoor living room"—that the architect announced would have an abundance of luxuriant shrubbery.[3]

Silver birch trees, similar to those at the Hughes estate in Bedford Hills, dotted the hedge-enclosed lawn. Rupert bought twenty-five trees from a nursery that had imported them from Oregon but had been unable to sell them because no one thought they would live in Los Angeles. He gave them special care, and all survived.

The main entrance to the house, through an arch in a grille that extended to the top of second-floor windows, led to a large carved door, then into the great hall, adorned with paintings and tapestries.[4]

After Retta Badger visited in 1932, she wrote for the *Los Angeles Times Sunday Magazine* that a person could spend all day looking at the pictures. One that impressed her was by Ernest L. Blumenschein, who had come from the East to paint the scenery and people of Taos, New Mexico. His painting in the Hughes home was "The Plasterer," depicting a Hopi Indian holding a trowel in front of a fireplace at Blumenschein's Taos home. After seeing a reproduction, Hughes wired the artist, asking to buy the original painting. There is no doubt that he made a wise choice, for "The Plasterer" was one of three Blumenschein paintings featured in the 1955 book *Pioneer Artists of Taos*.[5]

The living room, large but not austere, was equipped with sofas, lounge chairs, tables, paintings, mementoes, bookshelves, and a grand piano at which Rupert composed music.

This room was also the setting for a stunning piece of sculpture showing the head of a young lady. The sculptor was Rupert himself, who for many years had found it relaxing to try to create beauty with his hands. Once he produced a figure of a Revolutionary War soldier with head thrust forward, prompting Gutzon Borglum to agree with Hughes that the throat provided a unique medium of expression.[6] And so it was with the young girl, whose head reclined as if she were asleep. The resulting sculpture, titled "Nocturne," was a strikingly beautiful piece and undoubtedly the best example of Rupert's work in that medium.

But of all the rooms, the one most important to Rupert and Patty was the studio in which they spent most of their time, except in summer when they sometimes would walk up the outside stairs from the second floor to the flat-topped roof to enjoy an evening breeze. The study was the last major part of the house to be completed, after a special permit was issued two years later than the original building permit. The only other important change would be a twenty-foot-square, one-story addition in 1933 to enlarge the garage to accommodate six cars.[7]

The favorite room of Rupert and his wife was described at times as a study, a library, a workroom, a workshop, a studio room, or a den. Measuring about twenty-five by forty feet, it was, said Rupert, "where we sit, work, and dream."

Book shelves—some reaching almost to the two-story ceiling—provided space for 15,000 volumes, but Rupert emphasized that despite the handsome bindings and rarity of many of them this was not a book collection but a much-needed reference library. The placement of leaded windows high above the shelves provided adequate space for books below and helped protect Pat's fair skin from sunlight. Indirect lighting fixtures hanging from the white ceiling brightened the room for nighttime work.[8]

A stairway at one end led to a second floor gallery where additional books reaching to the ceiling were easily accessible. From this balcony, just off the bedrooms, one could look down and see French doors on the left, leading to the patio and pool, and the carved stone fireplace at the far end of the study. When one magazine writer visited, there was a large lounge at each side of the fireplace, but another wrote in 1935 that "near the fire are soft chairs and a sofa and odd leather chair." Rupert had seen a chair like it in New York, but its $1,500 price was too high, so he had a replica built. Bookmakers had used the original two hundred years earlier to record cockfight bets. It was designed to be straddled, and, as a writer described the replica: "A flat, padded top on the curved-around back was made for elbows, and a book rest fastened to the back held whatever you put on it." [9]

Although it was a curiosity and reportedly Rupert's favorite "writing chair," in later years he named it "Hughes's Folly" because he never could adjust the writing stand to the proper angle. "Now I use it to get photographed in," he said.[10]

This chair-desk was not, however, the only work surface in the room. At first there were three large desks—one for Rupert, another for his secretary, and the third for Patty. But, as time went on, there were five—some fine antiques, but others of plain mahogany. Rupert found good use for them all: one for his George Washington research and writing, another for novels, still others for short stories or articles. Thus he could leave notes and reference materials for a specific project on a certain desk and know that everything would be undisturbed. Often he would tire of working on a novel or the biography and would decide to finish an article or short story, moving in that manner from one desk to another and back again. When he finished something he could clear off a desk and start another project.[11]

There was another feature of the library-workroom that caused comment: the abundance of paintings of his wife. During the 1930s Pat would say that she was glad the Depression came along because Rupert otherwise would have covered the walls with her likeness and she would have spent all her time posing for portraits. The fact was that he regarded her as a woman of great beauty, and so he commissioned artists to capture that beauty on canvas. One portrait, painted by Leon Gordon, hung against the balcony railing, and was Rupert's favorite. Above the fireplace was a full-length portrait by Ben Ali Haggin hanging between two large Armin Hansen canvases whose rich blue colors were called "complementary to the lovely Titian-haired figure of the portrait."

Three interviewers who wrote about the Hughes residence commented on Rupert's friendliness, Pat's beauty, and the warmth of the welcome they provided. The *Better Homes & Gardens* writer took the title for her article, "We Create Beauty Ourselves," from a comment he made:

"No matter where we live, and believe me, Hollywood is no worse or no better than any other city or village in the world, there is beauty all around us. We create it ourselves. And in the creation lies our happiness."

Upon departing from the home, the *Los Angeles Sunday Times Magazine* interviewer concluded, "There has been so much to see and your host and hostess so delightful, but even the most enthralling experiences must end. The carved door swings wide and you step out among the eerie trunks of the birch trees." [12]

In an article headed "Rupert Hughes: Informal Portrait of a Paradox," published in *The Family Circle*, Ilka Roberts went into much detail about the subject's personality. She discussed his home life, writing accomplishments, and aspirations, then said:

"And there you have Rupert Hughes: Sympathetic to individuals he would hate in a crowd. Generous to individual distress that he would crusade against if it became a 'cause.' The heart of a sentimentalist—the mind of an iconoclast. Loved by those who know him best. Admired by those who disagree with his ideas. Completely sweet—irritatingly paradoxical. But first, last and always an individual . . . and a most interesting one." [13]

Life on Los Feliz Boulevard settled down to a steady round of work for Rupert during the waning years of the 1920s. Some of his friends, including Charlie Chaplin and Cecil B. DeMille, had built homes nearby in the Los Feliz area, where since 1916 the Los Feliz Improvement Association had worked to enhance and protect the beauty of the neighborhood.

At the Hughes home there was much less entertaining of guests than in earlier years when Rupert and Adelaide had lived on Western Avenue. Patty was more reserved than Adelaide had been, and now she and Rupert limited their invitations mainly to small groups of friends and seldom attended large parties, despite the fact that one writer described Rupert as having "almost more friends than any man in town." [14] Although neighborly and involved with the community, the Hugheses were not much interested in society events.

At times, however, Rupert was included in important social happenings, such as the 1926 wedding of Eleanor Boardman and director King Vidor. The ceremony at the Beverly Hills home of Marion Davies was supposed to be a double wedding, with the mysterious Greta Garbo and screen lover John Gilbert intending to take their vows at the same time. But Garbo never showed up and the spurned actor got into a fist fight with Louis B. Mayer after the producer made a slurring remark about her.[15]

Otherwise, it was a festive occasion, with eighty of Hollywood's leading lights in attendance—Charlie Chaplin, Mary Pickford and Douglas Fairbanks, Joan Crawford, Norma Shearer and Irving Thalberg, to name a few—as Miss Boardman and Vidor went ahead with the ceremony. A photo of the wedding party showed Rupert Hughes in a prominent position on the front row.[16]

Rupert's intimate knowledge of what went on in southern California during the 1920s provided the background for a new novel he wrote, called *We Live but Once*, published in 1927 by Harper & Brothers. Similar in some ways to his earlier books with a New York setting that provided details of social customs and fashions, this time the heroine was a wealthy young Santa Barbara woman, Valerie Dangerfield, who had a penchant for fast driving and fast living, as her surname implied. As the author described her, "If Valerie had any religion, it was an implicit faith in her impulses" . . . . Her "salvation or her damnation" depended entirely upon whatever struck her fancy, wrote Rupert. "If it were something noble, she would storm heaven; if ignoble, hell." [17]

What strikes her fancy in *We Live but Once* is a handsome defense attorney, Blair Fleming, whom she first sees in a Santa Barbara restaurant; the fact that he is married makes him more interesting to her.

A *Boston Transcript* reviewer thought that with a lighter touch Hughes could have made the story into a farce, or with a stronger treatment could have given it "true dramatic intensity." [18]

The appearance of the novel on bookstore shelves in May preceded by about seven months the publication by William Morrow & Company of the second volume of the Hughes biography of Washington. By now the first volume, after thirteen months, had tapered off in sales but would go into a fifth printing in early 1928. The new book, *George Washington: The Rebel and the Patriot, 1762-1777*, ran more than a hundred pages longer than the first one, although it covered only half as long a span of Washington's life.

Quoting from Washington's diaries and account books, Hughes showed his interest in theater, dancing, fox hunting, liquor purchases, and playing cards for money. He also revealed Washington's generosity to family, servants, and beggars. The book traced Washington's role as a delegate to the Continental Congress, then as Commander-in-Chief of forces fighting for liberty, and ended with the Delaware crossing and the raid on Trenton that gave him his first victory.

Critics hailed the book as a great improvement over Hughes's earlier volume about Washington. He had covered the ground amply, leaving no doubt about his admiration for his subject, said J. T. Adams in the *Herald Tribune's* Books section. N. W. Stephenson, in the *New York World*, declared, "For many readers, on whom hitherto a fictitious Washington has been imposed, illumination has come." [197]

By now it seemed certain that the Hughes biography would continue for another two or more volumes, and some critics looked forward to the prospect. "If Mr. Hughes maintains the standards of the first two volumes in those that are to follow we shall have the most illuminating, scholarly, definitive biography of Washington yet written," said C. G. Bowers in *The Nation*.[20]

As with the first volume, the *New York Times* treated the publication by Morrow as a news event, with headlines summarizing what the author said of his subject:

PAINTS WASHINGTON
AS GREAT BUT HUMAN

Rupert Hughes in New Book Calls Him Noble Soul, but
Also Frail and Erring 'PATHETIC, LONELY FIGURE'
Much of American History Infamous In Its Dishonesty,
He Says, Defying Critics of His First Volume

The news story pointed out that while the author had been frank in telling about his subject's personal failings, early military mistakes and indecisions, he had concluded that Washington "was the one great soul who had a vision of a united country and whose patriotism was beyond reproach." Such a conclusion prompted Don C. Seitz to declare in *The Bookman* that the new book proved that "George Washington has conquered Rupert Hughes." [21] But Rupert, in fact, had always admired Washington tremendously; if any conquering was done, it had taken place decades ago.

Soon after the second volume was released it went into a second printing and continued to win attention, including another *New York Times* review on December 11. Covering more than a page, it was illustrated with two portraits of Washington and a map of his early travels; its banner headline trumpeted: "MR. HUGHES STRIKES HIS STRIDE IN HIS LIFE OF WASHINGTON. The Second Installment of His Four Volume Biography Is Much Superior to the First." The article mentioned five other recent

Washington books, including a new version of the Parson Weems fable-filled biography, and said none of the five could equal Hughes's honest treatment of his subject. The biography was apparently intended to include four volumes, the reviewer said, and "as the record now stands, there is good reason to believe that Rupert Hughes will make a really valuable addition to the literature about Washington." [22]

This near unanimity of praise from critics did much to redeem Hughes's reputation and helped overcome the harsh words that had greeted his speech a year and a half earlier.

While in New York in December, Rupert received a letter of congratulations from historian John Corbin, who himself would write a biography of Washington; over the years the two would carry on an extensive correspondence. Hughes thanked him for his praise and said he was leaving the next day for "Loze Anglaze" but hoped to see him on a return trip to New York in February. He liked Corbin's suggestion of a different interpretation of a paragraph in his book and said he would reword it in the next edition, "which at the present rate should be coming along shortly."

Hughes also took another swipe at an old critic, telling Corbin that "everybody who ever experienced Albert Bushnell Hart at his hartiest seems to have loathed the old spider," and added, "It is funny to have him jumping me while being himself threatened with the flames by the still more jingoistic." [23]

These two adversaries, Hughes and Hart, faced a common foe in the form of Mayor William Hale Thompson of Chicago, whose belligerent article on "Shall We Shatter the Nation's Idols in School Histories?" appeared in the February, 1928, *Current History*. The same issue carried responses from Hughes and Hart, named in Thompson's indictment with other prominent historians.

"American patriotism rests upon the nobility of George Washington, father and founder of the nation, and the righteousness of the cause of freedom and independence that he led . . . . Drop the heroes from the country's histories; and you take the stars out of the firmament of patriotism," the mayor warned. [24]

The words were anathema to Hughes, whose response titled, "Plea for Frankness in Writing History," chastised Thompson for charging that pro-British forces had brought about a falsification of school history books and that such books were "treason-tainted." As for himself, Hughes declared:

Mayor Thompson has honored me by including me in his sweeping denunciations, and thereby put me in far more excellent company than I deserve. Because of my compilation of Washington's actual writings and deeds, Mayor Thompson is quoted as dubbing me "a cheap skate looking for publicity." He is quoted by the press as going so far as to call me "a damned liar." He admitted when questioned that he had not read my book. He has indeed been quoted as boasting that he does not read books . . . . I have no complaint to make of his abuse. It warms me. It would, indeed, be almost fatal to the reputation of any historical writer to receive a kind word from Mayor Thompson, since his ideals are the very opposite of the ideals of any truth-seeking scholar.[25]

While Thompson saw the Hughes biography as part of a dark plot to ruin the reputation of a national hero, another observer, Will Rogers—by 1927 considered America's greatest humorist and on his way toward becoming the nation's most popular citizen—viewed Rupert and his book in a different light.

This chronicler of daily events, deeds and misdeeds, famous for poking fun at politicians and royalty, seized upon the controversy surrounding the Rupert Hughes biography and made it the subject of one of his syndicated weekly articles. Earlier, however, before publication of the second volume, Rogers had hinted to newspaper readers that Hughes was up to something. Under the heading of "Movie Stars Mob 'Lindy,'" he reported on a Los Angeles reception for Charles Lindbergh after the aviator's historic solo flight across the Atlantic. Rogers wrote that all the stars were gathered at the Ambassador Hotel, where "Lucky Lindy" was seated between Mary Pickford and Marion Davies while signing everything the movie folk, from Louis B. Mayer to Tom Mix, handed him.

"I will give Rupert Hughes credit," wrote Rogers. "He wasent in the autograph line. Being just a struggling author maybe he dident have anything for poor 'Slim' to write on. Personally I think Rupert was just sitting there thinking up some devilment that George Washington had got in, that the daughters of the Revolution hadent heard about, and he was on the verge of telling 'em."[26]

On December 18, the Rogers weekly article titled "Will Turns Literary Critic" was devoted entirely to Hughes and Washington. Distributed by McNaught Syndicate to newspapers throughout the country, it started with Rogers's comment that he had never attempted book reviewing, but now, he had decided to "take up this critic business serious"—the reason being the Hughes version of Washington's life.

Rogers referred to the author as "Rupert Hughes, an old friend of mine, that is, he used to say hello to me when we used to work at the Goldwyn studio." He continued:

He was the original eminent author, and the only one who re-mained eminent after his first picture. Now Rupert is just about one of our greatest humorists in America. He is right in a class with Cobb . . . But like Cobb he don't like this funny man business, so they now write stories and try and put in enough plot that it will drown the humor out . . . . But hear either one of them at a banquet when he knows it's not going to be published in book or magazine form and the old humor will crop right out.

Well, about a year or more ago Rupert, you remember, wrote a book exposing (well not exactly exposing), but kinder giving Washington's other side. They say every man has two sides and Rupert is the first one to roll Washington over.

Well it kicked up quite a furor. The Daughters of the Revolution started revolting. Most of the organization had traced kinship back to George, and they wanted him to stay like McGuffy had put him. But Rupert's humor cropped out and he dug out all this other and put it into print. . . . Well, people that hadn't read anything about Washington in years except the Cherry Tree and hatchet episode started in new. Course it kicked up a lot of fire, and Rupert, seeing he had the blaze started, certainly never had been accused of being a poor showman that he didn't know when to throw on more wood when he saw the blaze going good, so the rascal up and hits 'em with another volume, and it's this second volume that I am starting in my career as a critic on.

Liquor, and cards, and dances. Well you just got to read it . . .

What I want to know is why Hughes keeps picking on Wash-ington. He couldn't do all that devilment alone he had to have fellows with him. Why don't Hughes write about Jefferson? I bet he could dig up some scandal on him. You know what I think it is. I think it's politics. Hughes is a Democrat. That's about what's the matter with him, and he won't tell things on Jefferson because he was a Democrat . . . .

It's politics, that's whats doing it. He is trying to show that the Republicans were not decent from the start. Now no man can do two volumes worth of scandal. Why don't he hop on Andy Jackson? There's a lad that never missed a shot or a drink while in the White House, but he was a Democrat, that's why Hughes is trying to protect him. . . . And if Hughes keeps on putting out these volumes slamming the Republican party, why I am going to do a little research work and tell something on the Democrats. I'll show 'em some dirt.[27]

The irony of this article by Rogers, whose friendship with Rupert would continue to grow, was that it humorously chided him for being a Democrat. Rogers, of course, considered himself to be a "member of no organized party— I'm a Democrat," but Rupert had been brought up as a Republican and would later become active in Republican circles, although he supported several Democrats for President and could see the good and bad in leaders of both parties. The irony would continue when Hughes, chastised for unconventional and liberal views as a young man, vilified as an iconoclast and agnostic in his middle years, and the author of stories and novels some critics considered risque and too modern, would someday be labeled a conservative and smeared by opponents who would misunderstand his patriotic motives and reasoning.

MARY
PICKFORD
IN
JOHANNA
ENLISTS

BY RUPERT HUGHES
SCENARIO BY FRANCES MARION
DIRECTED BY WILLIAM D. TAYLOR

CHAPTER EIGHTEEN
WAR FILMS AND STORIES

"It will be a surprise."

A renewed interest in stories and movies about the World War became evident in the United States nearly a decade after the 1918 Armistice agreement was signed.

One of these was a tale of battlefield cowardice and heroics written by Rupert Hughes and made into a silent film by First National Pictures. It is not known exactly when he wrote *The Patent Leather Kid*, but Grosset & Dunlap published it in 1927—along with four Hughes short stories—in a book with the same title. There were at least two editions: one without illustrations, and the other a photoplay edition.

There was a significant difference between the original story and the filmed version. The book's main character was an attractive young cabaret dancer, Fay Poplin, who wore an outfit made of patent leather.

Rupert wrote, "The Kid danced wildly well in a shady cabaret where her only protection from herself or her company was the understanding that she was the special sweetie of the up-and-coming young prize-fighter 'Curly' Boyle, known in the perverse accent of certain native New Yorkers as 'Coily Berl.'" [1]

In a strange twist, the motion picture's title role was changed to that of the fighter, played by Richard Barthelmess, a popular actor whose part was considered "more picturesque." [2] Thus, the prizefighter became "The Patent

Leather Kid"—so called because of his smooth, shining black hair—while the female lead, now known as Curly, was "The Golden Dancer," a role played by Molly O'Day, sister of Sally O'Neil, who starred in Rupert's *Don't*.

The Kid is fearless in the boxing ring but cowardly at the thought of war. But after enlisting in the Army he is sent to France, where he sees his trainer fall under German fire. He then saves his lieutenant's life and is critically injured. He is taken to a hospital where Curly is a nurse, and she vows to spend her life taking care of him.

Opening night on August 15 at the Globe, a legitimate theater in New York, brought an enthusiastic review from the *New York Times*, which called *The Patent Leather Kid* "an emphatically human chronicle . . . . filled with incidents that are true to life and some really good comedy." [3]

The Hughes novel described war scenes in vivid terms, and to depict them in the film the producers enlisted the aid of the War Department and officers and soldiers at Camp Lewis, Washington, where filming took place. According to the book's foreword, a dozen cameramen sixty feet above the battlefield, recorded action involving "three thousand U. S. regulars, 600 civilians as German soldiers and five million dollars' worth of U.S. army guns, tanks and equipment." [4]

It was an expensive and highly advertised film. Adela Rogers St. Johns was credited with the screen adaptation and Winifred Dunn the scenario. But there was no doubt as to who was the star. When moviegoers arrived at the Globe, 200 stills of Barthelmess—each of him by himself—greeted them in the lobby. The film proved to be one of the two most popular motion pictures Barthelmess made. [5]

Another war movie, *Wings*, starring Clara Bow, Charles "Buddy" Rogers, and Gary Cooper, had opened two days earlier. Its screenplay was by John Monk Saunders, whose marriage to Avis had ended in divorce; two months later, he married actress Fay Wray. Meanwhile, Howard Hughes was preparing to film a spectacle of the sky called *Hell's Angels*.

While working on a third volume of the George Washington biography, Rupert was drawn into a debate on the subject of "Should Capital Punishment Be Retained?" His views were published in the *Congressional Digest* after being stated in the *Washington Herald*.

Taking a strong negative stand, he likened laws punishing murder to divorce laws, pointing out that in both cases some states were lenient and others extremely strict. He contended that it was wrong for the upper class-es to have an advantage, saying, "If anybody is ever going to be put to death for murder, I should think the professional good man should be put to death first." He asked, "Does it not seem unfair and heartless as well as horribly futile to put to death here and there some wretch whose chief guilt is that he committed his crime in the wrong state or picked the wrong lawyer?" [6]

Other subjects on which he wrote and corresponded covered a wide range, often involving a critique of another author's work. In June, 1927, he complimented Jim Tully, the "hobo writer" he is credited with discovering, on a new book that contained what Hughes called "some of your best best, and that is a superlative indeed." Tully had asked for corrections on some galley proofs, and Rupert, noted for the scarcity of mistakes in his own writings, pointed out a few typos and suggested one clarification.

Their friendship had developed after Tully came to his home one evening to discuss an idea for a book. When Rupert found out that the young man had not eaten dinner, he asked his cook to fix him something to eat. Fascinated by Tully's tales of hobo life, he encouraged him to write the book and later spent "hours and days" helping to see it through to publication. [7]

His willingness to provide advice to aspiring authors sometimes meant risking damage to a friendship, as when Marian King asked him to criticize a short story she had written. She was a friend of Rupert and Pat as well as of Elspeth, and he mailed his reply to her in care of his daughter in Washington, D. C. While praising the plot, he went on for three pages to suggest improve-ments, pointing out that she would need to do considerable work before her story would have a chance of being published. He apologized, afraid of being too harsh, but told her it would be dishonest and not "true friendship" to praise her work unduly. He offered to read the manuscript again after she made changes.

Another letter to her a few weeks later indicated the effect of his criti-cism and showed the diplomatic manner in which he handled such matters: "Your tennis-playing has not been wasted, for you are a most excellent sport as is shown by your letter of thanks for the lambasting I gave your story. It did not compare with many of the roastings I have had and still get, but you are not as practised in taking punishment without ether as I am." [8]

Among his writings that saw their way into print in 1927 was a treatise he had written a few years earlier. It bore the strange title of "The Ghastly

Purpose of the Parables" and apparently was printed first in the *Haldeman-Julius Monthly*. In this brief tract he contended: "The important inescapable fact is that if you believe in Christ at all or in his words as they are given in the *Bible*, you cannot honestly—you cannot safely—doubt what he says: viz., that he came to save only a few Jews; that he purposely disguised his message to prevent its being understood (and he certainly succeeded in that); that only a few people are saved, and the rest are tormented with infinite everlasting agony, just because Christ did not happen to like them . . . ." [9]

If there was any adverse reaction to this, it would not have been unanticipated. But sometimes he was surprised at an unexpected turn in the public's response, as indicated in a 1927 interview with a columnist for *The Bookman*, who described the setting for their New York meeting:

> Late one cold afternoon I trotted up to the swank Hotel Elyseé to call on Mr. and Mrs. Rupert Hughes. Settled back in one of those seats which are so much easier to get into than get out of, I smoked excellent cigarettes and ate peppermints out of a glass jar while Mr. Hughes told me sadly that he seemed to do good in spite of himself. Some time ago he wrote a story about superannuated clergymen which was warranted to make the ministers mad. On the contrary. A large and prosperous Methodist church made him an opulent offer for many copies, so that they might put one in every pew of their flourishing edifice.[10]

The story referred to, "When Crossroads Cross Again," first published by *Collier's* in January, 1921, dealt with the poverty of an old preacher, Jordan Loomis, and the kindness of an actress, Fanny Keeney. It was highly critical of the almost penniless situation in which many retired ministers found themselves after long years of service. When Luther E. Dodd, secretary of the Board of Finance of the Methodist Episcopal Church, South, read the story he was so touched by Rupert's portrayal of the preacher that he asked and received permission from *Collier's* to republish it.[11]

But that was not the end of the story. E. J. Fleming, secretary of the Department of Ministerial Relief of the General Board of the Church of the Nazarene, was so impressed when he read the Methodists' reprint that he also asked *Collier's* for permission to republish it for his denomination. He received a "very nice letter" from Rupert Hughes granting permission for it to be reprinted in the interest of the Ministerial Relief Fund of the Church of the Nazarene. It was published as a forty-five page booklet, with a foreword by Fleming.[12] The story and reprints had appeared several years before Rupert had criticized churches in his *Cosmopolitan* article.

He now told the columnist for *The Bookman* that the editors of *The Red Book*, in which his stories had been running for as long as he could remember, wanted to sign him to a ninety-nine year contract. He also revealed that he was working on a new book but would not tell its title, saying, "It will be a surprise." [13]

Visits to New York had become an established routine for Rupert and Pat, who usually packed up each January for an extended stay there. They would occupy a large suite in a quiet, conservative hotel—usually the Elysee on East 54th Street, between Madison and Park Avenues—in a convenient location for concerts, plays, and other events they both enjoyed.

It was no small matter to prepare for such treks, for they would take along Rupert's secretary, a maid, and Pat's Pekingese dog. Rupert would also take hundreds of books, which he called the tools of his trade. But as an interviewer reported, "more often than not, only one out of perhaps five cases of books is opened" during their stay in the city.[14]

Although Hughes's output of short stories had been slowed by his attention to the George Washington biography, an earlier story, "The Stick-in-the-Muds," named one of the best short stories of 1920, was now included in *The World's 100 Best Short Stories*. Classics by Dickens, Tolstoy, and Hawthorne were also published in the five-volume and ten-volume sets by Funk & Wagnalls Company, with Grant Overton as editor-in-chief, in 1927. That same year, *Collier's* published another story by Rupert, and within the next year he also provided fiction for the latest version of *McClure's*, now called the *New McClure's—A Man's Magazine!* He was in good company there, with many other highly regarded authors.[15]

Hughes felt honored and proud when named an honorary vice president of the Mark Twain Society, headed by Cyril Clemens, a relative of the famous Missouri author. He told Clemens what a thrill it had been for him as a boy to meet Mark Twain in Keokuk.[16] Hughes's acceptance of the honor led to an involvement with the society that would continue for years.

The novel Rupert had referred to in *The Bookman*'s interview came out in mid-1928 as *The Lovely Ducklings*, a lighthearted story of a Los Angeles couple, the Todds, whose five children, ranging in age from early teens to late twenties, give them no end of troubles. The mother is shocked when her off-spring succumb to temptation.

Reviewers called the book cleverly done, pointing out that Hughes seemed to understand the younger generation and its slang. A *New York World* critic thought there was too much moralizing, but said Hughes had done a "fairly entertaining job in reclaiming each one of these wild cubs from the menace of perdition." [21]

Certainly no one believed *The Lovely Ducklings* ranked with Rupert's best novels, but writing it must have been a reprieve from the tedium of researching and evaluating the numerous facets of Washington's life. As for moralizing about the younger generation, Rupert no doubt intended instead to reveal the outmoded attitudes of some parents who failed to understand their children.

A quote from a 1928 article about him in a Western Reserve University alumni publication reflected his view of modern life: "Rupert Hughes is an optimist, and protests against the incessant talk of growing evils of our age. He declares that history shows human nature to be the same—development has lessened the evils of each succeeding age." [22]

Rupert had family concerns of his own in 1928, mainly in connection with his mother's failing health. In mid-September he wrote to her before leaving for New York to arrange the details of two contracts for stories that were expected to bring him about $100,000 the next year. His letter to "My own darling Mimi" told her, "I hadn't the heart to tell you goodbye for fear it might upset you at a time when you need all your strength and cheer, so I have asked Felix to read you this letter when you begin to worry about my absence."

He had been so distressed by her illness that he slept in her house and could do almost no work; Felix, too, had been there or nearby night and day. "Then your marvellous turn for the better not only rejoiced my soul but enabled me to get back to my labors," Rupert said, urging her to follow the orders of the nurses who were providing around-the-clock care. Patty, of course, was going to New York with him, and she "sends her dearest love and I send you a million kisses," Rupert said, assuring his mother that they would keep in touch with her by letter and wire. [19]

But the improvement in her condition was not long lasting, and less than two months later, on November 14, Jean Amelia Summerlin Hughes, the beloved "Mimi," died of intestinal cancer. [20]

198

Though her life had been one of love and unselfish devotion to her own children who had stood by her without fail, she had remained bitter toward her grandson, Howard, for refusing to follow the well-meaning advice of his relatives. Although at first she had overlooked his selfishness, her attitude was reflected in her will, signed on February 16, 1928, which bequeathed to Felix her beautiful home at 204 North Rossmore, along with household furniture, utensils, and other personal property used in connection with the house. All other property—real, personal, tangible, and intangible—was to be divided equally between Rupert and Felix.

There was a specific reference to her grandson: "I mention the name of my grandson, Howard R. Hughes, Jr., to show that I have not forgotten him and that I purposely have not given him anything in this my last will and testament." [21]

By now Felix had moved to Los Angeles and had become well established there, turning his talents to a new field in addition to the teaching of singing. With the rush by motion picture studios to turn out talking pictures, brought on by the success of *The Jazz Singer*, starring Al Jolson, there was a demand for actors and actresses whose voices had audience appeal.

Sound motion pictures quickly took their toll of stars whose speaking voices did not match their appearances: virile males with high-pitched voices and beautiful females whose accents or dialects marred the impression moviegoers had of them from their silent screen images.

Highly-advertised studios or colleges of voice culture—seven by mid-1928—were quickly established in order to teach movie people how to say their lines, and elocution teachers from across the nation rushed to Hollywood. But Felix Hughes was already there and was well known among stars, producers, and directors. Possessor of a rich, cultured speaking voice, this baritone singer was now called upon to provide instruction to leading lights of Hollywood and soon became known as one of the two most eminent "voice teachers to the stars." [22]

His many famous pupils included: Anita Page, Nancy Carroll, Jean Harlow, cowboy Hoot Gibson, and female stars of *The Desert Song*. In later years, another pupil was Betty White, who would star in "The Golden Girls" on television in the 1980s and 1990s. She credited Felix for having instructed her in both operatic singing and voice. [23]

The name of another Hughes made news in a less exemplary way several times during the 1927-28 period. Rush Hughes was accused in May, 1927, of an attempted attack on a sixteen-year-old chorus girl, Adele Smith, at his Great Neck, Long Island, home. Both the girl and Rush's wife, Marion Harris, were members of the cast of *Yours Truly*, then playing in Manhattan, and Mrs. Hughes had invited Miss Smith to spend the night at the Hughes home. The *New York Times* reported, "Mrs. Hughes, who testified before the Grand Jury, is said to have made the statement that she and her husband quarreled on Wednesday morning. According to the District Attorney's office, Hughes said that when he left the bedroom he went downstairs to get a drink."

Rush pleaded not guilty before a Justice of the Peace, was freed on bail, waived immunity, then went before the grand jury to deny the accusations. After the testimony, charges were dismissed. That evening Mrs. Hughes and Miss Smith went back to work in *Yours Truly* and refused comment on the grand jury's action.[14]

Less than eight months later, the *Times* carried a brief Associated Press account:

DIVORCES RUPERT HUGHES' FOSTER SON

Chicago, Jan. 5—Mary Ellen Bissel Hughes, known on the stage as Marion Harris, obtained a divorce today from Rush Hughes, adopted son of Rupert Hughes, the novelist. She testified they were married in 1923 and separated in 1925 and that she supported her husband during their married life. Custody of a two-year-old son was granted to her.[25]

Although the item said the couple had been separated since 1925, the previous account of the dismissal of the Smith girl's charges indicated that Rush and his wife were together in 1927, and the newspaper erred in calling him Rupert's "adopted son," which he was not. Later, there would be irony in the title of the next motion picture in which Rush appeared: *Beware of Married Men*.

Rupert again took up the theme of modern youth in a novel published in newspapers in March, 1929. Called *Carter and Daughter, Incorporated*, it was heralded by the *Cleveland Plain Dealer* as a story about a "sophisticated college graduate who comes home to find her mother in the throes of a near-disastrous flirtation." It was called a never dull tale about modern youth versus "mischievous age," told with deft touches. The newspaper published it in six daily parts as the third in a series of "modern fiction masterpieces." Advance publicity called Hughes "almost a Clevelander." [26]

A decidedly more ambitious effort came in writing his next novel, published in June, 1929, by Harper & Brothers. *Mermaid and Centaur* is a tale of striking contrast between the exciting but seamy world of a carnival and the peaceful but relatively dull life on a farm. The story centers around Jason Brafford, a well-to-do farmer whose devotion to his deformed sister, Rita, has kept him from marrying. Unable to walk, Rita sees publicity about a carnival seal act and asks her brother to bring her a picture of the seal. Instead, he arranges for the beautiful trainer, a diver, to bring the seal to the farm to perform for Rita. Jason and the diver marry, but the carnival life is too alluring, and the mermaid leaves the farm and the centaur.

Although some reviewers thought Hughes had not made any great contribution to literature with *Mermaid and Centaur*, they praised its entertainment value. A *New York Herald Tribune* review declared: "The novel has an undeniable fascination, in part due to the elements which enter into it, and in part to the descriptive powers and unfailing dramatic sense of the author." [27]

Writing novels did not keep Hughes away for long from the Washington book; he continued to delve into every conceivable facet of his subject's life, attempting to put together an accurate account of the period covered. His correspondence with other experts occupied much time.

In a letter thanking John Corbin for "generous references to me" in an essay Corbin had written for *Scribner's*, Hughes wrote, "I am having hell finishing the Revolution. There is infinitely much stuff that has never been treated or treated with any element of fairness, and I hate to miss anything." As for the criticism he had endured, he added, "My skin looks now like a piece of very loose crochet-work—or fish net." [28]

A September 30 letter to Corbin continued the discourse about Sally Fairfax:

> Years ago Eugene Prussing brought me the Sally Fairfax story and asked me to make a movie of it with him. It was news to me but I said that since it was a love story in which nothing happened, it didn't make very good drama, though excellent morals.
>
> Later I asked John C. Fitzpatrick what he thought of Prussing's book.

He answered that it was pretty but could not be proved since he gave no evidence that the letter was written to Sally.

Then (I rather flatter myself about it) I dug up the letter written by Billy Fairfax, which fitted Washington's letter perfectly and stated that Sally was writing by the same impatient courier . . . .

Concerned about not having completed the biography, he told Corbin that the problem in regard to Washington was that "every day I run across something absolutely unheard-of about his deeds or his expressions of opinion. He led a hundred lives!" [29]

"He led a hundred lives!" It was reflective of statements Rupert often made about his own personal wish—that *he* could live a hundred (or, as he sometimes expressed it, a thousand) lives. And now he said it about Washington—that the great hero did, in essence, live a hundred lives through his many accomplishments.

It was obvious that the third volume would not be published in 1929, due not entirely to the complexity of his subject. Other writing was also involved. *Cosmopolitan* published one of his favorite stories, "The Baby's Shoes." Decades later, he contributed its manuscript to the Special Collections Department at the University of Iowa Libraries for its Iowa Authors Collection.

Another of his favorites, "The Father of Waters," was honored by publication in a ten-volume compilation as one of *The World's 50 Best Short Novels*. This 1929 Funk & Wagnalls anthology, with an introduction by Grant Overton, placed his story in the company of such all-time classics as Charles Dickens's "A Christmas Carol."

A Hughes story, "Naked Truth," published in February, 1929, in *Hearst's International and Cosmopolitan*, was listed by *O. Henry Memorial Award Prize Stories of 1929* as one of a select 120 from among 2,000 stories published in American magazines. A secondary list in the same book included "Baby's Shoes" and another Hughes tale, "The Rented Body." The latter, published in *Cosmopolitan* in November, 1928, was described by the magazine as "a story of a mind to which all things were pure—and of an opposite." The 1929 *Index to Short Stories Supplement* listed thirteen Hughes stories published in magazines between 1925 and 1927.

There was further recognition in 1929 in the Macmillan Company's *A Guide to the Best Historical Novels and Tales*, which provided a summary of his novel *The Golden Ladder*, republished by Hurst & Blackett in England and by A. L. Burt Company in New York. It was listed as one of a select number of historical books that were of "special worth."

At around the same time, an article Rupert wrote on "Washington as His Contemporaries Saw Him," excerpted from his second Washington book, was published in *The American Scrapbook*. The same publication included a simile attributed to Hughes—"Restless as spilled mercury"—in a page of best similes.[30]

During the waning days of 1929 Rupert wrote an essay on "The Debutante Industry," ridiculing a tradition of the social set: "Of all the silly survivals of ancient custom the 'coming out party' of the young girl is surely the silliest. In every imaginable case it is the coming out of somebody who has been out for years. By the time the girl of eighteen or more has reached that age in this age there is mighty little that she does not know as much of as she wants to; and she is either a timid imbecile or an experienced veteran." [31]

Although Rupert's personal involvement with motion pictures had slackened while he devoted time to the Washington manuscript, his name continued to be associated with the movie industry, largely because of films made from stories he wrote.

The first of these was *The China Slaver*, a Trinity Pictures offering that came out in January. Sojin played a Chinese island ruler noted for white slavery and narcotics trafficking.[32] A month later, *The Girl on the Barge*, based on Rupert's "A Girl on the Barge" (published in *Hearst's Cosmopolitan* in 1927), had its first New York showing at the Colony Theater on Broadway. The Universal Pictures production featured two well-known stars: Jean Hersholt as a bewhiskered, hard-drinking barge captain, and Sally O'Neil as his daughter who had been born and reared on the vessel and had never learned to read.

The *New York Times* thought the scenes of barges and tugboats were "admirably pictured, even those in which miniatures were used." As for what apparently was the first full-length silent movie with talking sequences made from a Hughes story, the *Times* called the result "another melange of dialogue and silence." [33]

Rupert wrote the screenplay for what is believed to have been one of the earliest talking pictures, a two-reel short subject titled *The Dancing Town*. The 1928 Paramount film, directed by Edmund Lawrence, was #3 in a series of shorts called "Great Stars and Authors." [34]

Silent films were becoming almost obsolete in 1929, and the public's demand for movies that could be heard as well as seen had a distinct impact upon producers who had planned silent movies or already had them in production. This was especially true of Howard Hughes, who had worked since October, 1927, on what he hoped would be the most significant air spectacle ever filmed. Much has been written about the making of Hell's Angels, the idea for which had been suggested by director Marshall Neilan. After buying the plot, Howard proceeded to write the scenario himself and supervise its production by the Caddo Company, which he owned.

According to Rupert's account, Howard originally estimated the cost of the motion picture at $600,000, but it ended up costing millions. After hiring Lewis Milestone as director, then giving the assignment to former aviation editor Luther Reed, he decided to direct it himself, causing problems with actors James Hall and Ben Lyon, who resented his inexperience as a director. For the female lead, Howard chose the beautiful Swedish actress Greta Nissen.

In a quest for authenticity, he had a miniature version of London built and brought in fifty planes, many from abroad, for air battles. Costs mounted as he moved from one California location to another, seeking the right cloud formations. When stunt pilots balked at a low-flying maneuver, Howard—who had learned to fly several years earlier—did it himself. But the plane crashed, and he was taken unconscious to a hospital. Surgeons repaired damage to his face, but he would suffer pain from the injury for years. The crash was one of a series of plane accidents, four of them fatal, during filming of Hell's Angels.[35]

At an audience preview in March, 1929, the verdict was obvious. As Rupert put it, "It was a silent picture, and the audience received it in silence. The public had turned against the silent drama almost overnight." He added, "Howard's high hopes went into a tail spin and crashed."

The young producer then decided to redo Hell's Angels in sound, which required virtually everything except aerial shots to be filmed again. It was also necessary to replace Greta Nissen, whose accent was too obvious. After numerous screen tests took place, the dynamic and beautiful Jean Harlow, previously seen in Laurel and Hardy comedies, won the part. Howard had her bleach her hair, gave her a long-term contract, and his press agent publicized her as a "platinum blonde," thereby starting a fashion craze.

By the time Hell's Angels, complete with sound, was again ready for public showing, Howard had spent two and a half years with the movie. It had become the most expensive ever made up to that time—a record that would stand for years. Publicity claimed that it had cost four million dollars, but Rupert thought the actual cost was a little more than half that.[36]

A half-million was spent on promotion and advertising for the film,[37] which opened in Hollywood in May, 1930, at Grauman's Chinese Theater. Critics called it the greatest of all air pictures, and crowds flocked to see it throughout the United States and England. As Rupert later wrote, this was "pretty good for a young man of twenty-four." [38] For Howard, however, there would be more motion pictures. Even while making Hell's Angels, he had produced two others, and within the year after its release turned out five more.

Despite the success of his movie career, however, Howard's marriage to Ella foundered. He had bought a home, but his preoccupation with planes, movies, and personal interests—including starlets—left Ella to seek her own diversions. Once when she entertained at a formal dinner party, Howard was not there; finally he showed up in old clothes, ate quickly, and went upstairs.[39]

A few weeks later Ella left him, returning to Houston where she divorced him in 1929 with a settlement that provided her with five annual payments of a quarter of a million dollars each. She later remarried, had children, and apparently was happy,[40] while Howard would become known for his relationships with a succession of glamorous Hollywood women.

One who occupied much of his attention was actress Billie Dove, who seemed most likely to become his next wife. Eleanor Boardman recalled that, while Howard was dating Miss Dove, Rupert Hughes made a surprising comment about his nephew: "He'd throw his mother down the stairs if it was to his advantage." [41] Later, however, Rupert would write admiring articles about Howard.

Before the release of Hell's Angels, another motion picture with a wartime theme was made from a short novel Rupert wrote, called She Goes to War. It was an Inspiration Pictures film distributed by United Artists, directed by Henry King, with dialogue and titles written by John Monk Saunders—Avis's former husband. The heroine is Eleanor Boardman, and John Holland and Edmund Burns are rivals for her affection. Her patrician looks were well-suited to her role as a socialite who volunteers as a "Y" helper in France. When a sergeant becomes too drunk to answer the call to battle, she puts on his uniform, takes his place at the front, and performs heroic deeds.

The New York Times praised King's "extravagant picturization" and said he had "elicited a fine and sensitive performance from Eleanor Boardman, whose beauty and intelligent acting are too good for the narrative, which is often wearying because of its unbelievable incidents and its indelicate comedy." Miss Boardman herself, in a later year, recalled that she did not enjoy wearing a uniform, although it is obvious from the film that her attractiveness was not disguised. She also remembered that "they sprayed the whole set with glycerine to make a mist and then I had to have my hair done six times a day and wade in the mud and messes like that." [42]

She Goes to War became the first talkie of the World War, and although *Motion Picture Magazine* said the dialogue and sound obviously had been put in afterwards, it called the action "exciting," an impression a viewer would share, despite the film's faults.[43]

Rupert's short novel from which the movie was made had been published first in *Red Book* magazine, and soon after release of the motion picture, Grosset & Dunlap published the story in the 1929 illustrated photoplay book *She Goes to War, and Other Stories*. The remainder of the volume includes three Hughes tales: "A Girl on the Barge," "The River Pageant," and "A Daughter of Today."

On the evening of May 19, 1929, many of Hollywood's leading producers, directors, screen stars, writers, and others turned out for the presentation of the first Academy Awards during a banquet in the Blossom Room of the Hollywood Roosevelt Hotel. Awards honoring achievement in twelve categories, plus two special awards, were handed out by Douglas Fairbanks, Sr., president of the Academy of Motion Picture Arts and Sciences. Winners received still-unnamed gold-colored statuettes, later to become well-known as "Oscars."

Nominations were for work done on motion pictures during 1927-1928, and by comparison with the spectacular shows put on for Oscar presentations in later years the proceedings were simple—what actress Janet Gaynor, the Best Actress award winner, later called "more like a private party than a big public ceremony." [44]

The Rupert Hughes movie *The Patent Leather Kid* was in the running with nominations for two Academy Awards: Rupert himself in the category of Writing (Original Story) and Richard Barthelmess for Best Actor. Barthelmess was also nominated in the same category for his performance in another movie, *The Noose*.

In the vote tabulation, Rupert lost out to Ben Hecht, author of the original story for *Underworld*, and Barthelmess came in a runner-up. *Wings*, written by John Monk Saunders, was named Best Picture, and Lewis Milestone took top honors as Best Comedy Director for *Two Arabian Nights*, produced by Howard Hughes.

CHAPTER NINETEEN

THE EARLY THIRTIES

*"I still get a good many showers of brick but
almost altogether from people who do not trouble
to read my own words."*

Shortly after the start of the 1930s, Rupert again visited New York, where he continued his correspondence with John Corbin. Each had a new volume about Washington soon to be published. At 2 a.m. on January 11, 1930 (the time indicated on his letter), Rupert wrote from the Hotel Elysee that he had received a second batch of galleys for Corbin's book and had made notes on them as requested.

He considered portions of the book to be "beautiful and very touching," but suggested caution in the treatment of those who had opposed Washington. He thought it should not be assumed that Washington's opponents were traitors.

In a postscript, Hughes told Corbin: "I send you my third volume herewith. Please don't sell it to a second hand bookstore before publication date Feb. 6th." [1]

On the day before the official publication date, he spoke at a luncheon gathering of Delta Upsilon, his own fraternity; again the subject was Washington. The *New York Times* headlined its story "WASHINGTON PRAYER IS TERMED A MYTH," with the subhead "Rupert Hughes Denies Valley Forge Story—Questions President's Religious Faith." This was nothing new, although it may have been the first time Hughes had stated these views publicly in such forthright terms. In 1926, after a long meeting with John C. Fitzpatrick in the latter's Library of Congress office, he had jotted a note to himself to the effect that Fitzpatrick, who had edited Washington's diary, had told him "he had never found the name of Christ in Washington's writings."

Now Hughes told fraternity members that he was convinced that the story that Washington had prayed at Valley Forge was a myth like that of the cherry tree. Questioning whether Washington was "even a Christian believer" and pointing out that the general had "repeatedly refused to say that he believed in Christ," Hughes urged the college men and graduates to support truth in historical research.[2]

The third volume, published by William Morrow & Company, was titled *George Washington: The Savior of the States, 1777-1781*. In an Afterword, Hughes noted that his first volume had barely covered the first three decades of Washington's life and the much larger second volume had dealt with fifteen years. Now, "this third volume, still longer, is strained to embrace four years. I might seem to be working out the exact formula of Achilles and the hare, but the worst is over now." At first he had intended to write a single-volume study of certain neglected phases of Washington's life. But, "It seems doomed to go on forever and forever, piling up tomes of increasing bulk and diminishing scope."

In expressing appreciation to numerous libraries and individuals for providing access to manuscript collections and other help, Rupert thanked one other person: "I am again, and more than ever, grateful for my wife's tireless aid, enthusiasm and keen-eyed zest for accuracy."[3]

A *New York Times* review said the author had supplied a long overdue biography that depicted Washington against a realistic background of his time. "As he proceeds with his work, Mr. Hughes acquires greater poise in the field to which he has almost abruptly transferred himself from his earlier vocation of writing fiction."[4]

Historian Henry Steele Commager, writing in *Books*, declared that Hughes had "gained in understanding, in clarity of judgment, in scholarship and in literary grace" with each volume about Washington. In fact, said Commager, "This work, which at first aroused mainly the indignation of professional patriots and the supercilious wonder of some professional historians, has now justly earned the encomiums of all students of history, of all lovers of truth."[5]

It seemed apparent that Rupert's latest effort had won overwhelming approval by historians and critics, as well as readers; at last, the author who had suffered abuse that only a masochist could have enjoyed had become recognized as a serious student and an authority on the life and times of George Washington. Of greater importance was that more people now understood the real George Washington.

He told "Prexie" Thwing, "It has been pleasant to have my third volume on Washington so generally hailed as a sincere tribute of praise," although "I still get a good many showers of brick but almost altogether from people who do not trouble to read my own words." He added, "Still, it is almost pleasant to be tarred and feathered for an honest effort to tell the truth, instead of being lynched for some of the odious things I have really done with evil intent." [6]

Soon after the Hughes volume appeared, Charles Scribner's Sons published Corbin's *The Unknown Washington*, and Rupert wrote a generally favorable critique for *Current History*. Before the review was published, he sent Corbin a typed copy and explained that the editor had limited him to 1,200 words, which was not a tenth enough. "I put in one jab to make it look unlike log-rolling," he told Corbin, "but I told him to cut it out if he wanted to." [7]

Neither Corbin nor Hughes had reason to be happy about comments from Albert Bushnell Hart, whose summary of recent volumes about Washington appeared some months later in *The Publishers' Weekly*. Hart, in his capacity as Historian of the George Washington Bicentennial Commission, included both authors among "a group of Washington biographers who started out with the conviction that Washington has been much overrated, that there is a shady side of his life which has never been acknowledged, and that in many ways he was a failure." [8]

Hart's opinion was definitely in the minority, however, and the vindication Hughes received from the favorable response to his third volume encouraged him to proceed with research for the next Washington book.

In his May 2 letter to Corbin he had mentioned that he and Patterson would sail that day on the *Paris*, heading for "the city named after it." The trip was not only for pleasure but also to research the opinions of Washington's French and British contemporaries in regard to happenings during the post-Revolutionary War period. Upon their return to New York, they stayed at the Hotel Elysee for several weeks.

The Elysee, with its comforts and convenient location, had become almost a second home for the couple, and New York provided cultural attractions and an excitement that Rupert could not resist. For years he had longed to spend more time in New York, and he and Pat had finally made a decision, albeit a tenuous one.

A few days before leaving for Europe, he had confided to Dr. Thwing that when they came back to the United States they would stay in California only until about December 1. They would then return East to live, said Rupert—adding, "I hope." [9]

It was a hope that was not to be fulfilled, for whatever reasons. Perhaps the Depression made selling their home and moving across the country seem unwise just then. They did not move East in December, nor would they in years to come. Instead, they would remain in their Arabian Nights mansion in Los Angeles, but would make frequent and lengthy visits to New York. However, Rupert would never give up entirely on his desire to move back to the city where he had started his career, and at times would come close to making his home there again.

In one letter, Dr. Thwing had mentioned the possibility that Western Reserve might grant an honorary degree to Rupert. The mere suggestion was immensely flattering to Hughes, who had shown great loyalty to the university. He had supported it in many ways and had stayed in touch with some of his classmates.

"As for the degree: it is like you to think of it," Rupert wrote. "I can't imagine what degree the university would dare give me unless it would be the Third Degree or something sub-zeronian. But I can only say that in a long and eventless life I have never refused anything, from insults plainly meant for me to laurels plainly meant for somebody else." [10]

The suggestion for the honorary degree had reached him before he and Pat left for Europe, and although Thwing had hinted that it might be granted the following year, nothing was done about it then.

Two days before the *Paris* sailed for Europe, Rupert's newest novel about New York, published by Harper & Brothers, was reviewed. Called *Ladies' Man*, it had started running in *Cosmopolitan* during the latter part of 1929, and its story of high society life in the big city provided escapism for readers tired of the realities of hard times. The book was a "Harper Sealed Mystery," with its final eight chapters enclosed in a lightweight paper wrapping which proclaimed "A Sporting Offer" that stated, "As one of the horrified thousands of onlookers you have witnessed James Darricott's awful death. In ten minutes time the scene will be re-enacted behind the locked door of the hotel room— and behind this thin paper seal. If you can resist the desire to complete your work as a detective, return this book to your bookseller with the seal unbroken and your money will be refunded." [11]

The problem with this enticing offer was that there had been little suspense in Hughes's story about the tossing of James Darricott from a hotel window in Times Square. That was the principal fault a *New York Times* reviewer found, otherwise applauding the action and descriptions of New York night life. [12]

Mystery author Dashiell Hammett reviewed *Ladies' Man* for the *New York Evening Post* and pronounced it "the stuff movies are made of, with gorgeous pageants, wild doings in night clubs, lovely gowns . . . and neither subtlety nor consistency of characterization to hamper its adaptation to the screen." But the problem was, according to Hammett, that "it is written in Mr. Hughes's unfortunate later style, hysterically at the top of his voice." [13]

Hammett was not the only one who saw in the novel the elements that made it a natural choice for motion picture production; within a year it would be brought to the screen by Paramount with some of Hollywood's leading stars in main roles. It would also be published in the east German city of Leipzig under the title of *Der Fraulenliebling* and would undergo a Czech translation. [14]

Even while *Cosmopolitan* was running the serialized version of *Ladies' Man*, Hughes was working on another novel with a New York setting that would appear in the same magazine beginning in November, 1930. *No One Man* was based on the premise that a woman is not satisfied with just one man. In this instance the wealthy young girl is Penelope Newbold, whose ultramodern ways suit her surname. After Harper & Brothers published it as a book in 1931, critic Niven Busch, Jr., wrote for the *Saturday Review of Literature* that Hughes apparently had taken his theme from Boccaccio's statement that "ten men are sorely tasked to satisfy one woman," and thought Rupert had developed that theme as might have been expected. [15] This novel, too, was destined to become a motion picture within a short time.

Rupert was not involved with the making of either film, spending time instead on other activities. When he was not in New York, he devoted considerable attention to a Los Angeles-based organization he had founded in the early 1920s, called The Writers (also referred to as the Writers' Club), a group that held regular weekly meetings at which members could hear well-known speakers and entertainers. There were also special events, such as one in 1931 that featured the staging of a one-act play he wrote and directed called "Prohic-bition," about a heavy drinking senator in favor of prohibition.[16]

Another play Rupert had written many years earlier was published in 1930 by Samuel French, Inc., in a book titled *Hollywood Plays: 12 One-Act Plays from the Repertory of the Writers' Club of Hollywood.*[17] The Hughes play, "On the Razor Edge," was first published in January, 1910, in *Lippincott's* magazine.

Its first stage production had been by the Writers' Club, with Rupert directing and Eleanor Boardman starring, on June 12, 1925. An amusing tragicomedy, it was published separately in booklet form by Samuel French, Inc., in 1930. In the following year another Hughes one-act play, "The Ambush," depicting an incident during Sherman's march to the sea, was included in an anthology titled *Short Plays for Modern Players*, published by Appleton.

Meetings of The Writers enabled established and aspiring authors to discuss mutual concerns, keep up with each other's current activities, and provide a helping hand when needed. Hughes was especially interested in encouraging young talent, but his assistance was not confined to Hollywood writers; he often responded to requests for advice from young authors elsewhere. In 1930 he praised and gently criticized a story sent to him by a Dallas youth, and closed with a word of encouragement: "You have ability and it needs only hard work and persistence to succeed. You are only eighteen and you have done splendidly for that age. Do not begrudge your art years of toil and postponement of hope." [18]

Hughes's own prestige had been boosted by the favorable response to the third Washington volume. Recognition of various sorts now came his way, including a request in 1930 to serve on the advisory board of radio station WGBS as a programming consultant. It was an invitation he accepted with pleasure and one that would foreshadow a later involvement in network radio.[19]

In St. Louis the Pictorial Map Company published in 1930 a large four-color Pictorial Map of Missouri that included 200 pen sketches of points of interest. One was the Rupert Hughes birthplace in Lancaster, a house still standing and considered a tourist attraction. A year later, an abbreviated but accurate account of his life was included in *Living Authors*. John Albert Macy, author of an admiring biographical pamphlet about Hughes that Morrow published after the second Washington volume was issued, included a piece by

Rupert with Charles Chaplin and Paulette Goddard.

Fredric March, Rupert Hughes (standing) and Ronald Colman.

Rupert Hughes, Irvin S. Cobb, and author and actor Will Rogers.

Rupert working on one of his musical compositions.

Rupert with the M-G-M lion.

Known for his scholarly
attention to detail,
Rupert Hughes examines
a volume from his library.

Rupert Hughes delivers
the eulogy for Will
Rogers at memorial
services attended by
25,000 in the Hollywood
Bowl in 1935.

Rupert Hughes stands in front of a bookshelf containing novels, stories, and other works he wrote. He considered his three-volume biography of George Washington his greatest achievement.

Left to right: Authors Rupert Hughes, Lloyd C. Douglas and Sean McManus, enjoy a skit at the Writers' Club in Hollywood at a dinner honoring Douglas. Hughes founded the club and was its president for more than three decades.

Three generations (left to right): Rupert's granddaughter Barbara; his daughter, Elspeth Hughes Lapp; granddaughters Agnes Christine "Chris" and Elspeth (Beth); and his first wife, Agnes.

More than 500 admirers attended a 1950 testimonial dinner for Rupert Hughes. Front row (left to right): Eloise O'Brien, wife of actor Pat O'Brien, with Hughes and his granddaughter, Barbara Cameron. Back row (left to right): Fletcher Bowron, California Governor Earl Warren, Lew Lauria, Wes Cameron (Barbara's husband), and emcee Pat O'Brien.

Hughes had this unusual writing desk made for him after seeing one like it
in a museum. He wrote all of his books and stories in longhand.

Rupert Hughes.

Rupert in the 1931 book *American Writers on American Literature*, which Macy edited for H. Livermore, Inc.[20]

In the first two years of the 1930s the topics Hughes covered in his writings and speeches were far-ranging. *Cosmopolitan* published his serials and such modern short stories as "Lovely Liar," about a young woman unable to tell the truth, and "Lovelady #99," the story of a man who falls in love with a mannequin.[21] The cover of the July, 1931, issue publicized fourteen writers, whose stories and articles appeared in that issue, as "The 'Who's Who' of Literature"—among them Hughes, Sinclair Lewis, Irvin S. Cobb, W. Somerset Maugham, George Ade.

American Magazine in August, 1930, published Hughes's article "Getting Paid for Having a Good Time," which traced the career of Lawrence Tibbett, who had become an opera singer, motion picture star, and recording artist. *American* also carried the author's disclaimer that he was the discoverer of Tibbett—although the magazine reported that the singer himself gave him much credit for his spectacular career.[22]

In a *Ladies' Home Journal* article, "George Washington's Letters on Love," Hughes provided an insightful view into a phase of the first President's personal life: letters to his adopted daughter and stepchildren in which he attempted to guide them toward what Hughes termed "the sane, sound happiness" Washington had found in his own marriage." Rupert, himself a stepfather, wrote that "Washington was not only the best father any country ever had, but was as good a stepfather as any stepchildren ever had." [23]

Shifts in emphasis back and forth from Washington's time to present-day events and customs, as demonstrated in Rupert's concurrent writing of a biography and modern novels, were also indicated in his speeches. Among subjects he covered on the lecture circuit was "The Woman of 1931," in which he applauded the emancipation of modern woman, saying that "when woman cut her hair and her skirts she also began cutting her wisdom teeth." Speaking at the Fortnightly Forum in New York, in the appropriate setting of the George Washington Hotel, he told an audience of several hundred that smoking was an example of new privileges for women—a practice almost unheard of a few years earlier.

"My only suggestion now is that they smoke less cigarettes and more cigars," he said. "I tried to get my mother to take up smoking—when she was 80—for I thought it would cheer her mind. But she had been brought up by another age and would not. I think smoking is a good thing, however, and certainly if men do it, women should be allowed the privilege." [24]

His willingness to join in unpopular causes was further evidenced when he advocated the release of convicted labor leader Tom Mooney, serving a life sentence in San Quentin Prison for the 1916 Preparedness Day bomb murders. Rupert's opinion was expressed at a "Tom Mooney convention" in San Francisco in October, 1931.

On the speakers' stand at the rally of 5,000, columnist Paul Bern, who headed the story department at Metro-Goldwyn-Mayer, read to the crowd a letter from Hughes contending that Mooney had been held prisoner for fifteen years without any evidence to connect him with the crime. Hughes wrote: "Eminent jurists and citizens of the most unquestioned virtue abhor such crimes as Mooney is charged with, but abhor still more the methods by which the crime was fastened on him and the refusal to undo the injustice disclosed by the amazing amount of new light thrown on the whole procedure." [25]

In the years following the deaths of his parents, Rupert had continued to have a close relationship with his younger brother, Felix, the only one left of his immediate family. The handsome and athletic Felix by now was married to Ruth Stonehouse, who had started her career as a professional dancer but had gone on to acting roles in silent movies and had been part owner of the Essanay Studios in Chicago. She was described as a charming actress who often played comedy roles. Items about the couple appeared in 1930 in the "Society in Cinema-land" column of a fan magazine, Screen Play Secrets.[26]

Felix was now well-established as a singing teacher and voice coach in Hollywood, and Rupert was too busy researching and writing to devote much time to movies. But their nephew, Howard, flush with the success of Hell's Angels, rushed five more films to the screen. He had chosen capable directors for two of his best motion pictures—Lewis Milestone for The Front Page, a lively newspaper story with the principal character patterned after Colleen Moore's famous uncle, Walter Howey; and Howard Hawks for Scarface, based upon the lawless career of Al Capone and his mob.

The choice of Hawks for the gangster picture was surprising, because Howard Hughes had sued him for allegedly using portions of Hell's Angels in the movie Dawn Patrol. Authors of one Howard Hughes biography thought the lawsuit provoked another chapter in the deteriorating relationship of Howard and Rupert, because John Monk Saunders had written the Dawn

Patrol script. But Saunders had been divorced from Avis since 1927, and in later years Rupert would write glowing accounts of his nephew's successes. As for the lawsuit, Howard Hughes agreed to drop it, then played a round of golf with Hawks. Hawks won the match, despite Hughes's golfing prowess, and said he would direct *Scarface*.[27]

Although Rupert was not involved in the production of *Ladies' Man*, the film based on his recent novel, Walter Wanger had paid him $75,000 even before the second installment of the serial was published—the highest amount paid up to that time for screen rights to a novel that had not been produced as a play.[28] The Paramount production, released in the spring of 1931, starred the dapper William Powell in the leading role of James Darricott, the gigolo. Carole Lombard and Kay Francis also star in the story of a salesman who is unsuccessful because women prefer him to the bonds he sells.

The opening at the Paramount Theater in New York brought mixed but generally unfavorable reviews from city newspapers. Although one critic praised Powell's acting and the dialogue by Herman J. Mankiewicz, he did not like Lothar Mendes's direction. Another reviewer thought the film was "good enough to be better." [29]

Rose Pelswick of the *Journal* considered it fair entertainment and a likely forerunner of other gigolo films. While criticizing the director and screenwriter for the movie's artificiality and "overstuffed dialogue," she placed no blame on Rupert Hughes, whose *Ladies' Man* she considered "an excellent novel." [30]

As summer neared in 1931, five weeks after *Ladies' Man* hit the screens, Rupert had a sad task to perform, but one he had known he must do eventually. He and Felix had agreed that the final resting place of their deceased parents should be the Midwestern town where the couple had lived for forty-five years. Although the aged Judge Felix Hughes and his wife Jean had lived out their last years in Los Angeles, their roots were in Keokuk, and both Rupert and Felix knew their parents wished to be interred in the family plot there. Now, more than four and a half years after the death of their father and two and a half years since their mother's demise, the dutiful sons arranged for the remains of "Daddy" and "Mimi" to be moved from California to Iowa, to be reinterred in Keokuk's Oakland Cemetery.

Although Felix was unable to go to Keokuk for the June 5th committal service, Rupert arranged to be there on his way back to California from New York. The Keokuk American Legion Post provided military honors, and judges and family friends were pallbearers.[31]

The sons provided an imposing and handsome monument for the deceased members of their family who were buried in a prominent location at the edge of the tree-shaded cemetery. Headstones mark the location of each of those buried there: Felix Turner Hughes, 1838-1926, and Jean A. Summerlin Hughes, 1842-1928, along with their youngest children—Reginald, 1876-1881; Jean, 1880-1880; and Baby Hughes, 1883-1883. The remains of the judge and "Mimi" were reunited with those of their three children who never grew up to leave home—all together again in Keokuk.[35]

CHAPTER TWENTY

GOING LIKE SIXTY

*"Countless pitfalls pockmark the field of biography.
I think I have fallen into most of them, but I am
going on though my head is muddy and bowed."*

Three weeks and a day before the 200th birthday anniversary of George Washington, Rupert Hughes turned sixty. His hair with its often uncontrollable forelock was still brown, and he neither looked his age nor had slowed down.

He continued the upside-down schedule of working from about 10 p.m. to 5 a.m., after which he would sleep six hours or less. Breakfast usually consisted of "coffee and cigars." An interviewer, Ilka Roberts, commented that he drank more coffee than any eight men she knew. But his fondness for the beverage was not to stay awake; instead, he once said, "It's my way of drinking water."

He laughed at the notion some people had that he never slept at all. He would fight sleep as long as possible, but when it came it was usually deep and uninterrupted by dreams. If he awakened, he would return to his desk to write or read, and soon would be sleepy again.

He told Miss Roberts, in all sincerity, that he seldom worked hard, but she noted that he always seemed to be writing a number of things at once.[1]

After six decades, in 1932 he was—in the expression of the day—still "going like sixty."

During the Washington Bicentennial he was in much demand as a speaker and head table guest at February luncheons and banquets. Having done his best to counteract fables about George Washington, he took note of the theme at these functions: "cherry ornaments, cherry boutonnieres, cherry ice cream, cherry pie and little hatchets, even ice cream in hatchet form"—proof that old legends die hard.[2]

The February, 1932, issue of *American Magazine* published his article on "When Washington Laughed and Cried," in which he provided proof of Washington's warmheartedness as opposed to the popular notion that he had been aloof and cold. Examples were Washington's grief when his little step-daughter died; his love of the theater; his enjoyment of revelry at the tavern; and even some cheerful moments at Valley Forge.[3]

While in the middle of a lecture series, mainly about Washington, Rupert told Western Reserve's "Prexy" Thwing, "My magazine articles and my lectures have done a good deal to dissipate the amazingly widespread story that I am a debunker . . . . It is wonderful to receive the astounding tributes that come to me from great historians and the touching letters from the laity who say that I have made them, for the first time, really love Washington." [4]

But Hughes was not one to let such approval go to his head. He once said, "I modify my transports of joy and keep my pride low by realizing how petty a thing a 'little triumph is on this small anthill in which we swarm." [5] It was now his fervent hope, he told Thwing, "to have the fourth volume out this fall after two years work and the fifth will follow in a year or two more." [6]

His determination to carry the Washington biography forward through two more volumes was contrary to the trend among other biographers to present Washington's life in a single book. But short biographies were "already legion," according to Henry Steele Commager, who reviewed four such books in the *New York Herald Tribune*. In contrast, Commager wrote, "Rupert Hughes has undertaken the courageous task of a full-length portrait, and for this there is a real need . . ." [7]

Rupert's lecture tour included speeches in Chicago through February 22 when Washington's birth was celebrated, then on to Pittsburgh, Erie, and Grand Rapids, Michigan. Along the way, he stopped off in Lakewood, Ohio, near Cleveland, to visit his daughter Elspeth, her husband, Edward Lapp, and their "three little children," as Rupert described his granddaughters, who by then were eight, nearly seven, and five and a half years old.[8]

Visits with his daughter and her family, though infrequent, were regarded as special occasions by his granddaughters. One of them, Elspeth (called "Beth" to distinguish her from her mother), recalled an instance in which the family went to the railroad station to meet "Gramps" when he stopped over in Cleveland. The train arrived late at night, but Rupert arranged for the toy shop at the Harvey House to open especially for the three girls. He then told each of them to pick out any toy she wanted and he would buy it for her.[9]

Not all of his speeches on the 1932 tour dealt with Washington; other topics included "Modern Tendencies in Literature" and "Sentimentalism in America."[10] In a return visit to the Midwest a month later, when he spoke in Indianapolis on "Movie Censorship," columnist George Davis of the *Cleveland Press* reported that he had called movie censors "complete imbeciles."

Hughes said, "Movie censorship is a scheme for giving a lot of jobs to people who could not earn as much money in any other way. I don't doubt that some movie producers should be horsewhipped for scenes they put on the screen. But this is no reason why three or four people should decide what is literary and artistic fare for an entire commonwealth."[11]

His lecture topics seemed almost limitless, and the same was true of his writing. He could write at great length on many subjects. He told an interviewer that he once wrote a story about two girls that was supposed to run 2,000 words, but it took him twice that length just to get their parents up and dressed in the morning.[12]

Another writer, Gove Hambidge, in a lengthy profile published by the *New York Herald Tribune*, noted that Rupert could say something interesting on almost any subject. Hambidge described him as "a shortish man with well developed jowls and an Irish look to his mouth; brown eyes behind rimmed glasses; brown hair, not at all gray, and with baldness still in the future; rather deaf; dressed from necktie to shoes like coffee enriched with cream." His only exercise, said the article, was taking a walk when his work was finished, at about the time most people were getting ready for breakfast. The profile, titled "The World Is His Grab-Bag," added that from the way he told a story it was apparent that "only lack of time prevented him from being an actor."

"He has reduced to powder an American rule that specialization is necessary to success," wrote Hambidge. "He illustrates a more valid rule—the creative mind ranges restlessly, finds all kinds of things provocative, stirring, tempting. It is often capable of creating in more than one medium."[13]

Static, referring to the kind that interferes with radio reception, was a novel Rupert wrote while working on the Washington biography. It ran as a serial in *Cosmopolitan*, then Harper & Brothers published it as a book in 1932. Later, it was adapted for radio as a soap opera. Billed by *Cosmopolitan* as "The First Romance of Radioland," [14] it was the story of a small-town girl who became a network singing star in New York and then got involved in a triangle with her hometown boy friend and a radio station executive.

Other published writings by Hughes during this period included a 1933 novel, *The Uphill Road*.[15] A nonfiction book, *The Art of Hope*, was published the same year by Delta Phi Lambda sorority. It contained his tribute to Milton Berry and additional material about Berry's rehabilitation work and the proposed Milton H. Berry Institute for Paralysis Correctment. The sorority also published a shorter version of the book, consisting of Hughes's open letter to parents of paralyzed children, a year later.[16]

A renewed interest in the theater was indicated when he offered Barrett H. Clark, an authority on drama and its history, a dramatic version of *The Golden Ladder*, telling him it would require "a rather expensive production and an actress who can go from a young girl to an old woman, so it is not selling like hot cakes. If you want to put it on, as you doubtless do from this description, the Play Co. (the American Play Company) would doubtless split commissions with you, unless you split sides first." [17]

He also wrote a brief dramatic sketch during the 1930s, called *On the Road to Yorktown*, published in New York for the National Conference of Christians and Jews. His interest in history also prompted him to write a three-part series for *Good Housekeeping* about early days in California. It was illustrated by Dean Cornwell's working drawings for murals he was painting for the rotunda of the new Los Angeles Public Library. The magazine series, "Pilgrims to the Sunset," traced the conquest of the far west from the days of exploration, through the gold rush era, and on up to the California of 1932.[18]

Hughes praised the city of Los Angeles for choosing to celebrate neglected explorers and thought it ironic that "we dwell in the Golconda they dreamed of, and yet we are not content. We tremble and wail at a depression that would have been to them inconceivable prosperity." [19]

In one instance Rupert combined two interests—short story writing and music—for *Family Circle* Magazine. "It Isn't Forgiven Unless It's Forgotten" was a clever tale about a struggling night club singer whose husband, her piano accompanist, writes songs that are flops until he starts putting her corny comments to music; then he and his wife hit the big time in a hurry.[20]

In the same issue the magazine published the Ilka Roberts profile of Rupert, "Informal Portrait of a Paradox," along with two photos of the author, one of him reading a newspaper and the other showing him seated beside Pat on a rocky hillside while they examine a manuscript. The latter's caption: "When Rupert Hughes writes a story his first reader is his wife, Patterson Dial. Here they're vacationing at Lake Arrowhead, California." [21]

In 1932 he was honored by inclusion of a story, "The Rented Body," in a volume titled *20 Best Short Stories in Ray Long's 20 Years as Editor*. In an introduction to the book, Long said he had read thousands of stories while editing *Red Book*, *Cosmopolitan*, and other magazines. Authors of those he liked best and included in the volume were Hughes, Ernest Hemingway, W. Somerset Maugham, Fannie Hurst, and sixteen others.

Long called Hughes the most unusual of all the writers he had known— "a most indefatigable worker." Yet, wrote Long, "So far as appearances or good humor go, I've never seen him in the least worn out." Citing Hughes's accomplishments as a novelist, biographer, composer, sculptor, and author of *Excuse Me* (which Long considered "one of the most intelligently humorous plays ever to appear on Broadway"), he said that some of the films Hughes directed were "beautifully done and greatly successful." [22] The Hughes story Long selected concerned an artist who saved a beautiful young woman from suicide and then talked her into becoming his model—hence the title.

Also in 1932, two Hughes short stories, "Michaeleen! Michaelawn!" and "At the Back of God Speed," both written in the teens and considered among his best, were listed in Alexander Jessup's book *Representative Modern Short Stories*.[23]

Early the same year the Paramount Publix production of *No One Man*, directed by Lloyd Corrigan, opened at the Paramount Theater on Times Square in New York, starring Carole Lombard and Ricardo Cortez. The *New York Times* said that in the movie version the Hughes novel had been "converted by a pedestrian hand to the requirements of a society scenario." [24]

Two other motion pictures based upon Rupert Hughes stories were also released in 1932. One, produced by World Wide and directed by Paul L. Stein, was *Breach of Promise*, from a story called "Obscurity." Chester Morris and Mae Clarke headed the cast. The other was another remake of *Tess of the*

Storm Country, based on the play Rupert had written in 1911 from the Grace Miller White novel. The Fox film starred Janet Gaynor and Charles Farrell. Sonya Levien and S.N. Behrman wrote the screenplay.[25]

The reincarnation of *Tess* was a source of amusement and financial gain for Hughes and Mrs. White. They had made $12,500 when Miss Pickford produced the 1922 film, and now when Fox bought the rights from her, they were paid the same amount again. Looking ahead another eleven years, Rupert said, "We are pinning fresh hopes now on 1944." *Tess of the Storm Country*, in fact, did not fade away; it would live again in still another revival in 1960, starring Diane Baker, Lew Phillips, and Wallace Ford. The 20th Century-Fox film, in Cinemascope and color, was called by Leonard Maltin "leisurely paced, nicely done." [26]

Another Paramount picture to which Rupert's name was attached was accompanied by great fanfare in March, 1933. Titled *The Woman Accused*, it featured Nancy Carroll, Cary Grant, Louis Calhern, Jack LaRue, and John Halliday. Its most unusual aspect was that it was based upon an original story written for *Liberty* Magazine by what were billed as ten of the world's greatest authors. The name of Rupert Hughes headed the list that included Zane Grey, Vicki Baum, and Irvin S. Cobb. Paul Sloane directed the film in which Calhern is Miss Carroll's former lover whom she is accused of murdering. LaRue, his henchman, is a key witness.

The *New York Herald Tribune* reviewer thought "ten celebrated authors" had wasted time on a "feeble and unconvincing little tale," although he praised Miss Carroll and Cary Grant. *Variety*'s critic commented, "It took ten pretty well-known authors to turn out this story for *Liberty* and Bayard Veiller, vet playwright-scenarist, to put it in screen form. Result as reflected by the picture may convince producers and exhibitors that new writing talent should be encouraged." [27]

These negative comments were echoed by those that followed the story's publication in book form by Ray Long and Richard R. Smith, Inc., less than two months later. A *New York Times* book review declared, "If a machine existed for the production of novels without the hindrance of an artist's imagination, its work would resemble this collaboration of ten successful writers . . ." [28]

Much more cordial was the reception granted another motion picture adaptation of a Hughes short story, a Paramount production of a W. C. Fields comedy called *Tillie and Gus*, co-starring Alison Skipworth and Baby LeRoy. In this yarn, Fields and Skipworth are a married couple of card sharks who return from Alaska to help their niece save a dilapidated ferryboat, the Fairy Queen, the only thing left of her father's estate. They challenge owners of a rival boat to a race, but when firewood for the Fairy Queen falls overboard, Fields tosses in boxes of fireworks to provide power.

It is a clever story, highlighted by hilarious acting by Fields and Skipworth, with Baby LeRoy's escapades adding to the film's entertainment value. Leonard Maltin's *Movie and Video Guide*, six decades later, gave it three and a half stars out of a possible four and pointed out that it was the first motion picture in which Fields was pitted against Baby LeRoy.[29]

Meanwhile, the work on volume four of the Washington biography was not going well. Distractions of other activities, including an increasingly heavy schedule of lectures, were partly to blame. But the major problem was assimilating the vast amount of material available on the next phase of Washington's life.

There were other complications, too. Much of Hughes's research involved an analysis of Washington's own writings, which were being compiled by John C. Fitzpatrick of the Library of Congress. In a letter to Fitzpatrick Rupert complimented him on the "splendid edition" of a portion of Washington's writings, saying he was flattered to find his own work mentioned, but added that he awaited with impatience the other volumes Fitzpatrick was editing. He added, "My own work has been so delayed by such numbers of things that I am quite as unhappy as Kings." [30]

Fitzpatrick blamed legal restrictions for the delay in distribution of those volumes of the Bicentennial edition of Washington's writings that were already completed; only Congress could straighten out the mess, he said, and that would probably take years.[31]

At the end of 1932, the nation's political situation was in a state of anxiety, with Hoover serving out his lame-duck months before the accession of the newly-elected Franklin D. Roosevelt to the presidency. No one knew what the leadership change might mean, but the uncertainty brought on by the deepest depression in history was bound to continue as the new administration and a preponderantly Democratic Congress prepared to take over.

Looking at conditions from a historical perspective, Rupert saw similarities between early 1933 and the difficult times in which George Washington had led the nation. On Washington's 201st birthday, the *New York Times*—

after an interview at the Ritz Towers—reported that "Rupert Hughes, novelist and historian, who startled many persons a few years ago by declaring that George Washington had some of the vices of many of the gentlemen of his time mixed with uncommon virtues, told . . . yesterday of Washington's fight to right a national depression."

The headline was "WASHINGTON HERO OF ANOTHER SLUMP," and a subhead referred to Hughes as an "Iconoclastic Biographer." He called the American Revolution the result of a depression and said that poverty caused colonists to take their anger out on the British Crown. Hughes noted that Washington and Franklin Roosevelt were both "aristocrats, gentlemen farmers." [32]

He had never doubted Washington's sterling qualities but had felt obligated to provide an honest assessment of him, he explained in a *Los Angeles Examiner* article, "Duty of a Biographer," in which he remarked on two schools of thought regarding biographies: one, a selling job to present the subject as faultless; and the other, to tell the truth. In his opinion, the biographer who suppresses facts insults the memory of a great man or woman. [33]

He elaborated on this in a lengthy paper he wrote, titled "Pitfalls of the Biographer," for presentation before the Pacific Coast Branch of the American Historical Association at Occidental College on December 30, 1932. After the paper was read, it was discussed by historians Professor Nathaniel W. Stephenson of Scripps College, Eugene E. Prussing of Hollywood, and Dr. Louis Knott Koontz of the University of California at Los Angeles. Later, it was published in the *Pacific Historical Review*.

A scholar's "chief lacerations" after writing a biography usually come from other scholars, Hughes contended. "It is a constant astonishment to observe the magnificent carnage that results when historians raven on each other's books, articles, and convictions." Professional historians probably regarded him "more as a curiosity than a menace," he thought, but said that while criticism of his work had often been unfair and based upon misunderstanding, much of it had been generous and tolerant. "Countless pitfalls pockmark the field of biography," he said. "I think I have fallen into most of them, but I am going on though my head is muddy and bowed." [34]

In early 1933, Hughes again was making speeches, but most were now unrelated to Washington. In January he was back in Cleveland, speaking at the Ohio Theater on "Men, Women and Marriage." He protested divorce laws that differed from state to state; some states had as many as seventeen or eighteen grounds for divorce, but South Carolina had only one. Marriage laws were just as absurd: "In one state you can marry a girl of twelve if she consents. But if you try that in another state, you are a criminal and go to jail."

The speech also dealt with current economic conditions, and Hughes expressed disenchantment with President Hoover, then serving the last few weeks of his term, for insisting that there was no depression when "everything was going to pot."

"All the little fellows who had lost their shirts when the bottom fell out of the market, took the 'Great Engineer's' word for it that business had, or soon was going to turn the corner, and they went home and got their babies' shirts. Then they lost the babies' shirts, too," Rupert declared.[35] In a later year it would be said of Hughes that by inheritance and conviction he was a Republican, but in 1928 he had voted for Al Smith against Hoover and later voted for Franklin D. Roosevelt in two elections.[36]

The trip to Cleveland provided another opportunity to visit Elspeth and Ed and their daughters, and it also meant Rupert could stop by the Delta Upsilon house, where classmates from the early 1890s, including Frederick Waite—by then a professor of histology at Western Reserve's School of Medicine—greeted him. Members of the student chapter were also there to hear what a famous author had to say, but he mainly wanted to talk about football and Western Reserve athletics.[37]

His visit was an occasion for an interviewer from the *Reserve Record* to ask about his days at Western Reserve Academy, before he had entered Adelbert. Hughes recalled enjoyable times at little "Hardscrabble Academy" and admitted to some mischief. The lead paragraph of the student newspaper's report on the interview was:

"In the stone window sill of the second floor room in the northwest corner of North hall may be seen the weather-beaten initials 'R. H.', carved there 45 years ago by a man who was recently named on *Liberty*'s list of the ten greatest living authors—Rupert Hughes." The reporter called attention to Rupert's "ungrayed" hair and the black cigar he smoked "with which he gestures as he talks." [38]

It came natural to him to emphasize points of importance in speeches and conversation, and such gesticulation was remarked upon at other times. Ilka Roberts, describing him as a graceful man, said he would usually stand while telling a story, acting it out with sweeping arm gestures that would sometimes "clear an end table of its vases, ash trays and cigarette boxes, or a mantle of all its knick-knacks." Knowing about this, she added, "The thoughtful hostess who would enjoy Rupert's stories carefully puts her most prized—and breakable—possessions away before arrival." [39]

Since college days he had been described as witty, interested in what others had to say, and gracious in dealing with people in all walks of life. The well-known New England novelist Gladys Hasty Carroll, author of As the Earth Turns and other popular books, recalled a half-century later her first and only meeting with him. "I was surprised to find the famous debunker such a charming, gentle man who seemed to enjoy a quiet corner and one-on-one conversation." [40]

Unlike most celebrities on the lecture circuit who restrict speeches to one or a few subjects, he would sometimes ask the group that booked him to suggest one. When invited to speak at the Faculty Club at the University of Southern California, he wrote:

I am greatly flattered by your invitation to address the Faculty Club on April 19th and I shall be proud to accept, though I am at something of a loss what to talk about. There's always George Washington though a bit old. There is the whole problem of biography. There is the world of fiction and writing for publication

Perhaps you would be good enough to suggest something that your fellow victims would find least offensive. [41]

Requests to speak on literary subjects were not surprising, and some of his lectures dealt with modern trends in literature, or how to write fiction or biography. As president of the Writers' Club, he was considered the dean of the Hollywood writing colony and "the official Wailing Wall and father confessor to many young writers." He also lent his name in 1932, as did Gertrude Atherton, to an endorsement of the Palmer Institute of Authorship's writing course, advertised in The Bookman[42] and other magazines.

To some colleagues who knew Rupert only in later years and regarded him as an unabashed conservative, it would have been a surprise to learn that in 1933 he was named to a position in the National Recovery Administration during the early months of President Roosevelt's New Deal. The NRA, headed by Hugh S. Johnson and established to fight the depression by carrying out plans included in the National Industrial Recovery Act, set up and enforced codes of fair competition for industries and businesses. Although many Republicans and conservatives condemned the far-reaching act, calling it unconstitutional and socialistic, Rupert enthusiastically took up his new responsibilities and enlisted the support of other writers. Among those whose help he sought was Hamlin Garland, to whom he sent a telegram in August, 1933:

I HAVE BEEN DRAFTED AS CHAIRMAN OF THE AUTHOR'S LEGION OF THE NRA STOP THIS IS AN ORGANIZATION OF WELL KNOWN WRITERS WHO WILL BE ASKED TO CON-TRIBUTE IN MODEST WAY TO THE SUCCESS OF NRA NATION-AL CAMPAIGN BY USE OF THEIR NAME AND THEIR LOYAL SUPPORT TO THE GOVERNMENT STOP WANT YOU AS A MEM-BER OF THIS PATRIOTIC BODY STOP WILL APPRECIATE YOU ATTENDING LUNCHEON NEXT TUESDAY AT ONE O'CLOCK WITH YOUR CHAIRMAN AND THE CALIFORNIA STATE CHAIR-MAN OF NRA JACK L. WARNER AT WARNER BROS STUDIOS BURBANK STOP PLEASE PHONE ACCEPTANCE TO WRITERS CLUB STOP MANY THANKS

RUPERT HUGHES[43]

As matters turned out, his involvement and that of other writers and Hollywood executives would be short-lived; the United States Supreme Court declared the recovery act unconstitutional and the President abolished the NRA in 1935.

Some of Rupert's friends wondered how he could manage to make so many public appearances and become involved as a toastmaster and head of such organizations as The Writers, considering the hearing loss he had suf-fered over a period of many years. Others in a similar situation might have turned down invitations to speak, but not Hughes. For one thing, he was an early advocate of hearing aids and was willing to wear one from the time such a device required the use of a heavy battery pack. But there were special tech-niques he employed to minimize the effects of his growing deafness.

O. O. McIntyre, the syndicated columnist whose writings acquainted mil-lions of readers with goings-on in New York, wrote a column in August, 1933, in which he touched on the subject of deafness, using his friend Rupert as an example. While undoubtedly exaggerated, his comments showed how Hughes had made the best of a bad situation:

Of all hard of hearing, Rupert Hughes has been most accomplished sur-
mounting his handicap. Immediately he mastered lip reading and never
fails to catch every shred of conversation. Furthermore he salvaged out
of deafness, an ability for after dinner and public speaking he never
exhibited before. When he enters a filled room he does most of the
talking and makes it so extraordinarily interesting no one cares to talk.
Thus Rupert does not have to try to catch what others are saying.[44]

Ray Long, the magazine editor who published dozens of Hughes's serials and
short stories, wrote that he sometimes thought deafness had been an advantage to Rupert. "It has made possible concentration which would be impossible to a person subject to distracting noises." But, Long added, "his ability to
write as he does lies much deeper than that. It grows from the fact that he is
thoroughly an artist at heart, and that he simply chose writing as the principal expression of his art.[45]

CHAPTER TWENTY-ONE

A SPECIAL FRIEND

"People don't realize how important it is to laugh
often and to laugh at themselves. Dignity is all
right, but not the dignity which is near pomposity."

Will Rogers said he had joked about every prominent man of his time, "but I never met a man I didn't like." [1] This feeling was reciprocated by those with whom he came in contact, including members of The Writers and that organization's president, Rupert Hughes. Everyone liked Will Rogers.

Rogers and Hughes, who saw each other often at meetings of The Writers and at other functions, shared a mutual admiration that became apparent in their writings and speeches. Rogers found column material in Rupert's revelations about George Washington, but he also had an appreciation of Hughes as a speaker and humorist, as indicated in his nationally syndicated Weekly Article on Christmas Day, 1932. The article reported on the dedication of a building for writers at the Fox studio, where Rogers starred in pictures.

"Mr. Rupert Hughes the eminent author come over and spoke in behalf of the authors," wrote Rogers. "I know you have all read Rupert Hughes, but you missed much if you have not heard him in one of his delightful speeches. He was at his best on this day," Rogers said.

Recalling that he was working at the Goldwyn studio when Hughes came to Hollywood, Rogers wrote, "Well, Rupert Hughes stuck out here, and it's part and parcel of our industry. We hate to call it that, it sounds so sordid. He is really a co-artist with us, in this constructive photography we carry on."[2]

Rogers's "Will Rogers Says" daily telegrams and longer weekly articles were published unedited by newspapers, for he had insisted that the McNaught Syndicate not correct his punctuation, spelling, or grammar. In October, 1933, he touched on a dinner the Writers' Club sponsored in honor of Walt Disney. The entertainment, he said, included remarks by Disney, a pantomime by Charlie Chaplin, and his own "nonstop speech." He added, "Rupert Hughes, that clever writer, is a wonderful toastmaster."[3]

It was becoming increasingly apparent that Hughes's reputation as a clever wordsmith would be based upon his public appearances as well as by what he wrote. For the time, however, writing occupied most of his attention. He finished a novel and worked on another, but also turned out short stories, including "Where There's Smoke," published in *Good Housekeeping* in January, 1934. A key part of the story was the reference to "Little by Little," the first play Rupert wrote as a boy.

At about the same time, *Cosmopolitan* finished serializing his newest novel, *Love Song*, scheduled for book publication by Harper & Brothers. It was the story of Meriel Lawton, a young singer from the Midwest, whose voice shows great promise but is nearly ruined by faulty teaching methods. She is rescued from this fate and becomes an opera star but not without encountering numerous problems of romance.

In *Love Song*, Rupert returned again to subjects and places dear to his heart. His sister, Greta, had undergone her share of triumphs and obstacles in a singing career, including serious damage to her voice. His younger brother, Felix, had become expert in the proper methods of training singers for operatic roles, while Rupert himself knew well the arduous work and sacrifices required in order for musicians to succeed.

The book, published in August, brought an enthusiastic response from critics, especially in regard to the plot background. A reviewer for the *Boston Transcript* wrote about the author: "It is when he deals with music, and musicians at work and musicians at play, that he writes with the firm touch of a master who loves the task he has set for himself." Lisle Bell, in *Books*, declared, "What Rupert Hughes knows about music would fill an encyclopedia—has, in fact, done so. But his knowledge of vocal methods and the techniques of teachers is fused with his story."[4]

The most enthusiastic review was from Margaret Wallace in the *New York Times*, who wrote "Without doubt, *Love Song* is the best novel Rupert Hughes has given us, and it has an excellent claim to the further distinction of being the best musical novel so far produced in America." [5]

The book was also popular with readers, going through a number of Harper editions, and in January, 1935, Jarrolds published its first Great Britain edition.

W. G. Chapman of the International Press Bureau in Chicago wanted to buy the second serial rights to *Love Song*, but the author had to turn him down, pointing out that he did not own them for this book or others published recently.[6] Other syndicates also showed an interest in Hughes's work. In response to a request from the Chicago Tribune-New York News Syndicate, he submitted a 70,000-word novel, saying, "If you get half the pleasure of reading this story that I got out of writing it, you will not be bored. But alas, there is no discoverable relation between an author's delight and a reader's." [7] It is not known which novel he sent or whether it was accepted for syndication.

Samuel French, Inc., brought out a standard library edition of *Excuse Me* in 1934—not the novelized version, published in 1911, but the three-act farce that had been so successful in New York and on tours throughout the United States and in other countries.[8]

At around the same time, when a friend suggested a subject for a novel, Hughes said he liked the idea but did not have time for it, having just agreed to write a series of five other novels along a certain line. In his same letter, he said that although he would be flattered to serve on a Serra committee— apparently to honor Junipero Serra, a missionary who founded the first mission in California—he begged off because "I am such a notorious heathen and anti-religionist that I'd look funny there." [9]

In 1934 Paramount released a movie, *Miss Fane's Baby Is Stolen*, based on one of his stories. Adela Rogers St. Johns wrote the screenplay and Alexander Hall directed the film starring Baby LeRoy, Dorothea Wieck, Alice Brady, Jack LaRue, and Alan Hale. In the plot, Madeline Fane (Wieck) discovers her baby is missing, but decides not to tell police, hoping to pay ransom without publicity. However, when the kidnappers contact her she notifies authorities, the crime is publicized nationally, and the film ends happily.

Child kidnapping was still a sensitive subject as a result of the 1932 abduction and killing of the infant son of aviation hero Charles A. Lindbergh, and some people thought a movie dealing with such a matter was in bad taste.

Rose Pelswick of the *New York Journal* considered the melodrama emotionally disturbing, although "dramatically it is vividly developed with mounting suspense." [10] In the *New York Times*, Mordaunt Hall provided a positive review of the movie. He thought it dealt with kidnapping in an intelligent and restrained fashion, and he termed Hughes's work a "stirring narrative." [11]

Despite a lessening involvement in movie-making, Hughes continued to chronicle the happenings of the film community. This was especially true in an article he wrote for the *Saturday Evening Post*, published in March, 1934. Titled "A Brief for Hollywood," it was a strident defense of the movie business, its stars, producers, and others working to provide entertainment through the medium of films. Hughes contended that Hollywood had been for years a meek victim of critics who were sure they knew "just what is high art, pure morals and true intelligence." Meanwhile, Hollywood had led "a vastly busy life on a plane probably quite as high as that of her critics. And that is not saying much."

He was tired of Eastern writers who had worked on films and returned home to whine that "'Hollywood tempted me,' blaming Hollywood for their love of money, fair women, what not." Hughes reminded readers that movies had entertained, comforted, and educated audiences. "Take the motion picture from the world and imagine the ghastly void it would leave." [12]

Whether Rupert's article persuaded many readers is not known, but it was not the only essay about Hollywood that he wrote for the *Saturday Evening Post*. A year later, his splendid two-part "Early Days in the Movies" provided an entertaining look at the film industry from the time he had become associated with it until 1935. Anecdotes were told in an amusing and informative style.

Movie stills and other photos, including one of Rupert directing a scene from inside a fireplace for *Remembrance* and another of him with well-known writers and artists acting in the Dutch Treat Club motion picture, illustrated "Early Days in the Movies." The article ranks as one of the most lively and interesting accounts of the early motion picture industry ever published, while also providing fascinating and revealing sidelights of Hughes's own life and film career. [13]

In a typed manuscript for another lengthy article now in the library at the University of Southern California, Hughes told numerous other stories about Hollywood people. Believed to have been written in the mid-thirties, there is no indication that "Behind the Scenes" was ever published, but it is especially interesting because of inside information Rupert provided.

He recalled an incident in the early 1920s about silent film star Rudolph Valentino, who knew that Hughes had attended a private showing of *Blood and Sand*, starring the actor. After the screening at producer Jesse Lasky's house, Valentino asked Hughes his reaction to an episode in which the star was gored by a bull. When Hughes said he liked the scene, Valentino told him it was going to be cut and urged him to advise Lasky to leave it in. After first declining, Rupert finally wrote an apologetic letter to Lasky, which the producer ignored. When the scene was eliminated, Valentino abandoned his contract, temporarily giving up his career, and began a tour as a dancer.

In the same manuscript, Hughes wrote about actresses:

I have had Greta Garbo on the running board of my car making up a conspiracy against a woman she did not like . . .

I have had Pola Negri cooking a supper for me in my kitchen and sobbing in my arms because she had just finished a picture and as usual wanted to commit suicide.

I have had the then unheard-of Norma Shearer telling me of her desperate eagerness to get a part to play and then getting one in my farce, *Excuse Me* . . .

I have had Lucille Lesueur timidly taking a test for a part in a picture of mine and being crowded out of it, to gain fame later as "Joan Crawford." [14]

The non-fiction writing Rupert did in the mid-thirties was not confined to movie reminiscences. He also wrote a tribute to Mark Twain for a late 1935 issue of *Good Housekeeping* in connection with the centennial of the humorist's birth. Called "I Heard Mark Twain Laugh," it included Hughes's remembrances of his boyhood in Keokuk when Twain's mother and brother lived there. [15]

The piece was published about a half year after Hughes himself was the subject of the article "We Create Beauty Ourselves," written for *Better Homes & Gardens* by Margaret McOmie. Although it concentrated mainly on the Hughes home on Los Feliz, it provided a good description of Rupert and his work schedule. By then his brown hair had begun to turn silver, but there was "a vitality and eagerness in his voice that is wide-awake with much variety in it," she wrote. She liked him at once, "for his large deepset brown eyes have a kindly gleam of humor." [16]

Some letters he wrote during this period contained amusing insights into his life and habits. Such a letter went to a Miss Shirley Spencer, who had asked for a sample of his handwriting. "But I don't know how to," he protested (in a handwritten response). "When I have time and am trying to be very polite I write exquisitely like this," his letter suddenly becoming almost indecipherable as he continued, "When I am in a hurry I write like this"—(with strikeovers and lines going uphill and down). "When I am composing under" (illegible words follow with lines in all directions, some words marked out, etc.) . . . "to the back of the page." He concluded, "So I hope you will excuse me from sending you a sample. There is no such thing." [17]

In correspondence with author Julian Street he made plain his views about alcoholic beverages, after Street sent him a book about wines. Hughes called it a volume of poetry, saying he found the "various gleaming, bubbling stanzas" fascinating, but added, "I drink very little alcohol because it makes me sleepy and my effort is to keep awake; but I love to read about the beautiful manifestations of the vintners' art." [18] In later years, however, Wes Cameron, husband of Rupert's granddaughter Barbara, would recall that Rupert would often write all night, armed with coffee and brandy. [19]

Although he was unable to concentrate solely on the Washington biography, he willingly responded to other writers' requests for information uncovered in his research. One of those he assisted was John Hyde Preston, who was working on a biography of Benedict Arnold. Hughes sent him a lengthy letter providing the whereabouts of information—cited by author, book or magazine title, and page—and offered more assistance if needed. [20]

Although such attention to scholarly matters took a backseat to fiction writing, Rupert combined both in his 1935 book *The Man Without a Home*. It was a historical novel about John Howard Payne, the American actor and playwright who wrote the words to the song "Home Sweet Home." The story centers around the nineteenth century romance of Payne and Mary Godwin Shelley, attractive widow of English poet Percy Bysshe Shelley. She herself had written the horror story *Frankenstein* while still in her teens. Hughes based his novel mainly on Payne's letters to Mary Shelley, who was more interested in Washington Irving, while Irving loved another woman. [21]

The Man Without a Home was published serially in *This Week*, the Sunday magazine supplement to numerous metropolitan newspapers, and then as a book by Harper & Brothers. Margaret Wallace, in the *New York Times*, called it "a more than usually fascinating bit of historical research" which the author had presented with charm and eloquence. She considered the book "less a novel than a slice of literary history." [22]

Hughes was also involved in writing another novel published in 1935—this time a collaboration with five authors. As in 1933 when he had been a part of a team writing *The Woman Accused*, it was also published in *Liberty Magazine*.

The origin of the story was most unusual. President Franklin Roosevelt, an avid reader of mystery fare, suggested the plot idea during a White House conversation with Fulton Oursler, longtime editor of *Liberty*, saying that he had devised the plot some years earlier but had been unable to solve the mystery it posed. The question was whether it would be possible for an unhappy rich man to convert his wealth into cash, then disappear and start a new life doing something worthwhile without being traced. Oursler thought of several possible solutions, but the President shot them down. Finally the editor suggested inviting six prominent mystery writers to try their hand at the plot, and Roosevelt agreed.[23]

Oursler approached the authors and they agreed to write a six-installment serial, which *Liberty* published as "The President's Mystery," with a subhead of "Plot by Franklin D. Roosevelt." Oursler wrote in his autobiography that he was the only one who knew what it was all about, and the authors "were as much surprised as the public when they saw the opening chapters following a laughing Roosevelt picture on the cover."

Rupert wrote the first installment, and others were by Samuel Hopkins Adams, Anthony Abbot, Rita Weimann, S. S. Van Dine, and John Erskine. *The President's Mystery* was soon published as a book by Farrar & Rinehart, but, as Oursler recalled, "in those early days—when the John Farrars of the world were still anti-Roosevelt—only about two thousand copies were sold," and "collectors have grabbed them all." [24]

The title and the story's association with President Roosevelt made *The President's Mystery* seem a natural for motion picture production, and a film by that title was released in the fall of 1936, a month before the election in which Roosevelt sought a second term. Produced by Nat Levine for Republic Pictures, it starred Henry Wilcoxon as a lawyer and lobbyist for National Canneries, who tires of his work after blocking a Senate bill that would have permitted small companies to shut down and reopen as cooperatives. After he sells his securities and disappears, his faithless wife, played by Evelyn

Brent, is murdered. He then decides to advance the cause of cooperatives and help reopen a cannery owned by Betty Furness.

The screenplay by Lester Cole and Nathaniel West was unabashed propaganda for the cooperative movement, and *New York Times* reviewer Frank S. Nugent reported that the two had "used the President's question as a springboard of their own, and have plunged from it into the swifter current of a topical problem." But, Nugent added, "although there is no disputing the propagandist intent, the film—unlike the Soviet lectures—has not reduced its narrative to a moralizing bludgeon." [25]

Hughes no doubt was distressed with changes made by the script writers, despite his belief that a studio had the right to do as it pleased with a story it purchased. Also, by now Hughes and Cole were on opposite sides in a dispute over unionization of writers, and they would clash often in future years in an escalation of differences that would become part of a larger controversy.

But in the mid-thirties, despite a growing rift among motion picture writers, there was a camaraderie among members of the Writers' Club, over which Hughes continued to preside. There were happy occasions, such as a dinner the club sponsored in honor of *Los Angeles Times* columnist Lee Shippey when his novel *Where Nothing Ever Happens* was published. Hughes had reviewed the publishing contract, offered to help promote the book, organized the dinner, and asked Will Rogers and Irvin S. Cobb to speak. [26]

When invitations went out from Hughes, Shippey was overjoyed by his kind words and immediately thanked him. Hughes responded that he hoped Shippey's novel would be immensely successful "and that many others may follow it with fame and fortune for you." [27] There was nothing Rupert enjoyed more than seeing someone else receive deserved credit. Unlike some authors who envy and downplay another's success, he rejoiced upon such an occasion and sent a congratulatory letter.

The friendships Hughes formed through The Writers were especially deep and lasting, and his long tenure as president was proof of his popularity. He enjoyed the lighthearted banter with other members, including Will Rogers.

There was a special place in his heart for Rogers, whose down-to-earth humor and honesty appealed to Hughes. He knew the famed Oklahoma cowboy philosopher as a person, as well as a celebrity, and found him to be a warmhearted and courageous soul.

He later wrote about an incident that occurred when he and Rogers toured the Milton H. Berry Institute, where infantile paralysis victims were rehabilitated. Rogers had a clever remark for everyone he met, with each cheerful comment bringing laughter. Rupert recalled that after the tour, when Will went to wash his hands, Milton Berry, the director, left to get him a towel, then returned to find Rogers "leaning against the wall, his head in his arms. He was sobbing like a child." The director left without saying anything, and soon "Will was back again, bright-eyed and gay, and tossing jokes about as if there were no suffering before him." [28]

In 1935 Rogers was at the zenith of his career, having reached the top in just about everything he had tried to accomplish: he was being paid $500 a minute as a radio speaker—a record amount; his columns were in hundreds of newspapers; during the previous year he had been the number one box office draw as a screen actor; his six published books were exceedingly popular; and he was in demand more than any other public speaker. He handled these assignments in an offhand, "aw shucks" way that made everything he did seem easy.[29]

Around the world, Will Rogers was better known than any other United States citizen. No other public figure was more willing to take off in an airplane to visit a place where he thought there was a good story or an opportunity to assist in disaster relief. He not only reported, but made news, and Americans had become accustomed to reading about his travels.

And so it was that they read with anticipation in the summer of 1935 about a trip he planned to make with another famous Oklahoman, the record-breaking pilot Wiley Post. They would fly to Alaska and then to Siberia in the *Winnie Mae*, a new red monoplane equipped with pontoons.

They took off from Renton, Washington, on August 3 for Juneau, Alaska, where they stayed until August 9, then made several stops before flying to Fairbanks on August 13. From there, Post decided to head for Point Barrow in northern Alaska. After leaving Fairbanks at 2 p.m. on August 15, they landed six hours later on a lagoon, where Post checked with natives as to the direction to fly to reach nearby Point Barrow. Concerned about the craft's tendency to be nose-heavy during takeoffs and landings, he examined it carefully before taking off.

The plane began to lift, but soon started falling. The *Winnie Mae* crashed, and both occupants died—the world-renowned and skilled pilot and his lone passenger, the most famous and popular citizen of the United States.[30]

An Eskimo who saw the disaster raced fifteen miles to Point Barrow to tell officials, who immediately alerted news media and others about the deaths of Will Rogers and Wiley Post. Everywhere, shocked people stopped and wept, unable to imagine a world without the humor of Will Rogers to lighten their daily lives.

Messages of sympathy poured out from statesmen and leaders, as well as humble citizens, to help assuage the grief of Betty Blake Rogers and her family. Among telegrams sent to the grieving widow was a brief one from Rupert Hughes: "Just not to be absent from the multitudes sending you their sympathies I remind you of how I loved and admired Will and that I share your heartache." [31]

From early morning until noon on August 22, an estimated 150,000 persons filed past the casket of Will Rogers at Forest Lawn Memorial Park. Attendance at the 2 p.m. funeral service in the Wee Kirk o' the Heather at Forest Lawn was limited to 125 family members, friends, studio executives, actors, and actresses. Rupert and Patterson Hughes were among the invited, as was Howard Hughes. [32]

Simultaneously, a much larger memorial service took place at the Hollywood Bowl, planned by a committee headed by Mary Pickford, Rupert Hughes, and Conrad Nagel. A throng of 25,000 people attended the service that was broadcast by the Mutual Broadcasting System, National Broadcasting Company, Canadian Radio Commission network, and two Los Angeles radio stations. [33] Rogers's friend, Rupert Hughes, gave the eulogy.

Newspaper reports indicate that Hughes's voice was "threaded with emotion" as he spoke: "We are mourning one of the outstanding characters of our time. He believed in the equality of man. His philosophy was that he was as good as any king and any high officer, and any king and any high officer was as good as he."

Rupert's remarks also pointed up an attribute of Rogers that he himself shared: "People don't realize how important it is to laugh often and to laugh at themselves. Dignity is all right, but not the dignity which is near pomposity." [34] Both Rogers and Hughes knew the importance of laughter and humor.

CHAPTER TWENTY-TWO

RECOGNITION AND CONTROVERSY

*"The men and women of a nation cannot be expected
to meet the great obligations of the present if they refuse
to exhibit honesty, charity, open-mindedness, and free
and growing intelligence toward the past. . ."*

Even before the body of Will Rogers was laid to rest, suggestions were being made for the creation of a suitable memorial. Within a month after the funeral, a national group called the Will Rogers Memorial Commission was organized, with Vice President John Nance Garner as chairman. Two hundred and fifty prominent Americans were appointed to the commission, including Henry Ford, Herbert Hoover, Alfred E. Smith, and Rupert Hughes, who was one of thirty-six Executive Committee members.[1]

Hughes also became the commission's California state chairman and lost no time in starting the solicitation of funds. The big money-raising event he planned was a "Show of Shows" to be staged in the Shrine Auditorium in Los Angeles. He reported that the talent would include a "who's who" of the motion picture, stage, and radio world, and predicted a sellout.[2]

Nearly a month before the show occurred, an event spotlighting Rogers's career took place on the fifty-sixth anniversary of his birth, and again

Hughes was involved. November 4, proclaimed Will Rogers Day by most governors and mayors, served as the official opening of the national fund-raising campaign scheduled to end on Thanksgiving Day. The highlight of the day was an hour-long radio program broadcast nationally on both NBC and CBS, with appearances by Hollywood celebrities and political figures. Speakers included some of Rogers's closest friends: Rupert Hughes, humorist Irvin S. Cobb, actor Fred Stone, speed pilot Capt. Frank Hawks, and comedian Eddie Cantor. Among others on the program were former President Herbert Hoover, publisher Arthur Brisbane, Charlie Chaplin, George M. Cohan, Eddie Rickenbacker, Amos 'n Andy, and Rudy Vallee.[3]

On the same day, Hughes announced that banks and newspapers would accept contributions to a memorial fund. He urged Californians to lead all states in "today's great national festival of affection." [4]

The next important occasion honoring Rogers was the dedication of a $200,000 Will Rogers sound stage at the Twentieth-Century-Fox studio, broadcast coast-to-coast by both NBC and CBS. Hughes presided, with more than 300 of Rogers's friends, the governors of California and Arizona, four United States senators, and civic leaders attending. Beloved child star Shirley Temple opened the dedication service, and while Irvin Cobb held her in his arms, she pulled a cord, unveiling a plaque, and said in a choking voice, "I loved Uncle Will."[5]

From then on, Hollywood events paying tribute to Rogers—with Hughes usually involved—were held at frequent intervals. The single most impressive benefit, the "Show of Shows," more than lived up to its name with an astounding array of entertainers in the Shrine Auditorium on Sunday night, December 1. As state chairman of the memorial fund Rupert had enlisted the help of impresario Sid Grauman to serve as director general for the extravaganza, featuring "All the Stars-All the Studios." [6]

Never before had so many stage, screen, and radio personalities appeared in a single performance, attracting a sellout crowd of more than 7,000. Proceeds from the show that began at 8:30 p. m. and lasted until after midnight swelled the fund by some $20,000, by depression standards a sizeable amount.[7]

The program opened with an overture of "The Last Round-Up" by a 100-piece orchestra, the singing of the national anthem by Mme. Ernestine Schumann-Heink, and brief speeches by Hughes, Fred Stone, Will Hays, and silent picture western star William S. Hart. An array of seventeen masters of ceremonies included such stars as Warner Baxter, Clark Gable, Tom Mix, and Spencer Tracy. Fourteen composers of popular songs performed in teams of two on seven pianos, playing their hit tunes and then a finale together.

But the emphasis was on big name entertainers whose faces and voices were familiar to the audience. Among those participating in twenty-two separate acts were: Shirley Temple and Bill Robinson repeating their famous stairstep dance performance; May Robson as the Old Lady Who Lived in the Shoe, aided by child star Mickey Rooney; Bing Crosby singing "Home on the Range"; and Joe E. Brown and an acrobatic team. The list went on: Ronald Colman, Jackie Cooper, Billie Burke, Edward Arnold, Boris Karloff, Bela Lugosi, Myrna Loy, Fredric March, Cesar Romero, Barbara Stanwyck, the Three Stooges, Sophie Tucker, Mae West, Paul Robeson, Dick Powell, Edgar A. Guest, Eddie Cantor, and many more.

In a fight between James J. Braddock and an opponent, the judges were Rupert Hughes, Cecil B. DeMille, and Sid Grauman; one of the seconds was Tom Mix.[8]

Newspaper reports were unanimous in calling the show a great success. One paper said Will Rogers had been honored as no other man in life or death in what was undoubtedly "Hollywood's most lavish and pretentious display of talent in history." [9]

In the months that followed, Rupert's fund-raising efforts and those of 2,000 committees across the nation continued, although in a less spectacular way. By August 15, 1936, exactly a year after the plane crash that killed Rogers, Hughes reported that the national committee had raised about $250,000 for a memorial, including $40,000 raised in California.[10]

While Rupert was making certain Will Rogers was accorded the honor he was due, a movement was underway at Western Reserve University to recognize Hughes himself, that institution's best-known graduate, whose ties with the university and especially its Adelbert College had remained strong. He contributed to fund-raising campaigns, and continued to sponsor poetry prizes bearing his name.[11]

Although the former president, Dr. Thwing, had hinted earlier that Western Reserve might grant Hughes an honorary degree, nothing had come of it until 1936, when on the morning of June 10, the university awarded him the degree of Doctor of Letters. The *Cleveland Plain Dealer Sunday Magazine* heralded the occasion with a feature article headed "Reserve,'92, to

Welcome 'Railroad' Hughes," referring to one of his nicknames while a student at Adelbert.

"Western Reserve University has many famous alumni and some have won acclaim in more serious fields of endeavor than Mr. Hughes," said the *Plain Dealer* writer. "But it is doubtful if anyone who went to Reserve, and there are 50,000 such living today, is as well known. Nor has any of them chosen to win fame in a more difficult or overcrowded trade—writing." [12]

At the Commencement ceremony in Severance Hall on the university campus in Cleveland, Hughes was introduced by faculty representative H. W. Taeusch, who traced his accomplishments in music, literature, history, the theater, and motion pictures. He added:

Much of this work reflects the interest which even in college days prompted his nickname, History Hughes. His greatest professional achievement is his life of George Washington, of which three of the proposed five volumes are already published. In this work he bears out the quotation he chose for his motto: "the men and women of a nation cannot be expected to meet the great obligations of the present if they refuse to exhibit honesty, charity, open-mindedness, and a free and growing intelligence toward the past that has made them what they are." [13]

In presenting the diploma, President W. G. Leutner read a citation:

RUPERT RALEIGH HUGHES—a son of the "Middle Border" you came to the Western Reserve and went later to New England and the Atlantic Coast to let the roots of your being tap again the older sources, and you are now an adopted son of the golden west, critic, scholar in music and biography, dramatist, author whose ironic humor can at once prick the bubbles of pretension and cheer the weary heart, on recommendation of the University Faculty and by vote of the Board of Trustees I do admit you to the honorary degree of Doctor of Letters with such rights and privileges as pertain to this degree. In token of this act we bestow upon you the hood of your Alma Mater and grant you this diploma. [14]

Although Hughes was accustomed to speaking to audiences of all sorts and sizes, it was with special pride that he delivered the Commencement convocation address. His extemporaneous remarks brought a commendatory letter from former President Thwing, for which Rupert thanked him: "Bless you for your kind words about my crazy speech! They are all the more pleasant from my feeling that your kindness would overlook any badness in my oratory." [15]

In addition to Western Reserve, others sang his praise in 1936, including H. L. Mencken, whose fourth edition of *The American Language* called attention to Hughes's contributions in promoting the American language as opposed to a stilted British-style of speech. "Hughes has written on the subject more than once, and always with great vigor."[16] Another 1936 book, *The Great Biographers*, discussed problems biographers encountered in writing about George Washington. Said author Albert Britt, "Perhaps the most significant thing that has yet been done is Rupert Hughes's *George Washington*." [17]

Meanwhile, there were some authors who thought less highly of his work and opinions, and their disdain and criticism were reciprocated in kind as Hughes again became involved in an exchange of lengthy letters. The first of these came about when Chicago critic and editor Burton Rascoe recalled in *Esquire Magazine* Hughes's "dog-fight" with southern author James Branch Cabell. This revived an argument of eighteen years earlier and brought a heated reply from Rupert. In a three-page, single-spaced typed letter he told Rascoe, "Your talent for getting things wrong amounts to infallible genius."

Hughes said he had accused Cabell of "putting forth the false banalities that the Greeks found nothing immoral in nudity and that medieval people were more interested in ballads than in money." After he had disproved "these old misunderstandings," Hughes said, Cabell had expressed amazement that "such a person as I should have ideas about Greeks and the middle ages, when I was supposed to be merely a person who wrote trashy stories in which rich brokers seduced poor stenographers." Hughes told Rascoe:

I answered that Mr. Cabell plainly had read neither my works nor Greek history. I said that I had never written a story of a rich broker seducing a poor stenographer, and that if I ever brought two such people together I should have had the poor stenographer seduce the rich broker.

I did not say . . . that I learned Greek at my mother's knee . . . . I said that I had studied Greek art at my mother's knee and was not the illiterate ignoramus Mr. Cabell treated with such lofty derision but a lifelong student of the subjects on which I found Mr. Cabell ignorant and fatuous—as he was . . . .

Hughes suggested that Rascoe document his references more carefully. "You have always swung your broadsword with a lusty fearlessness . . . but you do knock so many things off the shelf." He signed the letter, "Yours from the depths of devastation." [18]

Rascoe promptly took up the cudgel again, replying with a letter that matched Rupert's for length. Accusing Hughes of self-eulogy and being touchy, Rascoe said he had published both sides of the Hughes-Cabell argument. He thought Rupert should be satisfied with the success he had achieved and the money he had made, and not fly into a rage just because it had been implied that he had lost out in a disagreement with Cabell so many years ago. [19]

There is no doubt that Hughes was sometimes touchy about criticism, but usually he would shrug it off as something to be expected. Before long, however, he was involved in another disagreement with much greater ramifications.

From 1936 until late 1938 Hollywood was abuzz with talk about "the fight between the Left and Right to gain control of all the writers at the studios," according to Hollywood columnist Sheila Graham. "The announced aim of the Screen Writers Guild was to better the working conditions for them all, and especially for hacks who were poorly paid. To combat this dangerous idea, the producers organized the Screen Playwrights under the presidency of Rupert Hughes." [20]

This was an oversimplification of the issues involved in the dispute. Hughes could foresee immense problems for individual writers arising from the type of union some of them favored, and he especially resented an attack upon him by Heywood Broun in *The Nation*'s "Broun's Page."

Broun's blast followed comments Hughes made after being asked by publisher Roy Howard of the *New York World-Telegram* to tell why he had resigned from the Screen Writers Guild. [21] Broun accused Hughes of fighting for "free speech, free press, and Metro-Goldwyn." He called him the leader of the Guild's "white-mouse faction" and "a connoisseur of buttered bread" who had caved in to pressure from employers. Broun recalled that Hughes had written a penetrating book about George Washington that had disturbed some patriotic people, "but now he tends to conformity"—writing "from his cubicle on the lot" about the freedom of writers. [22]

Hughes, visiting in New York, could not stomach this attack, and he quickly responded in kind with a letter to *The Nation*:

In all the years I've been reading Heywood Broun, this is the first time he ever held me up to scorn and ridicule. And for a whole page in *The Nation*!

But he appears to be serious when he calls me "the leader of the white-mouse faction" . . . and describes me as trying to curry favor with the picture producers—a "man running for his life."

But I was not running for my life or even my livelihood. Producers have never controlled my life or livelihood, and have never even tried to. I have never occupied "a cubicle on the lot." In all my life I have worked for the studios on a salary for only one period of four weeks two years ago, and another of six this year. In both cases I did all my work at home on my own hours . . .

Hughes said that sixty other screen writers had resigned from the Guild of their own volition and not as "white rats." His own revolt had been as a member of the council of the Authors' League (of which he was one of six honorary vice-presidents) after realizing that what was being contemplated was "a gigantic plan to organize and combine all writers in every field into one vast closed shop."

He recalled his lengthy union involvement as a founder of the Authors' League, the Dramatists' Guild, and the Screen Writers Guild, "old and new." He told about serving on an NRA committee "in open war with the producers," and as a member of a committee of dramatists that had brought an end to the Actors' Equity strike "in hot opposition to the managers."

Even if producers had barred him from the studios, he could have written other types of material. "But if that amalgamation had succeeded and I had offended the ruling writers, I could have been debarred from shooting off steam not only in the movies, but in magazines, newspapers, pamphlets, books, plays, the radio, television, everywhere," he contended.[23]

Accounts of the Guild's formation and its later opposition from the Screen Playwrights can be found in *The Hollywood Writers' Wars*, by Nancy Lynn Schwartz, and in *The Inquisition in Hollywood*, by Larry Ceplair and Steven Englund. There had been an attempt to form a union called the Photoplay Authors' League in 1914-1916 and an effort to gain support for a Screen Writers Guild in the 1920s, but neither had won a contract with studios. The writers' branch of the Academy of Motion Picture Arts and Sciences had handled labor relations, but many writers were unhappy when it agreed to layoffs and pay cuts while studio executives received bonuses.

Out of this discontent had come a meeting in February, 1933, of ten screenwriters, several known for leftist leanings, to consider reviving the SWG. Their goals were to form a union strong enough to back its demands; to become allied with the Dramatists' Guild and other writers' organizations; and to seek royalty payments for writers.[24]

The Hollywood Writers' Wars recalled that the Writers' Club, which Hughes headed, had been affiliated with the Authors' League of America since the 1920s and was all that remained of the screen writers' subsidiary of the Dramatists' Guild, but it was not a union and its membership was mostly made up of established writers. The committee organizing the Screen Writers Guild decided to negotiate with the Dramatists' Guild in New York to try to have its subsidiary revived and turned over to the new Guild.[25]

At succeeding meetings, after studios cut wages, attendance grew, and by the time the SWG of the Authors' League of America was reorganized, 173 charter members each paid a membership fee of $100. Members elected leftist John Howard Lawson as president, adopted a new constitution and bylaws, and named a committee to draft a working rules code. Among committee members was Rupert Hughes, who in 1934 also served on the Board of Directors.[26]

But after Hughes broke with the Guild, philosophical differences separated Guild members from those leaving to join the Screen Playwrights. Hughes, in opposing the SWG, was known as one of the "Four Horsemen"—the others being Walt Disney, James Kevin McGuinness, and Howard Emmett Rogers.[27]

In believing that the Communists wanted to control Hollywood writers, Hughes had good reasons for concern. As Ceplair and Englund wrote, "No single person better incarnates the values, aspirations, and durability, as well as the doubts and hesitations, of the Hollywood 'career' Communist than Jack Lawson, for two decades the most respected Red in the movie industry." In time, they wrote, he progressed from "political rhetorician" to "part-time Communist to full-time Party loyalist." [28]

To Rupert Hughes, the thought of turning the leadership of Hollywood writers over to such individuals was intolerable, and he continued to be in the forefront of the so-called writers' wars for as long as they raged. But it was not only the Communists against whom he fought. He also stood firm against the menace of fascism then gaining strength in Europe, and he despised the ideas and actions of Nazis. The formation of the Hollywood Anti-Nazi League in 1936 found him among film community leaders who banded together to show their disdain for Nazism and to call attention to the menace of Hitlerism in the United States. Organized by writers Donald Ogden Stewart and Dorothy Parker, actor Fredric March, composer Oscar Hammerstein, and director Fritz Lang, the League grew quickly to 5,000 members. The wide diversity of political beliefs among leaders and members, including stars such as Eddie Cantor, movie moguls Jack Warner and Carl Laemmle, and radical writers Lawson and Sam Ornitz, was surprising, but it indicated the strong opposition to fascism. Among the League's activities were a boycott of Nazi goods, publication of a weekly newspaper, and mass rallies.

As one of the League's most outspoken members, Hughes sought to change its name to the Hollywood Anti-Nazi and Anti-Communist League, to demonstrate opposition to what he perceived as the two main threats to the American way of life. His efforts were unsuccessful, due no doubt to the presence in the League of members who supported the Communist movement.[29]

In mid-summer 1936, Hughes began a new phase of his career that put him in a national spotlight. The *New York Times* carried a portrait of him at a radio microphone, with a caption: "Rupert Hughes, author, turns master of ceremonies on Tuesdays, 9:30 p.m., for an hour, WABC variety show, originating in Hollywood."[30]

The first broadcast of the weekly Camel Caravan show aired June 30, and was carried nationally over the Columbia Broadcasting System. Announcer Bill Goodwin introduced Hughes as "distinguished for his career as author, scholar and soldier." The program featured two well-known musical groups: Benny Goodman and his Swing Band and Nathaniel Shilkret and his Orchestra.

Hughes praised the sponsor, saying it was "especially pleasant to be on a tobacco program. For this country of ours was founded and fathered by a tobacco planter. It was his tobacco crop that enabled George Washington to serve as our Commander-in-Chief without pay." Adding a note of patriotism, he reminded listeners that it would soon be the Fourth of July, and urged, "For a moment, let us close our eyes and tell ourselves how good it is to be alive, here and now in this, our beloved country."

When he introduced singer Gladys Swarthout, he rhapsodized: "Missouri has given to the world some of its most beautiful women—none more exquisite than Gladys Swarthout." After Miss Swarthout sang, Hughes introduced movie stars Clark Gable and Madeleine Carroll for a scene from "Men in White." [31]

Rupert handled the star-studded show in a manner both lighthearted and serious—the sort of treatment readers had come to expect of his writing and audiences had experienced in his speeches.

In the second show, he introduced Rosalind Russell and Spencer Tracy with references to his own ambitions and shortcomings: "There are times when I'd give my right arm to be able to sing high 'A's' like a great tenor. I long to be terribly funny and can only be terrible. I long to bring tears to the eyes by telling of things that make my soul weep. But I can't sing, I can't act for comedy or pathos. So I go to see and hear those who can express me— release me. Others must feel the same. Hence these splendid artists."

After the second show, a *Variety* critic thought some improvements in the pace were needed: "Biggest hitch develops in allotting Rupert Hughes the right amount of patter without letting him run off with the clock, and in making something of the expensive orchestras without turning the stanza into a straight musical." He added that "Hughes m. c.'s in a highly literary manner, which could be okay except that he lets things get out of hand. Patter frequently runs to great lengths, taking the edge off his carefully selected words and thus wearying." The critic also thought some heavier fare could be included among the dramatic offerings. [32]

The pace picked up somewhat for the succeeding programs in the time slot opposite Fred Astaire's National Broadcasting Company program. The third Camel Caravan show featured John Barrymore, and those that followed presented other celebrities—Robert Taylor, Carole Lombard, the Marx Brothers, Jimmy Cagney, Joan Bennett, and flying ace Col. Roscoe Turner, to name a few—but one show was cut to a half hour from Hollywood and then switched to New York for the Jack Sharkey-Joe Louis heavyweight prizefight. By October, George Stoll's orchestra had replaced that of Nat Shilkret.

The December 22 broadcast—26th in the series Hughes emceed—featured Ruth Chatterton and Otto Kruger. Rupert then announced that a program change would take place, saying that "the Caravanites of 1937 will begin with a new master of ceremonies, the brilliant screen comedian, Jack

Oakie." There would be a new format; it would be called Jack Oakie's College and would feature performers from a different college each week.[33]

The reason for the change was not stated, but there was no doubt that it would save money to substitute collegians for the top stars who had graced the program while Rupert was emcee. Although it marked the end of his role in a variety show, he would eventually return to radio in a different type of program that would provide him with a greater opportunity to express his views.

Ironically, a few weeks after his six-month stint with the Camel Caravan ended, a photo of Hughes appeared in *Liberty* with Clara Beranger's article on "Who Will Be the New Movie Stars of 1937?" The caption for Hughes's picture, one of sixteen, was "Rupert Hughes, on the air and a coming ace." In the same issue, *Liberty* gave *The President's Mystery* a three-star movie rating out of a possible four.[34]

A second movie that year, *It Had to Happen*, was based on one of Hughes's short stories and was produced by 20th Century-Fox. The big-name cast included George Raft, Rosalind Russell, Arline Judge, Leo Carrillo, and Alan Dinehart, with Raft playing an Italian immigrant who becomes a powerful union boss and tries to romance society matron Miss Russell.[35] Leonard Maltin's 1995 edition of *TV Movies and Video Guide* rated it with two stars out of a possible four.

Near the end of the radio series, Hughes described himself, in a questionnaire completed for artist Dean Cornwell, as a "Jack at all trades and good at none." In reply to a question about his heritage, Rupert said his ancestors on both sides were "largely Welsh," adding that "Welshmen usually begin to talk Welsh to me but I don't know a word of it." As for his hobbies, Hughes responded, "Smoking, piano playing (privately). I've given up all forms of athletics, as I do all my writing by long hand."

Cornwell also asked Hughes to note anything pertaining to him that would lend itself to "symbolic pictorial representation typical of the devices traditionally used in coats of arms." Hughes's answer: "Pat suggests that two Pekingese rampant would be in order. We have a sable brown one called Jinka and a biscuit-colored one called Taffy. They're all over the place. Fountain pens couchant."[36]

The description of himself as a "Jack at all trades" was one he often used, but "good at none" was far from the truth; he was, in fact, much better than good at nearly everything he attempted. But there was always the desire to try something new, which meant he would then spend less time on work already in progress, such as the Washington biography.

The attention Rupert gained for his activities in the middle thirties did not compare with that which focused on the exploits of his nephew Howard, who had turned toward the development of an airplane capable of setting speed records. After he and a team of engineers worked a year and a half on the "mystery ship," he piloted it to a world record of 352 miles per hour on September 12, 1935. But the motor cut out and he had to land the craft on its belly in a field, fortunately without injury to him.

His next assault was on the transcontinental speed record, taking off from Burbank on a secret flight in a standard mail plane equipped with an engine designed for high altitudes, on January 13, 1936. With a broken antenna and a compass that malfunctioned, he flew as high as 18,000 feet and occasionally used oxygen to stay awake. When he arrived at Newark, he had bested the record by more than a half hour. Then, after flying to Miami for a rest, he learned that another pilot had flown there from New York in slightly more than five hours, so Howard flew nonstop to New York in four hours, twenty-one minutes and thirty-two seconds.

Having established two records, he headed toward home, stopping for lunch in Chicago where a friend bet him fifty dollars that he could not reach Los Angeles by dinner time. Howard took him up on it, leaving at 1:05 p. m. Chicago time. His radio quit, he had no maps for much of the trip, his oxygen supply cut off, and at times he flew at 20,000 feet to avoid heavy winds, but the plane arrived in Los Angeles at 7:15 p. m., in time for dinner.[37]

His record-setting flights added to the fame he had attained as a film producer, and soon Howard Hughes was regarded as a legendary figure capable of doing anything he set out to do.

Liberty Magazine recognized the public interest in the heroic Howard and asked his Uncle Rupert to write a biographical sketch about the famous pilot. Rupert agreed, and his two-part article on "Howard Hughes—Record Breaker: The Story of an Exciting Life" was published on February 6 and 13, 1937. As Rupert put it, the editor had called Howard "the most picturesque young man in the country today." By accepting the invitation to write his life story Rupert had been placed in a strange situation:

"This puts me in the two paradoxical positions of being the poor uncle of a rich nephew, and the biographer of one who, instead of being dead, is only half my own age. But what of it?"

The account, written in an entirely different tone than Rupert's scathing letters to Howard in 1924, traced Howard's movie career and said he had inherited his father's mechanical bent. But Rupert denied that Howard was a reckless daredevil: "The truth . . . is that no aviator on earth—or off it— plans more carefully, takes more thought of design and efficiency, or is better informed of everything about a plane . . . . If, at times, Howard takes a chance, forgets everything but the goal and pushes on to success—why, that's the only way success is ever won." [38]

On January 31, 1937, Rupert reached the age of sixty-five, a landmark becoming accepted as retirement age in business and industry, but it was no time for him to slow down. His intention to complete one project was indicated in a letter to Cyril Clemens in March, in which he accepted the Honorary Vice Chairmanship of the Western Branch of the International Mark Twain Society:

"I hope to get the final volume of George Washington off my conscience within the next year or two, but it is an old hope, which, like tomorrow, is always just over the horizon." [39]

It is noteworthy that he now thought in terms of the "final volume" of the biography; previously he had planned to write both volumes four and five before he was finished with the project.

Some of Rupert's earlier writings were now being given new life, including his short novel The Gift Wife, for which William G. Chapman of the International Press Bureau paid him $100 for newspaper rights in 1937. In acknowledging receipt of the check, Hughes told Chapman that various magazines had purchased all serial rights to most of his short stories, except for Collier's Weekly, but stories written for that publication had since been syndicated. As for other short stories, they were "too old or stupid to send you." [40]

Jarrolds, a London company, published a novel he wrote, called Double Exposure, about Irish people in the United States, but it bears no publication date. In the book, Jarrolds listed certain other Hughes works, including two that are relatively unknown—The Thousandth Girl and True Lover's Knot. [41]

As always, Hughes answered letters from persons seeking his advice or information. He agreed to serve on a committee sponsoring the publication of a poet's work.[41] But his response to a New York woman applying for a job as his secretary in Los Angeles seemed out of character for a man who was a champion of women's rights. He thanked her, but wrote, "I am already provided with a secretary and even if he should break under the strain I should secure another man to replace him. I feel I have no right to drag a poor woman through the sort of work falls on my secretary." [43]

But that was not the last of the matter. A year and a half later he answered a second appeal from the same woman: "In reply to yours of the 21st, I still have to say that I know of nothing in your line of work or anyone's else. My own secretary does all the work I have, and I judge from the advertisements, and from what I hear, that there are many, many efficient secretaries unable to find jobs here. Yours with regrets and best wishes." [44]

Although the tone of his second letter to the persistent job seeker was businesslike—even though courteous—in other letters he could praise profusely, as in one he wrote to Maine author Gladys Hasty Carroll: "It was a delight to see your beautiful handwriting which always writes such beautiful things. We should have enjoyed very much more seeing your beautiful self . . . . Hoping that we may see you out here again, and with all admiration for your gorgeous work, I am yours faithfully, Rupert Hughes." [45]

The year 1937 marked the fiftieth anniversary of his graduation from St. Charles College, the military school. The *St. Charles (Missouri) Cosmos-Monitor* recalled that Rupert Hughes, the well-known story writer, had captured two medals at the 1887 Commencement. Throughout the article he was called Rupert R. Hughes. Two weeks later, the newspaper published a letter from him: "Many thanks for the copy of the paper containing your account of that Commencement. It brought back vivid memories of a great night in my life, and a most picturesque year." [46]

The winner of silver medals for an essay and highest scholarship had more than lived up to his promise during the half century that followed.

AN EPIC NOVEL

*"While this book is offered as a novel, not a
history, I have done what I could to keep it as true
to fact as only history can be, while making it as
true to life as only fiction can be."*

Rupert Hughes was never reluctant to debate historians whose opinions
differed from his, but at times the truth was difficult to determine. Early
in 1938 he confessed to Max Farrand of the Henry E. Huntington Library: "I
should love to talk with you sometime about your interpretations. You say you
differ with me upon some of mine. That is not strange, as I differ with myself
from day to day; but I should value your wise and learned comments." [1]

In writing about current events, Hughes often viewed them from the
standpoint of history, as in a *Liberty* essay on "Why Our Girls Won't Behave."
He wrote that women had made much progress toward emancipation that
provided greater opportunities and enabled them to compete in sports and
business. As for misbehavior:

It is self-respect, carried at times to excess, that makes so many
women prefer alliances with men they love to marriages with men
they don't. They feel it decenter to give themselves than to sell
themselves. Rather than sneak to their sins they go brazenly to them.

Sin is sin and I'm not defending it, but I do maintain that sin plus hypocrisy is two sins for one.

There's no denying that our women are not what they ought to be, but let us not forget that they never were as good as all that—or so near to it as they are today.[2]

When he wrote this piece, he was deeply immersed in one of the most important writing projects of his career: a novel whose setting was colonial New England during a period in which extreme penalties were imposed upon persons suspected of the slightest infractions of moral and religious codes. After many years of research, he had begun the first draft in 1933 or 1934.

Believing that early New England and its people had too often been portrayed as frigid and narrow, he hoped to breathe life into that era by telling the story of Seaborn Fleet, a romantic figure who rebelled against oppression in and around Boston, where he grew up in the mid-1600s. But Hughes was concerned that New Englanders might regard him as an outsider, so he enlisted the services of Clifford K. Shipton, a recognized scholar of Massachusetts history, to check the manuscript for inaccuracies or misinterpretations.[3]

The publisher was to be Charles Scribner's Sons and the editor the highly esteemed Maxwell E. Perkins, a legendary figure in publishing circles. Correspondence in the Charles Scribner's Sons Archive at the Princeton University Library reveals the painstaking manner in which Hughes brought *Stately Timber* into line with Perkins's recommendations. The first draft was a voluminous 410,000 words, jam-packed with descriptive material and episodes of Fleet's life and romances in Boston and his adventures in such places as Virginia and the Barbados. When Perkins suggested some cuts, Hughes went to work with a vengeance to reduce the verbiage.

"I have been devoting my all-days and all-nights to a furious onslaught on 'Stately Timber' with axe, crosscut saw, pruning hook, plough, sickle, scissors, and eyebrow pluckers," he wrote to Perkins on July 11, 1938. He cut more than 100,000 words and said, "Even as the sensitive author who put all those words in with so much care, I believe they are better out." He regretted a major deletion, concerning a slaveship, but thought he could use it in his next novel, which would deal with the Revolutionary War period.

Shipton, the Massachusetts history expert, at first thought some parts of *Stately Timber* were unfair to New Englanders, so Hughes changed them.

Later, Shipton suggested other alterations, and Hughes gave in without argument; now, he declared, "I fear no historical critic." And when Shipton told him his fee for the assistance, Hughes thought it too small and paid him twice that amount.[4]

In July, 1938, Hughes told Perkins that the revised manuscript would be in his hands within a few days, but a week later he sent the editor a telegram:

EXCITEMENT OVER MY NEPHEW HOWARD'S AIR RACE AND INSISTENCE BY *COSMOPOLITAN MAGAZINE* THAT I RUSH THEM A BRIEF ARTICLE ON HIM BROKE INTO MY AXE SWINGING ON STATELY TIMBER BUT IT WILL LEAVE HERE IN A FEW DAYS CORDIAL GREETINGS.

RUPERT HUGHES[5]

During the two years since setting aviation speed records, Howard had continued to win acclaim as a pilot. In 1936 he had won the Harmon Trophy and was voted the world's number one flier by the Ligue Internationale des Aviateurs.[6] He continued to make news as a rich and eligible bachelor seen with such top motion picture actresses as Ginger Rogers and Katharine Hepburn, but devoted most of his attention to designing and building airplanes. In 1937, and again the next year, he sought permission to fly around the world in a twin-engined amphibian plane, but federal officials doubted that the craft could stand such a long flight. He then attempted to win approval for an around-the-world flight in a Lockheed 14, which he equipped with three radio transmitters and two supercharged engines. Meanwhile, he drew up a new version of his will, leaving most of his estate to medical research.[7]

Even though he did not yet have an okay for the flight, he took off on July 4 for New York to make final preparations. Finally the permission came, and on July 10 the plane carrying Howard and the four-man crew lifted off at 7:20 p.m. They reached Paris sooner than predicted, but takeoff was delayed eight hours for landing strut repairs. Then, after a brief stop in Moscow they flew to Omsk in western Siberia, where they took on a large load of fuel. Ten and a half hours later they landed at Yakutsk in Siberia. Meanwhile, the American public kept up with their progress by radio and newspaper accounts, waiting anxiously for the latest news of the multimillionaire pilot and his crew.

Taking off over high mountains near Yakutsk, they flew to Fairbanks, Alaska, and on to Minneapolis. Then came the last leg, the flight to New York. Finally, at 2:37 p. m. on July 14, 1938, they landed at Floyd Bennett Field in New York, where a crowd of 25,000 cheered their arrival. With Howard at the controls all the way, they had set a record for an around-the-world flight: three days, nineteen hours, and seventeen minutes. Near pandemonium broke out when the tired, unshaven Hughes emerged from the plane.[8]

More than a million admirers lined streets the next day when he rode up Broadway in the largest ticker tape parade in Manhattan's history. This was followed by parades in other cities, including Houston. In what would be his last visit there, events included a banquet attended by relatives, boyhood friends, and civic leaders. He spent the night at the family home on Yoakum Boulevard, and the next day toured the Hughes Tool Company plant.[9]

The flight that stirred the nation and elevated Howard to heroic proportions prompted *Cosmopolitan* to ask Rupert to write an article about his amazing nephew, causing the interruption in the *Stately Timber* revisions.

By July 23, Rupert had completed not only the *Cosmopolitan* piece but had the reduced version of the *Stately Timber* manuscript on its way to Scribner's. Altogether, he had cut it by 112,000 words, and the result, he thought, was an immense improvement. Now, he told Perkins, "Heaven give you strength to wade through this shattered and splintered forest!" [10]

Having made the changes, Rupert and Pat headed for a respite at Pebble Beach and Del Monte. But soon after their return home he began receiving letters from Perkins concerning the novel. On August 25, he told the editor he had done some more slashing, although he protested slightly some suggested cuts. By his count, he had reduced the manuscript to 260,000 words from the original 410,000.[11]

When *Stately Timber* reached bookstores in February, 1939, it was a handsome volume of 638 pages, plus an Author's Note in the front. In the note, Hughes wrote:

"While this book is offered as a novel, not a history, I have done what I could to keep it as true to fact as only history can be, while making it as true to life as only fiction can be." Once again he gave credit to Pat, "For her unflagging help from the first conception of the story to the casting of its pages, I am infinitely indebted to my wife, Patterson Dial." [12]

He had devoted more time to researching and writing *Stately Timber* than to any other novel, and there is no doubt that it ranks among his best. Seaborn Fleet emerges as one of the most unforgettable characters in a Hughes book.

The critical reaction to *Stately Timber* was enthusiastic, with reviewers treating it as a major novel. Writing in the *New York Times*, Margaret Wallace said:

> Rupert Hughes brings to this colorful chronicle of the Massachusetts Bay Colony a vast experience as a story-teller, and some rather unusual personal qualifications. His abilities as a dramatic—sometimes as a melodramatic—writer have been demonstrated in scores of scenarios and short stories . . . His interest in American history, which considerably antedates the present wave of enthusiasm for historical fiction, has already gotten him the name of a notable debunker.

But, she added, it was his "host of imitators" and not Hughes who had been responsible for the worst excesses of debunking. She called *Stately Timber* historically truthful and, "as we should have expected from Mr. Hughes, a first-rate story, crammed with dramatic incident and colorful characterizations."[13]

John P. Marquand's review in *The Saturday Review of Literature* commented that in the "long and somewhat rambling book that deals with the adventures amatory and spiritual of a maladjusted and humane Bostonian named Seaborn Fleet" Hughes had "brought together studiously and realistically the exotic details of a vanished and misinterpreted period. The only social phase which he seems to have omitted is bundling."[14]

Fulton Oursler, editor-in-chief of *Liberty*, praised the novel as Hughes' greatest and said he had experienced a wide range of emotions while reading it and had felt that he was, in fact, living the life of Seaborn Fleet.[15]

Buoyed by comments from readers and booksellers, Hughes accepted invitations for speaking engagements and radio interviews, including an appearance on Rudy Vallee's broadcast. Meanwhile, *Cosmopolitan* published an excerpt from the book, and by early March sales of the novel had amounted to 5,100 copies, with many additional copies in bookstores on consignment.[16]

When Hughes told Perkins that he and Pat planned to visit New York soon, Perkins invited them to lunch in order to hear about plans for the Revolutionary War era novel. He thought that if Scribner's published it he could offer a better deal than on *Stately Timber*, in which Hughes took the risks. As things turned out, however, Pat did not feel like making the trip, so Rupert and his secretary went alone.[17]

In early May he made plans for another stay of ten to twelve days in New York. Although he had not mentioned the nature of Pat's illness, he told Perkins, "I am glad to say that my wife is so much better that she is coming with me." [18] Schedule conflicts prevented their meeting with Perkins, but at the end of May Rupert told him they might return again in late July or in August. By then, however, he had put off the writing of the Revolutionary War novel in order to work on something saleable, as he put it.[19]

Although *Stately Timber* had occupied most of his attention for a long period, he handled other writing assignments, including completion of a novel by Robert W. Chambers, whose writing he had championed in the dispute with Burton Rascoe. After Chambers's death, Hughes finished *Smoke of Battle*, the book Chambers was working on before he died. Hughes's name is not in the book, but an inscription in his handwriting, telling about his role in completing the novel, appears in a copy of the 1938 Chambers book in the Rupert Hughes collection at the University of Southern California.

Late in September, 1938, Daniel Henderson, editor of *Progress*, a Hearst house magazine, invited him to write a sketch about his longtime friend Irvin S. Cobb, and asked Cobb to prepare a similar article about Hughes. Rupert agreed, and his "Tribute to Cobb" poked fun while showing admiration for his subject. He wrote:

"We were quotes gentlemen farmers unquote in Westchester County together . . . . We are now Hollywoodsmen together, and they tell me he's a grand actor. I wood not know. And I know nothing of his formative years. But from the look of him they must have been exceedingly formative." Hughes followed these comments about the portly Cobb with more tongue-in-cheek remarks.[20]

By 1938 the name of the Writers' Club had been changed to the Authors' Club, with Rupert still the president and Cobb the honorary president. Lee Shippey, Gene Lockhart, and James Swinnerton were vice-presidents. An Advisory Board included such prominent names as Charles Chaplin, Walt Disney, Lloyd C. Douglas, Harold Lloyd, Ernst Lubitsch, and Hal E. Roach.[21]

Hughes's life at times seemed a curious contrast of scholarly research and the enjoyment of fellowship at the Authors' Club and other social and business gatherings. He appeared as toastmaster at the forty-eighth annual banquet of the Los Angeles Chamber of Commerce, a formal occasion marking the 107th anniversary of George Washington's birth. More than a thousand civic leaders and other prominent Los Angeles citizens gathered for the occasion.[22]

In another appearance, he spoke on a New York radio broadcast on behalf of 380 social service and health agencies, urging contributions to a $10 million fund campaign. He called the New York Fund a "scientific, dynamic, effective engine for the decrease of misery and the increase of happiness." He contrasted the social service effort with what had happened in the past, saying, "The more I read about the good old days the less I believe that they were so good and the gladder I am that they are old." [23]

Shortly after publication of his novel about Puritans, one of his earliest books came out in revised form. The *Music Lovers' Cyclopedia*, recognized as the standard, handy reference book on music, had sold nearly 100,000 copies, but he had been unable to find time to update it. To fill the need, Doubleday invited music critic and composer Deems Taylor to work with Russell Kerr, associate editor of the *Musical Courier*, to revise the book. In doing so, they mainly provided additional biographical information about composers and musicians and described operas and other musical compositions written since publication of the earlier editions. The resulting book had a slightly different title: *Music Lovers' Encyclopedia*. Credit was given on the cover, dust jacket, and title page: "Compiled by Rupert Hughes. Completely revised and newly edited by Deems Taylor and Russell Kerr." [24]

Taylor and Kerr retained, and in some cases revised, the charts and tables Hughes had prepared. Such items were useful, wrote Taylor—"particularly the table showing the pronunciation of the various letters of the alphabet as they occur in sixteen modern languages. There may be a similar chart published elsewhere; if there is, I am unfamiliar with it."

They also kept, verbatim, Hughes's prefatory "An Introduction to Music," and Deems Taylor explained the reason:

Mr. Hughes, who is chiefly known to the world as a novelist, is a musical amateur in the finest sense of the word, a music-lover who has studied and practiced the art of music all his life, purely for the fun of it. To realise that profound scholarship can be coexistent with an amateur standing, you have only to read his chapter. Naturally the science of music has progressed . . . . Nevertheless the *fundamentals* of music remain constant, and almost any literate and intelligent lay music-lover should be able to obtain the foundation of a music education by reading this *Introduction to Music*. Written thirty-five years ago, it remains a sound and useful little treatise.[25]

A trade edition, differing from the Doubleday version only in its binding, was also published in 1939 by Garden City Publishing Company.

The *Subscription Books Bulletin* recommended the *Music Lovers' Encyclopedia* as "a handbook for the personal library of the individual interested in music," and "for supplementary purposes in the public library, where its pronouncing feature should be especially valuable." According to the *Boston Transcript* reviewer, "For an up-to-date book of reference in a single volume it will be hard to surpass." [26]

In 1940, Blue Ribbon Books, Inc., published a major part of the *Encyclopedia* as a separate book, *The Biographical Dictionary of Musicians*. It contains the revised biographical sketches plus Hughes's pronouncing dictionary, table of pronunciations in sixteen languages, and list of abbreviations.[27]

Hughes's attention during the final year of the 1930s was not directed toward a novel about the Revolutionary War period, as he had planned, nor did he complete a volume about Washington. Instead, he wrote about the recent past and a different personality—the crusading district attorney of New York County. He had in mind what he had mentioned to Maxwell Perkins: something saleable.

That a market existed for his biography of the crime-fighting Thomas E. Dewey there seemed no doubt. Several publishers expressed an interest in a book about the popular Dewey, who, despite his comparative youth, was being talked about as a possible Republican candidate for the nation's presidency. At age thirty-seven the Michigan-born Dewey had established a notable record in prosecuting crime figures while he was United States attorney for the Southern District of New York and later a special prosecutor and then New York County district attorney.

In an introduction to *Attorney for the People: The Story of Thomas E. Dewey*, Hughes pointed to Dewey's accomplishments, organizational skills, and eloquence as qualities that had made him the subject of consideration for the presidency.[28] The biography is a fascinating tale of racketeer-fighting in

New York and other places. Detailed descriptions of celebrated cases, such as the prosecution of "Lucky" Luciano, are provided, and although the author lets the facts speak for themselves and does not unduly glorify his subject, Dewey emerges as a highly admirable attorney for the people.

The book was a rush job for Hughes, who in 1939 made frequent trips to New York for lengthy talks with Dewey and his top staff members. When Maxwell Perkins learned what he was working on, he asked to see the manuscript for possible publication by Scribner's. But there were problems in this. Fulton Oursler, who had invited Hughes to write a Dewey biography for serialization in *Liberty*, had read the first 35,000 words and was anxious to publish the serial as soon as possible. Publisher Houghton Mifflin also wanted a look at the manuscript.

Hughes told Perkins there were some strings attached to the biography: "Dewey not only has the final say on it but on the publishing house. His uncle was a vice president of Houghton Mifflin for many years. Furthermore it is understood that after the book is published, a condensed version of it may be used without royalty in case a campaign biography is desired for public release by the party." In addition, another publisher planned an unauthorized biography of Dewey by another author, thus making the timing of the Hughes book more urgent. For those reasons, Rupert doubted that Perkins would want to enter into "such a helter-skelter arrangement." But as soon as he finished the Dewey book, he said, he intended to get to work on the Revolutionary War novel.[29]

Although the arrangements with Dewey and Houghton Mifflin could have jeopardized the objectivity of the biography, Hughes apparently did not feel restricted in writing his version of Dewey's life. By the time the book was published the two had developed a mutual admiration that grew into a life-long friendship.

The speed with which Hughes could produce a manuscript was evident when "Attorney for the People: The Life Story of Thomas E. Dewey" was rushed into print by *Liberty*. When the first weekly installment was published on October 21, 1939, the magazine's front cover heralded it as a "great biography."

The Houghton Mifflin book, with the slightly shorter title of *Attorney for the People: The Story of Thomas E. Dewey*, was in bookstores within months and was reviewed shortly after the first of the year. The *New York Times* reviewer, who remarked that if Republicans decided to nominate

Dewey for president they undoubtedly could count on a vote from Hughes, called the book a "sympathetic, lively and lucid narrative." [30]

The *New Yorker* critic described it as "colorful, journalistic, and shrewd writing, intended to show that Dewey's experience is broad enough to fit him for national office," but there was some disappointment on the part of Hughes's own college fraternity publication, the *Delta Upsilon Quarterly*. It called the book an interesting campaign document but said the reviewer "is left with deep regret that Brother Hughes should turn from Washington whose greatness was beyond question, to a public figure whose real greatness is still to be proved." [31]

Ever since Hitler's forces invaded Poland on September 1, 1938, and England and France declared war against Germany two days later, there had been much talk about possible U.S. involvement in another world war. Hughes followed such events closely and expressed his opinion about them, based upon his military experience and knowledge of history.

On February 18, 1940, when the *New York Times Magazine* published his full-page article on "Washington—and 'Entangling Alliances,'" he recalled the views expressed by the nation's first president and related them to world events taking place at the beginning of the 1940s. He quoted Washington as saying, "The most sincere neutrality is not a sufficient guard against the depredations of nations at war." [32]

A month later, a *Liberty* article by Hughes strongly condemned those persons in the United States who supported causes detrimental to American freedom. Titled "When Tolerance Is Treason," it warned that the nation's ideals were protecting the very people who aimed to destroy them.

Rupert wrote that nobody believed more completely than he in "free thought, speech, and press, and in universal tolerance." But now, "I am beginning to wonder if tolerance of the intolerant is not treason." He had come to this point only after speaking at a meeting of the Steuben Society about Baron von Steuben's Revolutionary War contributions. Shocked to find members saluting each other with "Heil Hitler," he reminded them that a Jew, Haym Salomon, had saved Steuben from starvation and said he doubted that they really believed in "such imaginary nonsense as an Aryan race." Hughes learned later that one Nazi had to be restrained from trying to throw him out.

He argued that those claiming the right of free speech and free press to propound Nazism or Communism should be asked if their philosophies include the same rights. And then: "No? Then you shall not have freedom here. You shall have the gag and the cell and, if need be, the death that you would mete out to those who disagree with you," he declared.[33]

This patriotic message stirred hundreds of readers to write letters of praise for his point of view. *Liberty* published eight of them in its May 18 issue, including one urging that the article be published on the front page of every newspaper in the United States. The Vox Pop editor remarked that the response showed "which way the wind blows." [34]

Hughes's belief in the need to protect and nurture the ideals and freedoms upon which the nation had been founded was expressed in essays and speeches on the subject, and in a stirring song, "Our Forever United States," published a year earlier by Robbins Music Corporation.

Although the war in Europe and growing tension in the United States brought to a standstill his work on the George Washington book, he told John Corbin on June 14, 1940: "When this war is over, if ever, I hope to get on with my biography. I have thousands of notes and an enormous library collected, but I don't seem able to get the leisure to devote uninterruptedly to the shaping and selection and writing of the infinite material." [35]

Indeed, Hughes would find himself back in uniform without any progress being made on the Washington biography.

Rupert Hughes'
SOULS FOR SALE

Eleanor Boardman

Frank Mayo

Lew Cody

Mae Busch

Richard Dix

Barbara La Marr

She waited breathlessly for the next move of the intruder.

A Goldwyn Picture

CHAPTER TWENTY-FOUR

BACK IN UNIFORM

*"Here nobody is so humble that he may not aspire to
the peaks. I am as good as anybody, but no better."*

While becoming increasingly concerned about U.S. military unpreparedness, Hughes put finishing touches on a novel that was much different
from the one he had written about Colonial New England.

A modern narrative about Los Angeles, it told the story of a handsome
lifeguard who saves a businessman from drowning; the resulting publicity
leads to a movie contract for the rescuer, followed by his meteoric rise to
stardom and a studio-inspired romance that competes with his real love for
another girl.

Rupert knew that most fiction about Hollywood had been written as
satire, while the rest of the Los Angeles area had been ignored. Believing
that better treatment was deserved, he began writing a serial about the metropolitan area for *Cosmopolitan*, but halfway through got sidetracked with
the Dewey biography. Then the magazine editors decided they would prefer
publishing a short version of the Los Angeles story in a single issue.

Convinced that the tale should cover a wider scope, Hughes sent the
entire manuscript to Maxwell Perkins, explaining that it was based on actual
occurrences and that "the inside workings of the studios and the various people in the factory are taken from real and reel life as I have known them so

well and so long." [1] Perkins readily accepted the novel for publication by Scribner's, offering a ten percent royalty on the first 3,000 copies sold, with the usual fifteen percent above that number.[2] Rupert agreed to the terms, saying, "If it doesn't sell there is misery enough for all; if it does, glory enough. And as you suggest, Hitler may be in the White House by 1941."

The selection of an appropriate title for the novel baffled Hughes, his wife, and Perkins. At times both he and Pat liked "Los Angeles" or the original working title of "The Los Angelesians," but at other times he preferred "The City of Angels" or "The Lights o' Los Angeles." [3]

Finally, when Charles Scribner's Sons published the book in January, 1941, it bore the title *City of Angels*. "Glamour Boy," the shorter version, had already appeared in *Cosmopolitan*, and permission had been granted for the Illinois School for the Blind to reproduce it in braille.[4] At some point, Hughes also wrote the words and music for a song called "City of Angels." [5]

Rupert was delighted with the novel's physical appearance, except for the back of the dust jacket. He told Perkins, "I seriously feel that anyone who might be tempted by the front of the jacket or even the contents would be frightened off by a glimpse of the terrible and fatuous face on the rear." He hated to overwork the editor's generosity, "but if the chance should arise to change the jacket, please put almost anything there except my face." [6]

Margaret Wallace of the *New York Times* noted that the plot, though seemingly improbable, was based on fact. As for Warren Thorburn, "the idolized glamour boy turned overnight into the derided pretty boy," she said that Hughes was "too good a screen writer to leave things at this. A natural disaster in the final reel—which probably is being filmed already—helps Mr. Thorburn out considerably here," she added.[7]

In *City of Angels* Hughes provided his views on the international situation and the need for preparedness. One character in the book, a U. S. Navy admiral, predicts that Los Angeles "will be the plague spot of our next war, which will probably be with Japan." [8]

It was the war in Europe that put a halt to Hughes's work on the Revolutionary War novel. He wondered now if he would ever get around to writing it, but this uncertainty was not due to a lack of desire to complete the project. "The material is collected and the plot pretty clear," he told Perkins, "but I cannot abide the thought of writing or publishing at this time a story in which England plays the villain." [9]

Deeply concerned about the threats to the free world, he saw the need for a substantial buildup of U. S. defenses and was determined to do what he could to help. And so, at the age of sixty-eight, Lt. Colonel Rupert Hughes of the U. S. Army Reserves, who had enlisted in the New York National Guard forty-three years earlier, turned his efforts toward the founding of the California State Guard. Soon the Guard would occupy most of his time, but now he maintained a heavy schedule that was typical of his usual activity.

His concern for the future of the world was expressed as one of a hundred prominent writers who signed an Authors' Manifesto in opposition to the Hitler regime. Stating that writers had been among the first to "feel the growing darkness" of Nazism, the manifesto called for immediate aid for the embattled Britain.[10]

There were refrains of freedom, too, in a memorial inscription Rupert wrote in 1941 after the death of a friend, the renowned sculptor Gutzon Borglum, whose most notable work was the Mount Rushmore Memorial in South Dakota, portraying the heads of four U.S. presidents.

Borglum, who years earlier had praised a piece of sculpture by Hughes and had created a tribute to Adelaide, was one of the "immortals" buried in the Memorial Court of Honor in the Great Mausoleum at Forest Lawn Memorial Park, Glendale, California. A plaque in memory is inscribed:

GUTZON BORGLUM
1871—SCULPTOR—1941

His birthplace was Idaho. California first taught him art. Then France who first gave him fame. His genius for the exquisite as well as the colossal gave permanence in bronze and marble to moods of beauty or passion, to figures of legend and history. As patriot he stripped corruption bare. As statesman he toiled for equality in the rights of man. At last he carved a mountain for a monument. He made the mountain chant: "Remember! These giant souls set America free and kept her free. Hold fast your sacred heritage. Americans: Remember! Remember!"

RUPERT HUGHES
Author[11]

On February 11, 1941, the American Academy of Public Affairs presented Hughes with the Award of Merit, 1939-41, for "outstanding public service as founder of the California State Guard."[12] Within a few months, on May 2, he was commissioned a colonel and put in command of the Second Regiment of the California State Infantry,[13] a Guard unit, after having served as inspector general. From then on, he devoted nearly all of his time to the buildup of volunteer forces.

In keeping with his belief in the equality of women, he wrote an article titled "Shall We Have a Woman's National Guard?" that was highlighted on the front cover of *Liberty* magazine.[14] In "The End of Hitler," an article in the September, 1941, issue of *Esquire*, Hughes declared that no punishment could fit Hitler's crimes and warned that unhappy deaths had befallen "other conquerors, greater than he."

In a remarkable sense of timing, the December, 1941, issue of *The American* magazine published a short essay by Hughes entitled "I Am an American." Accompanying the essay were his portrait and a description of him as a "versatile American—novelist, dramatist, song writer, motion picture director, Army officer." Hughes stated that American ideals had been instilled in him in early childhood and in competition for a livelihood, and he declared that "here nobody is so humble that he may not aspire to the peaks. I am as good as anybody, but no better."

Government, he said, was the protector of its citizens. "I am a part of it and owe it my allegiance and my service." He urged:

Let this then be our vow:
By the blood that stained the snow of Valley Forge, and crimsoned the seas, the prairies, and the mountains; by the voices that cried "Liberty or Death;" by the inspired documents that make our history; by the graves of our heroes and heroines; we swear to uphold our country in our lives and defend it with our lives, that we may earn from those who come after us the gratitude and the honor we owe to those who went this way before us.[15]

The vow was real for Hughes, who was determined to devote his all, if necessary, to his beloved country. And by the time the Japanese attack on Pearl Harbor stunned the nation on December 7—within days after the *American* article was published—he had been a regimental commander for more than five months, striving to make ready the ill-prepared forces under his command.

Although many Americans in 1941 seemed oblivious of the signs of impending trouble, others—including some in the film industry—led double lives, as Jesse L. Lasky, Jr., son of the pioneer film producer, put it in his 1975 book *Whatever Happened to Hollywood?* After working all day as an MGM scriptwriter, he would drive to the Los Angeles Armory to don the uniform of an enlisted man in the Second Regiment California State Infantry. Somehow it seemed unreal to write escapist film scripts and then rush off "to present arms to our ancient colonel, Rupert Hughes, otherwise a renowned novelist. And knowing there was not one single cartridge in the whole regiment!"

In order for the Guardsmen to learn what war was like, Lasky recalled, Colonel Hughes "somehow contrived to get a few rounds of live ammunition, which I suppose he paid for himself, and complex logistics were worked out to portage a few hundred of us into the Mojave Desert for a weekend of bivouacking and maneuvers."

The scene from then on, as Lasky described it, had elements of hilarity. Everyone thought the first sergeant was joking when he solemnly announced on Sunday morning that the Japanese Air Force had sunk the American fleet at Pearl Harbor and that their regiment had been ordered back to Los Angeles, where "the fate of Southern California may rest in our hands." Not until they turned on the radio did they believe the truth.[16]

With war against Japan a reality in the wake of the Pearl Harbor attack, the importance of the volunteer forces of the Guard became apparent, despite their unpreparedness for battle. There remained the possibility of a Japanese attack on the West Coast. The responsibilities of Colonel Hughes increased substantially on April 9, 1942, when he was placed in command of all California State Guard troops in southern California, with eight regiments in the southern division reporting to him. It was more than a full-time job for the seventy-year-old Hughes.

In September, 1942, he described his demanding schedule in a letter to Bernhard Knollenberg, Yale University librarian. He told what it was like to command eight regiments with "thousands of men on guard at bridges, dams and defense plants scattered through mountains, deserts and cities. Motor trips of two days and two nights do not suffice to visit the remotest of them." He added, "Last night was the first night I have slept at home for nearly six months." As for the future, "I still hope to finish the biography, then go over it and correct the many blunders and stupidities, and add new light thrown on the subjects by later publications such as your fine volume."[17]

At some point Hughes found time to write a chapter about George

Washington for *There Were Giants in the Land*, a 1942 book published by Farrar & Rinehart, Inc., consisting of essays, written at the request of the United States Treasury Department, by twenty-eight well-known writers to pay tribute to an equal number of "giants of the past." The purpose, Treasury Secretary Henry Morgenthau, Jr., wrote in the introduction, was to show the manner in which each of the described men and women had met a crisis with a brave and bold decision.[18]

The book, the frontispiece of which was a portrait of Washington, included essays by Stephen Vincent Benet, Alexander Woollcott, Carl Van Doren, Carl Sandburg, and other noted authors. The Hughes chapter reminded readers that "Washington had his Pearl Harbor—whole series of Pearl Harbors" and had faced problems of untrained and ill-equipped forces: "When Washington took command at Boston in 1775, he inquired how much powder there was. When he heard how little, he nearly fainted." [19]

While on duty with the Guard, Hughes received less public attention than at any time for years. An exception was a portrait in *Better Homes and Gardens* for February, 1942, to illustrate Sigmund Spaeth's article on "You Can Make Music." The picture showed him at a piano, with a cigar jutting from his mouth; the caption read: "Rupert Hughes has done more than most, having composed several songs." And, too, the 1941 edition of *Missouri, a Guide to the "Show Me" State*, an *American Guide Series* book, included references to Hughes and his accomplishments, with a description of his birthplace as a point of interest on a tour of the state.[20] But no motion pictures were made from his stories during this period, nor were any new Hughes novels published. Anyone who knew him, however, could predict that this relative dearth of material would not continue for long—only until his wartime responsibilities would come to an end.

That point was reached early in 1943, when he resigned his military command at the age of seventy-one. During the two years of his command, even though he was stationed in California instead of a faraway land, he had spent little time at home and had slept in an armory almost every night for at least a year. But now, instead of retiring to a life of leisure when his military duty ended, he plunged immediately into an entirely new phase of his career.

Having had experience in radio broadcasting while emceeing the Camel Caravan, he eagerly accepted an invitation from the National Broadcasting

Company to do a weekly commentary on national and world affairs. The show was to be broadcast on Sundays (at 1 p. m., New York time) beginning in April, 1943.[21] After many years on the lecture circuit, he now was assured of a national audience.

His correspondence reflected his thinking on internationalism and the possibility of world government—topics about which he would continue to speak and write. He agreed with a woman who wrote to him that most Americans opposed the internationalists, but he was surprised that more of them did not speak up. "We cannot have too many or too loud voices to drown out those who would sell us out, or give us away," he told her.[22]

To those with opposing views, such as H. C. F. Bell, a history professor at Wesleyan University in Connecticut who advocated a League of Nations, he explained his position: "The history of the world is packed with leagues and federations pledged to perpetual peace. None of them lasted. All of them fomented jealousies and feuds." [23]

No less pronounced were his opinions on the need for military preparedness, as expressed in an essay, "M-Day Was Two Years Ago." Pointing to the need for more anti-aircraft guns, airplanes, tanks, and other equipment, he urged: "Mobilize! Mobilize! Mobilize!" [24]

Meanwhile, his radio broadcasts brought such a wave of approving letters that he told Maxwell Perkins he would like to write a book stating the reasons he opposed a world alliance. "Practically nobody is standing up for the continued separateness of our country," he said. "I have never been an isolationist when it came to trade or to war. But I opposed our entry into the League of Nations . . . . I believe that any attempt at a permanent world-alliance would only hasten the next war." [25]

He enclosed two pages of brief excerpts from favorable letters he and the network had received. Some of the comments were:

The most remarkable and inspiring speech I ever heard. Courage, common sense, and the attribute for which you are so famous—humor . . . .

Such subtle humor, such conservation of words! I have heard Roosevelt, Churchill, Wilson years ago; but they are dwarfed . . . .

Almost every one I know listens to you. You open amazing new vistas for thought . . . .

Why, oh, why don't we have somebody in Congress like you?[26]

A cordial reply from Perkins encouraged him to move ahead on the book.[27] But although he had thought it would be easy to write, he was unable to devote sufficient attention to it just then.

Although his reputation was increasingly that of a conservative, he went on record on national radio as favoring the passage by Congress of an Equal Rights Amendment to the United States Constitution. The endorsement brought praise from a leader in the women's rights movement.[28] But Hughes's efforts and those of others in favor were decades ahead of the required endorsement by the states, a majority of which had still failed to ratify such an amendment by the 1990s.

Much of his writing now was devoted to radio scripts and responding to correspondence about his commentaries. It is difficult to know what he wrote in 1943 or in any other year, because many of his manuscripts bear no evidence as to when they were written. But it is known that a short book he wrote, *His Fabulous Fortune*, was published by Jarrolds in London in 1943.[29]

He also wrote *In a Blaze of Glory*, a novel syndicated to metropolitan newspapers with a total circulation in the millions. It appeared in fourteen weekly installments beginning October 10.[30] It is the story of a small-town girl who goes to Hollywood determined to meet stars and to spend in a "blaze of glory" the wealth she has inherited from her father. But she donates her inheritance instead to Hollywood's patriotic causes intended to support the war effort. In love with an Army sergeant, she is accused of a murder and becomes a blackmail victim, but by then she has no money left.

It seems the sort of tale that could be made into a movie, and Rupert wrote a proposal for such a film, saying that it would tell an interesting and romantic story while providing an understanding of the motion picture industry's enormous contribution to the war effort.[31] There is no evidence that the picture was made, but Hughes's attempt to sell the idea showed that he was still a champion of Hollywood and thought it important to depict what the film community was doing to support the nation's fighting men.

His recent years in uniform had required him to be away from Pat most of the time, and it was good to be back home again. The armory and outposts had not compared with the luxury of the Los Feliz mansion or with the elegant and dignified New York hotels in which the couple often had spent weeks at a time.

He regarded Pat as a partner in his research and writing, and valued her judgment and discerning eye in checking facts and proofreading. Unlike Adelaide, who had been listed as co-author of some films, Pat had not been credited as a co-author of any of Rupert's motion pictures or fiction, although he often acknowledged her assistance. As with Adelaide, however, he encouraged her in her own writing.

While Adelaide's ambitions had run to poetry, Pat preferred to write short stories, for which she had begun to achieve recognition more than a dozen years earlier—almost immediately after her first story was published in *American Magazine* in February, 1931. Called "Putty in a Woman's Hands," it was illustrated with a photo of the author. An editor's note told how the story had come about:

One day not so long ago I sat down at luncheon with Rupert Hughes and his charming wife, who once was Patterson Dial. We talked of this and that, mostly of six-day bicycle races, which Mrs. Hughes adores. Incidentally—and most incidentally—Mrs. Hughes mentioned her interest in young folk of college age. And from that incidental remark sprang this story, the very first Mrs. Hughes ever wrote; and it is the first of several stories about Emmy and her young friends which you are to enjoy in *The American Magazine*.

The Editor[32]

After the Emmy stories, there had been numerous others in national magazines—some intended for adult readers and others for young people, such as "The Great Theodosia Plot" published in *Scholastic*; it was one in a series of Isabelle stories that appeared in *This Week*, a Sunday magazine distributed with leading newspapers.[33] By then Pat had become known not only as Mrs. Rupert Hughes, the novelist's wife and a former silent screen actress, but as an author of importance in her own right. This pleased her husband exceedingly.

Rupert had not been close to other members of his immediate family for many years, with the exception of his brother Felix. However, he kept in touch, sending occasional letters and inscribed photos to Elspeth and sometimes birthday gifts to his granddaughters, who were all in their teens by the time the United States entered the war. While their grandfather was still in uniform, the eldest, Agnes Christine Lapp, nearly nineteen, was married on November 24, 1942, to George W. Roberts.[34]

Rush Hughes, meanwhile, had appeared in the 1938 motion picture *Love and Hisses*, and in 1939 had become host of the NBC radio program "Pot O' Gold," featuring the orchestra of Horace Heidt and His Musical Knights—a game show in which phone calls were made to listeners, who were given a chance to answer questions and win money. In 1944 Rush would join the cast of the popular Danny Kaye show on CBS as a featured player.[35]

Felix's wife, the former Ruth Stonehouse of the silent screen, had died on May 12, 1941, of a cerebral hemorrhage at age forty-eight.[36] After that, Felix and Rupert continued to see each other often. Their interest in music was a strong bond, and they had many of the same friends in the film community and in the arts. Felix, however, was more active in athletics than Rupert, playing golf regularly and bringing home tournament trophies and awards.

On October 22, 1943, the handsome Felix, at the age of sixty-nine, married Ruby Helen (McCoy) Parrott in a ceremony in Santa Ana, California.[37] It was the start of a life together that she later would describe as "one of the most beautiful, contented, inspirational, and happy marriages any one could desire or hope to have." [38] Although she was considerably younger than Felix, they had much in common. Her intelligence, modesty, and graciousness were in keeping with his personality traits that had helped him become such a popular and effective teacher.

Ruby met Rupert for the first time on the day of her wedding and became better acquainted two nights later when he and Patty invited the newlyweds to dinner. From the start, Ruby felt at home with her new in-laws; it was obvious to her that they were close and that Patty understood her husband completely. Rupert, she thought, seemed "a very warm person. You felt like you knew him." [39]

As Rupert grew older, his brother and Ruby would become increasingly important in his life.

CHAPTER TWENTY-FIVE

THE DIFFICULT YEARS

"I hope you are having no more pain and weariness than your bravery can take care of, and I wonder at your sweet cheerfulness. All my love to you, darling child. Your devoted Daddy."

The favorable reaction to his radio broadcasts continued to be an amazement to Hughes. School teachers reported that the programs dealing with history proved useful as classroom teaching aids; the American Economic Foundation printed a thousand copies of one broadcast; and there was talk of producing a series of recordings by Rupert for radio airing and use in schools. In April of 1944 he assured Maxwell Perkins that he still hoped to visit with him about the possibility that Scribner's might publish a volume "along the line of my Gospels."

More importantly, however, he wanted Perkins to take a look at a short novel Patterson had written. In Rupert's view, the tale about a boy who grows up to become a war hero compared favorably with Mark Twain's *Tom Sawyer*. He reminded Perkins that Pat's short stories had been immensely popular and that magazine editors had asked for more than she had been able to write—"in her cautious and conservative spirit." The editor of *This Week*, he said, considered her "the female Booth Tarkington." [1]

There was no decision about the novel for nearly two months, but when it came Pat made the best of it, telling Perkins: "Your letter rejecting my story cheered me up more than an acceptance from some other house. I never thought I'd live to see the day when I'd receive a kind word from you about my writing. Again may I tell you how extremely gracious it was of you to read the manuscript and how grateful I am." [2]

There is no doubt that her appreciation of kind words from Perkins was genuine, but the rejection of the manuscript must have been a considerable disappointment. As Rupert had indicated, she was careful in her writing and held herself to high standards.

His own idea of writing a book about the folly of world government never reached fruition, but he continued with his radio commentaries as World War II wore on during the remainder of the year.

In his personal life during this period, Rupert grew closer to his daughter, Elspeth, as evidenced by their correspondence during 1944 and 1945. Just as he had called upon his own father for help when it was needed most, Elspeth and her husband, Edward Lapp, found it necessary to ask for assistance. There had been other such requests in the past, which Hughes had granted, and now it was a matter of Elspeth's health that caused Ed to seek his father-in-law's financial support.

There were indications early in 1944 that Elspeth was ill, and Rupert wrote her a cheerful letter telling her that while in Bakersfield addressing a women's political club he had met a woman who had known her years earlier at the National Cathedral School in Washington, D. C.[3]

Rupert's second granddaughter, Elspeth Summerlin Lapp, at the age of nineteen, married John De Pould on July 8, 1944.[4] In his correspondence with her, the grandfather called her "Sis," "Sister," or "Beth," to distinguish her from her mother. At times, when thanking a granddaughter for a gift sent to him at Christmas or some other time, he would protest that he was unworthy of such attention. Most often he signed his letters "Gramps." [5]

With the earlier marriage of Agnes Christine, known as Chris, and now that of Beth, the only one of his grandchildren still single was the youngest, Barbara. In the fall of 1944 she became ill, and Rupert helped out with her medical bills.[6]

His sympathetic nature became evident when he sent messages of consolation and cheer to friends who met with tragedy or losses.

Such it was when the wife of novelist Lloyd C. Douglas died. He wrote to Douglas on December 31, 1944:

"My heart aches for you in your heartbreaking loss. It has been a cruel ordeal for you to be so ill yourself for so long, and to be tortured with anxiety and grief for your dearly beloved. No one has less deserved such double affliction." [7]

Meanwhile, Rupert's own wife had suffered bouts of illness from time to time and had started taking a sedative in 1944 to enable her to sleep after spending long hours at her writing. According to Rupert, at times she worked so hard that she became overwrought, and although the medicine seemed to help, he often became concerned about her well-being. [8]

It was on such a night, on March 23, 1945, that he came home from a lecture at about 10:30 p. m., at which time he visited for awhile with Patty. She said she was tired after having spent much of the day in the garden, doing some pruning and routine landscaping. But she seemed to be in a good frame of mind when she told him she planned to take a sleeping pill in order to have a good night's rest.

As usual, he went to his study to do some writing and remained there until about 3:30 in the morning, but before retiring he looked in on her and saw that she was sleeping. She looked a little pale, so he felt her pulse, which seemed "vibrant, almost racing," but he thought nothing of it and went to bed in his own room.

About six hours later, a maid stopped by where his wife had been sleeping—in a room painted dark blue—and discovered that she was unconscious. An ambulance was summoned immediately to take her to Hollywood Receiving Hospital, and the alarmed Rupert followed close behind in a friend's car. But before they reached the hospital his beloved Patty had died.

Stunned at the news, he told reporters at the hospital that he was certain that the death of his forty-two-year-old wife was accidental: "She couldn't have planned to take her own life, as we had made plans for today and only a few hours before she had seemed in the best of spirits."

Newspapers headlined the news of the tragic death with such captions as the *Los Angeles Times*'s "Sleeping Pills End Life of Rupert Hughes' Wife." A published photo showed the grieving Rupert looking dazed, with hair awry, cigar in one hand and coffee cup in the other, as he sat in the hospital giving his view of what had happened.

"She had no fear of death," he said, "and occasionally remarked that she was ready to pass on at any time," but had never threatened suicide. Even when she had become moody and depressed because she thought her writing did not meet her own high standards, she had "always brightened up."

Police were puzzled as to whether the death was accidental or a suicide, according to the *Times* report, which noted that her passing broke up a well-known writing team. It added that "Hughes called her his 'right arm,' saying she aided him in his own work, as well as carrying on her own." [9]

The *New York Times* stated the decision as to whether an inquest would be held was delayed until after an autopsy was performed. [10] But the autopsy failed to reveal the cause of death, the coroner reported. He announced that further inquiry would be made to determine the strength of the sedative she had taken, but ruled that no inquest would be conducted and that the body could be released for burial. [11]

The death certificate stated that the death was an accident, caused by barbiturate poisoning. [12]

Arrangements were made for Patty's body to be cremated and for the remains to be inurned in a niche in the Columbarium of Memory section, not far from the "Last Supper" stained glass window, in the Great Mausoleum at Forest Lawn Memorial Park, Glendale. In making the necessary decisions at such a time of grief, Rupert showed an ability to cope that was an inspiration to his new sister-in-law. The shock of Patty's death was sudden, Ruby Hughes later recalled, "but I learned a lesson from the way Rupert handled it. He didn't get hysterical. He had command over everything that had to be done. It was a good lesson to learn." [13]

The difficult times that followed were indicated in a letter he wrote to Ed Lapp in response to a letter of condolence. Rupert appreciated the sympathy, as well as offers from granddaughters "Sister" and "Bobbie" to come to Los Angeles to help out.

"There is nothing anybody can do," Rupert said. "Physically, I seem to be able to take care of everything that comes and am extremely fit except for overwhelming mental depression. I keep busy because there are so many things that have to be done."

He told Ed, "The colored man who has been with us for twenty years is still here and his wife gets the meals and takes care of the house," and as for himself, "I seem to be made of leather and iron and am not worth fretting over." He asked Ed to "please consider this a letter to Elspeth as well as to you, and read it to her with my dearest love." [14]

Less than a week later came the news that President Franklin Roosevelt had died of a cerebral hemorrhage in Warm Springs, Georgia. As the nation mourned his loss and the world wondered what sort of President the relatively unknown Harry Truman would make, Rupert went on the air with an NBC broadcast on Saturday, April 21, attempting to put the matter into perspective.

He applauded Truman's speech to the nation and predicted that "this Truman of Missouri is not saying 'Show me!' He is going to show *us*—show us the way back into the old high-road that led us to our present glory, under leaders who felt themselves the servants of the people, and whose highest pride was their lofty humility." [15]

Although the optimistic tone of the broadcast gave no hint of sorrow over the loss of his wife or concern about his daughter's illness, the intensity of his mourning was evident in a letter he wrote the same day to Elspeth. Addressing her as "Dear Elspethkins," he promised to stop in Cleveland to see her on Wednesday, May 2, on his way to New York. He looked forward to the visit "after so long a time and after so many cruel sufferings for both of us." He signed his letter: " . . . always with oceans of love, dear sweet child, I am your worthless old Daddy". [16]

After the visit took place, other letters to "Dearest Elspethkins" followed in quick succession. She was about five and a half years older than Patty had been when she died, and would soon have her forty-eighth birthday. The knowledge that she was growing weaker, coupled with his deep sense of loss over his wife's death, brought him much closer to his daughter, as revealed in a letter he wrote her on May 6 from the Gotham Hotel in New York:

For a long time it looked as if I would never get to Cleveland to see you. Then suddenly the opportunity and the necessity for this trip arose and I had the sweet privilege of an hour with you after long years of separation.

It grieved me deeply to find you in bed and undergoing so great a martyrdom; but I was immensely comforted to find you so brave and philosophical about your terrific ordeal and still able to laugh and be the gay and defiant Elspeth of old.

I am proud of you and you ought to have a medal of honor with a purple heart for putting up such a good fight . . . .

It is too early to say just when I can get back to Cleveland since it is almost impossible to get near a railroad train these days; but I have asked for tickets leaving here May 27th on a Sunday, and stopping over in Cleveland on Monday, the 28th, so you'd better postpone your plans for doing a good day's washing on that day, though something may turn up to change my plans . . . .

So save your strength for May 28th and we will have another chat. Certain possibilities have arisen already here to make it probable that I shall have to return East again before very long; so I am counting on being almost a commuter to Cleveland.

All love to you, my brave darling.

Your devoted
Daddy[17]

These were days of excitement and anticipation for the United States and the free world, as events moved rapidly toward the end of war in Europe. Allied armies were closing in on the Germans, and demands were being made for surrender on all fronts. In late April, news of Italian dictator Mussolini's execution was followed by the suicide of Hitler. Then, on May 2, Berlin fell to the invading Russian forces.

Within two days after Hughes's letter to Elspeth telling of his plans to visit her again, the Germans surrendered unconditionally and the free world celebrated V-E Day. Rupert went on the air on Sunday in a debate on the network radio program "Wake Up America," then penned a long letter to his daughter, full of joy at the news from Europe and expressing hope that Japan would surrender before long. He warned, however, that the Russians seemed determined to make things difficult for everyone.

In telling Elspeth about his broadcast praising Truman, he recalled having been the toastmaster at a Los Angeles banquet honoring Truman and members of the Senate's Truman Committee. He added that he was amazed recently to get a letter from the White House in which President Truman thanked him for his comments on the radio and said he would never forget their "very pleasant visit" in Los Angeles. In Rupert's opinion, "He has done wonderfully well and has saved the country from dismay and disunity . . . . It only goes to show that what we really needed in the White House was somebody from Missouri. Thank God, it's not me."

Hughes told Elspeth that Governor Dewey had telephoned him after hearing about Pat's death and had invited him for a visit in Albany. Rupert planned to spend a night there before stopping in Cleveland on the return trip to Los Angeles. But now he was uncertain when that would be, for it was getting more difficult to book transportation now that the Army was disbanding so quickly.

> I hope you are having no more pain and weariness than your bravery can take care of, and I wonder at your sweet cheerfulness. All my love to you, darling child.
>
> Your devoted Daddy.[18]

Apparently that was to be his last letter to his "Dearest Elspethkins." On May 14, however, he wrote to Ed Lapp and asked for a suggestion as to what sort of gift he could send for her birthday, coming up on May 23.[19] But just a day after his note to Ed, Elspeth died, scarcely a week before her forty-eighth birthday. Her death certificate declared the immediate cause to be cerebral apoplexy due to hypertension, from which she had suffered for several years, and collapsed lungs, for which she had undergone surgery in February.[20]

It was impossible for Rupert to make travel arrangements from New York to Cleveland for the funeral because of enormous transportation problems. But Ed wrote to him about the service, and Rupert responded with a letter expressing once again the love he felt for his daughter:

> Thank you for your letter telling me of the last things about our poor dear Elspeth—the throngs of friends and the flowers. I didn't send any from here because I understood that the blanket of flowers was included in the account I am to pay.
>
> Your tribute to the sweet girl was beautiful, and she deserved it all. It was cruel that I could not get to the funeral; but it is practically impossible to move by train or plane. The demobilization of the troops adds to the difficulty . . . . So I could not reach Cleveland in time for the final rites in spite of being so near.
>
> Yes, indeed, I want you to keep in touch with me, and write me often. Please tell the girls to do the same and not to wait always for an

answer. I am writing day and night and the radio brings in an appalling mass of letters, hundreds of which I cannot answer for lack of time and strength in spite of the high compliments they pay me.

I have not tried to describe my feelings about the loss of darling Elspeth—In a very brief period I suffered the sudden and accidental loss of my wife and the slow and merciless loss of my only child. Words have been my life long business and speech making my second trade; but there are no words for such sorrow and regret. Even to try to speak of them wrecks me altogether. I have always said that the crowning cruelty of life is to have some beloved soul endure such torment that death comes as a blessing. That was poor Elspeth's fate and, even at a time when millions have been dying in agony, it is no less terrible. But what can we say?—or do?—Nothing but endure as best we can, and stumble on till we drop by the wayside.

Love to the girls and to you.,

Devotedly,

Rupert[21]

Despite spending "day and night" at his writing, as mentioned to Ed, he made little progress toward having much of value published during this period. But in England, Jarrolds published his novel *In a Blaze of Glory* in 1945, after its U. S. newspaper syndication, and he wrote the foreword to a book called *Teachers Are People*, published in Santa Barbara the same year.[22] Some copies of his books still sold—even those about the Lakerim Athletic Club boys. He was amazed that a few copies of his first published book were being purchased after nearly a half century.[23]

Although at first he had seen no reason for any of his granddaughters to stay with him in Los Angeles, in August he invited Elspeth (Beth) De Pould out for a visit and told her that "it's fine to see all of you grow up to be beautiful ladies and living life to the fullest." [24]

The brave front he had put up in telling Ed how busy he was at his work appeared less positive in September, after Lapp had found it necessary to ask his father-in-law for financial help. Rupert turned him down once, saying that he had sold almost nothing for six months, but a few weeks later, in response to another request, sent fifty dollars. He advised Ed to "make it go as far as you can, for as I explained, I am getting in next to nothing." He then told some bad news: He had lost his weekly radio program. Although the NBC people assured him that they loved his work, and he continued to receive enthusiastic letters, the network had been unable to sell the program to a sponsor. Times were difficult and were certain to become more so, he predicted, putting much of the blame on labor bosses.[25]

His situation had not improved as Christmas approached. He had done "little work of value during the year" and had undergone expensive surgery, he told Ed, although he did not say what sort of an operation was involved.

His correspondence with his son-in-law continued, and in the spring of 1946 he said he planned to stop in Cleveland on his way to New York; he signed the letter "Devotedly, Dad." [26]

By autumn, however, he was so elated about a project he was working on that he wrote to Beth to tell her about it. He was planning a book about the work being done by Warden Clinton Duffy at San Quentin penitentiary and had just returned home after three days there as the warden's guest. He had been impressed by the affection with which inmates regarded Duffy and his wife, despite the fact that there was no mollycoddling by officials. Informing his granddaughter that he planned another trip East in late October or early November, he said, "I do hope that this time I shall not be denied the blessing of meeting you all as I was before." [27]

He was delighted when Barbara went to New York to see him during his stay there. After her return to Cleveland, he told Beth about their pleasant visit and again expressed happiness over having such beautiful ladies for granddaughters.

"You should be most thankful you didn't turn out to look like me." [28]

Soon after, Barbara went to California for an extended stay with her grandfather, and he was elated by the change in atmosphere that immediately took place at the Los Feliz Boulevard home. He wrote, "She lights up this lonely old house with her beauty and her high spirits." In a later letter he told the De Poulds ("Johnny and Beth"), how much her companionship meant to him: "Barbara has been blooming and beautiful and making a great hit with everybody old and young. It has been a great happiness to me to have her here and I was greatly relieved when she decided not to go back to Cleveland." [29]

In earlier years, Rupert had owned a number of different kinds of automobiles and had driven them himself, but more recently he had a driver named John Burnham, who also served as his secretary. When Barbara arrived on the scene, she wanted to make herself useful, and so was given the assignment of taking over Burnham's duties as her grandfather's driver. In later years, she recalled that it was a remarkable experience for a young girl of nineteen to chauffeur him around in his 1941 Chrysler to various concerts, parties, and events at such places as the Authors' Club and at the homes of his friends, many of whom were well-known celebrities.[30]

Before long, her grandfather decided that she could also serve quite capably as his secretary, so she also replaced Burnham in that capacity, taking over the task of typing Rupert's manuscripts and letters. This was no easy assignment, considering his handwriting was considered notoriously difficult to read. But she managed to figure it out and soon was an indispensable aide to her illustrious "Gramps."

Even before Barbara's arrival, he had begun writing the Warden Duffy biography and was making plans to get back to unfinished work, including the long-delayed George Washington biography. His interest in this important project was still strong, even though he had postponed its completion many times, and he occasionally still became involved in disagreements over certain aspects of Washington's life and career. It seemed that the Sally Fairfax matter would never be resolved.

Lt. Col. Roy G. Fitzgerald of the Dayton Historical Association in Ohio told him about a woman who said she possessed the disputed Fairfax letters and was convinced that Hughes was a liar. The charge brought a response from Hughes that "a liar, as I understand the word, is one who deceives intentionally. I certainly did not lie about Sally Fairfax. I found the letters in Ford's edition of Washington's writings and much comment on them elsewhere."

His letter continued for more than four single-spaced pages, elaborating on points in question. "I sincerely believe," he wrote, "that Washington loved Sally Fairfax desperately. I sincerely believe that he came to love Martha profoundly." He said he would appreciate anything Fitzgerald might turn up that would help him in the completion of his fourth and fifth volumes and the revision of the first three.[31]

But he did not seem so optimistic when he wrote to Fitzgerald again ten days later. He clarified some references cited in his earlier books and added, "If I live to make a revision, I hope to correct many errors found by me and other readers of the early volumes." [32] It was the first time he had expressed doubts about updating the Washington biography.

CHAPTER TWENTY-SIX

A MENACE PERCEIVED

"They've been powerful in Hollywood for years, both secretly and openly. They've attacked me and anything else that ever opposed them."

Having been involved in a number of controversies during his career, it was not surprising that in the last half of the 1940s Hughes again took a leading role in verbal battles with other writers.

In 1946 he objected to novelist James M. Cain's proposal that the Screen Writers Guild join with the Authors' League in setting up an American Authors Authority for the avowed purpose of enabling writers to lease their material through the authority instead of selling it outright. All rights would go to the authority, which would copyright the material and lease it to editors, producers, or others for a separate fee each time it was used, thereby enabling writers to share in profits from remakes and resales of their work as well as from the first usage.[1]

Many writers endorsed the plan, but Hughes roundly denounced it. With the backing of fifty prominent authors—including Louis Bromfield, Bruce Barton, John Erskine, Katherine Brush, and Clarence Budington Kelland— he formed the American Writers Association to combat the proposal. Calling it "an attempt to establish a monopoly of all literary material," Hughes recalled the earlier effort by a group of screenwriters to "Stalinize"

American literature when they drafted a twenty-page constitution to cover all forms of literary expression. He now argued:

> The seven-year itch has broken out again . . . . Now, seven years later, a group dominated by the same majority of Communists proposes to take over all copyrights of every kind . . . .
>
> The American Authors Authority ought to be laughed out of existence before it has to be howled and fought down by believers in the Bill of Rights, the freedom of the individual and the right of authors to own their own property and their own souls.[2]

As a result of widespread criticism, including denunciations by studio heads and authors H. L. Mencken, Dorothy Thompson, and James T. Farrell, a new version of the plan, intended to soften opposition, was announced in March, 1947. But it did not satisfy Hughes and the American Writers Association board of directors. As president, Hughes issued a statement, backed by the board, in which he called the Cain plan "dictatorial and monopolistic and the brain child of Communists and their fellow-travelers."[3]

Cain was quoted later as saying that the fact that the Screen Writers Guild was Communist-inspired was "irrelevant." Contending that the plan was his and not the Guild's, he said he had supported Republicans Earl Warren and Thomas Dewey in their election campaigns. Although Hughes agreed that Cain was not a Communist, he said it was hard to find anyone who would admit to being one, "though the sprawling world known as Hollywood is lousy with holders of cards and their side-kicks."[4]

Hughes had charged that the only change made by the revision was the translation of the original plan into a legal document. That attack was refuted by Emmet Lavery, president of the Guild, who contended that the new plan gave assurance of guarantees against interference with the contents of literary works. Hughes and the AWA argued, however, that a small minority could easily capture control of the authority—a dangerous situation in the hands of either right or left. "But it happens to be a notorious fact that those who hatched the plan and those most energetic in pushing it are of the pro-Communist persuasion."[5]

With the new wave of opposition stirring doubts about the proposal, support weakened among members of the Screen Writers Guild. As a result, the plan eventually lost the Guild's backing, but even as the argument died down, Hughes became embroiled in a larger controversy.[6]

It involved some writers with whom he had tangled a decade earlier when he and others left the Guild. Since then, the rift between left and right wings in Hollywood had lessened during World War II when Communist Russia teamed with democratic nations. But in 1944 Hughes and James K. McGuinness had helped organize an anti-Communist organization called the Motion Picture Alliance for the Preservation of American Ideals, which continued to attack the Guild. Director Sam Wood was the first president of the Alliance, Walt Disney was one of three vice presidents, and Hughes was an Executive Committee member. Alliance members included such other prominent Hollywood names as King Vidor, Gary Cooper, Adolphe Menjou, John Wayne, Robert Taylor, Charles Coburn, and Hedda Hopper. Union leaders recruited producer Walter Wanger to join in denouncing what they regarded as irresponsible statements by Wood and the MPA, but five years later Wanger would admit that "time and history" had proved the Alliance was correct in its foresight.[7]

After World War II, amid reports that Communists were infiltrating key industries in the United States, the Un-American Activities Committee of the United States House of Representatives began holding hearings to ferret out names of those known or believed to be Communist Party members.

In May, 1947, a subcommittee of HUAC, headed by Representative J. Parnell Thomas of New Jersey, went to Los Angeles to take a look at the motion picture industry. In closed door hearings at the Biltmore Hotel, the committee interviewed "friendly" witnesses —among them actors Adolphe Menjou, Robert Taylor, and Ronald Reagan. Others were producers Jack Warner and Leo McCarey, and writers Rupert Hughes, James Kevin McGuinness, and Howard Emmett Rogers.

Veteran actor Menjou called Hollywood "one of the main centers of Communist activity in America" because of the prominence of the motion picture industry. He declared that it was the "desire and wish of the masters of Moscow to use this medium for their purpose—which is the overthrow of the American Government." Thomas stated that Menjou and Warner had given the committee the names of hundreds of Hollywood Communists—mostly writers.

The congressman reported that Rupert Hughes had provided not only the names of writers who were Communists but also their Communist Party membership numbers. Hughes told reporters that the Screen Writers Guild he had helped found was "lousy with Communists." He said, "They began to take over the guild in 1937. They've been powerful in Hollywood for years, both secretly and openly. They've attacked me and anything else that ever opposed them." [8]

The Los Angeles hearing set the stage for a full-scale investigation of Communist infiltration into the motion picture industry. Subpoenas were issued to forty-three producers, actors, writers, and directors to appear as witnesses at October hearings before the full committee in Washington, D. C. Some, including Menjou and Hughes, had testified in Los Angeles; nineteen of those subpoenaed, including sixteen writers, were "unfriendly" witnesses.

The hearing in the Caucus Room of the old House Office Building began on October 21 before a large audience, and, as a front-page story in the *New York Times* reported, it "had the elements of a lively Hollywood script. It had humor, anger, glamor, climactic action and cheers for the star (Menjou)." But there were some from Hollywood who were hostile toward Menjou, who urged the industry to make some anti-Communist films.

Hughes testified that Warner Brothers had paid him $15,000 to write a plot for a movie attacking Communism, but an agent had then told him that "stinkpots" would be placed in every theater that showed the film. As a result, it was never produced. Calling screenwriter John Howard Lawson a leading Communist, he accused him of trying to make the SWG "an instrument of Communist power." There was no question that Communists dominated the Guild, Hughes declared, but he added that democratic forces were trying to take it back.

Another witness, John Charles Moffitt, *Esquire Magazine* film critic and a former screenwriter, told the committee that when the *Hollywood Reporter* had asked certain writers whether they had Communist Party cards with numbers on them, none of the writers replied. Eleven such names, along with card numbers for eight of them, were then provided to the committee.[9]

By the next week the committee charged eight Hollywood writers with contempt for refusing to tell whether they were Communists. Meanwhile, Screen Writers Guild president Emmet Lavery, claiming that Hughes had accused him of being "a Communist masquerading as a Catholic," asked to establish in the record "how far from the truth Mr. Hughes is." He acknowledged that there were Communists in the Guild but thought their influence had been overstated.

The committee's demand that writers reveal whether they were Communist Party members brought a protest from the American Veterans Committee, which charged that the probe had shown "such crass disregard of constitutional rights that the committee should be abolished." Similar sentiments were expressed in a statement from a number of writers, producers, playwrights, and others who protested what they regarded as an invasion of personal rights.[10]

Regardless of the motives of those who testified against the accused, a backlash began to develop that would grow to much larger proportions in the 1950s when Senator Joseph McCarthy's accusations of Red infiltration in the United States would bring about a wave of protest against his methods of questioning witnesses. Later, in the 1970s, the question of whether such investigations had unjustly destroyed the reputations and careers of writers and others who refused to testify would become the subject of several books, including Robert Sobel's *The Manipulators: America in the Media Age*. Sobel quoted Hughes as calling Lavery of the Screen Writers Guild "a man whose views are Communist, whose friends are Communists, and whose work is communistic." Although Hughes did not actually tag Lavery a Communist, Sobel wrote, "The industry knew that Lavery was a mild liberal, who on occasion had criticized even the New Deal as being too advanced." [11]

By the time the hearings were concluded, two more unfriendly witnesses had been charged with contempt, and they along with the other eight became known as the Hollywood Ten. Meanwhile, as the Guild's influence weakened and Lavery neared the end of his second term as president, he condemned the radicals and urged that the organization disassociate itself from those charged with contempt. Even James M. Cain declared that while he considered Rupert Hughes, Parnell Thomas, and others reprehensible, "these gentlemen say we are loaded with Communists, and whether we like it or not, this charge is true." [12]

On November 24, 1947, in a special session of Congress, Representative Thomas called for a contempt citation against Alfred Maltz, one of the Hollywood Ten. Only seventeen of 463 Congressmen present voted against the citation. This was followed by similar lopsided margins on the other nine accused.

The Motion Picture Producers Association promptly declared that its members would fire or suspend without pay any of the Hollywood Ten who worked for them and would not rehire them until they were acquitted or purged of contempt citations and declared under oath that they were not Communists. The producers said they would not knowingly employ any Communist or member of any organization that advocated the overthrow of the U. S. government.[13]

Gradually the support of the Ten, once so vocal, faded away as it became less popular to rally to left-wing causes. But in later years many Americans— including some authors writing about the period—would regard the accused as martyrs.

In separate trials in federal court, all those charged were found guilty. Lawson and Dalton Trumbo were turned down on appeals and the Supreme Court refused to hear their cases. In June, 1950, they began serving one-year terms at a federal penitentiary. Six others were handed one-year terms and two received six-month sentences.[14]

Some people no doubt wondered how a champion of freedom such as Rupert Hughes could have been a party to what so many considered an invasion of personal rights. But as one of the earliest foes of Communism, he was determined to help prevent its spread. For him, it was a patriotic duty to tell what he knew about subversives in the film industry. Years later, his sister-in-law, Ruby Hughes, stated it succinctly when asked to comment on his view of those whom he believed to be Communists or Communist sympathizers: "He fought them and went to Washington to testify." [15] Likewise, actress Colleen Moore, recalling the same period and Hughes's earlier battles with the Screen Writers Guild, said: "Rupert was very brave. He put himself right out on a limb, because so much control at that time was held by the Communists. He was a good American. He was a patriot." [16]

Words of commendation also came for Hughes on January 6, 1948, from Hollywood Post No. 43 of the American Legion, which presented him a "Citation of Citizenship" for "patriotism meriting special confidence and esteem because of outspoken Americanism before Congress in opposing the subversive Communist menace in our country." [17]

Although the battle over supposed Communists in the film industry was of prime interest to Hughes, so was the political picture during the late 1940s. Invited by Cyril Clemens to state his views of Franklin D. Roosevelt, he replied, "I am afraid that if I sent my true opinion of FDR the symposium would turn into a riot." [18]

The Republicans seemed almost certain to win back the White House in 1948, and Rupert was elated when they nominated Dewey again. Democrats were badly split, despite their first-ballot choice of Truman at the national convention, when Senator Alben W. Barkley of Kentucky was nominated as his running mate. Liberals who left the party in disgust formed the Progressive party, with former Vice President Henry Wallace as its presidential nominee.

In speeches during the heat of the campaign, Hughes could be blunt, as in his remarks to the Electric Club. A newspaper headline, "RUPERT HUGHES FAVORS EGGING," referred to his comments about an incident in which Henry Wallace was a target during a trip down South. Hughes, who urged that Communists be run out of the country or jailed, was quoted as saying, "One disappointing phase of the Henry Wallace egging was that the Southerners, supposed to be crack shots, missed their target so often." [19]

Although he had praised Harry Truman during the early days of his presidency, there was no doubt in Hughes's mind that Dewey was much better qualified for the position. Therefore, Truman's surprise defeat of Dewey, after a whistlestop "Give 'em Hell, Harry" campaign, deeply disappointed the author of an admiring biography of the losing candidate.

Hughes denied a rumor that he would write a biography or sketch about his fellow Missourian, Truman. He told Cyril Clemens, "The statement that I was writing something on Truman was incorrect . . . . I feel he is doing terribly badly." [20]

Shortly after Truman's reelection, Hughes could focus his attention on a pleasant event—the wedding of his youngest granddaughter, Barbara, now twenty-two. Her presence in his household for more than two years had enabled him to recover from the sadness of the loss of his wife and daughter. Barbara had done his typing and served as his driver, and she had often accompanied him to various events and had lunch with him at his favorite table at the Brown Derby. But now she was to establish a home of her own with her husband, Wesley Colin Cameron.

The marriage ceremony was a formal affair at the Beverly Hills Community Presbyterian Church on December 9, 1948. A family portrait taken at the wedding showed a beautiful bride and her proud grandfather with the handsome bridegroom and his mother. [21]

Rupert had been protective of his granddaughter while she lived in his home, insisting on a midnight curfew whenever she went out for the evening. But he thought highly of Wes Cameron, and he and Wes came to enjoy a close friendship even before the wedding took place. Once, when Wes did not return to his own home until after 4 a. m., his mother said he should not be keeping Barbara out so late. His reply: "Oh, I took her home at midnight. I've been talking with Rupert."

After the wedding, Barbara continued to type manuscripts and letters for her grandfather, and she or Wes would drive him to meetings of The Authors and other events. Decades later, she recalled how much her husband and her grandfather enjoyed being together. "They had a special relationship," she said, noting that her husband, with a background in advertising and sales, enjoyed telling stories about things that went on at the Authors' Club and at meetings he attended with Rupert.

Barbara and her sister Beth could also remember humorous incidents involving their grandfather. One that Barbara recalled was the time when Rupert arrived at a meeting of authors and was given a standing ovation. His immediate reaction was to tell them, "Kneel, my subjects!" Beth remembered another occasion when a group of writers decided that each would try to write a headline that would be front-page news all over the world. Rupert won easily with his headline: POPE ELOPES.[22]

Although Rupert saw Barbara and Wes frequently after their marriage, his visits with his other granddaughters were rare occasions. In April, 1949, he told Beth he had hoped to stop in Cleveland to see her while on a trip to New York, but had been unable to arrange it.[23]

He kept busy with his work, including unusual projects such as walking a police beat and riding in a patrol car with a woman sergeant in preparation for writing a story about his experiences.[24] An article he wrote for The Rotarian, "They Don't Make the Headlines," was described as a short "biography of a certain young girl of our day whose good deeds are blessedly obscure." [25]

Hughes's classic reference book, Music Lovers' Encyclopedia, as revised by Deems Taylor and Russell Kerr in 1939, was republished in 1947 by Garden City Publishing, Inc. A year earlier he had been given credit for his own compositions and books about music in John Tasker Howard's Our American Music.[26] Recognition also came from the Mark Twain Society. He told Cyril Clemens in early 1948 that he was flattered by election to "knighthood" in the society.[27]

Meanwhile, his novel *Static*, about a small-town singer who becomes a network radio star, was picked up by the National Broadcasting Company for a soap opera sponsored by General Mills. When published serially in *Hearst's International-Cosmopolitan* the story had been touted as "the amazing career of Holly Sloan, fascinating heroine of Rupert Hughes' novel of Radioland." And now, nearly sixteen years later, the characters in this tale of the air waves were themselves introduced to a listening audience on September 1, 1947. The soap opera was called *The Story of Holly Sloan*, and the title role was played by a well-known singer, Gale Page. Although the show ran only one season, it won a "respectable" listener rating. [28]

The Hughes name was associated with a broad range of material, from soap opera to epic poetry, during the late forties. "Gyges' Ring," the lengthy dramatic monologue written while he was a Yale graduate student and published a few years later to excellent reviews, was included in a 1949 book of his poetry entitled *Gyges' Ring and Other Verse*. The publisher, Murray & Gee, Inc., of Culver City, California, called the volume "a gallimaufry"—a term borrowed from Hughes—"of all sorts of verse, some of it in lighter vein." [29]

Included were eighty-four offerings, ranging in length from a few lines to twenty-nine pages. Thirty-four were classified as "Varia," including "The Man Who Looked at Godiva" and one called "Jean Summerlin," about his mother. Among eight sonnets were Rupert's touching tribute to his sister, titled "Greta," and his oft-published "Decoration Day." There were four haunting elegies, including "At Kensico," which described his sister's beauty and the cemetery in which she was buried. "Cremation" made an unabashed statement in favor of cremation instead of burial.

The remaining verses were classified as "Free Verse," "Quatrains," "In Dialect," "Translations," "Patriotisms," and "Frivolities." The last part of the 154-page book was devoted to "Portraits," a total of three, called "Cain," "The Hero and the Hulk. A Little Epic," and, of course, what Hughes considered his major poetic work, "Gyges' Ring."

Most of the pieces had been penned decades earlier and some, such as "The Happiest Man in I-O-Way," had been published in other anthologies. Hughes had set several of the poems to music, including "Cain" and "My Forever United States."

Gyges' Ring and Other Verse, a compendium of what Hughes undoubtedly regarded as his best verse, became a popular seller and soon went into a second edition published by House-Warven, Publishers, of Hollywood, which stated that "critics rate it as some of the best of contemporary poetic writing" and called the book "a perpetual favorite among those who enjoy poetic expression." [30]

There was also talk of publishing *The Patent Leather Kid* as a paperback. Hughes thanked agent Harry Lichtig for his letter "with its announcement of the annual announcement" that the book is to be "re-soled," and adding that "I should, of course, love to see it issued as a Pocket Book." Although the novel was submitted to a publisher of paperback books, there is no indication that it was accepted. [31]

Meanwhile, Hughes wrote an introduction to Marie (Hays) Heiner's 1949 book *Hearing Is Believing*, recalling that false pride had at first prevented him from taking advantage of devices for overcoming impaired hearing. [32] A photo of Hughes, with his hand cupping his ear, illustrated his article on the same theme for *Woman's Day*. Published in February, 1949, it was titled "Save Your Voice!...I Hear You Now." A caption stated, "A hard-of-hearer confesses that for years he put the burden of affliction on others." The article told what his first hearing aid had done for him, even though it was heavy and awkward: "It was like Columbus discovering America."

He also worked during this period on several books—nonfiction and fiction, including a novel begun in 1946. And he still had not given up entirely on the George Washington biography. One newspaper, on Washington's birthday in 1949, credited Douglas Southall Freeman and Hughes with making the public aware that "Washington was far from being the chilly and aloof figure pictured by legend. He was, in fact, as real as the boy who lives next door." [33]

Washington was still the topic of much of Hughes's correspondence with historians and other biographers. During the latter part of 1949, he wrote, "I am still cherishing the hope of finishing the Washington biography, and making a much needed revision of the three published volumes." [34]

LONG OVERDUE

"I'm all swole up."

Since the early days of his career, Rupert had helped provide recognition for numerous authors, often presiding at banquets and other functions in their honor. Now it was his turn to be the center of attention.

Shortly before his seventy-eighth birthday, many of the great and near-great of Hollywood and elsewhere gathered in the Embassy Room of the Ambassador Hotel in Los Angeles to pay tribute to him for lifetime achievements during a long and varied career.

His appreciation of the honor was indicated in a letter to Lee Shippey, the *Los Angeles Times* columnist for whom he had arranged a similar event some fifteen years earlier. He told Shippey three days before the banquet:

> Thanks for the ad!!! and "right next to the reading matter."!! I'm all swole up. The fact that your eulogy was largely fiction puts me all the deeper in your debt.
>
> It is wonderful how generous the *Times* has been with its announcement of the testimonial dinner, and now it is topped by your magnificent feat of imagination and charity.[1]

It was a widely heralded occasion, with journalists in New York as well as Los Angeles taking note of the plans. Danton Walker's Broadway Column in the *New York News* announced: "Rupert Hughes to get a testimonial dinner at the Ambassador Hotel, with all branches of show business represented." [2]

Newspapers also provided extensive follow-up coverage, with a *Los Angeles Times* headline of "Rupert Hughes' Services Lauded at Dinner Fete," and the *Los Angeles Examiner* reporting that "500 Attend Dinner Here in Honor of Rupert Hughes." Sponsors were three Hollywood organizations representing top talents of the motion picture industry—The Authors, The Lambs, and The Masquers. Many of those attending brought their spouses.

In the view of actor Pat O'Brien, master of ceremonies, the January 9 banquet was "long overdue"—an opinion shared by many others. More than 375 messages of praise and congratulations for Hughes had poured in from friends in theatrical, literary, military, and political fields, but Lew Lauria, event chairman (listed in the printed program as Chancellor-in-Chief), ruled that there were too many to be read. Instead, O'Brien called upon some of the honoree's close friends for three-minute testimonials. [3]

One lifelong friend called Hughes "the outspoken champion of freedom in America," and another lauded him as "one of the outstanding Americans to whom more honor is due than he can ever be accorded." [4]

Governor Earl Warren, who later would become the Chief Justice of the United States, cited the honoree's wartime activities: "Rupert Hughes did our state and country a great service during World War II when he helped found the California State Guard." He added that as a colonel and regimental commander Hughes "helped guard our airplane factories, railroads and war facilities . . .—and at a time when he had reached his three score and 10." Brigadier General LeRoy H. Watson presented Hughes with an Army commendation for his services during both World Wars and his work with the State Guard. [5]

The three sponsoring groups gave Hughes a large console television set with a plaque affixed to it that read: "To Rupert Hughes, a great American, for your devotion to your country and your fellow men, with deepest affection from your many admirers."

Those eulogizing him included movie producers Louis B. Mayer, Jack Warner, and Jesse L. Lasky; comedian Ed Wynn; Los Angeles Mayor Fletcher T. Bowron; Sheriff Eugene W. Biscailuz; actors Edward Arnold, Jean Hersholt, Leo Carrillo, and Fred Stone; industrialist Donald M.

Nelson; impresario Sid Grauman; author Paul Wellman; detective Raymond Schindler; and many others.[6]

A dozen speakers were seated on the dais, along with producers Samuel Goldwyn and Cecil B. DeMille and industrialist Eric Johnson. Author Clarence Budington Kelland shared emcee honors with O'Brien.[7]

The attractively printed program, bound with a ribbon, carried a portrait of Hughes on the front cover.[8] Inside were names of sponsors and participants, including three Chancellors of the Exchequer, a Trumpeteer-in-Chief, nine Trumpeteers (including Wesley Cameron, husband of Hughes's granddaughter Barbara), and seven Executors (among them Grauman and author Paul Wellman). Several individuals served in dual roles; for instance, Cameron was also one of a half-dozen Gatehouse Guardians.

But it was The Royal Guard that included most of the big names. Besides Governor Warren, other political figures were Governor Thomas E. Dewey of New York, the Secretary of State, the mayor and sheriff. Military leaders included three generals, a colonel, and the American Legion State Commander. The rest of The Royal Guard was a veritable Who's Who of the entertainment world. Among those on the list of 120 were:

Gene Autry, Warner Baxter, Jack Benny, Edgar Bergen, Joe E. Brown, Billie Burke, Eddie Cantor, Bing Crosby, Marion Davies, Cecil B. DeMille, Jack Dempsey, Walt Disney, Lloyd C. Douglas, Donald Douglas, Erle Stanley Gardner, Sam Goldwyn, Edmund Gwenn, Hugh Herbert, Jean Hersholt, Bob Hope, Hedda Hopper, Walter Huston, George Jessel, Frances Marion, Robert Montgomery, Victor Moore, Ralph Morgan, Alan Mowbray, Pola Negri, Louella Parsons, Mary Pickford and husband Buddy Rogers, Joseph M. Schenck, Raymond C. Schindler, Lee Shippey, Preston Sturges, Gloria Swanson, Lawrence Tibbett, Jack Warner, and Walter Winchell.

Rupert's brother, Felix, and sister-in-law, Ruby, were present, as was his granddaughter Barbara. Among photographs taken was one published in the *Los Angeles Times* showing Mrs. Lew Lauria, the emcee's wife, planting a kiss on the honoree's head.[9]

Letters and telegrams provided more tributes.[10] From Samuel Goldwyn came a telegram saying, "I am very happy to join in honoring a valued friend who is a distinguished writer, a famous historian, an outstanding citizen and a great American. Rupert Hughes' single-minded devotion to the cause of American democracy and to the principles on which our country is based have made him an example of outstanding citizenry to the entire nation."

Cecil B. DeMille's telegram told Hughes: "The world knows you as a great story-teller. Our country knows you as an outspoken champion of freedom. I know you as an old and dear friend, to whom I send warm greetings on this occasion in your honor."

Some regretted they could not attend, including Louella Parsons: " . . . am so happy you are getting recognition you so justly deserve." Joe E. Brown, calling Hughes "a great American," said, "all members of the entertainment world are proud of Rupert Hughes humanitarian." From Joseph Schenck came a wire: "Your pen and your character have been an asset to Hollywood and to our country. You have been a fine humanitarian and a contributor to progress, socially and in literature."

Walt Disney telegraphed that "I know no man who exemplifies more the real spirit of America. His trenchant pen and forthright speech have made him a leader in the fight for liberty and the freedom of peoples the world over . . . . He is a really great American."

Expressions of appreciation came also from organizations with which Hughes had close ties, including the Friends of Poland, which he headed as president. Another was the Blue Bird Camp Association, Inc., a California group that provided recreational opportunities for deafened boys and girls; its letter said Hughes had been on its advisory board for fifteen years and "has been an inspiration to all of us who have a similar hearing handicap."

And so it went: speeches and written messages in tribute to Rupert Hughes. It was an evening to be treasured, and he beamed at the praise accorded him. Then, after the speaking ended and the audience began to leave, he posed for pictures with Governor Warren, Pat O'Brien, and others, including his granddaughter. He graciously inscribed her program with a tribute: "To the beautiful Barbara from her proud ancestor. Rupert Hughes." And on her husband's program he wrote: "Wesley Cameron with the devotion and gratitude of Grampa Hughes." [11]

For some time Rupert had considered selling his Arabian Nights home, which, after the loss of Patterson, had been too large for him, especially now that Barbara was established in a home of her own. There was also the expense factor to consider.

In early 1950 he sold the Los Feliz Boulevard mansion, and in March accepted the invitation of Felix and Ruby to move into a separate wing of their Mediterranean-style residence at 204 North Rossmore. At first he intended to stay only temporarily, planning to live again in New York. Ruby later recalled that even though he was very fond of Los Angeles he especially loved New York, regarding it as an exciting place to be.

After a few months, he began to prepare for his move to the city where he had begun his career. "I can still see him packing his trunk and getting ready to leave," his sister-in-law reminisced. He did go there, but stayed only a short while before returning to Los Angeles, mainly because of a producer's promise that he would make a film from some Hughes short stories. But the producer had trouble arranging financing—a familiar problem in Hollywood—and never made the movie, although he did turn one of Rupert's short stories, "The Lady Who Smoked Cigars," into a film that was never released.[12]

Again, Rupert settled in at the spacious house on Rossmore, where he lived with Felix and Ruby in a relationship built on affection and mutual esteem. Years later, Ruby wrote about the "great admiration, love and devotion between Rupert and Felix as brothers," pointing out that "in the early days when Felix was getting established in the teaching profession, it was Rupert who was successful who helped his younger brother, and in the later years of Rupert's life after his wife had died, it was Felix who opened his heart and our home to Rupert." [13]

The productive years, however, were not over for Rupert, who still had many writing projects in the works—some half-finished and others near completion. The year 1950, in fact, was a good one for him. Buoyed by the adulation heaped upon him at the testimonial banquet and apparently happy in his new surroundings, he was inspired to bring to fruition some of his activities.

One manuscript that had occupied much of his attention might have seemed out of character for Hughes, who by this time usually supported the side of business in disputes involving workers versus management. The book upon which he now put finishing touches was *The Giant Wakes*, a novel based upon the life and career of Samuel Gompers, the

London-born labor leader who had become the first president of the American Federation of Labor and had served in that capacity for nearly four decades. Gompers, an independent-minded leader not involved with political parties, had urged unions to bargain with employers. A champion of laws to regulate working conditions of women and minors, he had helped bring about legislation establishing the U. S. Department of Labor. But if Gompers's views seemed in conflict with those of Hughes, a reading of the author's early novels would have been a reminder that he also had called for improvements in working conditions.

Even before its July 17 publication date, *The Giant Wakes* won recognition, when Hughes received the Tamiment Social and Economic Institute's 1950 book award. Eugene Lyons, associate editor of *The Reader's Digest*, presented the award of distinction at the institute's annual conference in Tamiment, Pennsylvania, during the Gompers centennial celebration, attended by several hundred trade union leaders. Hughes was cited for portraying "with sympathy and insight the heroic and moving story of the life of Samuel Gompers and his struggle to win for labor its rightful place in our national life." [14]

Mixed reviews greeted the novel's publication by Borden Publishing Company of Los Angeles. John Cournos, admitting in the *New York Times* that he was "allergic" to biographical novels, said he "came to curse and remained to bless. There is something in the story preponderantly ardent and just; the founder of the American Federation of Labor emerges as a living personality." [15]

Soon after the book came out, Hughes responded to repeated requests from the University of Iowa to provide a manuscript for the university's Special Collections Department as part of its Iowa Authors Collection. His lengthy and apologetic handwritten letter to Grace Van Wormer discussed his current state of affairs:

> Among the multitudinous things I have to be ashamed of—and am—there is hardly anything that is so inexcusable as my failure even to acknowledge your most courteous and flattering letters.
>
> People have insulted me with violence and virulence and promptly received an answer. You honored me by an invitation to deposit one of my worthless manuscripts in your honorable library, and have never had so much as a Thankyouma'am out of me . . . .

I meant to send you something at once; but I could not decide what to send. I write everything in long hand and have 3 or 4 copies typed. Then I destroy my manuscript as a rule. So I had few manuscripts remaining.

This year I decided to sell my house and move to New York, where I was spending a good deal of my time. I moved over to my brother's at this new address in late March. I had such a vast accumulation of things, and was moving into such limited space that I made a holocaust of manuscripts in long hand and typescript. A truck load was carried away. Then I went to New York. Returning, I find practically no manuscripts at all, though there must be many in storage, where I have sent tons.

He said he would try to go through his stored things to find something interesting or representative, but at the house he had found only one complete manuscript—a short story, "The Baby's Shoes," one of his favorites, published in *Cosmopolitan* in 1929. He hoped to find others in storage, but in the meantime he enclosed the manuscript and a Christmas poem he had just written. Hoping this action would show that he was not "wholly unresponsive to human kindness and generosity," he concluded the letter, "Please forgive my unforgivableness." [16]

The poem he sent, "Christmas Rendezvous," was published in *Good Housekeeping* in its Christmas issue. It was a poignant reminder that even though long distances might separate loved ones, it is still possible to meet again on holidays—through the miracle of shared memories. [17]

Meanwhile, one of his early short stories, a fairy tale about a poor lawyer's son, "The Latest News About the Three Wishes," was republished in *The Second St. Nicholas Anthology*. It was in *St. Nicholas* magazine that his Lakerim Athletic Club series had appeared before the turn of the century, thus launching him on a career as a fiction writer. [18]

There was a 1950 edition of *Music Lovers' Encyclopedia*, the Deems Taylor-Russell Kerr revision of his book. It bore his name prominently— "Compiled by Rupert Hughes."

He also completed another biography in 1950—a straightforward treatment, rather than a novel. The subject was Raymond C. Schindler, the brilliant detective who had been among those honoring Rupert at the testimonial banquet. No fictionalization was needed to make *The Complete Detective* a thrilling story. Its subtitle, *Being the Life and Strange* and *Exciting Cases of Raymond Schindler, Master Detective*, provided a clue as to what readers would find among Hughes's accounts of the more prominent of the 10,000 cases Schindler had tackled. The best-known was the solving of the murder of Sir Harry Oakes.

With a foreword by Erle Stanley Gardner, Sheridan House published the biography in October, 1950. The dust jacket recalled that "during the many years that he has known Ray, Rupert Hughes has made a hobby of recording the most fascinating of Mr. Schindler's cases, as a faithful 'Dr. Watson.'"[19]

Opinions of reviewers varied. *The Chicago Sunday Tribune* pointed out that "this exciting collection of true law-breaking episodes has more shivers to the page than any fiction whodunit you ever read," and the *Springfield Republican* declared, "The Schindler story has been told before, but as a personal friend and an established writer Mr. Hughes has an edge that enables him to attain new heights."[20]

A review in *The New Yorker* called Hughes's prose style "rather primitive (there is probably no author with a greater weakness for exclamation points and for capitalizing common nouns)," but termed the book lively and fascinating.[21]

It was not surprising that Rupert had chosen a detective as the subject of a biographical novel. Long interested in mysteries and innovative methods of solving them—his own action-packed thriller, *Empty Pockets*, dating back to 1915—he now turned to detective fiction, writing a story about a private eye. Distributed by the NEA Service to newspapers nationwide beginning in February, 1950, *Fingerprints Don't Lie*, a serialized murder novel set in Los Angeles, introduced the character of Martin Queripel, publicized as the "Very Private" detective who, "contrasting greatly with the modern, swashbuckling hero of detective fiction, is quiet, cultured and pleasant, after the manner of the old-time storybook sleuths."[22]

While involved with the Schindler biography and the murder mystery, Hughes had continued to work on a novel that had occupied much attention for nearly five years. Finally, the lengthy manuscript, typed by his granddaughter Barbara, was ready for publication.

With the intriguing title of *The Triumphant Clay*, it is a love story about an architect, David Vibbard, who becomes involved with three women of distinctly different types. One is Mary Sprague, wealthy and irresistibly attractive because of her amorality and a willingness to provide him with lucrative commissions to design her apartment and country home; Aniela, a beautiful and earthy Polish servant of voluptuous proportions; and Hazel Allen, a Puritanical soul who carries prudery to an extreme.

Hughes provides an insight into the workings of Vibbard's mind, showing his susceptibility to the wiles of Mary, the simple and selfless appeal of Aniela, and even the virtue and straitlaced religious fervor of Hazel. After he fathers a child by Aniela, who is betrothed to another man, he takes Hazel as his wife in a marriage without love or passion— but one that brings him acclaim as an architect of New England churches. In order to find release from the conventionality of his career and a married life without meaning, Vibbard turns to sculpture.

The novel, though crammed with descriptive passages, nevertheless is fast-moving, as David's involvement shifts from one woman to another. Especially vivid is the account of a disaster that befalls the Polish woman and Stefan, the son she has borne David. After Hazel forces Aniela and Stefan to leave the Vibbard home, the boy's foot gets caught in the railroad track. When a train bears down upon them, Aniela is unable to shield Stefan from the oncoming engine and both lose their lives. Filled with admiration for her deed, David creates a majestic sculpture of the woman and boy that is so lifelike and heroic that the rich Mary Sprague, back in the village after years in Europe, insists that it be erected in a public place. Even Hazel, seeing the triumphant clay statue and realizing that her husband possesses an exceptional talent, agrees that the work he has created is one of great art and beauty.[23]

On the dust jacket of *The Triumphant Clay*, published by House-Warven, Publishers, of Hollywood in mid-1951, is a stunning portrait of the Polish peasant girl, a reproduction of a drawing by W. T. Benda, who used a live model to depict Aniela's radiant beauty. The original drawing became the property of Hughes, and decades later it would hang in the home of his sister-in-law, Mrs. Felix Hughes.

The *New York Times* review, headed "Victory of the Spirit," was generally favorable: "At a time when most creative artists have closed the book on their active careers Rupert Hughes, now 79, has returned to the literary lists with a novel of considerable dramatic power." The reviewer, Henry Cavendish, wrote, "There is a poetic cadence in the long line of the author's prose, a broad sweep and colorful descriptiveness that points inevitably to the grand scale of Homeric writing." But Hughes was hardly another Homer, he said, noting that the book was "so melodramatically overwritten as to be reminiscent of the florid language of Southern orators a generation ago." [24]

The novel won for Hughes a Certificate of Award on November 14, 1952, from the Manuscripters of Los Angeles, a writers group, as the most outstanding novel of the month.[25] There is no doubt that *Triumphant Clay* is a powerful novel that ranks among the author's best.

In 1951, other organizations honored Hughes for long and diligent service in advancing the cause of freedom. In a ceremony at the University of Southern California on April 5, the Freedoms Foundation presented him a Certificate of Recognition that cited his contribution to "our American concept of freedom." He also received a 1951 Citation from the Crusade for Freedom, and in 1952 was honored with a life membership in Sigma Tau Sigma, National Social Science Honorary Society.[26]

In June, *Coronet* magazine published Hughes's essay on "Comedians Have Courage," in which he related anecdotes about his comedian friends of the past and present—Will Rogers, Jimmy Durante, Fred Allen, Eddie Foy, W. C. Fields and others. Paying tribute to their art and courage, he wrote that "in every home, there is someone who grieves, or is frightened, or in agony," but when a comedian comes on television or radio "immediately there is helpful laughter. The tragedies are dispelled and, for a while, at least, life is worthwhile again." [27]

By 1951 Rupert had become convinced that television was a medium of great promise and a means of education and enlightenment. In March the magazine *Films in Review* published his essay on "TV Won't Ruin Everything," a condensation of a larger piece he had contributed to the forty-fifth anniversary edition of *Variety*. He decried the attitude of those who contended that television had turned viewers away from the arts and conversation and had drained sports arenas, churches, theaters, and lecture halls. He said such critics did not mention the churches still packed, many motion picture houses jammed, books with enormous sales, magazines with millions of readers, and newspapers "almost too heavy to lift." [28]

In the early days of television programming, he made frequent appearances on local panel shows in discussions of current affairs. His sister-in-law, Ruby, later recalled, "He gave many a young participant a grueling time," and added, "He was in his late seventies when he entered upon this new career, but he attacked it with the same gusto he had brought to earlier endeavors." [29]

He wrote a number of proposals for television, preparing outlines and synopses for a series on "Great Moments in Great Lives," beginning with a program about George Washington, and a half-hour series of classical dramas with well-known stars in "The Rupert Hughes Playhouse of the World," in addition to individual programs on various subjects.

There was also a presentation script, prepared and offered by Donald Clark and Edward Verier, for a radio and/or TV series titled "Story . . . by Rupert Hughes," starring Charles Coburn. The script consisted of introductions by Hughes and Coburn of an adaptation of a Hughes *Saturday Evening Post* story, "The Heart Mender," with well-known actors and actresses featured. Other programs in the series included six more of his published stories.[30]

As he approached his eightieth birthday, he responded to the question "Are you a humanist?" that was posed to him and other authors. The results were published in *The Humanist* magazine in October/November, 1951. The article, "Authors and Humanism," quoted such writers as Conrad Aiken, Sinclair Lewis, and Albert Schweitzer—each considered by the magazine to be affiliated with the philosophy of humanism, a term that has been subject to many interpretations. In his published reply, Hughes stated, in part:

> I am a "humanist" as opposed to "divinist," may I say? I am an atheist. I am certainly not theistic. As for existentialism I have read reams about it without getting any . . . mental grasp of just what it is supposed to be . . . . My attitude toward man is neither optimistic nor pessimistic. I am a very cheerful person because I always expect the worst and never quite get it. I believe in uniting for the happiness of humanity, in at least its physical and other comforts; but I have no hopes of Utopia, perpetual peace, one world, the millennium—or any radical change in human nature or its response to "improvements." [31]

Although Hughes was still an influential member of the Hollywood community, his name had not been associated with any motion pictures during the

past decade and a half. He had been involved with a number of film proposals, such as a movie that would be made by the Lambs, based upon a magazine serial, and another that would use the Lambs as a plot background.[32]
None of these projects materialized.

But the situation changed in 1951 with the release of *FBI Girl*. The
title on the screen proclaimed "Robert L. Lippert presents Rupert Hughes'
FBI GIRL. Screenplay by Richard Landau and Dwight Babcock, Based on
a Story by Rupert Hughes." A black and white film directed by William
Berke, it starred Audrey Totter, George Brent, and others with familiar
names—Cesar Romero, Raymond Burr, and Tom Drake. Burr is a mob
leader who dominates the governor, Raymond Greenleaf, who is wanted
for a murder committed earlier under a different name. Brent and Romero
are FBI agents, and Miss Totter, an FBI clerk, helps solve the case.

In their 1987 book *The Great Gangster Pictures, II*, James Robert Parish
and Michael R. Pitts called the low-budget *FBI Girl* "pleasant fare," and
especially praised Burr—best known for his later television role as attorney
Perry Mason—for his effectiveness in the role of the "slimy gangster." [33]

Hughes's fascination with the FBI was also indicated in another
novel, *McFarren of the FBI*, distributed in ten installments by the New
York News-Chicago Tribune Syndicate and published in newspapers with
a combined circulation of five million copies.[34]

In other matters, Hughes wrote the foreword to *Kabah -Adventures in
the Jungles of Yucatan* by Stacy-Judd, published in 1951 by House-Warven.
The same publisher came out with a book called *Royal Vistas* by Van Royhl
and Rupert Hughes. Published as volume ten of a series, it was based on
poems by Hughes.

On November 8, 1951, Harry H. Lichtig, an agent who had represented Rupert, died, and the estate requested that all literary materials be
returned to owners. Lichtig, of the Hollywood-based Lichtig-Englander
agency, had represented prominent authors and artists for motion pictures,
television, and radio. Rupert replied that he would like for his material
held by the agency—specifically *The Patent Leather Kid* and *City of
Angels*—to be returned to him.[35] Decades later, a grandnephew of Lichtig
would purchase and move into Rupert's former Los Feliz Boulevard home.

In the early 1950s Hughes still read with great interest the work of
other biographers and historians concerning George Washington and

his contemporaries. One of them, an admirer of Hughes's work, was Douglas Southall Freeman, who in his 1951 *George Washington, Volume Four, Leader of the Revolution* noted that "Hughes's research uncovered several sources not previously known. In the present study, the fullest, most grateful use has been made of some of this material." [36]

IN HIS EIGHTIES

*"It is a vast luxury to walk through the world
feeling that everybody means well."*

The year 1952 dawned with hopeful signs. Rupert would reach his eightieth birthday at the end of January, and he had completed work on another book.

War of the Mayan King, a Story of Yucatan was an adventure tale seen through the eyes of Ulil, a teenaged apprentice to a sculptor. Like Hughes's first published volume of fiction fifty-four years earlier, (the Lakerim Athletic Club stories), it was written for young readers. Again, his vivid style provided an aura of excitement and drama.

Published by The John C. Winston Company of Philadelphia as one in a series of Winston Adventure Books, *War of the Mayan King* was illustrated with Edward J. Smith's drawings of jungle scenes and athletic contests engaged in by young Mayans.

A dozen years later a bibliography of historical fiction would recommend the book for reading by junior high school students.[1]

Although Hughes had been the object of a lavish outpouring of affection by hundreds of admirers only two years earlier, friends were determined not to let his eightieth birthday slip by unnoticed. In recent years some had made it a practice to get together with him on each of his birthdays, but now the landmark observance of the "big eight-oh" brought about two separate celebrations on January 31, 1952.

First of these was the party sponsored annually by a longtime friend, George Hussay. More than a half-hundred invited guests gathered at the fabled Brown Derby in Hollywood to pay tribute to Hughes. The *Los Angeles Times* reported, "Presents piled high on the table before the guest of honor were topped by a caricature drawn by Gordon Currie. Each guest autographed the sketch." [2]

An even bigger event took place that night in clubrooms of The Writers Round Table, at 1776 North Highland in Hollywood, where more than two hundred of Hughes's friends honored him at a reception. Miss Jaime Palmer, club president, presented him a gold-engraved memory book containing testimonial letters and signatures of hundreds of admirers, including Governor Dewey of New York and former President Herbert Hoover, who told Rupert that they both might "yet see a Republican president." [3]

The *Los Angeles Evening Herald & Express* reported that the 8:30 p. m. "soiree" was staged against "a background of red, white and blue floral decorations, symbolizing the uncompromising Americanism of the historian, novelist and military leader." [4] Among notables attending were actors and authors; Mayor Fletcher Bowron; lecturer Burton Holmes; detective Ray Schindler; and producers Jesse Lasky, Sam Goldwyn, and Jack Warner.[5]

Rupert was in fine form as he accepted the memory book from Miss Palmer. He repeated what had become an old saw—long ago attributed to Mark Twain—that the secret of his longevity was the strict rules he followed: "Never go to bed as long as there is someone to stay up with. Never smoke while sleeping, and never smoke more than one cigar at a time."

The move to the home of Felix and Ruby had not hindered Rupert's social life, which still included a round of concerts, lectures, and meetings. Several times, Ruby invited Aileen Pringle, for many years a close friend of Rupert and Patty, to dinner at the Hughes household; she was also a friend of Ruby and Felix, so these were evenings of pleasant reminiscences.[6] Miss Pringle, who had played leading roles in more than sixty silent movies—including Rupert's *Souls for Sale*—had been married to James M. Cain, with whom Rupert had disagreed so vigorously about the

Cain Plan, but she and Cain had divorced in 1946.

Rupert also continued to be involved in organizations, still heading The Authors and maintaining an active interest in veterans groups; he regularly attended meetings of the American Legion and the Veterans of Foreign Wars.

One evening, upon returning from a dinner meeting, he heard Felix improvising at the piano on a theme Felix had composed. Rupert paused to listen, then suggested his brother continue to work on it; Rupert, in turn, would write some lyrics to go with the music. Out of this collaboration came two songs, "Soul of My Soul" and "Tomorrow," apparently the only compositions the two wrote together. They dedicated both songs to Ruby, who later copyrighted them and had the thrill of hearing them performed by leading orchestras in southern California.[7]

In reflecting upon the years when Rupert lived with her and Felix, Ruby would later recall that Rupert still devoted several hours each day to the creative process. "I would see him gazing out over our patterned California garden and the huge Arizona cedars which his mother had planted as a backdrop in 1924." Much of his time was now spent writing for *Center of Light*, an inspirational magazine House-Warven had begun publishing in Hollywood in 1950. It often featured articles by Hughes and other well-known writers.[8]

His views and philosophy about life and its meaning had undergone a change in recent years, according to his sister-in-law. Although her interpretation of this seems somewhat at odds with his statement *The Humanist* quoted in 1950—which might have been written at an earlier date—she was convinced that there was a real evolution in his beliefs.

She believed that into the essays he wrote for *Center of Light* he "put the wisdom attained in living to his advanced age—wisdom which had taken him through unbelief to acceptance of a Great Authority." It became customary for him to use the expression "God bless you, Ruby" in everyday conversation.[9] To her this seemed not a glib comment, but an indication that he honestly sought blessings from the Almighty upon one whom he wished well. It was hardly the language of a confirmed atheist.

It is unlikely that he ever returned to a conventional view of the religion he had castigated three decades earlier. The dogmas and practices he had condemned could never have much meaning to him again, but his experiences and observations of life had enabled him to develop a spiritual philosophy of his own.

"I believe he was convinced that the true meaning of life is creation— with which everyone is gifted in one form or another, to use or neglect," Ruby wrote many years later. "If he had a fear it was that some day the view might arise among the young that life has no meaning, no purpose—leading to a nihilism which could end in unspeakable chaos, the utter destruction of human society, and perhaps even the extinction of man himself."

"Rupert's antidote," she added, "would be . . . to let the glimmering forces of creation light us as brightly as may be along the path to the Golden Age, which, we are told, will replace the Age of Gold." [10]

It had been Rupert's good fortune to have enjoyed a healthy life, with only occasional physical problems, throughout most of his first eighty years. He once observed, "I have had few illnesses, but I do not complain of the dearth. My hearing is bad. I wear glasses, but I have almost all my teeth and most of my hair." [11]

Although he enjoyed sports, he rarely participated in them. But he had his own way of keeping fit. He once wrote, "I keep my muscles pretty strong . . . by flexing exercises, by exerting all of the power of one muscle against another and going along the whole line of muscles from scalp to toes. I carry a heavy walking stick and use it as a gymnasium."

He did not approve of suffering if it could be avoided, knowing that "whether it is only a cinder in the eye, a pebble in the shoe or a thorn in the thumb, the body cannot serve the soul any better than an automobile can carry you till you take the tire lock off the wheel." Such thinking led to a theory about human personality:

"Similarly, the soul should have such cinders and thorns removed as can be reached. The sense of inferiority, the delusion of persecution, the feeling that one is kept back by conspiracy, or that one's critics have some secret motive, the magnifying of a failure, the idea that one is being watched and derided—all these things are torments and they prevent many noble souls from accomplishing their best and from enjoying what they achieve."

These convictions, established many years earlier, had kept him from despair over the opinions of others regarding his work. As he had put it:

"When I am soundly trounced by a critic, I get no comfort from the thought that he has a personal spite against me, or is actuated by envy. Why should he like my work? Why shouldn't he say he hates it, if he does? It is a vast luxury to walk through the world feeling that everybody means well."[12]

He had learned to accept rejection philosophically—realizing that nothing personal was meant by the turndown of a manuscript by a publisher. His granddaughter Barbara recalled his saying, in regard to rejection slips, "I have wiped every part of my anatomy with them." [13]

Ruby Hughes came to know and understand her brother-in-law as few others did, and she became aware of his faults as well as the strengths of his character and his exceptional talents. "To meet him in person," she wrote, "Rupert Hughes could appear extremely aloof . . . . His main fault was that he would tend to reject outright what didn't chime with his mind, although he did this as gracefully as he assimilated what he found attractive." [14]

In differing with contemporaries over literature and history, he could argue convincingly or write heated letters in an exchange of views, but then would lock arms with his adversary and they would go out together for dinner.[15] That was part of the "vast luxury" of which he wrote—the feeling that everybody means well.

Despite having had arteriosclerosis and hypertension since a year or so after the end of World War II, Rupert seemed to be in good physical shape until after he turned eighty in 1952. But his condition that year suddenly deteriorated when he suffered a stroke and was diagnosed as having chronic myocarditis[16]—an inflammation of the middle muscular layer of the heart wall.

Later, just two days before his birthday in January, 1953, the Hollywood Citizen-News reported that he had suffered two broken ribs in a fall at his home and that his doctor had told him to "go easy" on celebrating his 81st birthday. But the resilient Rupert was undaunted by the mishap. The newspaper reported that he expected to be back with the Authors' Club in a few weeks.[17]

Although the output of his work had slowed considerably, with nothing meaningful to show for his recent efforts, some of his early writings were being published in new forms and he attained a certain amount of recognition for work done in the past. One of his earliest poems, "With a First Reader," was published in 1953 in Burton Stevenson's second edition of *The Home Book of Modern Verse*. A year earlier, Franklin P. Adams's collection of famous sayings, *FPA Book of Quotations*, included the poem's first four lines.[18]

In 1953, author Asa Don Dickinson listed Hughes's Washington biography among the three thousand best books written during the past three thousand years, a significant tribute. The choice of volumes mentioned in *The World's Best Books, Homer to Hemingway* was based on a consensus of expert opinion, according to the compiler, as "most worthy of the attention of today's intelligent American readers who are equipped with at least a high school education or its equivalent." The description of Hughes's *George Washington* stated: "This biography was frowned upon by some as an attempt to smear a national hero. It is really a successful and praiseworthy effort to restore the breath of life and virile humanity to one who had become to many an insensate stone image." [19]

In 1954 Garden City Books published still another edition of the Deems Taylor-Russell Kerr revision of Hughes's *Music Lovers' Encyclopedia*. By now it was a "must" on many shelves, and Hughes had established an enduring reputation as a music authority. The 1954 edition of *Our American Music* recalled that he had been "a musician, composer, and writer on musical subjects" before becoming a novelist. After his early music, it said, "he became something of a modernist, showing investigation of dissonance in his dramatic monologue *Cain* and in his *Free Verse Songs*." [20]

In 1955, a book of memorable quotations, *The American Treasury, 1455-1955*, cited "Her face was her chaperone" [21]—a quote from his book *The Last Rose of Summer*.

Decades later, another famous quote from Hughes would be published in *Forbes* Magazine: "A determined soul will do more with a rusty monkey wrench than a loafer will accomplish with all the tools in a machine shop."

Despite optimism expressed so often in years past, Hughes had resigned himself in the mid-1950s to a realization that the fourth volume of his George Washington biography would never be completed during his lifetime, nor would the earlier volumes be revised as he had so fervently hoped. He now knew that his work on Washington, which he considered his most notable achievement, would stand as it had been published. The partially written volume four must now become in itself a part of history—perhaps to be finished someday by another biographer, younger and with more time to devote to the uncompleted task.

The *Honnold Library Annual Report, 1954-55*, published by the Honnold Library for the Claremont Colleges in Claremont, California, carried news of an important acquisition by the Honnold Library Society:

> *The Rupert Hughes Collection of Material on Washington.* In the years 1926-1930 Rupert Hughes published a three-volume life of George Washington. In the course of writing these volumes the author gathered together the collection of 270 volumes and sixty pamphlets on Washington and his times which the Society has purchased for the library. In addition, the collection includes six boxes of clippings from newspapers and magazines, and transcripts of letters in the Clements and Huntington libraries, all concerned with Washington. Many of the pamphlets date from Washington's own time, including an anti-Washington pamphlet, *Remarks occasioned by the late conduct of Mr. Washington . . . .*[22]

The acquisition thus placed the bulk of Hughes's Washington research papers in a library where they could be made readily available to other historians and biographers interested in the George Washington era.

Hughes suffered a second stroke in 1953 which signalled he should put his affairs in order. Early in 1954 he signed a last will and testament that would leave his entire estate, including "any and all income from literary, dramatic, musical compositions, productions, manuscripts, whether finished or unfinished, and from all other sources of whatever type, nature or description to my brother Felix Hughes if he be living at the time of my death. Should my brother Felix Hughes predecease me, or die prior to the final distribution of my estate, then I hereby give, devise and bequeath my entire estate as aforesaid, to his wife Ruby H. Hughes." Felix was named executor, with power to sell or otherwise dispose of any and all property as deemed advisable for the best interests of the estate.

The will made known Hughes's family connections: "I state that I am a widower, that no children survive me, that I have three grandchildren, the children of my deceased daughter Elspeth Hughes Lapp, namely, Mrs. Wesley Cameron of Los Angeles, Mrs. William Roberts of Cleveland, Ohio and Mrs. John De Pould of Cleveland, Ohio; that I have a brother, namely Felix Hughes."

The will also stated:

"Except as herein specifically provided, I have intentionally and with full knowledge omitted to provide for my heirs including but not limited to my granddaughters and their children.

"I have intentionally left my entire estate to my brother Felix Hughes and to his wife Ruby H. Hughes . . . in deep appreciation of the loving care and maintenance with which they have provided me during the latter part of my life." [23]

The signature, in the now shaky handwriting of the man who had written millions of words by hand for publication, was dated January 8, 1954.

Because of his health problems, Hughes requested in November, 1954, that he be permitted to step aside from the presidency of the Authors' Club, knowing that he could no longer handle its responsibilities. The club members reluctantly agreed, but elected him president-emeritus. He had founded the club as The Writers in 1922, and, aside from a six-month period in which Irvin S. Cobb had headed it, had been its only president.[24]

By the mid-1950s his physical condition had worsened and he required more attention. From 1955 on he did hardly any writing, although he often sat absorbed in his thoughts, sometimes striving to put them down on paper.

By mid-1956 he could no longer walk by himself, so it was necessary for him to be confined to his room, although he was never bedridden. His writing ceased, but he did a little reading. When taking care of him became too much of a burden, a full-time nurse was brought in. As Ruby described Rupert's situation, it was a "complete letdown" for the man whose entire life had been one of vigor and almost ceaseless activity. His granddaughter Barbara would come by to visit and cheer him up, and she recalled decades later that he continued to be mentally alert despite his physical condition.[25]

On Sunday morning, September 9, 1956, Rupert had breakfast in his bedroom and seemed in good spirits. In the afternoon, when his nurse,

William E. Brockwell, returned to the room at about 2 p. m., Rupert was sitting as usual at the table where he ate meals and read, beside a window overlooking the garden.[26]

Luncheon trays had been sent in, and when Brockwell entered, Rupert greeted him "smilingly and warmly," as Felix later reported. The nurse proceeded to arrange the food and utensils on the table for the meal, and then, just when they had begun to eat, Rupert was seized by a heart attack.

Brockwell immediately summoned Felix and Ruby, who managed to reach Dr. Lorenz M. Waller, Rupert's physician, by telephone at his home. He rushed to the Hughes household, but within five minutes of his arrival—at about 3 p. m.—Rupert died. With him at the time were the doctor and nurse and his beloved Felix and Ruby.[27]

The patriot who as a young poet—at a time when wars still seemed glorious—had written that he wanted to die on a "battlefield of victory," had passed away quietly in a comfortable room, attended by loved ones. As Felix wrote in a letter, "God was very merciful to him because he endured no suffering at the end." [28]

The remarkable Rupert, the author who had often expressed a desire to "live a thousand years and a thousand lives" was now gone, having crowded into a single lifetime of more than eighty-four years and seven months an incredibly large number of creative accomplishments in a variety of fields.

In accordance with his wishes, Felix and Ruby arranged for his cremation. They also sent word of his death to his granddaughters, one of whom was in Cleveland and another in Europe with her husband.[29]

Sometime earlier, the founder of Forest Lawn Memorial Park in Glendale, Dr. Hubert Eaton, had requested Rupert's permission for his remains to be interred in the Memorial Court of Honor when he died. This was the final resting place, beneath the stained glass window of "The Last Supper," of many famous people—the "immortals," as Forest Lawn called them. But Hughes had declined this honor, choosing instead to have his ashes interred in the niche he had selected after the death of his wife, Patterson. Felix and Ruby followed Rupert's wishes that there be no funeral service, and they arranged for his remains to be inurned beside those of Patty in the Columbarium of Memory section in the Great Mausoleum at Forest Lawn.[30]

In newspapers of New York, Los Angeles, Keokuk, and other cities, the news of Hughes's death was given front page treatment; many papers carried his picture along with an obituary. The *New York Times* article cited his achievements as an author, citizen soldier, motion picture writer and director, radio commentator, and outspoken anti-Communist. It stated, "At the Lambs, oldest actors' club in the United States, it was said last night that Mr. Hughes joined in 1900 and was one of their members of longest standing." [31]

Some headlines used descriptive terms—"Noted Author, Soldier" or "Militant Writer." Most newspapers stated that he was best known for his Washington biography. The *Hollywood Citizen-News* described him as an "author-soldier-composer who called himself a jack-of-all-trades." The *Los Angeles Examiner* called him "for more than 50 years a towering figure in the literary life of the nation." The *Los Angeles Times*, citing his career and contributions as founder and president of the Authors' Club, reported that he was a popular dinner speaker and lecturer and was described by his friends as "Hollywood's wittiest toastmaster." [32]

Soon after Rupert's death, Felix said of his brother, "His body and mind may be stilled, but his greatness and beauty of character will always live." [33]

Most obituaries stated that Elspeth had been Rupert's only child, but that in addition to his brother he was survived by three granddaughters and nine great-grandchildren. References to Howard were incidental, if at all. A few weeks later, when the *Hollywood Citizen-News* reported that the author had left his estate—consisting "almost entirely of copyrights and manuscripts and yielding $500 income a year"—to his brother Felix, it noted that the will did not mention Howard.[34]

CHAPTER TWENTY-NINE

THE ESTATE BATTLE

*"I can get through to the Almighty by dropping to
my knees, but I don't know how to get in touch
with Howard."*

It had been a quarter of a century, almost to the day, since the death of
Rupert Hughes. His name was now mentioned infrequently—that is,
until certain circumstances that had begun with the 1976 death of his
nephew, reclusive billionaire Howard Hughes, unfolded into public view.

Since the 1940s, Howard's life had become so strange that Rupert
once said, "I can get through to the Almighty by dropping to my knees,
but I don't know how to get in touch with Howard." [1]

After Howard promised U.S. senators that a huge flying boat he
built could get off the ground, he flew it seventy feet high. In a battle
over Trans World Airlines, which he bought and sold, he defied an
order to appear in court, and while owning RKO Studios, he never set
foot on the lot.

He married actress Jean Peters in 1957, was not seen again in public,
and they were divorced in 1971. Meanwhile, he lived in secrecy in a Las
Vegas hotel and created an empire of hotels, casinos, aviation companies,
and land holdings. He later lived in hotels in other cities, amid rumors
that he was seriously ill.

On April 5, 1976, he died in an ambulance jet enroute to a hospital in Houston from Acapulco, Mexico. His funeral in Houston lasted three minutes and was attended by a sparse gathering, mostly relatives on his mother's side, including Aunt Annette Lummis.

Some headlines immediately after Howard's death stated that he left no known survivors. It seemed true that he died unmarried and childless—although both of those conditions were to be disputed later. But, in addition to his aunt, he had many first cousins on his mother's side, including William Rice Lummis, an attorney with the well-known Houston firm of Andrews, Kurth, Campbell, and Jones. Lummis, known as Will, had grown up in the Yoakum Boulevard home in which Howard's parents had lived, but he had only seen Howard twice. Nevertheless, when hospital officials called about arrangements for Howard's burial, he took over, and from then on his life would never be the same.[2] Within a short while he was appointed administrator and temporarily named sole stockholder of Howard's Summa Corporation; by early August he was chairman of Summa's Board of Directors.[3]

One of the first steps to be taken was to determine whether Howard had left a valid will; if not, there would be a need to find out who would inherit his vast estate. There appeared no doubt that his closest relatives were his Aunt Annette and the first cousins on his mother's side. Under Nevada law Aunt Annette would inherit everything, but in Texas the maternal and paternal heirs would share equally in the estate.[4]

Early news reports made no mention of possible surviving relatives on Howard's father's side, although an Associated Press obituary reported: "Young Howard grew up on movies. The orphaned scion of oil-drilling tool millions, he played hooky from an Ojai, Calif., school to visit his Uncle Rupert, a successful screen writer of the 1920s."[5] Will Lummis and his cousins were not aware of anyone related to Howard's father who would be entitled to any part of the estate.

To their great surprise, they soon learned that a claim to a portion of the Howard Hughes fortune was being made by three women on the paternal side of the family—the granddaughters of Howard's Uncle Rupert Hughes, who were being represented by Paul L. Freese of the Los Angeles law firm of Kindel & Anderson.

All three granddaughters—Barbara Cameron of Los Angeles, and

Agnes Roberts and Elspeth De Pould, both of Cleveland, were daughters of Rupert's only daughter, Elspeth. If it were determined that Howard's estate should be probated in Texas, they would most likely inherit half of it, but if probate took place in Nevada they would gain nothing at all. They first supported an attempt to have a neutral party named to search for a will, rather than Richard Gano, the court-appointed special administrator and a maternal first cousin of the deceased.[6] Then, in May, they filed suit claiming that Howard had died intestate and asked for a jury trial of their claim.[7] By then it was becoming apparent that legal maneuvers could become hopelessly snarled.

It was in this clouded environment that Will Lummis and his attorneys prepared a sixteen-page Settlement Agreement to make certain that the likely heirs on both sides of the family would share in the estate if no valid will was found. The largest portion would go to the Lummises, no doubt because of the possibility that probate would take place in Nevada, in which case Aunt Annette would be entitled to everything. In the agreement, after taxes were paid, she would receive 25 percent of the estate and 50 percent would go to other maternal heirs. Regardless of where the estate was probated, the remaining 25 percent would go to the paternal heirs. Mrs. Lummis, Sr., also was given the option of donating a quarter of the estate to charity before any division took place.[8] The agreement was signed in early July, 1976. With this smoothing out of possible problems, the main task appeared to be to find out whether any will that surfaced was valid.

But then something happened that threatened to wipe out the claim by the three granddaughters of Rupert Hughes. Suddenly, in August, two more persons filed a claim that they were entitled to a portion of Howard's estate because of their relationship with Rupert. They were Avis Hughes McIntyre, then seventy-six years old and living in Montgomery, Alabama, and her brother, Rush Hughes, seventy-four, of Palm Springs, California, the daughter and son of Rupert's second wife, Adelaide. If Avis and Rush could prove that they were "equitably adopted" heirs of Rupert Hughes they might inherit a large portion of the estate.

Most estimates of Howard's worth were about $2 billion or $2.5 billion. More than forty wills surfaced, but they were a bizarre lot, including one left in the Mormon headquarters in Salt Lake City that was ruled a fraud. There were also hundreds of prospective heirs, some of whom claimed to have married Howard and others who said they were his illegitimate children.

Meanwhile, the states of Texas, California, and Nevada fought over Howard's legal residence. A Houston jury ruled that he was a Texas resident for tax purposes, but the other states disagreed.

While the states battled, attorneys tried to work out a solution to the problem of what to do about the claim made by Avis and Rush, which their lawyer undertook to prove was valid even though they had not been adopted. He contended that they had used the Hughes name and that Rupert had provided for their education in private schools, had helped Rush find jobs as an actor, and had given Avis away in marriage—just as if they had been his biological children.

Agnes (Chris), Elspeth (Beth), and Barbara (Bobbie) at first fought the idea of "equitable adoption," but finally decided to settle the matter in order to avoid lengthy court proceedings. In the summer of 1977 they and the maternal heirs agreed to a new Settlement Agreement calling for twenty-two heirs to share in the distribution of the estate. Included were Howard's Aunt Annette Lummis; sixteen maternal cousins; and the five on the paternal side—Rupert's granddaughters and Avis and Rush.[9]

On July 13, 1981, Judge Pat Gregory of the Harris County, Texas, Probate Court No. 2 ruled that Howard Hughes had no close relatives and left no will at the time of his death. He threw out claims made by two women who said they had married Hughes and by two other persons claiming to be his children. The way was now set for a determination as to who were the actual heirs.

Judge Gregory had appointed O. Theodore Dinkins, Jr., a partner in the Houston law firm of Butler, Binion, Rice, Cook & Knapp, to be the "Attorney ad Litem for the Unknown Heirs of Howard Robard Hughes, Jr., deceased," and Dinkins had informed everyone indicating an interest in the proceedings that the hearing beginning August 24 would first consider the maternal claims and later those by persons on the paternal side of the family.[10] To ferret out the existence of all possible unknown heirs, he hired a certified genealogist, Mary Smith Fay, to trace the family background of Howard Hughes. While working on the case from 1977 until 1981, she and Suzanne Finstad, a law clerk and later a partner in the

Butler, Binion firm, had little difficulty finding out about family connections on the mother's side, but they ran into numerous controversies in regard to the Hughes side.[11]

Perhaps the most crucial dispute centered on the legitimacy of Elspeth Hughes, Rupert's daughter. Normally this would have been a mere formality, to be decided after examining Elspeth's birth certificate, but 400 rival claimants on the paternal side—ranging from second to fifth cousins—were determined to wage war over this matter with great vehemence.[12]

Among charges these detractors hurled at the hearing before Judge Gregory was that Elspeth was not Rupert's biological child but was born to his first wife, Agnes, as the result of an affair with another man. Another approach they took was that Rupert had been incapable of fathering a child because, they contended, a case of the mumps when he was a child had left him sterile.[13] Dinkins, Mrs. Fay, and Ms. Finstad diligently checked birth certificates and church, courthouse, and other records to try to determine the truth. Although there would be many unanswered questions, the evidence Dinkins presented to the jury bore out the claims made by Elspeth's daughters regarding their right to heirship.[14]

Attorney Paul Freese had assembled an impressive array of evidence to prove Rupert's acceptance of Elspeth as his daughter and her offspring as his granddaughters. Included were birth certificates, wedding documents, letters, notations in Bibles, newspaper clippings, and photographs. The granddaughters had provided ample confirmation of their relationship with Rupert—fond letters he had written to their mother when she was ill, and letters and notes he had sent them. These showed a deep and genuine love for his "Elspethkins" and a proud grandfatherly affection for her children.[15] There was also a deposition given by Ruby Hughes to help establish that the three women were the grandchildren of her late brother-in-law, Rupert.[16] In the face of so much proof, it would have seemed ridiculous for a jury to disregard such clear indications of family relationships and mutual love.

But the move to discredit Rupert's daughter was not the only tactic employed by opponents of his granddaughters' claim to kinship with the deceased Howard. Other distant cousins on the Hughes side, numbering about 160 and led by Robert C. Hughes of Alabama, told strange stories about Rupert and even about his father. They described a feuding

Kentucky family of Civil War days in which a one-eyed Felix Moner Hughes had robbed his brother (their ancestor, Daniel Freeman Hughes) of $140,000 and had later assumed the name of Felix Turner Hughes, then used the money to give his son, Howard Robard Hughes, Sr., a start in the oil tool business.

Mary Smith Fay, in a 1983 article on "Genealogy of Howard Robard Hughes, Jr." in the *National Genealogical Society Quarterly*, reported that she and Miss Finstad had found no census records that substantiated the claims. Other matters she declared were without proof were stories Robert Hughes and his fellow claimants told about Rupert. These included a tale that he had fathered a son by his first wife, Agnes, but that the child had died at an early age, and that Rupert also had a daughter, born in 1897 and named Lenora or Leila, who had "drowned in a swimming pool in Los Angeles about 1921." After the latter occurrence, according to the Robert Hughes story, Rupert had substituted Elspeth—supposedly the daughter of Patterson Dial from a previous marriage or affair—to take the drowned daughter's place. In attempting to confirm or refute this tale of intrigue, the genealogist found that in 1921 Patterson (who in 1917 was a high school freshman) would have been too young to have a daughter who could pass for Lenora or Leila, who by then would have been twenty-four years old.[17]

Later, in a 1984 book, *Heir Not Apparent*, detailing the findings of the investigation, Suzanne Finstad would imply that there was truth to some rumors about Hughes family members. Some of her conclusions, however, would seem as farfetched as the rumors themselves.[18]

Judge Gregory had stated that if the jury decided that Elspeth was not in the Hughes bloodline, a second nationwide search for heirs would take place.[19] Anyone seeking to discredit Elspeth, however, faced an uphill battle because of a Texas probate law that provides that any child conceived before or during a marriage is presumed to be legitimate.[20]

Finally, the matter was decided. The jury returned a verdict on September 4, 1981—just a few days before the twenty-fifth anniversary of Rupert's death—that Elspeth was indeed his daughter. The ruling brought newspaper headlines and national television coverage that included photographs of Rupert Hughes and of his granddaughters. The *New York Times* pictured the women with an enlarged photo of their mother.[21]

The verdict wiped out rival claims of more than 500 Hughes relatives and left only one additional matter to be decided on the paternal side. Judge Gregory scheduled a hearing to determine whether Avis Hughes McIntyre and her brother, Rush (who by then had died), had been "equitably adopted" by Rupert. Support for their claim had been provided by two stars of Rupert's silent movies. Both Colleen Moore and Eleanor Boardman gave filmed depositions indicating that he had introduced Rush to them as his son and that they later were told that he was Rupert's adopted son.[22]

Twelve days after the hearing began, Judge Gregory ruled that Avis and the estate of Rush were entitled to share in the Howard Hughes estate. He declared that although Rupert had not formally adopted Avis and Rush he had given them his name and had provided for their education and care.

Having previously determined that the maternal relatives of Howard would share in the estate, Judge Gregory's October 16, 1981 ruling meant that all twenty-two relatives who agreed to the settlement years earlier had now been declared heirs. In mid-November he signed the final judgment that seemed to bring an end at last to the five-and-a-half year battle to keep the estate from going to pretenders. Under the agreement formally approved, 25 percent of the estate would be donated to charity; of the remainder, 71.5 percent would be split among seventeen maternal heirs, and 28.5 percent would go to the five paternal heirs—9.5 percent to Avis and the estate of Rush Hughes and the other 19 percent to be divided among the granddaughters. Of the twenty-two heirs, four had died, which meant that their shares would go to their estates.

By 1990 the Howard Hughes estate was in various stages of distribution,[23] a process that would continue for some time. Fourteen years after the mystery man's death, his fortune at last was being passed along gradually to his heirs. But even after that, for the next several years, suits were still being filed by purported relatives seeking to share in the estate.

CHAPTER THIRTY

A LIFE IN PERSPECTIVE

"The Oaf who writes for posterity is mailing an anonymous letter with no address on it."

Fifteen years before Rupert died, he wrote a whimsical "auto-obituary" titled "The Happy Death of Rupert Hughes," published in *Coronet*. In it he wrote about himself:

"While he had become a general nuisance and his departure will not be lamented, he may be forgiven much now that he is out of the way because of his desire to hurt nobody and his futile eagerness to help everybody . . . . This would seem to leave us nothing to do but forget him." [1]

At times it has seemed that he has been forgotten, but there are signs of his rediscovery. Some of his early books about music and musicians have been reprinted, and he has been mentioned in many books about Hollywood. In St. Charles, Missouri, a proposal has been made to name him the town's literary "favorite son" and to restore the Opera House as a showcase for his films and plays. [2] Also in Missouri, the Rupert Hughes Roadside Park welcomes travelers to Lancaster, his birthplace.

In 1984, Ruby Hughes donated Rupert's manuscripts and literary correspondence to USC, and in 1990 an exhibit there honored his accomplishments. In the same year, the Arabian Nights home on Los Feliz Boulevard was included on a fund-raising tour sponsored by the Los Feliz Improvement Association. Ruby spoke about Rupert at both events.

When Rupert Hughes began his George Washington biography he intended it to be a single volume, but he expanded it into three published books, with a fourth volume partially written and another planned. Along the way, his opinion of Washington grew more favorable.

And so it has been with this study of the life and career of Rupert Hughes. The challenge proved more formidable than envisioned, but there came a realization that he truly was a man of exceptional talent and an amazing diversity of accomplishments. He was interested in everything and everybody and in always trying something new.

After reading his books, stories, essays, articles, poems, and letters, and listening to some of his music and viewing his films that are still in existence, it becomes obvious that he is entitled to a lasting place in the history of literature and the arts in America. Fortunately, those educational institutions that have acquired as much of his work as possible—most notably the University of Southern California and the University of Iowa—have taken steps toward providing him with such recognition.

A staff member of the Museum of Modern Art stated that Rupert Hughes has been neglected by too many film historians. Someday this may be rectified—even though Hughes said he included posterity among his "affectionate disrespects." [3]

When Rupert's death occurred on September 9, 1956, the two major Los Angeles newspapers ran editorials headed simply "Rupert Hughes." *The Examiner* declared that he had "performed illustriously in many roles—as an American patriot who never equivocated on any principle involving his beloved country; as a foe of Communism who devastated that movement with his penetrating analyses of its devious methods, and as a writer, lecturer and soldier." Noting that his lectures had "moved thousands upon thousands to new ideals," the editorial added:

> As a patriot, he never failed to stand up and be counted, in the cause of true Americanism—true Americanism, it must be noted, because no one was quicker than Rupert Hughes to debunk the hollow type of "patriotism" which consists merely of fine phrases, and no deeds.
>
> Our country has lost a stalwart figure in the passing of Rupert Hughes. And Los Angeles has lost a tireless contributor to its cultural growth. [4]

In a similar vein, the *Los Angeles Times* summed up his "distinguished career," numerous talents, and broad interests, repeating his statement that "I should like to live a thousand years and a thousand lives." Calling his Washington biography "a realistic appraisal of our first President as a man, rather than a legend," the *Times* continued:

> Besides his books, Mr. Hughes' pen produced hundreds of short stories, as well as serials, movie and radio scripts, poetry, and musical compositions. He was, at various times, a motion picture director, a soldier, sculptor, and at all times a scholar. Among the first to recognize the menace of Communism, he devoted the most active years of life to verbal and written opposition to it, whenever, wherever, and in whatever form it appeared.
>
> He was an extraordinary American and he made a mark on his times.[5]

A patriot, a stalwart figure, among the first to recognize the menace of Communism—these were terms that would have made Hughes proud.

Other words also come to mind: genius, brilliant, indefatigable, Renaissance man. They help sum up the life and career of one of the most remarkable persons in the history of American literature and in the patriotic life of the nation. Truly, Rupert Hughes was "an extraordinary American."

NOTES

CHAPTER ONE   THE FAMILY HERITAGE

1. Rupert Hughes (hereafter cited as RH) to Howard Hughes, Jr., 19 April 1924, Kimberley Cameron Papers.
2. Mary Smith Fay, "Genealogy of Howard Robard Hughes, Jr.," *National Genealogical Society Quarterly,* 71 (March 1983), 4.
3. RH, "My Father," *American,* Aug. 1924, 66.
4. Fay, "Genealogy," 4; *Portrait and Biographical Album of Lee County, Iowa* (Chicago: Chapman Brothers, 1887), 509.
5. *Biographical Album,* 509; RH, "My Father," 66.
6. Ruby H. Hughes (hereafter cited as RHH), "Loving Memories of Felix Hughes," *Shoppers Free Press,* Keokuk, Iowa, 28 Dec. 1977; RH, "My Father," 34.
7. Fay, "Genealogy," 5.
8. *Biographical Album,* 509.
9. *Dictionary of American Biography,* s.v. "Hughes, Howard Robard."
10. RH, "My Father," 66.
11. *History of Schuyler County, Missouri* (Trenton, Mo.: W. B. Rogers Printing Co., n.d.), 82.
12. RH, "How I Work," n.d., TS in Rupert Hughes Collection, Doheny Library, University of Southern California, Los Angeles (hereafter cited as RH Papers, USC).
13. RHH, "Loving Memories," 28 Dec. 1977; *Who's Who in America,* 1912-1913, s.v. "Hughes, Felix"; Fay, "Genealogy," 5.
14. RH, "My Father,"66.
15. RH, "My Mother," *American,* Sept. 1924, 16.
16. Poem read by RHH at opening of RH exhibit at Doheny Library, USC, 31 Jan. 1990.
17. *History of Lee County,* 260; RH, "My Father," 68.
18. Author visited Oct. 1983.
19. Dilly Tante, ed., *Living Authors* (New York: H. W. Wilson Co., 1931), 186.
20. Francis J. Helenthal, *The "Keokuk Connection": Howard Hughes* (n.p., 1976), 4.
21. RH, "My Father," 34; RH, "My Mother," 16.
22. RHH, "Loving Memories," 28 Dec. 1977.
23. Burns Mantle, *American Playwrights of Today* (New York: Dodd, Mead & Co., 1929), 246.
24. RHH, "Loving Memories," 28 Dec. 1977.
25. RH, "My Mother," 118.
26. George Gordon, *The Men Who Make Our Novels* (New York: Moffat, Yard & Co., 1919), 45.
27. Tante, *Living Authors,* 187.
28. RH to Dean Cornwell, 12 Dec. 1936, Iowa Authors Collection, University of Iowa Libraries, Iowa City (hereafter cited as Iowa Authors).
29. Visit to cemetery by author, Oct. 1983.
30. RH, "I Heard Mark Twain Laugh," *Good Housekeeping,* Nov. 1935, 44; *World Book,* 1963, s.v. "Twain, Mark."
31. RH, "Heard Mark Twain," 184-185.
32. RHH with Patrick Mahony, "Rupert Hughes [1872-1956]: Reflections on His Centennial," *Coranto* 8 (1973) 2:26; "Rupert Hughes, American," flyer (New York: Howard R. Peat, Inc., n.d.).
33 RH, "Why I Quit Going to Church, *Cosmopolitan,* Oct. 1924, 144.
34. RH, "My Father," 68, 70.

CHAPTER 2.   FROM ST. CHARLES TO NEW YORK

1. Mrs. Robert Rauch, "All in a Hundred Years," *Christian Advocate,* June 1940.
2 RH, "Where Are You, Tod Allerton?", *Cosmopolitan,* March 1924, 24.
3. Edna McElhiney Olson, *Historical Saint Charles, Missouri* (n.p., 1967), 21.

4. Rauch, "All in a Hundred Years"; Olson, *Historical Saint Charles*, 21; Olson, "Historical Series—St. Charles Opera House," *St. Charles Journal*, 14 Aug. 1960; Olson, "Historical Series—Numerous St. Charles Composers," *St. Charles Journal*, n.d.; Amy Scott and Erik Carlson, "St. Charles Needs a Favorite Son," *St. Charles Heritage*, vol. 10, no. 4, Oct. 1992, 92-93, 95-97.

5. Theodosia Rauch, "Biography of a Building," May 1954, TS in St. Charles County Historical Society Archives, St. Charles, Mo.

6. "St. Charles College Commencement Fifty Years Ago," *St. Charles Cosmos-Monitor*, 15 June 1937.

7. RH, "Where Are You?", 24.

8. Marie Kirkwood, "Reserve, '92, to Welcome 'Railroad' Hughes, *Cleveland Plain Dealer Sunday Magazine*, 7 June 1936, Case Western Reserve University Archives, Cleveland, Ohio (hereafter cited as CWRUA).

9. Ralph Portmann, "Rupert Hughes, '88 Recalls Girls, 'Spreads,' Student Speeches, *Reserve Record*, 27 Jan. 1932, CWRUA.

10. RH to Charles F. Thwing, 20 Sept. 1934, CWRUA.

11. Kirkwood, "Reserve to Welcome," 7 June 1936, CWRUA.

12. *The Reserve '91* (Adelbert College, Cleveland, Ohio, 1890); *The Reserve '92*; *The Reserve '93*; *Cleveland Plain Dealer*, 24 Feb. 1936, TS in CWRUA.

13. *The Reserve, '91, '92, '93*, CWRUA.

14. *The Best Short Stories of 1918 and the Yearbook of the American Short Story*, ed., Edward J. O'Brien (Boston: Small, Maynard & Co., 1919), 343; *The Reserve, '91, '92, '93*, CWRUA.

15. *Cleveland Plain Dealer*, 24 Feb. 1936; *The Reserve '92*, CWRUA; RHH at RH exhibit, USC, 31 Jan., 1990.

16. "Rupert Hughes, '92 Graduate, Visits School," *Reserve Weekly*, 17 Jan. 1933, CWRUA.

17. *The Biographical Dictionary of Musicians*, originally compiled by RH, revised and edited by Deems Taylor and Russell Kerr (Garden City, New York: Blue Ribbon Books, 1940), 410.

18. "Reserve to Welcome," *Cleveland Plain Dealer*, 7 June 1936, CWRUA.

19. *The Reserve '92*, CWRUA.

20. *Cleveland Plain Dealer*, 7 June 1936, CWRUA.

21. *The Reserve, '93*, CWRUA; *Cleveland Plain Dealer*, 7 June 1936, CWRUA.

22. RH, "My Father," 70.

23. RH, "How I Work," RH Papers, USC.

24. RH to Page, 2 Feb. 1893 and 10 March 1893, Fales Library, the Elmer Holmes Bobst Library, New York University (hereafter cited as Fales Library).

25. John Tasker Howard, *Our American Music, 3rd ed.* (New York: Thomas Y. Crowell Co., 1954), 570.

26. Gordon, *Men Who Make Novels*, 43.

27. RH, "My Father," 70; Marriage Register, St. George's Church, New York, Paul L. Freese Collection, Los Angeles (hereafter cited as Freese Papers).

28. Suzanne Finstad, *Heir Not Apparent* (Austin, Texas: *Texas Monthly Press*, 1984), 310.

29. RH, "My Father," 70; Fay, "Genealogy," 5; RHH, "Loving Memories," 28 Dec. 1977.

30. Marriage Register, St. George's Church, New York, Freese Papers.

31. RH, "Heard Mark Twain," 185.

32. RH to *Scribner's* 9 and 12 Sept. and 11 Nov., 1893, Charles Scribner's Sons Archive, Box 7, Manuscripts Division, Department of Rare Books and Special Collections, Princeton University Library (hereafter cited as Scribner's Archive). Published with permission of the Princeton University Library.

33. RH, "Why I Quit Church," 144, 146-147.

34. RH, "Happy Death of Rupert Hughes," *Coronet*, Oct. 1941, 28-29.

35. RH, "How I Work," 17, RH Papers, USC.

36. *The National Cyclopedia of American Biography, 1930*, s.v. "Hughes, Rupert"; RH, "My Father," 70.
37. RH, "Secret Societies at Yale," *Munsey's Magazine*, 292, 294.
38. RH, "My Father," 70.
39. Frank Luther Mott, *A History of American Magazines*, vol. 1, 1741-1850 (New York: D. Appleton & Co., 1930), 593; Gove Hambidge, "The World Is His Grab-Bag," *New York Herald Tribune*, 17 April 1932.
40. RH, "My Father," 70.
41. *New York Times*, Sunday, 1 Sept. 1895, 20.
42. T. Allston Brown, *A History of the New York Stage*, vol. 3 (New York: Benjamin Blom, 1903), 70.
43. John Chapman and Garrison P. Sherwood, eds., *The Best Plays of 1894-1899* (New York: Dodd, Mead & Co., 1955), 18.
44. Gordon, *Men Who Make Novels*, 43.
45. Burns Mantle, *American Playwrights of Today* (New York: Dodd, Mead & Co., 1929), 246.
46. Mott, *A History of American Magazines*, vol. 4, 1885-1905 (Cambridge: Belknap Press of Harvard University Press, 1938), 65-66.
47. Mott, *American Magazines*, vol. 4, 570; Mott, *A History of American Magazines*, vol. 5, Sketches of 21 Magazines, 1905-1930 (Cambridge: Belknap Press of Harvard University, 1968), 72.
48. RH, *The Lakerim Athletic Club* (New York: The Century Co., 1898), 4-9.

CHAPTER 3.   A WHIRLWIND IN MOTION

1. Copy of Elspeth Hughes birth certificate, Freese Papers; RH to R. U. Johnson, 13 June 1897, Fales Library.
2. *New York Times*, 13 Jan. 1916, 22.
3. RH, MS in RH Papers, USC. Handwritten note indicates "Written in my 20's."
4. Felix T. Hughes to L. M. Shaw, 3 March, 1898, State Historical Department, Division of Historical Musum and Archives, Des Moines, Iowa.
5. RH to Shaw, 29 April 1898, State Historical Department, Des Moines.
6. *Missouri and Missourians*, ed., Floyd Calvin Shoemaker, vol. 5 (Chicago: Lewis Publishing Co., 1943), 442.
7. *New York Times*, 13 Jan. 1916.
8. *An American Anthology*, 1787-1900, ed., Clarence Stedman (Boston: Houghton Mifflin Co., 1900), 736-737.
9. James Gibbons Huneker, *Steeplejack*, vol. 2 (New York: Charles Scribner's Sons, 1920), 189; Arnold T. Schwab, *James Gibbons Huneker: Critic of the Seven Arts* (Stanford, Calif.: Stanford University Press, 1963), 100.
10. Schwab, *Huneker*, 100; Huneker, *Steeplejack*, 191.
11. Schwab, *Huneker*, 100.
12. Huneker, *Steeplejack*, 191; Schwab, *Huneker*, 100.
13. Nicolas Slonimsky, *Baker's Biographical Dictionary of Musicians*, 6th ed. (New York: Schirmer Books, 1978), 783; RH, *Music Lovers' Cyclopedia* (New York: Doubleday, Doran & Co., 1912), 510.
14. RH to A. M. Foerster, 8 Nov. 1900, Iowa Authors.
15. RH, "A Eulogy of Ragtime," *Musical Record*, 1 April 1899.
16. RH, *Famous American Composers* (Boston: L. C. Page & Co., 1906), 424.
17. RH, *Famous American Composers*, 14.
18. Edward Jablonski, *The Encyclopedia of American Music* (Garden City, NY: Doubleday & Co., 1981), 1.
19. *Missouri and Missourians*, 441.
20. Tante, *Living Authors*, 186.

21. RH to William Lyon Phelps, 8 Jan. 1918, Yale Collection of American Literature, Beinecke Rare Book and Manuscript Library, Yale University, New Haven, Conn. (hereafter cited as Yale Collection, Beinecke Library).
22. Slonimsky, *Baker's Biographical Dictionary*, 783; Hughes, *Biographical Dictionary*, 329.
23. RH, *Music Lovers' Cyclopedia*, 464; *Missouri and Missourians*, 441; RH, "My Father," 70.
24. Fay, "Genealogy," 5; RH, *Music Lovers' Cyclopedia*, 464.
25. RHH, "Loving Memories," *Shoppers Free Press*, Keokuk, 28 Dec. 1977 and 4 Jan. 1978.
26. RHH, "Loving Memories," 28 Dec. 1977.
27. Fay, "Genealogy," 5-6.
28. *History of Lee County*, 260.
29. Helenthal, *Keokuk Connection*, 19-20.
30. RH, "Why I Quit Church," 147.

CHAPTER 4. BOOKS, PLAYS, REAL-LIFE DRAMA

1. RH, *Gyges' Ring: A Dramatic Monologue* (New York: R. H. Russell, 1901); it is possible there was an earlier printing, as Hughes mentions in "Happy Death" that it was his first published book.
2. RH to Phelps, 8 Jan. 1918, Yale Collection, Beinecke Library.
3. *National Cyclopedia*, 1930, s.v. "Hughes, Rupert."
4. RH, *Gyges' Ring and Other Verse* (Culver City: Murray & Gee, Inc., 1949), Foreword. The 1901 book sold "a few hundred copies," according to Gordon, *The Men Who Make Our Novels*, 42-43.
5. *Twentieth Century Authors*, 1942 ed., s.v. "Hughes, Rupert."
6. RH, ed., *Songs by Thirty Americans, for Low Voice* (Boston: Oliver Ditson Co., 1904), ix.
7. RH to Adolph M. Foerster, 27 Feb. 1903 and 11 March 1903, Iowa Authors.
8. RH, *Music Lovers' Cyclopedia*, 1.
9. RH, *Music Lovers' Cyclopedia*, v.
10. RH, *The Love Affairs of Great Musicians* (Boston: L. C. Page & Co., 1904).
11. *New York Times*, 15 Nov. 1902.
12. *New York Times*, 2 July 1904.
13. RH to Arthur Hoffman, 20 May 1905, Pennsylvania State University Libraries, University Park, Penn.
14. *Cumulative Book Review Digest*, 1905, 178.
15. *Dictionary of American Biography, Supplement* 6, 1956-1960, s.v. "Hughes, Rupert; *Who Was Who in the Theatre: 1912-1976*, s.v. "Hughes, Rupert."
16. *The Best Plays of 1899-1909*, eds. Burns Mantle and Garrison P. Sherwood (Philadelphia: Blakiston Co.; distributed by Dodd, Mead & Co., New York, 1944), 420.
17. Mantle and Sherwood, *Best Plays of 1899-1909*, 423.
18. *Who's Who in America, 1912-1913*, s.v. "Hughes, Rupert."
19. *Who Was Who in the Theatre, 1912-1976*, s.v. "Hughes, Rupert"; script in RH Papers, USC.
20. Gordon, *Men Who Make Novels*, 43.
21. Separation Consent Judgment, Agnes Hedge Hughes v. Rupert Hughes, 25 Nov. 1903, ordered by James Fitzgerald, Justice of New York Supreme Court, Freese Papers.
22. Hughes v. Hughes, Supreme Court of Queens County, New York, 12 July 1904, quoted in Fay, "Genealogy," 6 and 12; Finstad, *Heir Not Apparent*, 378-382, contains lengthy account of charges and counter-charges in the divorce case.
23. Fay, "Genealogy," 6.
24. *New York Times*, 30 Nov. 1903, 1.

CHAPTER 5. ALL FOR A GIRL

1. RH, "Heard Mark Twain."
2. RHH, "RH: Reflections," 29.

3. *New York Times*, 21 Feb. 1906, 9.
4. *New York Times*, 11 March 1906, 9.
5. RH to "Freddie" (no last name), 1 April 1906, Iowa Authors.
6. *History of Lee County*, 260.
7. *Musicians Since 1900, Performers in Concert and Opera*, ed. David Ewen (New York: H. W. Wilson Co., 1978), 953.
8. RHH, "Loving Memories," 4 Jan. 1978.
9. Fay, "Genealogy," 7; according to album cover for Cleveland Orchestra and Musical Arts Association's 1979 recording of *Celebrating the 60th Anniversary of the Cleveland Orchestra*, "The Cleveland Orchestra was founded in December of 1918 by Adella Prentiss Hughes, organizer of The Musical Arts Association."
10. Fay, "Genealogy," 7.
11. Donald L. Barlett and James B. Steele, *Empire: The Life, Legend, and Madness of Howard Hughes* (New York: W. W. Norton & Co., 1979), 31.
12. RH, "Howard Hughes—Record Breaker," *Liberty*, 6 Feb. 1937, 26, 28.
13. *Oil and Gas Journal*, Petroleum Panorama issue, 28 Jan. 1959, back cover.
14. *Missouri and Missourians*, vol. 5, 442; Mott, *American Magazines*, vol. 5, 30.
15. *Current Literature*, Dec. 1906, 697; Franklin P. Adams, *FPA Book of Quotations* (New York: Funk & Wagnalls Co., 1952), 116.
16. RH to George Horace Lorimer, 7 Dec. 1914, George Lorimer Collection, Historical Society of Pennsylvania.
17. *New York Herald*, Sunday, 10 June 1907, RH Papers, USC.
18. *Who Was Who in the Theatre: 1912-1976*, s.v. "Hughes, Rupert."
19. RH to Harrison Grey Fiske, 20 Nov. 1907, Minnie Maddern Fiske Papers, Manuscript Division, Library of Congress, Washington, D.C.
20. RH, "Early Days in the Movies," *Saturday Evening Post*, 6 April 1935, 19.
21. RH to Julia Marlowe, 22 Jan. 1908, Iowa Authors.
22. *Who's Who on the Stage 1908*, 30.
23. RH, comp., *The Poems of Adelaide Manola with a Memorial by Rupert Hughes* (New York: Harper, 1924), x.
24. *Poems of Adelaide Manola*, viii-x.
25. Fay, "Genealogy," 6 and 7.
26. Barlett and Steele, *Empire*, 590.
27. *New York Times*, 16 Aug. 1908, sec. 6, p. 6.
28. *New York Times*, Sunday, 23 Aug. 1908.
29. *Poems of Adelaide Manola*, x.
30. RH, "Early Days in the Movies," *Saturday Evening Post*, 13 April 1935, 121.
31. *Poems of Adelaide Manola*, x.
32. *New York Times*, 13 Jan. 1916, 22; RH later wrote, "having reached that dizzying height I resigned," RH to Mathews, n.d., CWRUA.
33. *Who's Who in America, 1912-1913*, s.v. "Hughes, Rupert"; *New York Times*, 30 Nov. 1910, 8.
34. *New York Times*, Sunday, 5 Sept. 1909.
35. *New York Times*, 11 Sept. 1909.
36. *New York Times*, 16 Sept. 1909.
37. William Glasgow Bruce Carson, *Dear Josephine* (Norman: University of Oklahoma Press, 1963), 93.
38. *Who's Who in America, 1912-1913*, s.v. "Hughes, Rupert."
39. *Delineator*, Sept. 1907; *Century*, Sept. 1908; *Ainslee's*, June 1909, June 1908; *Delineator*, clipping (n.d.) in RH Papers, USC.
40. *Saturday Evening Post*, 24 July 1909; Gordon, *Men Who Make Novels*, 49; letter quoted in Helenthal, *Keokuk Connection*, 13.

41. RH to William Gerard Chapman, 2 July 1937, Rupert Hughes Collection (#9348), Clifton Waller Barrett Library of American Literature, Special Collections Department, University of Virginia Library, Charlottesville, Va.

42. Frederic Taber Cooper, "The Factor of the Unusual and Some Recent Novels," *Bookman*, Dec. 1910, 431; *New York Times*, 21 Jan. 1911, 32.

43. *Book Review Digest*, 1910, 198.

44. Walter Williams, ed., *History of Northeast Missouri*, vol. 1, 1913, 134, Joint Collection, University of Missouri Western Historical Manuscript Collection-Columbia and State Historical Society of Missouri Mnuscripts, Columbia, Mo. (hereafter cited as Missouri Joint Collection).

45. *Cleveland Press*, 14 Nov. 1910, CWRUA; *Who's Who on the Stage 1908*, 77-78.

46. *New York Times*, 30 Nov. 1930, 8.

47. *The Best Plays of 1909-1919*, Burns Mantle and Garrison P. Sherwood, eds. (New York: Dodd, Mead and Co., 1933), 431; *Who's Who in America, 1912-1913*, s.v. "Hughes, Rupert."

CHAPTER 6. NEWFOUND SUCCESS

1. RH, "How I Write a Play," *Cleveland News*, 9 Aug. 1912, CWRUA.

2. *New York Times*, 3 Jan. 1911; advertisement in Liberty Theater program, 14 Aug. 1911.

3. Hambidge, "World Is His Grab-Bag."

4. "Life's Confidential Guide," *Life*, 4 Sept. 1911; Sigmund Spaeth, *A History of Popular Music in America* (New York: Random House, 1948), 91.

5. Ward Morehouse, *Matinee Tomorrow: Fifty Years of Our Theater* (New York: Whittlesey House, Division of McGraw-Hill Book Co., 1949), 107.

6. *Dictionary of American Biography*, Sup. 6, 1956-1960, s.v. "Hughes, Rupert"; Williams, ed., *History of Northeast Missouri*, 135 (Missouri Joint Collection).

7. Mantle, *American Playwrights*, 246.

8. Barlett and Steele, *Empire*, 590.

9. RH, "Early Days," 6 April 1935, 19.

10. RH, *Miss 318* (New York: Fleming H. Revell Co., 1911), 19, 125.

11. Gordon, *Men Who Make Novels*, 50.

12. RH, *Miss 318*, 6.

13. *Book Review Digest*, 1911, 244; *New York Times*, 3 Dec. 1911, 762.

14. RHH, "RH: Reflections," 28; Hambidge, "World Is His Grab-Bag."

15. RH to Charles F. Thwing, 13 Dec. 1911, CWRUA.

16. RH to Robert Bridges, 1 Feb. 1912, Scribner's Archive, Box 70, Princeton.

17. RH to Arthur B. Maurice, 14 Aug. 1922, Arthur B. Maurice Papers, A-T, Princeton (hereafter cited as Maurice Papers).

18. RH, *The Old Nest* (New York: The Century Co., 1912), 177-178.

19. "The Gossip Shop," *Bookman*, vol. 65, May 1927, 360.

20. *New York Times*, 17 May 1914; *Book Review Digest*, 1912, 229.

21. *Book Review Digest*, 1913, 269.

22. *Book Review Digest*, 1912, 229.

23. "The Gossip Shop, *Bookman*, vol. 65, May 1927, 360.

24. RH, "Early Days," 6 April 1935, 18.

25. RH to Thwing, 24 April 1912; Hughes biographical sketch, 1912; RH, "How I Write a Play." (All in CWRUA.)

26. *Book Review Digest*, 1913, 269.

27. RH to Walter Prichard Eaton, 26 Feb. 1912, Walter Prichard Eaton Collection (#6110), Clifton Waller Barrett Library of American Literature, Special Collections Department,

University of Viginia Library (hereafter cited as Eaton Collection, Barrett Library, U. of Virginia Library).

28. *Sadie* MS in RH Collection, USC; *Who's Who in America, 1912-1913,* s.v. "Hughes, Rupert."

29. Mantle, *American Playwrights,* 217 and 246; RH, "How I Write a Play," CWRUA.

30. *New York Times,* 19 Nov. 1912, 15; *Best Plays of 1909-1919,* 485.

31. *Who Was Who in the Theatre: 1912-1976,* vol. 2 (Detroit: Gale Research Co., 1972), 1235.

32. *The American Film Index,* 1908-1915, 531. Information supplied to author by Jack Spears.

33. RH, "Early Days," 6 April 1935, 19, 37, 39-40.

34. RH, "The Man That Might Have Been," *Cleveland Leader,* Sunday, 16 Feb. 1913.

35. *The Standard Index of Short Stores, 1900-1914,* Francis J. Hannigan, comp. (Boston: Small, Maynard & Co., 1918), 141.

36. *New York Times,* 23 Feb. 1913, sec. 7, 100.

37. *Book Review Digest,* 1914, 271; *New York Times,* 22 Nov. 1914, sec. 6, 517; *The American Treasury, 1455-1955,* Clifton Fadiman and Charles Van Doren, eds. (New York: Harper & Bros., 1955), 953.

CHAPTER 7. A NEW HOME, A NEW STYLE

1. "Lawyer Buys Estate," *New York Times,* 7 Feb. 1954, sec. 8, page 6.

2. *Bookman,* June 1914, 418; "Chronicle and Comment," *Bookman,* July 1915.

3. Hambidge, "World Is His Grab-Bag."

4. *Bookman,* vol. Sept. 1914-Feb. 1915; Gordon, *Men Who Make Novels,* 46.

5. Huneker, *Steeplejack,* 173.

6. RH, "Early Days," 6 April 1935, 40.

7. "Some Novels of the Month," *Bookman,* July 1915, 550.

8. *Book Review Digest,* 1915, 243; *Bookman,* July 1915, 550.

9. "Harper's Bookshelf" clipping, *Harper's,* n.d., CWRUA; Huneker, *Steeplejack,* 171.

10. RH, "Early Days" 6 April 1935, 40-41.

11. Kevin Brownlow, *Hollywood: The Pioneers* (New York: Alfred A. Knopf, 1979), 64-65.

12. RH, "Early Days," 6 April 1935, 43.

13. RH, "Early Days," 6 April 1935, 19.

14. Edward Wagenknecht, *The Movies in the Age of Innocence* (Norman: University of Oklahoma Press, 1962), 146.

15. RH, "Early Days," 13 April 1935, 19.

16. RH film credit list compiled for author by film historian Jack Spears, 1988.

17. RH, "Early Days," 13 April 1935, 30.

18. *AFI Catalog: Feature Films 1911-1920,* 68, cited in Spears film credits list; Spears to author, 1 Sept. 1993.

19. RH, "Early Days," 13 April 1935, 30.

20. RH to Sinclair Lewis, 29 March 1914, 22 July 1914, 11 Oct. 1915, Yale Collection, Beinecke Library.

21. Channing Pollock, *Harvest of My Years* (Indianapolis: Bobbs-Merrill Co., 1943), 255.

22. "Barker Urges Fund for Budding Genius," *New York Times,* 14 April 1915, 13.

23. Letter from RH and four others, N.d. (#9186), TLS from League of American Authors, Barrett Library, University of Virginia Library; Pollock, *Harvest of My Years,* 256.

24. Abel Green and Joe Laurie, Jr., *From Vaude to Video* (Henry Holt & Co., 1951), 195-196.

25. George N. Fenin and William K. Everson, *The Western* (New York: Grossman Publishers, 1973), 82.

26. Richard Schickel, "Doug Fairbanks: Superstar of the Silents," *American Heritage,* Dec. 1971, 93.

27. Leland L. Sage, "Iowa Writers and Painters: An Historical Survey," *Annals of Iowa,* 3rd ser., vol. 42, no. 4 (1974), 241.

CHAPTER 8. AND THEN THE WAR

1. *Who Was Who in the Theatre: 1912-1976*, vol. 2., 1236.
2. Gordon, *Men Who Make Novels*, 46-47.
3. *Bookman*, vol. 43, 118-120 and other monthly listings.
4. *Book Review Digest*, 1916, 283-284.
5. *New York Evening Post*, 5 Feb. 1916, sec. 3.
6. Gordon, *Men Who Make Novels*, 48.
7. *Bookman*, Sept. 1916, 580; "Rupert Hughes on the 13th Commandment," *New York Times*, 23 July 1916, Book Review section, 290.
8. RH to Phelps, 19 Oct. 1916, Yale Collection, Beinecke Library.
9. "Mrs. Greta Hughes Witherspoon," *New York Times*, 22 Feb. 1916, 11; Fay, "Genealogy," 5.
10. RH, *Gyges' Ring and Other Verse*, 48 and 56.
11. RH, "Early Days," 6 April 1935, 43; Raymond William Stedman, *The Serials: Drama and Suspense by Installment* (Norman: University of Oklahoma Press, second ed., 1977), 37.
12. RH, "Early Days," 6 April 1935, 43.
13. Printed program, Lorenz Theatre, 12 July 1916, Kemm Papers.
14. Stedman, *The Serials*, 37.
15. RH, "Early Days," 6 April 1935, 43; "Gloria's Romance Shown," *New York Times*, 23 May 1916, 13, 9.
16. RH, "Early Days," 6 April 1935, 43.
17. RH, "How I Work," RH Papers, USC.
18. RH, "M-Day Was Two Years Ago," MS, RH Papers, USC.
19. RH, "How I Work," RH Papers, USC.
20. RH, "Early Days," 13 April 1935, 31.
21. RH to Gordon Ray Young, 11 March 1917, RH Papers, USC.
22. "Tales of City, Town, and Country Life," *New York Times*, 18 March 1917, sec. 8.
23. RH to Young, 11 March 1917, RH Papers, USC.
24. *Missouri and Missourians*, 442; RH, "Early Days," 13 April 1935, 31.
25. RH to James M. Huneker, 14 Oct. 1917, Iowa Authors.
26. Gordon, *Men Who Make Novels*, 47.
27. RH, *We Can't have Everything* (New York: Harper & Brothers, 1917), 588-589.
28. *New York Times Magazine*, sec. 6, 13.
29. *Dictionary of American Biography*, Supplement 6, 1956-1960, s.v. "Hughes, Rupert."
30. RH to Mathews (no first name), n.d., CWRUA.
31. RH, "Early Days," 13 April 1935, 31; Jack Spears, *Hollywood: The Golden Era* (South Brunswick: A. S. Barnes & Co., 1971), 41.
32. RH, "Early Days," 13 April 1935, 31; Spears, *Hollywood: The Golden Era*, 41 and 179; Kevin Brownlow, *The War, the West and the Wilderness* (New York: Alfred A. Knopf, 1979), 141.
33. RH, "Early Days," 13 April 1935, 31.
34. RH to Edgar Selden, n.d., Iowa Authors Collection; RH to W. G. Chapman, 10 Aug. 1917, Hughes Collection (#9348), Barrett Library, University of Virginia Library.
35. Josephine Huneker, ed., *Letters of James Gibbons Huneker* (New York: Charles Scribner's Sons, 1922), 214-215.
36. RH to Huneker, 14 Oct. 1917, Iowa Authors.
37. RH, "Howard Hughes," 6 Feb. 1937, 28 and 26.
38. RH to Huneker, 14 Oct. 1917, Iowa Authors.
39. RH to Hamlin Garland, n.d. 1917, Hamlin Garland Collection, USC.
40. Nancy Johnson, Archivist/Librarian, American Academy and Institute of Arts and Letters, to James O. Kemm, 14 Aug. 1990.
41. RH to Phelps, 8 Dec. 1917, Yale Collection, Beinecke Library.

42. RH to Sinclair Lewis, 14 March 1917, Yale Collection, Beinecke Library.
43. Lewis to RH, 3 March, no year (Ca. 1917), excerpt in 1984 catalog, Paul C. Richards—Autographs, Templeton, Mass.

CHAPTER 9. A MILITARY CENSOR

1. RH to Phelps, 8 Jan. 1918, Yale Collection, Beinecke Library.
2. Hambidge, "World Is His Grab-Bag."
3. Ward Morehouse, *Matinee Tomorrow* (New York: Whittlesey House, McGraw-Hill Book Co., 1949), 60.
4. Scott M. Cutlip and Allen H. Center, *Effective Public Relations*, 2nd ed. (Englewood Cliffs, N.J.: Prentice-Hall, 1958), 38-39.
5. Form letter from M. Churchill, by RH, 4 Oct. 1918, Scribner's Archive, Box 70, Princeton.
6. Hambidge, "World Is His Grab-Bag."
7. "What to Read This Summer," *Bookman*, July 1918; *Book Review Digest*, 1918, 229.
8. "Censorship at Its Very Worst" editorial, *New York Times*, 3 Sept. 1918, 10.
9. *New York Times*, 4 Sept. 1918, 10.
10. Gordon, *Men Who Make Novels*, 48.
11. RH to Phelps, 8 Jan. 1918, Yale Collection, Beinecke Library.
12. RH, *Long Ever Ago* (New York: Harper & Brothers, 1918), 3.
13. RHH at RH exhibit at USC, 31 Jan. 1990.
14. *New York Times*, 24 March 1918, sec. 6, 123; *Book Review Digest*, 1918, 229.
15. Edward J. O'Brien, ed., *The Best Short Stories of 1918 and the Yearbook of the American Short Story* (Boston: Small, Maynard & Co., 1919), 377.
16. Mantle and Sherwood, eds., *Best Plays of 1909-1919*, 624; *New York Times*, 12 March 1918, 11.
17. *Index to Plays, 1800-1926*, Ina Ten Eyck Firkins, comp. (New York: H. W. Wilson Co., 1927), 88.
18. *Propaganda in Its Military and Legal Aspects* (Military Intelligence Branch, Executive Division, General Staff, U.S.A., n.d.). Handwritten note on first page indicates "written by Rupert Hughes," RH Papers, USC.
19. Donald Hayne, ed., *The Autobiography of Cecil B. DeMille* (Englewood Cliffs, N.J.: Prentice-Hall, 1959), 215-216.
20. *New York Times*, 15 July 1918, 9.
21. RH, "Early Days," 13 April 1935, 118; *Book Review Digest*, 1919, 249.
22. *New York Times*, 18 May 1919, sec. 7, 281.
23. *Who Was Who in America, 1951-1960*, s.v. "Hughes, Rupert."
24. RH, master of ceremonies, Camel Caravan radio program, Columbia Broadcasting System, 30 June 1936, TS, RH Papers, USC.
25. *Who Was Who in American History—the Military, 1975*, s.v. "Hughes, Rupert."

CHAPTER 10. EMINENT AUTHOR

1. RH, "Early Days," 13 April 1935, 31.
2. Spears, *Hollywood: The Golden Era*, 290.
3. RH, "Early Days," 13 April 1935, 31.
4. RH, "Behind the Screens," n.d., TS, RH Papers, USC.
5. Spears, *Hollywood: The Golden Era*, 290.
6. RH, "Early Days," 13 April 1935, 31, 118.
7. *Who Was Who in American History—the Military*, s.v. "Hughes, Rupert."
8. RH, "Early Days," 13 April 1935, 118.
9. "Eminent Authors Pictures Formed," *Moving Picture World*, vol. 40, no. 10, 7 June 1919, 1469.

10. Arthur Marx, *Goldwyn: A Biography of the Man Behind the Myth* (New York: W. W. Norton & Co., 1976), 98.
11. Charles C. Baldwin, *The Men Who Make Our Novels*, rev. ed. (New York: Dodd, Mead & Co., 1928), 41. The 1919 edition had been published under a pseudonym, George Gordon.
12. "Eminent Authors Pictures Formed," 1469; Marx, *Goldwyn*, 98-99.
13. RH, "Early Days," 13 April 1935, 120.
14. RH, "Author's Recognition in Movies," *New York Times*, 29 June 1919, sec. 3, 9.
15. RH, "Early Days," 13 April 1935, 120-121, 123.
16. RH, "At Home in Hollywood," RH Papers, USC.
17. Samuel Goldwyn, *Behind the Screen* (George H. Doran Co., 1923), 161.
18. RH, "Early Days," 13 April 1935, 118.
19. Frederick Palmer and Eric Howard, *Photoplay Plot Encyclopedia* (Los Angeles: Palmer Photoplay Corp., 1920), 78.
20. RH, "At Home in Hollywood," RH Papers, USC.
21. RHH, "RH: Reflections," 30; RH, Early Days," 13 April 1935, 120-121.
22. RH, "The Old First, and Last—Regulars," *New York Times Magazine*, 7 Sept. 1919, sec. 7, 3.
23. RH, "The Very Blue Book," *New York Times Magazine*, 14 Dec. 1919, sec. 4, 3.
24. *New York Herald Tribune*, March-June issues, 1910, RH Papers, USC.
25. Clippings in RH Papers, USC, and reviews in *Book Review Digest for 1919*, 249.
26. RH, "Viewing with Alarm," *Bookman*, May 1919, 263.
27. RH, "What Was Clytemnestra but a Stage Vampire?", *New York Times Book Review and Magazine*, 4 July 1920, 6.
28. RH to Mrs. Smith (no first name), n.d., Iowa Authors.
29. RH to John P. Toohey, 24 April 1919 and 19 Aug. 1919, Iowa Authors.
30. RH to Harold Waldo, 5 July 1919, Iowa Authors.
31. RH to Waldo, 11 June 1921, Iowa Authors.
32. RH to Walter P. Eaton, 31 Oct. 1919, Eaton Collection (#6110), Barrett Library, University of Virginia Library.
33. RH to Ferguson (no first name), 4 Dec. 1919, with scenario, Berg Collection of English and American Literature, New York Public Library.
34. RH to Channing Pollock, 20 Nov. 1919, Yale Collection, Beinecke Library.

CHAPTER 11. ON TO HOLLYWOOD

1. RHH, "Loving Memories," 4 Jan. 1978; Fay, "Genealogy," 7; RH, "Howard Hughes," 6 Feb. 1937, 26.
2. *Poems of Adelaide Manola*, x, viii.
3. *Poems of Adelaide Manola*, x-xi; RH to John Monk Saunders, 19 April 1920, Iowa Authors; *Book Review Digest*, 1920, 272; *Bookman*, Sept. 1920, 61.
4. Richard Le Gallienne, "'Love with Unconfined Wings' in Books of Poetry," *New York Times*, 18 Jan. 1925, sec. 3, 5.
5. RH to Saunders, 19 April 1920, Iowa Authors.
6. *Cleveland Topics*, 15 May 1920, CWRUA; RH to James B. Pond, 13 May 1920, Iowa Authors.
7. Edward J. O'Brien, ed., *The Best Short Stories of 1920 and the Yearbook of the American Short Story* (Boston: Small, Maynard & Co., 1921), 148-168, 383, 477.
8. RH, "How I Work," 11, RH Papers, USC.
9. *Bookman*, May 1920, 376.
10. *New York Times*, 30 May 1920, sec. 5, 280.
11. "Recent Books in Review," *Bookman*, Oct. 1921, 172; *Book Review Digest*, 1921, 209-210.
12. Gordon, *Men Who Make Novels*, 51-52.
13. RH, "How I Work," 4, RH Papers, USC.

14. RH, "In Praise of Harding's Style," *New York Times Book Review and Magazine*, »24 Oct. 1920, 6.

15. RH, "Our Statish Language," *Harper's Magazine*, May 1920, 849.

16. "Will the League Stop Wars?", *New York Times*, 17 Oct. 1920, sec. 3.

17. RH, "Imperialism in Reborn Poland," *New York Times Book Review and Magazine*, 18 July 1920, 9; RH, "The Third Russia," *New York Times Book Review and Magazine*, 15 Aug. 1920, 1.

18. *Show Biz: Vaude to Video*, 328; Raymond Moley, *The Hays Office* (Indianapolis: Bobbs-Merrill Co., 1945), 31.

19. *New York Times*, 17 April 1921, sec. 6, 2.

20. "Movie Men Favor a Federal Censor," *New York Times*, 2 Feb. 1922, sec. 2, 1.

21. Morehouse, *Matinee Tomorrow*, 184; RH to Frank (no last name), 22 Jan. 1920, Iowa Authors.

22. Alexander Woollcott, "The Play," *New York Times*, 17 Feb. 1920, 18; Woollcott, "Second Thoughts on First Nights," *New York Times*, 22 Feb. 1920, sec. 3, 6.

23. *The Best Plays of 1919-1920*, 335.

24. Title card for "The Thirteenth Commandment," Kemm Papers; *American Film Institute Catalog, Feature Films 1911-1920*, 922.

25. *AFI Catalog, Feature Films 1911-1920*, 810; Jacobs, *The Rise of the American Film*, 124.

26. *New York Times*, 5 June 1920, 19.

27. *Variety*, 11 June 1920; RH, "At Home in Hollywood," RH Papers, USC.

28. RH to Pond, 11 Nov. and 26 Nov. 1920, Iowa Authors.

29. Bruce Long, *William Desmond Taylor: A Dossier* (Metuchen, N. J.: The Scarecrow Press, Inc., 1991), 158, 202, 169, 182, 245.

30. RH, "At Home in Hollywood," RH Papers, USC; *American Film Institute Catalog of Motion Pictures Produced in the United States, Feature Films, 1921-1930* (New York: R. R. Bowker Co., 1971), 357; RH, "Early Days," 13 April 1935, 30.

31. RH, "At Home in Hollywood," RH Papers, USC.

32. *New York Times*, 21 Feb. 1921, 8.

33. *AFI Catalog, Feature Films, 1921-1930*, 561.

34. *New York Times*, 3 July 1921, sec. 6, 2.

35. RH to Jean Hughes, 29 May 1921, Kimberley Cameron Papers.

36. *Variety* review, 1921 volume, Margaret Herrick Library, Academy of Motion Picture Arts and Sciences, Beverly Hills (hereafter cited as AMPAS); *New York Times*, 29 June 1921, 10.

37. *Variety* review, 1921 volume, AMPAS.

38. *New York Times*, 29 June 1921, 10.

39. RH to Maurice, 14 Aug. 1922, Maurice Papers, A-T, Princeton; Hambidge, "World Is His Grab-Bag," 23; RH to Jean Hughes, 18 Sept. 1921, Kimberley Cameron Papers.

40. RH to Maurice, 14 Aug. 1922, Maurice Papers, A-T, Princeton.

41. Goldwyn, *Behind the Screen*, 245; *New York Times* advertisement, 29 June 1921, 10.

42. Goldwyn, *Behind the Screen*, 245.

43. RH to Jean Hughes, 18 Sept. 1921, Kimberley Cameron Papers.

44. *Variety* review, 1921 volume, AMPAS; *New York Times*, 3 Oct. 1921, 16.

45. RH to Thwing, 15 Oct. 1921, CWRUA.

46. RH to Jean Hughes, 18 Sept. 1921, Kimberley Cameron Papers.

47. Kilbee Brittain, "Nellie Durfee," *Terra*, Magazine of the Natural History Museum of Los Angeles County, vol. 18, no. 1, Summer 1977.

48. RH to Thwing, 27 Oct. 1921, CWRUA.

49. Copies of published songs and collections listed in this chapter are included in RH Papers, USC.

50. *Musical America*, 4 Dec. 1920, RH Papers, USC.

51. John Tasker Howard, *Our American Music, 3rd ed.* (New York: Thomas Y. Crowell Co., 1954), 570.
52. *Musical America*, 30 Oct. 1920, and *The Musical Courier*, 16 Sept. 1920, RH Papers, USC.
53. *The Etude*, May 1921, 224, 296.
54. *The Etude*, May 1920, RH Papers, USC; Berlin, *Ragtime*, 16.
55. *American Film Institute Catalog, Feature Films, 1921-1930*, 276; list of RH films supplied to author by Jack Spears.

CHAPTER 12. AND NOW A DIRECTOR

1. Colleen Moore, *Silent Star* (Garden City, N. Y.: Doubleday & Co., 1968), 19-27, 33, 109-110.
2. Moore, *Silent Star*, 117.
3. Colleen Moore Maginot, interview with author at El Ranchito, her home near Templeton, Calif., 7 June 1984.
4. RH to Jean Hughes, 18 Sept. 1921, Kimberley Cameron Papers.
5. *Variety*, 1922 volume, AMPAS.
6. Moore, interview with author, 7 June 1984.
7. RH to Jean Hughes, 18 Sept. 1921, Kimberley Cameron Papers.
8. RH, "Howard Hughes—Record Breaker," 6 Feb. 1937, 28.
9. Barlett and Steele, *Empire*, 49-50.
10. Moore, interview with author, 7 June 1984.
11. Barlett and Steele, *Empire*, 50.
12. RH to Jean Hughes, 18 Sept. 1921, Kimberley Cameron Papers.
13. Moore, interview with author, 7 June 1984.
14. *New York Times*, 26 June 1922, 16; *Variety*, 1922 volume, AMPAS.
15. Willis Goldbeck, "Mr. Hughes and the Photodrama," *Motion Picture Magazine*, Sept. 1922.
16. Goldbeck, "Mr. Hughes"; Moore, *Silent Star*, 117.
17. *New York Times*, 2 Oct. 1922, 21.
18. *New York Times*, 1 Oct. 1922, sec. 7, 3.
19. RH, "Behind the Screens," RH Papers, USC.
20. "Movie Making an Art," *New York Times*, 13 May 1923, sec. 8, 3.
21. William Drew, *Speaking of Silents* (Vestal, N.Y.: Vestal Press, 1989), 192.
22. Wagenknecht, *Movies in the Age of Innocence*, 147.
23. RH, "Early Days," 6 April 1935, 39; "Blanche Bates at the Palace," unidentified newspaper clipping in Rupert Hughes Papers at Honnold Library, Claremont Colleges, Claremont, Calif. (hereafter cites as Hughes Papers, Claremont).
24. Rudy Behlmer and Tony Thomas, *Hollywood's Hollywood* (Citadel Press, 1975), 119-120.
25. RH to Carl Van Doren, 27 April 1923, Carl Van Doren Letters, Box 16, Folder 12, Princeton.
26. RH, "Behind the Screens," RH Papers, USC.
27. MS for *Souls for Sale* trailer, 23 Feb. 1923, Cinema Section, Special Collections Dept., USC.
28. *Bookman*, June 1923, 493-494, 441.
29. *New York Times*, 9 April 1923.
30. *Variety*, 1923 volume, AMPAS; Eleanor Boardman (the Countess D'Arrast), interview with author at her home in Montecito, Calif., 9 June 1984.
31. RH, "At Home in Hollywood," RH Papers, USC.
32. Barlett and Steele, *Empire*, 51.
33. Goldbeck, "Mr. Hughes."
34. *New York Times*, 9 June 1923, 10.
35. Herald for *Gimme*, Kemm Papers.
36. *New York Times*, 15 Jan. 1923, 18; *Variety*, 1923 volume, AMPAS.
37. Screenplay MSS, Cinema Section, Special Collections, USC.

38. Moore, *Silent Star*, 117.
39. Moore, *Silent Star*, 128-129; Moore, interview with author, 7 June 1984.
40. Inside dust jacket for Moore, *Silent Star*.

CHAPTER 13. AT SUNDAY BRUNCH

1. Historical leaflet "The Villa Maria" (present name for the home) provided by Brothers of Saint John of God, 1990; RH, "Behind the Screens," RH Papers, USC.
2. Goldwyn, *Behind the Screen*, 245.
3. RH to Jean Hughes, 30 Jan. 1922, Kimberley Cameron Papers.
4. *Poems of Adelaide Manola*, vii, xiii; Boardman, interview with author, 9 June 1984.
5. *Poems of Adelaide Manola*, xiii; *Bookman*, Aug. 1922, 631.
6. *Poems of Adelaide Manola*, xiii.
7. *Bookman*, Nov. 1922, 384.
8. *Poems of Adelaide Manola*, xiv.
9. Barlett and Steele, *Empire*, 51; Boardman, interview with author, 9 June 1984.
10. Moore, interview with author, 7 June 1984.
11. RH, "How I Work," RH Papers, USC.
12. Goldwyn, *Behind the Screen*, 245.
13. RH to J. Murray Sandusky, 16 April 1922, Iowa Authors.
14. RH to Whitelock (no first name), 3 Jan. 1922, Rare Books and Manuscripts Department, University of Florida Library, Gainesville, Fla.
15. RH to Wilbur Cross, 19 Aug. 1922, Yale Collection, Beinecke Library.
16. RH, "An American Inferno," *New York Times*, 26 Feb. 1922, sec. 3, 11.
17. Will H. Hays, *The Memoirs of Will H. Hays* (Garden City, New York: Doubleday & Co., Inc., 1955), 343, 347.
18. *Bookman*, May 1923, 351-352; RH to Carl Van Doren, 21 April 1923, Van Doren Papers, Box 16, folder 12, Princeton.
19. RH to Van Doren, 27 April 1923, and Van Doren to RH, 25 April 1923, 3 May 1923, Van Doren Papers, Box 16, folder 12, Princeton.
20. *Bookman*, Aug. 1923, 601-603.
21. *Bookman*, Aug. 1923, 686; RH inscription in *Destiny*, State Historical Society of Missouri Research Library, Columbia, Mo.
22. RH, "On a Certain Condescension Toward Serials," *Bookman*, Dec. 1923, 378-383.
23. RH to Maurice, 4 Jan. 1924, Maurice Papers, A-T, Princeton.
24. *Bookman*, June 1923, 493.
25. *Book Review Digest* for 1923, 251; *New York Times*, 3 June 1923, sec. 3, 13.
26. RH to Marguerite Merington, 17 Sept. 1942, RH Papers, USC.
27. *New York Times*, 25 July 1923, 11.
28. *New York Times*, 8 Jan. 1924, 27.
29. *Variety*, 1923 and 1924 volumes, AMPAS.
30. *New York Times*, 8 Jan. 1924, 27.
31. *Variety*, 1924 volume, AMPAS.

CHAPTER 14. OF HAPPINESS AND GRIEF

1. Photostat of inscription in family Bible, Freese Papers; Fay, "Genealogy," 7.
2. RH to Jean Hughes, 18 Sept. 1921 and 30 Jan. 1922, Kimberley Cameron Papers.
3. *Who Was Who in America*, vol. 1, 1897-1942, s.v. "Saunders, John Monk"; RH to Jean Hughes, 30 Jan. 1922, Kimberley Cameron Papers.
4. Fay Wray, *On the Other Hand* (New York: St. Martin's Press, 1989), 85. Saunders married Miss Wray after his divorce from Avis.
5. "Divorces Rupert Hughes' Foster Son," *New York Times*, 16 Jan. 1928.
6. Fay, "Genealogy," 7.

7. Dale Carnegie, *Five Minute Biographies* (New York: Southern Publishers, 1937), 162.
8. Oscar Thompson, *The American Singer* (New York: The Dial Press, 1937), 363; RHH, "Loving Memories," 4 Jan. 1978, 2; *World Book Encyclopedia*, 1969 ed., s.v. "Tibbett, Lawrence."
9. RH, "Getting Paid for Having a Good Time," *American*, Aug. 1930, 90; Margaret McOmie, "We Create Beauty Ourselves," *Better Homes & Gardens*, April 1935, 86.
10. *Poems of Adelaide Manola*, xiv-xv; *New York Times*, Sunday, 16 Dec. 1923, 5.
11. *Poems of Adelaide Manola*, xv-xvi.
12. *New York Times*, 15 Dec. 1923.
13. *Poems of Adelaide Manola*, xvi.
14. *New York Times*, Sunday, 16 Dec. 1923, 5; *New York Times*, 17 Dec. and 20 Dec. 1923; *Poems of Adelaide Manola*, xvi.
15. Barlett and Steele, *Empire*, 52; Copy of death certificate of Howard Robard Hughes, Sr., Freese Papers.
16. Barlett and Steele, *Empire*, 51-52.
17. RH, "Howard Hughes," 6 Feb. 1937, 28; Barlett and Steele, *Empire*, 52.
18. Barlett and Steele, *Empire*, 54.
19. RH to Carl Sandburg, 3 Feb. 1924, Iowa Authors.
20. Copy of Howard R. Hughes, Sr., will, Freese Papers.
21. RH, "Howard Hughes," 6 Feb. 1937, 29.
22. Copy of Howard R. Hughes will, Freese Papers.
23. RH to Jean Hughes, 3 March 1924, Kimberley Cameron Papers.
24. RH to Howard Hughes, Jr., 19 April 1924, Kimberley Cameron Papers.
25. RH to Howard Hughes, Jr., 14 May 1924, Barbara Cameron Papers.
26. Barlett and Steele, *Empire*, 54-56.
27. Fay, "Genealogy," 7.
28. RHH, "Loving Memories," 11 Jan. 1978, and interview with author at her Los Angeles home, 21 Aug. 1986; RHH, "RH: Reflections" 32.
29. "In Old America," *New York Times*, 1 June 1924, sec. 3, 8; Hughes to H. S. J. Sickel, 5 Nov. 1936, Iowa Authors.
30. RH, *The Golden Ladder* (New York: Harper & Brothers Publishers, 1924), 181.
31. *Bookman*, Aug. 1924, 727, and Oct. 1924, 215; *Book Review Digest for 1924*, 300.
32. Jonathan Nield, *A Guide to the Best Historical Novels and Tales* (New York: Macmillan Co., 1929), 204; Ernest A. Baker and James Packman, *A Guide to the Best Fiction* (Barnes & Noble, 1967), 253.
33. *New York Times*, 7 June 1924.
34. RH, "Triumphant Hokum," *New York Times*, 24 Feb. 1924, 5.
35. RH, "My Father," 66, 70.
36. RH, "How I Work," 11, RH Papers, USC.
37. RH, "My Mother," 16, 120.
38. *Poems of Adelaide Manola*, xii, xvii, vii.
39. *Book Review Digest for 1925*, 329.
40. Alice Cecilia Cooper, ed, *Poems of Today* (Boston: Ginn & Co., 1924); Ernst C. Krohn, *Missouri Music* (New York: Da Capo Press, 1971), 50-51.
41. *Best Short Stories of 1924*, Edward J. O'Brien, ed (Boston: Small, Maynard & Co., 1924), 274, 343; 137-154.
42. RH, "Why I Quit Church," 44-45, 146, 148.
43. "Rupert Hughes Indicts Religion," *Current Opinion*, Dec. 1924, 754-755.
44. "RH Indicts Religion," 754-755.
45. RH to Grover C. Hill, 21 Oct. 1924, Grover C. Hill Collection, Alabama Department of Archives and History, Montgomery.

46. RH, "Am I an Atheist?", MS, n.d., RH Papers, USC.
47. *Dictionary of American Biography*, sup 6, 1956-1960, s.v. "Hughes, Rupert."
48. *Los Angeles Times*, 17 Dec. 1924.
49. Fay, "Genealogy," 7; *Who Was Who on the Screen, 3rd ed*, 1983, s.v. "Dial, Patterson."
50. Ilka Roberts, "Rupert Hughes, Informal Portrait of a Paradox," *Family Circle*, 27 Oct. 1923, 14-15, CWRUA.
51. RH to Jean Hughes, 3 March 1924, Kimberley Cameron Papers.
52. RHH, interview with author, 21 Aug. 1986; RH, handwritten 14-page autobiographical MS, untitled, n. d., RH Papers, USC.
53. "RH Marries Actress," *New York Times*, 1 Jan. 1925, 25.

CHAPTER 15. THE MID-TWENTIES

1. Barlett and Steele, *Empire*, 590.
2. Roberts, "RH, Informal Portrait," 14; RH, "How I Work," 14, RH Papers, USC.
3. "RH Named Guardian for Youth," *New York Times*, 18 April 1925, 17. In the cast list for *The Old Nest*, the brother is identified as Marshall Ricksen.
4. *A Catalog of Books Represented by Library of Congress Printed Cards*, vol 71 (Ann Arbor, Mich: Edwards Brothers, 1943); 1940 inscribed edition of RH book in Kemm Papers.
5. RH, "Early Days," 13 April 1935, 30.
6. *New York Times*, 27 Jan. 1925.
7. RHH, "RH: Reflections," 31; "Rupert Hughes Leaves Metro," *New York Times*, 28 June 1925, 20.
8. "Rupert Hughes Flatters the Human Race," *New York Times*, 24 May 1925, sec 3, 17.
9. *Book Review Digest for 1925*, 329.
10. RH to George Horace Lorimer, 11 July 1925, Wesley Stout Papers, Manuscript Division, Library of Congress, Washington, D. C. (hereafter cited as Stout Papers, LC).
11. RH to Lorimer, 2 May 1925, and Lorimer to RH, 11 May 1925, Stout Papers, LC.
12. Catherine Cranmer, "Rupert Hughes," unidentified newspaper reprint of *Missouri Historical Review* article, Oct. 1925, Keokuk Public Library.
13. RH to Henry E. Huntington, 26 June 1925, HEH 12365, Huntington Library, San Marino, Calif.
14. RH to George Sylvester Viereck, 31 March 1925, Iowa Authors.
15. RH to Viereck, 16 May 1925, Iowa Authors.
16. Frank Luther Mott, *A History of American Magazines*, vol. 4 (Cambridge, Mass: Belknap Press of Harvard University, 1957), 472.
17. Barlett and Steele, *Empire*, 56-59.
18. Barlett and Steele, *Empire*, 59-60.
19. Moore, interview with author, 7 June, 1984.
20. Barlett and Steele, *Empire*, 60-61; RH, "Howard Hughes," 6 Feb. 1937, 29.
21. *New York Times*, 11 May 1926, 24.
22. Mervyn LeRoy, *Mervyn LeRoy: Take One* (Hawthorn, 1974), 78-79.
23. *New York Times*, 16 May 1926, sec. 3, 8; *Book Review Digest for 1926*, 351; *Bookman*, Sept. 1926, 90.
24. RH to W. Orton Tewson, 28 Sept. 1926, William Orton Tewson Papers, Manuscript Division, LC.
25. RH, "Why I Am Still Going to School for My Country," *The American Legion*, July 1926, RH Papers, USC.
26. Fay, "Genealogy," 7.
27. Copy of Felix T. Hughes death certificate, Freese Papers. Birth year listed as 1837, but most sources show it 1838; copy of handwritten will of Felix T. Hughes, Freese Papers.

CHAPTER 16. THE GEORGE WASHINGTON FUROR

1. *New York Times*, 14 Jan. 1926, 1.
2. *New York Times*, 15 Jan. 1926, 14.
3. *New York Times*, 16 Jan. 1926, 16.
4. *New York Times*, Sunday, 17 Jan. 1926.
5. *New York Times*, 16 Jan. 1926, 1.
6. *New York Times*, 18 Jan. 1926, 24.
7. *New York Times*, 19 Jan. 1926, 26.
8. *New York Times*, 21 Jan. 1926, 20.
9. Hambidge, "World Is His Grab-Bag."
10. *Chicago Daily Tribune*, 14 Aug. 1926.
11. RH, *George Washington: The Human Being and the Hero, 1732-1762* (New York: William Morrow & Co., 1926), 487-492.
12. *New York Times*, 14 Oct. 1926, 14.
13. *New York Times*, 14 Oct. 1926, 14.
14. *New York Times Book Review*, Sunday, 24 Oct. 1926, 11, 30.
15. *Will Rogers' Daily Telegrams*, vol. 1., *The Coolidge Years: 1926-1929*, James M. Smallwood, ed. (Stillwater: Oklahoma State University Press, 1978), 151.
16. John Terbel, *A History of Book Publishing in the United States*, vol. 3, *The Golden Age Between Two Wars, 1920-1940* (New York: R. R. Bowker Co., 1978), 146.
17. Claude G. Bowers, "A Shelf of Recent Books," *Bookman*, Dec.1926, 502-503.
18. *New York Times*, Sunday, 19 Dec. 1926, 5.
19. RH, *Washington: Human Being*, 492-494.
20. *New York Times*, 21 Jan. 1927, 21.
21. *New York Times*, 23 Feb. 1927.
22. *New York Times*, 30 April 1927, 2.
23. *Book Review Digest for 1926*, 350-351.
24. *Publishers' Weekly*, 9 July 1927, 156.

CHAPTER 17. AN ARABIAN NIGHTS MANSION

1. Copy of building permit, 14 June 1925, in collection of Scott Lichtig, owner of the house in 1990; "Film Director Builds Home in Los Feliz Area," *Los Angeles Sunday Times*, 20 Sept. 1925.
2. McOmie, "We Create Beauty," 57.
3. *Los Angeles Sunday Times*, 20 Sept. 1925, 4.
4. Retta Badger, "The Workshop of a Hollywood Author," *Los Angeles Sunday Times Magazine*, 7 Feb. 1932; McOmie, "We Create Beauty," 87.
5. Badger, "Workshop"; Laura M. Bickerstaff, *Pioneer Artists of Taos* (Denver: Sage Books, 1955), following 22.
6. McOmie, "We Create Beauty," 54; Badger, "Workshop."
7. Badger, "Workshop"; copy of special permit in Scott Lichtig collection; Lichtig, interview with author, 3 Feb. 1990, at Los Feliz home built by RH.
8. McOmie, "We Create Beauty," 57, 54, 47; Roberts, "RH, Informal Portrait," 15.
9. McOmie, "We Create Beauty," 57; Badger, "Workshop."
10. Cutline for National Broadcasting Company photograph of RH seated in writing chair, 23 April 1943, Billy Rose Collection, New York Public Library at Lincoln Center, New York, N.Y.
11. Roberts, "RH, Informal Portrait," 15; Badger, "Workshop."
12. Roberts, "RH, Informal Portrait," 15; Badger, "Workshop"; McOmie, "We Create Beauty."
13. Roberts, "RH, Informal Portrait," 19.
14. Roberts, "RH, Informal Portrait," 15.

15. Garson Kanin, *Moviola* (New York: Simon and Schuster, 1979), 227; Kevin Brownlow and John Kobal, *Hollywood: The Pioneers* (New York: Alfred A. Knopf, 1979), 200.
16. Kanin, *Moviola*, 227; Boardman, interview with author, 9 June 1984.
17. RH, *We Live but Once* (New York: Harper & Brothers, 1927), 3-4.
18. *Book Review Digest for 1927*, 369.
19. *Book Review Digest for 1927*, 369.
20. *Book Review Digest for 1928*, 392-393.
21. *New York Times*, 21 Nov. 1927, 10; Don C. Seitz, "Figures from America's Past," *Bookman*, April 1928, 206.
22. *New York Times*, 11 Dec. 1927, sec. 4, 3.
23. RH to John Corbin, 14 Dec. 1927, Henry W. and Albert W. Berg Collection of English and American Literature, New York Public Library.
24. William Hale Thompson, "Shall We Shatter the Nation's Idols in School Histories?", *Current History*, 27:5 (Feb. 1928): 625.
25. RH, "Plea for Frankness in Writing History," *Current History*, 27:5 (Feb. 1928): 630.
26. *Will Rogers' Weekly Articles, vol. 3, The Coolidge Years: 1927-1929*, James M. Smallwood, ed. (Stillwater: Oklahoma State University Press, 1981), 87-88.
27. Will Rogers, "Will Turns Literary Critic," *Will Rogers' Weekly Articles*, vol. 3, 107-110.

CHAPTER 18.   WAR FILMS AND STORIES

1. RH, *The Patent Leather Kid and Other Stories*, photoplay ed. (New York: Grosset & Dunlap, 1927), 1-2.
2. RH, *Patent Leather Kid*, v. Background information in "Before You Begin" introduction by W.F.E.
3. Mordaunt Hall, *New York Times*, 16 Aug. 1927, 31.
4. RH, *Patent Leather Kid*, vi-vii.
5. *Variety* review, 1927 bound volume, AMPAS; Everson, *American Silent Film*, 200.
6. "Should Capital Punishment Be Retained?", *Congressional Digest*, Aug.-Sept. 1927, 239.
7. RH to Jim Tully, 10 June 1927, Iowa Authors; RHH, "Reminiscences of RH," at RH exhibit, USC, 31 Jan. 1990.
8. RH to Marian King, 29 June and 20 July 1927, Yale Collection, Beinecke Library.
9. RH, "The Ghastly Purpose of the Parables," *Haldeman-Julius Monthly*, n.d., 247-255, RH Papers, USC.
10. *Bookman*, May 1927, 360.
11. RH, *When Crossroads Cross Again* (St. Louis: Board of Finance of the Methodist Episcopal Church, South, n.d.), copy in New York Public Library.
12. RH, *When Crossroads Cross Again* (Kansas City: Department of Ministerial Relief of the Church of the Nazarene, 1921), Missouri Joint Collection.
13. *Bookman*, May 1927, 360.
14. Roberts, "RH, Informal Portrait."
15. Mott, *History of American Magazines*, vol. 4, 607.
16. RH to Cyril Clemens, 3 Jan. 1928, Cyril Clemens Collection, Missouri Historical Society, St. Louis.
17. RH, *The Lovely Ducklings* (New York: Harper & Brothers, 1928); *Book Review Digest for 1928*, 393.
18. "Alumni Sketches," *Western Reserve Weekly*, 6 March 1928, CWRUA.
19. RH to Jean Hughes, 19 Sept. 1928, Kimberley Cameron Papers.
20. Copy of death certificate of Jean Summerlin Hughes, Freese Papers.
21. Will Record No. 5, 418, Lee County District Court, Keokuk, Iowa; Barlett and Steele, *Empire*, 54-55.
22. Alexander Walker, *The Shattered Silents* (New York: William Morrow and Co., 1979), 76-77.
23. RHH, "Loving Memories," 11 Jan. 1978.

24. "Hughes Is Cleared," *New York Times*, 14 May 1927, 4.
25. *New York Times*, 6 Jan. 1928.
26. "Ex-Clevelander Writes of Modern Girl, in Plain Dealer," *Cleveland Plain Dealer*, 10 March 1929.
27. *Book Review Digest for 1929*, 462.
28. RH to Corbin, 27 Aug. 1929, Archives and Special Collections, University of Nebraska Libraries (hereafter cited as U. of Nebraska).
29. RH to Corbin, 30 Sept. 1929, U. of Nebraska.
30. *The American Scrapbook* (New York: Wm. H. Wise & Co., n.d.), 214, 377.
31. TS, RH Papers, USC. Notation "For Jan. 19, 1930" does not indicate where published.
32. AFI *Catalog of Feature Films, 1921-1930*, 125.
33. *New York Times*, 26 Feb. 1929, 31.
34. Spears to author, 30 Sept., 1991, quoting entry in *U. S. Catalogue of Motion Pictures*.
35. RH, "Howard Hughes," 6 Feb. 1937, 29-30; Noah Dietrich and Bob Thomas, *Howard: The Amazing Mr. Hughes*, rev. ed. (Greenwich, Conn.: Fawcett Publications, 1976), 70-71, 79.
36. RH, "Howard Hughes," 13 Feb. 1937, 28-29.
37. Dietrich and Thomas, *Howard: Amazing Mr. Hughes*, 52.
38. RH, "Howard Hughes," 13 Feb. 1937, 29.
39. Dietrich and Thomas, *Howard: Amazing Mr. Hughes*, 78-80.
40. Dietrich and Thomas, *Howard: Amazing Mr. Hughes*, 82.
41. Drew, *Speaking of Silents*, 50-51.
42. *New York Times*, 10 June 1929, 23; Boardman, interview with author, 9 June 1984; Drew, *Speaking of Silents*, 50-51.
43. *Motion Picture Magazine*, July 1929, 62.
44. Mason Wiley and Damien Bona, *Inside Oscar: The Unofficial History of the Academy Awards* (New York: Ballantine Books, 1986), 9.

CHAPTER 19.   THE EARLY THIRTIES

1. RH to Corbin, 11 Jan. 1930, Berg Collection, NYPL.
2. RH, handwritten note, 12 March 1926, Hughes Papers, Claremont; *New York Times*, 5 Feb. 1930.
3. RH, *George Washington: The Savior of the States, 1777-1781* (New York: William Morrow & Co., 1930), 688-689, 693-694, 696.
4. *New York Times*, 23 Feb. 1930, sec. 4, 3.
5. *Book Review Digest for 1930*, 518-519.
6. RH to Thwing, 17 April 1930, CWRUA.
7. *Current History*, June 1930, 418-420; RH to Corbin, 2 May 1930, U. of Nebraska.
8. Albert Bushnell Hart, "A Study of Washington," *Publishers' Weekly*, 119:822.
9. RH to Thwing, 30 April 1930, CWRUA; RH to John Hyde Preston, 8 June 1930, Iowa Authors.
10. RH to Thwing, 30 April 1930, CWRUA.
11. RH, *Ladies' Man* (New York: Harper & Brothers, 1930), opposite 402.
12. "New Mystery Stories," *New York Times*, 4 May 1930, sec. 4, 26.
13. *Book Review Digest for 1930*, 519.
14. Copies of translations in Doheny Memorial Library, USC.
15. *Book Review Digest for 1931*, 525.
16. Mailing to members from Writers' Club, with typed copies of script for "Pro-hic-bition," RH Papers, USC.
17. RH, "On the Razor Edge," *Hollywood Plays: 12 One-Act Plays from Repertory of the Writers' Club of Hollywood* (New York: Samuel French, Inc. 1930).
18. RH to (name illegible), 6 April 1930, Iowa Authors.
19. RH to Daley Paskman, 19 Feb. 1930, Iowa Authors.

20. Promotional letter from Pictorial Map Company to Mrs. Geo. W. McElhiney, 27 June 1930, St. Charles County Historical Society Archives; *Living Authors*, Dilly Tante ed. (New York: H. W. Wilson Co., 1931), s.v. "Hughes, Rupert"; *American Writers on American Literature*, John Albert Macy ed. (New York: H. Livermore, Inc. 1931).
21. "Lovely Liar" in May 1930 issue; "Lovelady #99," Oct. 1931.
22. RH, "Getting Paid for Having a Good Time," 42.
23. RH, "George Washington's Letters on Love," *Ladies' Home Journal*, Feb. 1931, 4-5.
24. "Hughes Urges Women to Smoke Cigars," *New York Times*, 2 May 1931.
25. "Spurn California, Mooney Asks as Aid," *New York Times*, 12 Oct. 1931.
26. *Who's Who on the Screen*, 1920 edition, s.v. "Stonehouse, Ruth," Spears Collection; *Screen Play Secrets*, May 1930, 102.
27. Barlett and Steele, *Empire*, 73.
28. RH, "Behind the Screens," RH Papers, USC.
29. *New York Times*, 1 May 1931, 30; *New York Sun*, 1 May 1931.
30. *New York Journal*, 1 May 1931.
31. Helenthal, *Keokuk Connection*, 26, 36.
32. Visit by author to Oakland Cemetery, 1983.

CHAPTER 20.   GOING LIKE SIXTY

1. Roberts, "RH, Informal Portrait"; Badger, "Workshop"; RH, "How I Work, 7-8, RH Papers, USC.
2. RH, "Pitfalls of the Biographer," *Pacific Historical Review*, 2:1, March 1933, 13.
3. RH, "When Washington Laughed and Cried," *American*, Feb. 1932, 42.
4. RH to Thwing, 15 Feb. 1932, CWRUA.
5. RH, "How I Work," 20, RH Papers, USC.
6. RH to Thwing, 15 Feb. 1932, CWRUA.
7. Henry Steele Commager, "For Washington's Bicentennial," *New York Herald Tribune*, 21 Feb. 1932, Books sec., 8.
8. RH to Thwing, 15 Feb. 1932, CWRUA.
9. Elspeth (Beth) De Pould, interview with author, 1 July 1994, Las Vegas.
10. RH to Thwing, 15 Feb. 1932, CWRUA.
11. *Cleveland Press*, 30 March 1932, clipping at CWRUA.
12. Badger, "Workshop."
13. Hambidge, "World Is His Grab-Bag."
14. *Hearst's International Combined with Cosmopolitan*, Oct. 1931, 2.
15. Floyd Shoemaker ed., *Missouri Day by Day* (Columbia, Mo.: State Historical Society of Missouri, 1942), 1:87.
16. RH, *The Art of Hope* (Van Nuys, Calif: Delta Phi Lambda Sorority, 1933 and 1934).
17. RH to Barrett H. Clark, 28 Nov. 1933, Yale Collection, Beinecke Library.
18. RH, "Pilgrims to the Sunset—A Story of the Conquest of the Far West," *Good Housekeeping*, Jan. 1932, 35.
19. RH, "Pilgrims to the Sunset—Gold-Seekers of Today," *Good Housekeeping*, March 1932, 256.
20. RH, "It Isn't Forgiven Unless It's Forgotten," *Family Circle*, Oct. 1933, CWRUA.
21. Roberts, "RH, Informal Portait."
22. *20 Best Short Stories in Ray Long's 20 Years as an Editor* (New York: Crown Publishers, n.d.; copyright, Ray Long & Richard H. Smith, April 1932), 35-37.
23. *Representative Modern Short Stories*, Alexander Jessup ed. (New York: Macmillan Co., 1932), 887.
24. *New York Times*, 23 Jan. 1932.
25. List of RH film credits compiled by Jack Spears.
26. RH, "Early Days," 6 April 1935, 19; *Leonard Maltin's Movie & Video Guide*, 1997 ed. (New York: Signet, 1996), 1335.

27. *New York Herald Tribune*, 11 March 1933; *Variety*, 14 March 1933.
28. "When Ten Collaborate," *New York Times*, 7 May 1933, sec. 4, 14.
29. *Leonard Maltin's Movie & Video Guide*, 1997, 1370.
30. RH to John C. Fitzpatrick, 26 Dec. 1932, John C. Fitzpatrick Papers, Manuscript Division, Library of Congress (hereafter cited as Fitzpatrick Papers, LC).
31. Fitzpatrick to RH, 30 Dec. 1932, Fitzpatrick Papers, LC.
32. *New York Times*, 22 Feb. 1933, 22.
33. RH, "Duty of a Biographer," *Los Angeles Examiner*, 4 March 1933.
34. RH, *Pitfalls of the Biographer* (Glendale, Calif.: Arthur H. Clark Co., 1933), 22, 24, 32.
35. *Reserve Weekly*, Western Reserve University, 17 Jan. 1933, clipping in CWRUA.
36. *Missouri and Missourians*, 5:442.
37. *Reserve Weekly*, 17 Jan. 1933, CWRUA.
38. *Reserve Record*, 27 Jan. 1932, CWRUA.
39. Roberts, "RH, Informal Portrait," 15, 19.
40. Gladys Hasty Carroll to James O. Kemm, 16 May 1984, Kemm Papers.
41. RH to John Daniel Cooke, 9 April 1937, HM 39604, Department of Manuscripts, Huntington Library.
42. Advertisement in *Bookman*, May 1932, xvi.
43. RH to Hamlin Garland, 25 Aug. 1933, Hamlin Garland Collection, Doheny Library, USC.
44. O. O. McIntyre, "New York," *Cleveland Press*, 23 Aug 1933, CWRUA.
45. Long, *20 Best Stories*, 37.

CHAPTER 21. A SPECIAL FRIEND

1. Joseph H. Carter, *Never Met a Man I Didn't Like: The Life and Writings of Will Rogers* (New York: Avon Books, 1991), 170, 270.
2. *Will Rogers' Weekly Articles*, vol. 5, *The Hoover Years: 1931-1933*, Steven K. Gragert, ed. (Stillwater: Oklahoma State University Press, 1982), 215-216.
3. *Will Rogers' Weekly Articles*, vol. 6, *The Roosevelt Years: 1933-1935* (Stillwater: Oklahoma State University Press, 1982), 65.
4. *Book Review Digest for 1934*, 466.
5. "Rupert Hughes's 'Love Song' and Other Recent Works," *New York Times*, 19 Aug. 1934, sec. 5, 6.
6. RH to W. G. Chapman, 20 Jan. 1935, Hughes Collection (#9348), Barrett Library, U. of Virginia Library.
7. RH to Mary King, 23 June 1935, Iowa Authors.
8. RH, *Excuse Me: A Farce-Comedy in Three Acts* (New York: Samuel French, Inc., 1934).
9. RH to Frank (no last name), 19 April 1934, Iowa Authors.
10. Rose Pelswick, "Laughter of Kidnaped Infant Eases Strain of Crime Film; Thrills a-Plenty on Bus," *New York Journal*, 20 Jan. 1934.
11. *New York Times*, 20 Jan. 1934.
12. RH, "A Brief for Hollywood," *Saturday Evening Post*, 3 March 1934, 23, 56-58, 60.
13. RH, "Early Days," 6 April and 13 April 1935.
14. RH, "Behind the Screens," RH Papers, USC.
15. RH, "Heard Mark Twain."
16. McOmie, "We Create Beauty," 54.
17. RH to Shirley Spencer, 28 Oct. 1935, Iowa Authors.
18. RH to Julian Street, 30 June 1935, Julian Street Papers, Box 28, Princeton.
19. Kimberley Cameron, conversation with author, 6 Dec. 1993, Beverly Hills, CA., quoting her father, Wesley Cameron.
20. RH to John Hyde Preston, 23 June 1934, Iowa Authors.
21. RH to Barrett H. Clark, 29 June 1936, Yale Collection, Beinecke Library.
22. *New York Times*, 18 Aug. 1935, sec. 6, 7.

23. Fulton Oursler, *Behold This Dreamer!* (Boston: Little, Brown and Co., 1964), 428-430.

24. Oursler, *Behold This Dreamer!*, 431.

25. *New York Times*, 19 Oct. 1936, 22.

26. RH to Stuart N. Lake, 1 June and 16 Dec. 1934, Lake Collection, Box 5, Department of Manuscripts, Huntington Library.

27. RH to Lee Shippey, 9 Jan. 1935, Lee Shippey Papers, MSS 147, Mandeville Special Collections Library, University of California, San Diego.

28. RH, "Comedians Have Courage," *Coronet*, June 1951, 53-54; RH, "When Will Rogers Wept," unidentified newspaper clipping, Will Rogers Memorial, Claremore, Okla. (hereafter cited as WRM).

29. Reba N. Collins, "Foreword" to David Randolph Milsten, *Will Rogers—The Cherokee Kid* (West Chicago, Ill: Glenheath Publishers, 1987).

30. Milsten, *Will Rogers—The Cherokee Kid*, 13-17.

31. RH telegram to Mrs. Will Rogers, 18 Aug. 1935, WRM.

32. *Los Angeles Evening Herald and Express*, 22 Aug. 1935; *Los Angeles Times*, 23 Aug. 1935.

33. United Press clipping from unidentified newspaper, WRM; New York Times, 23 Aug. 1935, 16; *Los Angeles Herald and Express*, 22 Aug. 1935, 16.

34. *Los Angeles Times*, 23 Aug. 1935; *Los Angeles Herald and Express*, 22 Aug. 1935

CHAPTER 22.   RECOGNITION AND CONTROVERSY

1. United Press, unidentified clipping 23 Sept. 1935, WRM.

2. *Los Angeles Herald*, 22 Nov. 1935.

3. *Los Angeles Herald and Express*, 2 Nov. 1935.

4. *Los Angeles Times*, 4 Nov. 1935.

5. Unidentified newpaper clippings, WRM.

6. Printed program for "The Will Rogers Memorial Show of Shows," Shrine Auditorium, Los Angeles, 1 Dec. 1935, Kemm Papers.

7. Clippings from unidentified newspapers, 2 Dec. 1935, WRM.

8. Printed program for "Show of Shows," Kemm Papers.

9. Clipping from unidentified newspaper, 2 Dec. 1935, WRM.

10. Associated Press, 15 Aug. 1936, unidentified clipping, WRM.

11. *Cleveland Plain Dealer*, 24 Feb. 1936, CWRUA.

12. *Cleveland Plain Dealer Sunday Magazine*, 7 June 1936, CWRUA.

13. TS, introduction of RH by H. W. Taeusch, 10 June 1936, CWRUA.

14. Typed copy of Rupert Raleigh Hughes citation by W. G. Leutner, 10 June 1936, CWRUA.

15. RH to Thwing, 18 June 1936, CWRUA.

16. H. L. Mencken, *The American Language*, 4th ed. (New York: Alfred A. Knopf, 1936), 77.

17. Albert Britt, *The Great Biographers* (New York: Whittlesey House, Division of McGraw-Hill Book Co., 1936), 102.

18. RH to Burton Rascoe, 18 April 1936, Cabell Papers (5947), U. of Virginia Library.

19. Rascoe to RH, 25 April 1936, Cabell Papers (5947), U. of Virginia Library.

20. Sheilah Graham, *The Garden of Allah* (New York: Crown Publishers, 1970), 178.

21. "The Shape of Things" column, *The Nation*, 27 May 1936, 662.

22. Heywood Broun, "Broun's Page," *The Nation*, 27 May 1936, 678.

23. RH, letter to editor, *The Nation*, 10 June 1936, 755-756.

24. Larry Ceplair and Steven Englund, *The Inquisition in Hollywood: Politics in the Film Community, 1930-1960* (Berkeley: University of California Press, 1983), 17, 20-21, 24.

25. Nancy Lynn Schwartz, *The Hollywood Writers' Wars* (New York: Alfred A. Knopf, 1982), 14-15, 18.

26. Schwartz, *Hollywood Writers' Wars*, 20, 321.

27. Anne Edwards, *Early Reagan* (New York: William Morrow and Co., 1987), 298.

28. Ceplair and Englund, *Inquisition*, 60.

29. Ceplair and Englund, *Inquisition*, 104-105, 107; Christopher Finch and Linda Rosenkratz, *Gone Hollywood* (Garden City, N. Y.: Doubleday & Co., 1979), 259.

30. *New York Times*, 5 July 1936, sec. 9, 10.

31. *Camel Caravan Programs* file, scripts for weekly programs 30 June-22 Dec. 1936, RH Papers, USC.

32. *Variety*, 15 July 1936.

33. *Camel Caravan Programs* file, RH Papers, USC.

34. Clara Beranger, "Who Will Be the Next Movie Stars of 1937?", *Liberty*, 23 Jan. 1937, 13; same issue, 43.

35. Carol A. Emmens, *Short Stories on Film*, (Littleton, Colo.: Libraries Unlimited, Inc., 1978), 151; Jack Spears, RH film credits list supplied to author, 22 Aug. 1988.

36. RH to Dean Cornwell, 12 Dec. 1936, Iowa Authors.

37. RH, "Howard Hughes," 13 Feb. 1937, 30-31.

38. RH, "Howard Hughes," 6 Feb. 1937, 24.

39. RH to Clemens, 16 March 1937, Clemens Collection, Missouri Historical Society.

40. RH to Chapman, 2 July 1937, Hughes Collection, (#9348), Barrett Library, U. of Virginia Library.

41. RH, *Double Exposure* (London: Jarrolds, n.d.). Copy in Library of State Historical Society of Missouri.

42. RH to Marie Gallagher, 29 June 1937, Iowa Authors.

43. RH to Lola L. Kovner, 11 Feb. 1937, Hughes Collection, (#9348), Barrett Library, U. of Virginia Library.

44. RH to Kovner, 26 July 1938, (#9348), Hughes Collection, Barrett Library, U. of Virginia Library.

45. RH to Gladys Hasty Carroll, 12 Oct. 1937, Special Collections, Mugar Memorial Library, Boston University, Boston, Mass.

46. *St. Charles Cosmos-Monitor*, 15 June and 29 June 1937, clippings in St. Charles County Historical Society Archives.

CHAPTER 23. AN EPIC NOVEL

1. RH to Max Farrand, 27 Jan. 1938, FAR Box 11 (46), Huntington Library.

2. RH, "Why Our Girls Won't Behave," *Liberty*, 26 March 1938, 50-51.

3. RH to Maxwell E. Perkins, 30 Nov. 1938, Scribner's Archive, Rupert Hughes (1), Princeton (hereafter cited as Scribner's Archive, RH (1).

4. RH to Perkins, 11 July 1938 and 30 Nov. 1938, Scribner's Archive, RH (1).

5. RH telegram to Perkins, 18 July 1938, Scribner's Archive, RH (1).

6. Ruth Reynolds, *The Life Story of Howard Hughes; Also the Amazing Story of Douglas Corrigan* (New York: Dell Publishing Co., c1938), 36.

7. Barlett and Steele, *Empire*, 89-91.

8. Barlett and Steele, *Empire*, 91-97.

9. Barlett and Steele, *Empire*, 98, 102-103.

10. RH to Perkins, 23 July 1938, Scribner's Archive, RH (1).

11. RH to Perkins, 25 Aug. 1938, Scribner's Archive, RH (1).

12. RH, *Stately Timber* (New York: Charles Scribner's Sons, 1939), vi-viii.

13. Margaret Wallace, "Rupert Hughes on Puritan Boston," *New York Times*, 19 Feb. 1939, 7.

14. J. P. Marquand, "Intolerant Puritans," *Saturday Review of Literature*, 18 Feb. 1939, 13.

15. Fulton Oursler to RH, 6 March 1939, copy attached to letter from RH to Perkins, 14 March 1939, Scribner's Archive, RH (1).

16. RH to Perkins, 25 Feb. 1939, 14 March 1939, 27 Dec. 1938, and Perkins to RH, 8 March 1939, Scribner's Archive, RH (1).

17. Perkins to RH, 8 March 1939, and RH to Perkins, 14 March 1939, Scribner's Archive, RH (1).

18. RH to Perkins, 4 May 1939, Scribner's Archive, Box 78.
19. RH to Perkins, 31 May 1939, Scribner's Archive, RH (1).
20. Daniel Henderson to RH, 27 Sept. 1938; RH, TS for "Irvin S. Cobb," *Progress*, n.d., RH Papers, USC.
21. Stationery used by RH in 7 Oct. 1937 letter to members, RH Papers, USC.
22. *Los Angeles Daily News*, 23 Feb. 1939, clipping in Hughes Papers, Claremont.
23. *New York Times*, 9 April 1939, sec. 3, 6.
24. RH, comp., Deems Taylor and Russell Kerr, eds., *Music Lovers' Encyclopedia* (Garden City, N. Y.: Garden City Publishing Co., 1939).
25. *Music Lovers' Encyclopedia*, viii-ix.
26. *Book Review Digest for 1939*, 485.
27. RH, comp., Deems Taylor and Russell Kerr, eds., *The Biographical Dictionary of Musicians* (Garden City N. Y.: Blue Ribbon Books, 1940).
28. RH, *Attorney for the People: The Story of Thomas E. Dewey* (Boston: Houghton Mifflin Co., 1940), vii.
29. RH to Perkins, 3 Aug. 1939, Scribner's Archive, RH (1).
30. Thomas C. Linn, "Books of the Times," *New York Times*, 5 Jan. 1940, 11.
31. *Delta Upsilon Quarterly*, April 1940, CWRUA.
32. RH, "Washington—and 'Entangling Alliances,'" *New York Times Magazine*, 18 Feb. 1940, sec. 7, 7.
33. RH, "When Tolerance Is Treason," *Liberty*, 23 March 1940.
34. *Liberty*, 18 May 1940, clipping in RH Papers, USC.
35. RH to Corbin, 14 June 1940, Archives and Special Collections, University of Nebraska.

CHAPTER 24. BACK IN UNIFORM

1. RH to Perkins, 2 July 1940, Scribner's Archive, Rupert Hughes (2), Princeton, hereafter cited as Scribner's Archive, RH (2).
2. Perkins to RH, 24 July 1940, Scribner's Archive, RH (2).
3. RH to Perkins, 10 Sept. 1940, Scribner's Archive, RH (2).
4. RH to Frauncie E. Moon, 19 Dec. 1940, Scribner's Archive, RH (2).
5. RH, "City of Angels," MS for music and words, RH Papers, USC.
6. RH to Perkins, 28 Feb. 1941, Scribner's Archive, RH (2).
7. Margaret Wallace, "A Hollywood Story," *New York Times Book Review*, 9 March 1941, sec. 6, 7.
8. RH, *City of Angels* (New York: Charles Scribner's Sons, 1941), 117-118.
9. RH to Perkins, 2 July 1940, Scribner's Archive, RH (2).
10. Copy of Authors' Manifesto signed by RH, Struthers Burt Collection, Box 18, Folder 5, Princeton.
11. Visit by author to Forest Lawn Memorial Park, June 1985.
12. Award, RH Papers, USC.
13. Commission certificate, RH Papers, USC.
14. *Liberty*, 8 March 1941.
15. RH, "I Am an American," *American*, Dec. 1941, 9.
16. Jesse L. Lasky, Jr., *Whatever Happened to Hollywood?* (New York: Funk & Wagnalls, 1975), 225-227, 229-233.
17. RH to Bernhard Knollenberg, 13 Sept. 1942, Yale Collection, Beinecke Library.
18. *There Were Giants in the Land* (New York: Farrar & Rinehart, 1942), vii.
19. RH, "George Washington, 1732-1799," *There Were Giants in the Land*, 191, 190.
20. *Missouri, A Guide to the "Show Me" State, American Guide Series* (New York: Duell, Sloan & Pearce, 4th printing, 1941), 148, 163, 460-461.
21. RH to Perkins, 11 July 1943, Scribner's Archive, RH (2).
22. RH to Mary Bourque, 30 July 1943, Iowa Authors.

23. RH to H. C. F. Bell, 29 June 1943, Special Collections & Archives, Wesleyan University, Middletown, Conn.
24. RH, "M-Day Was Two Years Ago," MS and TS, RH Papers, USC.
25. RH to Perkins, 11 July 1943, Scribner's Archive, RH (2).
26. Excerpts from listeners' letters attached to RH letter to Perkins, 11 July 1943, Scribner's Archive, RH (2).
27. RH to Perkins, 18 April 1944, Scribner's Archive, RH (2).
28. RH to Una R. Winter, 28 July 1943, with attached letters of Winter to RH, 6 July 1943, and Winter to N.B.C., 6 July 1943, UW 48, Department of Literary Manuscripts, Huntington Library.
29. *Twentieth Century Authors, First Supplement*, Stanley J. Kunitz, ed. (New York: H. W. Wilson Co., 1955), 468.
30. TS, proof sheets, and tear sheets for "In a Blaze of Glory," RH Papers, USC.
31. RH, typed proposal for motion picture version of "In a Blaze of Glory," RH Papers, USC.
32. Patterson Dial, "Putty in a Woman's Hands," *American*, Feb. 1931, editor's note, 24.
33. Patterson Dial, "The Great Theodosia Plot," *Scholastic*, 26 Feb. 1940, 30.
34. RH letters to Elspeth Hughes Lapp and granddaughters, Freese Papers; Fay, "Genealogy," 7.
35. Frank Buxton and Bill Owen, *The Big Broadcast*, 1920-1950 (New York: The Viking Press, 1972), 189, 66.
36. *New York Times*, 14 May 1941, 21.
37. Fay, "Genealogy," 7.
38. RHH, "Loving Memories," 11 Jan. 1978, 1.
39. RHH, interview with author, 21 Aug. 1986.

CHAPTER 25. THE DIFFICULT YEARS

1. RH to Perkins, 18 April 1944, Scribner's Archive, RH (2).
2. Patterson Dial Hughes to Perkins, 21 June 1944, Scribner's Archive, RH (2).
3. RH to Edward Lapp and RH to Elspeth Hughes Lapp, both 10 Jan. 1944, Freese Papers.
4. Photostat from family Bible, Freese Papers.
5. RH letters to granddaughters, Freese Papers.
6. RH to Edward Lapp, 12 Sept. 1944, Freese Papers.
7. RH to Lloyd Douglas, 31 Dec. 1944, Lloyd Douglas Papers, Cassel, Box 2, Bentley Historical Library, University of Michigan.
8. *Los Angeles Times*, 24 March 1945.
9. *Los Angeles Times*, 24 March 1945.
10. *New York Times*, 24 March 1945, 32.
11. *Los Angeles Times*, 25 March 1945, sec. 3, 6.
12. Copy of death certificate for Elizabeth Patterson Dial, Freese Papers.
13. RHH, interview with author, 21 Aug. 1986.
14. RH to Edward Lapp, 6 April 1945, Freese Papers.
15. Typed copy of RH address, 21 April 1945, CWRUA.
16. RH to Elspeth Hughes Lapp, 25 Feb. 1945, Freese Papers.
17. RH to Elspeth Hughes Lapp, 6 May 1945, Freese Papers.
18. RH to Elspeth Hughes Lapp, Sunday, n.d., Freese Papers.
19. RH to Edward Lapp, 14 May 1945, Freese Papers.
20. Copy of death certificate for Elspeth Hughes Lapp, Freese Papers.
21. RH to Edward Lapp, 20 May 1945, Freese Papers.
22. Virginia Woodson Church, *Teachers Are People*, foreword by RH (Santa Barbara: W. Hebberd, 1945).
23. RH to Lester Roberts, 13 Aug. 1945, Iowa Authors.
24. RH to Mrs. John De Pould, 11 Aug. 1945, Freese Papers.
25. RH to Edward Lapp, 23 Sept. and 8 Oct. 1945, Freese Papers.'

26. RH to Edward Lapp, 17 Dec. 1945 and 5 May 1946, Freese Papers.
27. RH to Mrs. John De Pould, 1 Sept. 1946, Freese Papers.
28. RH to Mrs. John De Pould, 1 Dec. 1946, Freese Papers.
29. RH to Mrs. John De Pould, 1 Feb. 1947, and RH to John and Elspeth De Pould, July 1947, Freese Papers.
30. Barbara Cameron, interview with author, 1 July 1994, Las Vegas.
31. RH to Roy G. Fitzgerald, 19 Aug. 1946, Iowa Authors.
32. RH to Fitzgerald, 29 Aug. 1946, Iowa Authors.

CHAPTER 26. A MENACE PERCEIVED

1. Schwartz, *Hollywood Writers' Wars*, 262.
2. Clipping from unidentified newspaper, 17 Sept. 1946, Rupert Hughes file, Margaret Herrick Library, Academy of Motion Picture Arts and Sciences, Beverly Hills, Calif. (hereafter cited as RH file, AMPAS).
3. Schwartz, *Hollywood Writers' Wars*, 262; *New York Times*, 8 May 1947, 14.
4. Roy Hoopes, *Cain* (New York: Holt, Rinehart and Winston, 1982), 399, 410.
5. *New York Times*, 8 May 1947, 14.
6. Hoopes, *Cain*, 410.
7. Ceplair and Englund, *Inquisition*, 192-193, 210-211, 214.
8. *New York Times*, 16 May 1947, 1, 19.
9. *New York Times*, 22 Oct. 1947, 1, 3.
10. *New York Times*, 30 Oct. 1947, 1, 4.
11. Robert Sobel, *The Manipulators: America in the Media Age* (Garden City, N. Y.: Anchor Press/Doubleday, 1976), 228-229.
12. Ceplair and Englund, *Inquisition*, 294-295.
13. Schwartz, *Hollywood Writers' Wars*, 277-279.
14. Ceplair and Englund, *Inquisition*, 346-349.
15. RHH, interview with author, 21 Aug. 1986.
16. Moore, interview with author, 7 June 1984.
17. Plaque, RH Papers, USC.
18. RH to Clemens, 28 May 1947, CWRUA.
19. Clipping from unidentified newspaper, 21 Sept. 1948, RH file, AMPAS.
20. RH to Clemens, 24 July 1949, CWRUA.
21. Barbara Lapp-Wesley Cameron wedding portrait, Freese Papers.
22. Barbara Cameron and Elspeth (Beth) De Pould, interview with author, 1 July 1994, Las Vegas.
23. RH to Mrs. John De Pould, 27 April 1949, Freese Papers.
24. RHH, "RH: Reflections," 31.
25. RH, "They Don't Make the Headlines," *The Rotarian*, Sept. 1947, 15.
26. John Tasker Howard, *Our American Music*, 3rd ed. (New York: Thomas Y. Crowell Co., 1946, 1954), 570.
27. RH to Clemens, 19 Feb. 1948, CWRUA.
28. John Dunning, *Tune in Yesterday* (Englewood Cliffs, N. J.: Prentice-Hall, 1976), 575.
29. RH, *Gyges' Ring and Other Verse* (Culver City, Calif.: Murray & Gee, 1949), inside dust jacket.
30. RH, *The Triumphant Clay* (Hollywood: House-Warven, Publishers, 1951), inside dust jacket.
31. RH to Harry Lichtig, 25 March 1949, RH Papers, USC.
32. Marie (Hays) Heiner, *Hearing Is Believing*, Introduction by Rupert Hughes (Cleveland: World Publishing Co., 1949).
33. Erie (Penn.) *Dispatch Herald*, 20 Feb. 1949, clipping in Hughes Papers, Claremont.
34. RH to Wilmer B. Leech, 12 Nov. and 22 Nov. 1949, Misc. Mss. Hughes, Rupert, courtesy of The New-York Historical Society.

CHAPTER 27. LONG OVERDUE

1. RH to Lee Shippey, 6 Jan. 1950, Lee Shippey Papers, MSS 147, Mandeville Special Collections Library, UCSD.
2. Danton Walker, Broadway column, *New York News*, n.d., clipping in RH Papers, USC.
3. *Los Angeles Times*, 10 Jan. 1950, 2; *Los Angeles Examiner*, 10 Jan. 1950, part 2, 1.
4. *Los Angeles Examiner*, 10 Jan. 1950, part 2, 1.
5. *Los Angeles Times*, 10 Jan. 1950, 2.
6. *Los Angeles Times*, 10 Jan. 1950, 2; unidentified clipping, RH file, AMPAS.
7. "Pat O'Brien to Preside at Hughes Dinner," *Los Angeles Times*, 1 Jan. 1950.
8. Printed program for Rupert Hughes Testimonial, 9 Jan. 1950, Freese Papers.
9. *Los Angeles Times*, 10 Jan. 1950, 2.
10. Letters and telegrams of congratulations to RH, "Testimonial Dinner" file folder, drawer 6, RH Papers, USC.
11. Printed programs, RH Testimonial, Freese Papers.
12. RHH, interview with author, 21 Aug. 1986.
13. RHH, "Loving Memories," 11 Jan. 1978, 2.
14 "Rupert Hughes' Novel Wins," *New York Times*, 26 June 1950, 25.
15. *New York Times*, 23 July 1950, sec. 7, 19.
16. RH to Grace Van Wormer, 5 Aug. 1950, Iowa Authors.
17. "The Poetry Page," *Good Housekeeping*, Dec. 1951, 115.
18. RH, "The Latest News About the Three Wishes," *The Second St. Nicholas Anthology*, Henry Steele Commager, ed. (New York: Random House, 1950), 151.
19. RH, *The Complete Detective* (New York: Sheridan House, 1950), inside dust jacket.
20. *Book Review Digest for 1950*, 457.
21. *New Yorker*, 7 Oct. 1950, 135.
22. "Murder Serial to Start Monday in the Enterprise," *High Point (N.C.) Enterprise*, 24 Feb. 1950, clipping in CWRUA.
23. RH, *The Triumphant Clay*.
24. Henry Cavendish, "Victory of the Spirit," *New York Times*, 24 June 1951, sec. 7, 16.
25. Award from Manuscripters of Los Angeles, RH Papers, USC.
26. Certificates and awards, RH Papers, USC.
27. RH, "Comedians Have Courage," *Coronet*, 53-55.
28. RH, "TV Won't Ruin Everything," *Films in Review*, March 1951, 24-25.
29. RHH, "RH: Reflections," 32.
30. Presentation script, proposals, outlines, and synopses in "TV Ideas and Radio Serials and Sketches" folder, RH Papers, USC.
31. Warren Allen Smith, "Are You a Humanist? Some Authors Answer," *The Humanist*, March-April 1981, 18, reprint of article with original title "Authors and Humanism," Oct.-Nov. 1951.
32. RH to John Golden, 12 Dec. 1944, John Golden Papers, Billy Rose Collection, New York Public Library at Lincoln Center, New York.
33. James Robert Parish and Michael R. Pitts, *The Great Gangster Pictures*, II (Metuchen, N. J.: Scarecrow Press, 1987), 140-141.
34. RH, *McFarren of the FBI*, undated MS, RH Papers, USC.
35. Mary Moon of Lichtig-Englander, Agency, to Dear Client, 27 Nov. 1951, inscribed with note from RH, RH Papers, USC.
36. Douglas Southall Freeman, *George Washington, Vol. 4, Leader of the Revolution* (New York: Charles Scribner's Sons, 1951), 475.

CHAPTER 28. IN HIS EIGHTIES

1. Hannah Logasa, comp., *Historical Fiction, McKinley Bibliographies, vol. 1* (Philadelphia: McKinley Publishing, 1964).
2. *Los Angeles Times*, 1 Feb. 1952, clipping in RH file, AMPAS.

3. *Los Angeles Times*, 1 Feb. 1952; *Hollywood Citizen-News*, 1 Feb. 1952, clipping in RH file, AMPAS.
4. *Los Angeles Evening Herald & Express*, 30 Jan. 1952, clipping in RH file, AMPAS.
5. *Hollywood Citizen-News*, 1 Feb. 1952; *Los Angeles Evening Herald & Express*, 30 Jan. 1952, clippings in RH file, AMPAS.
6. RHH to author, 30 Dec. 1989, Kemm Papers.
7. RHH to E. A. Ebersole, 7 March 1974, Rupert Hughes file, Keokuk Public Library; RHH, interview with author, 21 Aug. 1986.
8. RHH, "RH: Reflections," 32; copies of *Center of Light* are included in RH Papers, USC.
9. RHH, "RH: Reflections," 32, and telephone interview with author, 12 Dec. 1988.
10. RHH, "RH: Reflections," 33.
11. RH, ms of unpublished autobiographical sketch, n.d., RH Papers, USC.
12. RH, "How I Work," 14-16, RH Papers, USC.
13. Barbara Cameron, quoted by her daughter, Kimberley Cameron, in interview with author, 6 July 1994.
14. RHH, "RH: Reflections," 29.
15. RHH, interview with author, 21 Aug. 1986.
16. Copy of RH death certificate, Freese Papers.
17. *Hollywood Citizen-News*, 29 Jan. 1953, clipping in RH file, AMPAS.
18. Burton Egbert Stevenson, comp., *The Home Book of Modern Verse*, 2nd ed. (New York: Henry Holt and Co., 1953), 34; Franklin Pierce Adams, *FPA Book of Quotations* (New York: Funk & Wagnalls Co., 1952), 116.
19. Asa Don Dickinson, *The World's Best Books, Homer to Hemingway* (New York: H. W. Wilson Co., 1953), preface and 173.
20. John Tasker Howard, *Our American Music*, 570.
21. Clifton Fadiman and Charles Van Doren, *The American Treasury, 1455-1955* (New York: Harper & Brothers, 1955), 953.
22. *Honnold Library Annual Report, 1954-55*, Claremont, Calif.: Claremont Colleges.
23. Last will and testament of RH, signed 8 Jan. 1954, copy in Freese Papers.
24. *Los Angeles Times*, 10 Sept. 1956, 1, 18; *Los Angeles Examiner*, 10 Sept. 1956, 1, 16.
25. RHH, interview with author, 21 Aug. 1986; Barbara Cameron, interview with author, 1 July 1994.
26. *Los Angeles Examiner*, 10 Sept. 1956, 1; RHH to James O. Kemm, 9 Sept. 1985, Kemm Papers.
27. *Los Angeles Examiner*, 10 Sept. 1956, 1; RHH, quoting Felix Hughes, in letter to James O. Kemm, 9 Sept. 1985, Kemm Papers; *Los Angeles Times*, 10 Sept. 1956, 1.
28. Felix Hughes, quoted by RHH to James O. Kemm, 9 Sept. 1985, Kemm Papers.
29. RHH, interview with author, 21 Aug. 1986.
30. RHH, "Loving Memories," 11 Jan. 1978, 2; RHH to James O. Kemm, 9 Sept. 1985, Kemm Papers.
31. *New York Times*, 10 Sept. 1956, 1.
32. *Hollywood Citizen-News*, 10 Sept. 1956, clipping in RH file, AMPAS; *Los Angeles Examiner*, 10 Sept. 1956, 1; *Los Angeles Times*, 10 Sept. 1956, 1, 18.
33. Felix Hughes quoted by RHH to James O. Kemm, 9 Sept. 1985, Kemm Papers.
34. *Hollywood Citizen-News*, 25 Sept. 1956, clipping in RH file, AMPAS.

CHAPTER 29.   THE ESTATE BATTLE

1. Herbert S. Parmet, *Richard Nixon and His America* (Boston: Little, Brown and Co., 1990), 404.
2. Harry Hurt, III, *Texas Monthly*, Jan. 1977.
3. *Tulsa World*, 16 May 1976.
4. Hurt, *Texas Monthly*, Jan. 1977.

5. *Oklahoma City Times*, 6 April 1976.
6. *Tulsa Tribune*, 28 April 1976.
7. *Tulsa World*, 20 May 1976.
8. Hurt, *Texas Monthly*, Jan. 1977.'
9. Barlett and Steele, *Empire*, 590, 608.
10. O. Theodore Dinkins, Jr., to "Those parties interested in the heirship proceedings in the estate of Howard Robard Hughes, Jr., deceased," 29 June 1981. Copy in Kemm Papers.
11. Fay, "Genealogy," 3.
12. Fay, "Genealogy," 8; *Joplin (Mo.) Globe*, 1 Aug. 1981.
13. Fay, "Genealogy," 8.
14. *Houston Chronicle*, 8 July 1985.
15. Documents and letters presented by Paul L. Freese as evidence in Houston court case involving Howard Hughes estate, examined by author in Freese office, Los Angeles, 16 June 1984.
16. RHH, interview with author, 21 Aug. 1986.
17. Fay, "Genealogy," 8-10.
18. Suzanne Finstad, *Heir Not Apparent*.
19. *Joplin (Mo.) Globe*, 15 Aug. 1981.
20. *Tulsa World*, 24 Aug. 1981.
21. *New York Times*, 5 Sept. 1981.
22. Moore, interview with author, 7 June 1984; Boardman, interview with author, 9 June 1984.
23. Author's telephone conversation with John G. Grant, attorney for Barbara Cameron, 31 Jan. 1990.

CHAPTER 30. A LIFE IN PERSPECTIVE

1. RH, "Happy Death of Rupert Hughes," *Coronet*, Oct. 1941, 26.
2. Scott and Carlson, "St. Charles Needs a Favorite Son," 92-95.
3. Hughes, "Happy Death of Rupert Hughes," 28.
4. *Los Angeles Examiner*, 11 Sept. 1956.
5. *Los Angeles Times*, 11 Sept. 1956.

Abbot, Anthony, 252
Academy Awards, first, 206-207
Academy of Motion Picture Arts and Sciences, 206, 247
Adams, Franklin P., 44, 99, 314
Adams, John Wolcott, 59
Adams, J. T., 185
Adams, Samuel Hopkins, 235
Ade, George, 97, 213
Adelbert, The, 12, 13
Adelbert College, 14, 15, 19, 55, 58, 259-260
Aiken, Conrad, 116, 307
Ailen, Charles L., 17
Ainslee's (magazine), 48
Albany, N.Y., 48, 78, 81, 180, 283
A. L. Burt Company, 203
Alcott, Louisa May, 22
Alden, Mary, 112-113
Alexander the Great (RH play), 38
Allen, Fred, 306
Allentown, Penn., 51-52
All for a Girl (RH play), 46-47, 69
Ambassador Hotel, 121, 166, 189, 297-298
Ambush, The (RH play), 214
American (magazine), 58, 154, 159, 169, 202, 215, 220, 270, 275
American Academy of Public Affairs, 269
American Anthology, 1787-1900, An, 27
American Authors Authority, 287-288
American Economic Foundation, 297
American Federation of Labor (AFL), 302
American Historical Association, 226
American Language, The (Mencken), 245
American Legion, 218, 292, 297, 313
American Legion (magazine), 169, 179
American Library Association Booklist, 54, 57
American Play Company, 222
American Scrapbook, The, 203
American Treasury, 1455-1955, The, 316
American Veterans Committee, 291

American Writers Association, 287-288
American Writers on American Literature, 215
"Am I an Atheist?" (RH essay), 156-157
Amiable Crimes of Dirk Memling, The (RH novel), 61
Amos 'n Andy, 242
Anama Club, Hollywood, 134-135
Andrews, Kurth, Campbell, and Jones, 322
"Animal and Vegetable Rights" (RH essay), 32
Appleton, 214
Appleton's Magazine, 44
Arbuckle, Roscoe (Fatty), 125-126. 135
Arnold, Edward, 223, 298
Artcraft Pictures Corporation, 81, 89
Art of Hope, The, 222
Arts and Decoration (magazine), 124
Ashley, Fred, 14
Ashton, Sylvia, 111
Astor, Gertrude, 122
Astor Theater, 113-114
Atherton, Gertrude, 77, 95, 97, 228
"At Kensico" (RH poem), 74, 295
Atlantic City, N. J., 46, 109
Attorney for the People: The Story of Thomas E. Dewey (RH), 262-264, 267
Authors' Assurance Association, 69
Authors, The, 294, 298, 313
See also Writers, The
Authors' Club, 260, 286, 294, 315, 318, 320 . See also Writers' Club
Authors' League of America, 68, 95, 101, 128, 247-248, 287
Autry, Gene, 299

Babcock, Dwight, 308
"Baby's Shoes, The" (RH story), 202, 303
Badger, Retta, 182
Bahr, Herman, 111
Baker, Diane, 224

Balzac, Honore de, 73-74, 136
Bancroft, George, 168
"Barge of Dreams, The" (RH story), 72
Barker, Granville, 68
Barker, Reginald, 120
Barkley, Alben W., 293
Barlett, Donald L., 128
Barnes, T. Roy, 110
Barrymore, John, 167
Barthelmess, Richard, 157, 193-194, 206-207
Barton, Bruce, 287
Bates, Blanche, 45-46, 85
Bathing Girl, The (RH musical), 19-21
Baum, Vicki, 224
Baxter, Warner, 243, 299
Beach, Rex, 69, 95-97. 110
Beaumont, Texas, 32
Beauty (RH novel), 106
Bedford Hills, N.Y., 53, 55, 63, 68, 103, 110, 136
Beecher, Janet, 109
Beery, Wallace, 168
Behrman, S. N., 224
Belasco, David, 50
Belgium, La Juive, Liege, 31
Bell, H. C. F., 273
Bell, Lisle, 232
Benchley, Robert, 101
Benda, W. T., 305
Bennett, James O'Donnell, 175
Benny, Jack, 299
Beranger, Clara, 251
Bergen, Edgar, 299
Berke, William, 308
Bern, Paul, 216
Berry, Milton, 222, 239
Best Plays of 1894-1899, The, 21
Best Short Stories of 1918, The, 88
Best Short Stories of 1920, The, 105
Best Short Stories of 1924, The, 155
Best Short Stories of 1926, The, 169
Better Homes & Gardens, 182, 184, 235, 272
Beverly Hills Community Presbyterian Church, 293
Beverly Hills Hotel, 96, 104
Bibliotheque Nationale, 30
Bigger Man, The (RH film), 68
Bijou Theater, 46

Bill, Clarence, 15

Biographical Dictionary of Musicians, The (RH, Taylor, Kerr), 262

Birth of a Nation, The (film), 66-67

Biscailuz, Eugene W., 298

Bissell, George, 46, 53

"Bitterness of Sweets, A" (RH story), 129

Blood and Sand (film), 235

Blue Bird Camp Association, Inc., 300

Blue, Monte, 110

Blue Ribbon Books, Inc., 262

Blumenberg, Marc, 27

Blumenschein, Ernest L., 182

Boardman, Eleanor, 122, 126-127, 129, 132, 133-134. 153. 185-186, 205-206, 214, 3271

Bookman (magazine), articles about Hughes, 36, 63, 99, 116, 127, 133, 196-197, 228; Hughes essays, 99, 137; Hughes-Van Doren dispute in, 136-137; poem by Adelaide, 132; news and reviews of Hughes films and books, 49, 56-57, 64-65, 73, 86, 104, 106, 138, 152, 164, 168, 178, 187

Books (magazine), 210, 232

Borden Publishing Company, 302

Borglum, Gutzon, 154, 183, 269

Boston, Mass., 20, 34, 36

Boston Post, 105

Boston Transcript, 152, 186, 232, 262

Bow, Clara, 194

Bowers, Claude G., 178, 187

Bowron, Fletcher T., 298, 312

Boynton, H. W., 72-73

Braddock, James J., 243

Brady, Alice, 233

Brady, William A., 47

Braley, Berton, 89, 116-117

Breach of Promise (RH film), 223

Brent, Evelyn, 237-238

Brent, George, 308

Bridge, The (RH play), 44-45, 47-48, 68

Bridges, Robert, 55

Brisbane, Arthur, 242

British Museum, 30

Britt, Albert, 245

Broadway Theater, 94

Brockwell, William E. (nurse), 343

Bromfield, Louis, 309

Broun, Heywood, 263-264

Brown, Joe E., 259, 323, 324

Brown, T. Allston, 21

Brown Derby, 336

Brownell, Ed, 8

Browne's Chop House, 73

Brush, Katherine, 309

Burke, Billie, 79-80, 259, 323

Burke, Edmund, 181

Burnham, John (driver/secretary), 306

Burns, Edmund, 218

Burr, Aaron, 163, 164

Burr, Raymond, 332

Busch, Mae, 135

Busch, Niven, Jr., 226

Butler, Binion, Rice, Cook & Knapp, 348, 349

Cabell, James Branch, 97, 261-262

Cadman, S. Parkes, 183

Cain, James M., 309-310, 314, 337

"Cain" (RH song), 123, 166, 318

Calhern, Louis, 236

California Theater, 120

Camel Caravan (radio show), 266-268

Cameron, Barbara Patterson Lapp (granddaughter), 234, 278, 285-286, 293-294, 299-301, 304, 315, 318, 322-322

Cameron, Wesley Colin (Barbara's husband), 273, 293, 299, 300, 318

Camp Lewis, Wash., 294

"Canavan, the Man Who Had His Way" (RH story), 67, 111

Cantor, Eddie, 242, 249, 299

Capitol Theater, 110, 120, 122, 124, 127, 139, 153, 163, 167

Capper, Arthur, 180

Carnegie, Dale, 142-143

Carrillo, Leo, 251, 298

Carroll, Gladys Hasty, 228, 250

Carroll, Nancy, 199, 224

Carter, Mrs. Leslie, 50

Carter and Daughter, Incorporated (RH novel), 200

Carthage (fictional town), 56, 61, 168

Cat-Bird, The (RH play), 109

Cavendish, Henry, 305

Celluloid Sarah (RH vaudeville sketch), 133

Censorship, films and books, 86, 93, 103, 16, 108-109, 118, 125, 135, 221

Censorship, military, 85-86, 90-91, 93

Center of Light (periodical), 313

Century (magazine), 22-23, 25, 29, 48

Century Company, 23, 28, 49, 56

Century of Missouri Music, A (Krohn), 166

Ceplair, Larry, 247-248

Chadwick, Helene, 97, 110, 112, 115, 118, 129, 139-140

Chambers, Robert W., 260

Chaplin, Charles (Charlie), 97, 113, 126, 131, 133, 139, 185-186, 232, 242, 260

Chapman, W. G., 253

Charles Scribner's Sons, 211, 256, 258-259, 263, 268, 277

Chase, J. C., 61

Chase, Rhoda, 99

Chicago, 47, 120

Chicago Tribune, 75, 175, 234

Chicago Tribune-New York News Syndicate, 234

China Slaver, The (RH film), 203

Christy, Howard Chandler, 69

Churchill, M., 85, 100

Churchman (magazine), 156

Church of the Nazarene, 196

Cicconi, T., 47

City of Angels (RH novel), 268, 308

Civil War, 4, 10, 27, 36, 66, 152

Clansman, The, 66

Claremont Colleges, 145

Clark, Barrett H., 222

Clark, Donald, 305

Clarke, Jospeph I. C., 22

Clarke, Mae, 223

Clayton, Ethel, 110

Clemens, Cyril, 197, 253, 292-294

Clemens, Orion, 8, 175

Clemens, Samuel L., *See* Twain, Mark

Cleveland, Ohio, 43, 49, 105, 120, 143, 220-221, 226-227, 243, 281-283, 285, 294, 318-319, 322

Cleveland Orchestra, 43, 103, 142

Cleveland Plain Dealer, 200, 243-244

Cleveland Press, 49, 58, 221
Cleveland Topics, 105
Clipped Wings (RH novel), 71-72, 82
Cobb, Irvin S., 69, 88, 180, 190, 215, 224, 242, 259-260, 289
Coburn, Charles, 289, 307
Cody, Lew, 126, 139
Cohan, George M., 242
Cohen, Octavus Roy, 165
Cole, Lester, 238
Collier's, 80, 104, 165, 196-197, 253
Colman, Ronald, 243
Colonial Theater, Cleveland, 50
Coolidge, Calvin, 172
Come on Over (RH film), 119-120
Commager, Henry Steele, 210, 220
Commission on Training Camp Activities, War Department, 89
Complete Detective, The (RH book), 303
Concert, The (film), 111
Congregational Church, Keokuk, 8
Congressional Digest, 194
Conover, Arthur Vandeveer, 39
Contemporary American Composers (RH), 29-30, 49
Contemporary American Novelists (Van Doren), 136
Continental Newspaper Syndicate, 60
Contriband, The (writers' group), 101
Cooper, Gary, 194, 289
Cooper, Jackie, 243
Corbin, John, 188, 201-202, 209, 211, 265
Cornwell, Dean, 222, 251
Coronet (magazine), 306, 329
Corrigan, Lloyd, 223
Cort, John, 50
Cortez, Ricardo, 223
Cosmopolitan (magazine), 227; Hughes articles and stories in, 28, 118, 157, 202-203, 215, 223, 258, 302; Hughes attack on religion in, 155-156, 162, 197; Hughes serials in, 212-215, 222, 232, 267, 295; portions of Hughes books in, 259, 268
Costello, Dolores, 167
Cournos, John, 302

Coverly, Robert, 19-20
Crawford, Joan, 186, 235
Creel, George, 83, 85, 91
Criterion (magazine), 21-22, 27, 29-30, 36
Crittenden, Dwight, 112
Crosby, Bing, 243, 299
Croy, Homer, 137
Crusade for Freedom, 306
Cruze, James, 168
Cup of Fury, The (RH novel, film), 90, 96-98
Current History (magazine), 188, 211
Current Literature (magazine), 19
Current Opinion (magazine), 104, 156-157
Currie, Gordon, 312
Curtis, Holbrook, 36

Dancing Town, The (RH film), 203
Dangerous Curve Ahead (RH film), 112, 115
Danger Signal, The (RH film), 67, 111
Daniels, Bebe, 97
D. Appleton and Company, 56, 61
Davidson, Mrs. Grace L., 21
Davies, Marion, 185, 189, 299
Davis, Richard Harding, 63
Dawn Patrol (film), 216
Delineator (magazine), 48
Delmonico's, 41
Delta Phi Lambda, 222
Delta Upsilon, 15, 209, 227
Delta Upsilon Quarterly, 264
DeMille, Cecil B., 89, 185, 243, 299-300
DeMille, William, 89
Democrats, 191, 293
Dempsey, Jack, 97, 299
De Pould, Elspeth Summerlin Lapp (granddaughter), 220-221, 227, 275, 278, 281-282
De Pould, John (Elspeth's husband), 278, 285
Des Moines, Iowa, 69
Destiny (RH novel), 163-164
Detroit, 94
Dewey, Thomas E., 262-264, 267, 283, 288, 293, 299, 312
D. Fitzgerald, Inc., 59
Diantha Goes the Primrose Way, and Other Verses, 104, 154
Dickinson, Asa Don, 340

Dietz, Howard, 95
Dinehart, Alan, 251
Dinkins, O. Theodore, Jr., 324-325
Disney, Walt, 232, 248, 260, 289, 299-300
Dix, Richard, 115, 122, 126
Dixon, Thomas, 66
Dodd, Luther E., 196
Dodd, W. E., 180
Don't (RH film), 194
Doubleday, Doran & Company, Inc., 58
Double Exposure (RH), 253
Douglas, Donald, 299
Douglas, Lloyd C., 260, 279, 299
Dove, Billie, 203
Dozen from Lakerim, The (RH stories, book), 28
Drake, Tom, 308
Dramatists' Guild, 247-248
Dreiser, Theodore, 22, 48
Drew, John, 109
Drury, John, 117
Duffy, Clinton, 285
Dumay, Henri, 21
Dunn, Winifred, 194
Durante, Jimmy, 306
Dutch Treat Club, 59, 234

Eaton, Hubert, 319
Eaton, Walter Prichard, 58, 101
Edison, Thomas Alva, 57
Elysee Hotel, 197, 209, 211
Embury, Aymar II (architect), 63
Eminent Authors Pictures, Inc., 4, 94-96, 98, 110, 114,
Emmet, Katherine, 47
Empty Pockets (RH novel, film), 65-66, 82 89 304
Encyclopedia Britannica, 30, 34, 42, 44
Englund, Steven, 247-248
Equal Rights Amendment, 274
Ericksen, Samuel, 162
Erskine, John, 237, 287
Esquire (magazine), 243, 27, 290
Essanay Company, 45, 216
Etude (magazine), 117
"A Eulogy of Ragtime" (RH essay), 29
Evelyn College, 17
Everybody's Acting (film), 166
Everybody's Magazine, 22
Excuse Me (RH play, novel, film), 51-53, 59, 68, 89, 162-163

Fad and Folly (RH play), 38
Fairbanks, Douglas, Sr., 46-47, 68-69, 113, 182, 186, 206, 286
Fairfax, Sally, 176-179, 201, 206, 286
Fairy Detective, The (RH children's book), 99
Family Circle (magazine), 185, 222
Famous American Composers (RH book), 49
Famous Players Company, 67, 101
Famous Players-Lasky Corporation, 101, 110
Farrand, Max, 255
Farrar & Rinehart, Inc., 237, 272
Farrell, Charles, 168, 224
Farrell, James T., 288
"Father of Waters, The" (RH story), 105
Fay, Mary Smith, 324-326
FBI Girl (RH film), 308
Fields, W. C., 224-225, 306
Fifth Avenue Theater, 20
Films in Review (periodical), 306
Findlay, Ruth, 109
Fine Arts Pictures, 111, 119
Fingerprints Don't Lie (RH novel), 304
Finstad, Suzanne, 324-326
First National Pictures, 89, 193
Fiske, Harrison Grey, 44-45, 47
Fitzgerald, F. Scott, 130
Fitzgerald, Justice James, 40
Fitzgerald, Roy G., 286
Fitzpatrick, John C., 176, 201, 210, 225-226
Flagg, James Montgomery, 52, 60, 63-65, 77
Flaming Youth (film), 130
Fleet, Seaborn (fictional), 256 259
Fleming, E. J., 196
Fleming H. Revell Company, 54, 57
Foerster, Adolph M., 29, 34-35
Forbes (magazine), 316
Ford, Henry, 241
Ford, Wallace, 224
Forest Lawn Memorial Park, 240, 269, 280, 319-320
For She's a Jolly Good Fellow (RH play), 89
Fosdick, Raymond B., 107
Foy, Eddie, 306
FPA Book of Quotations, 44, 316
Francis, Kay, 217

Freedoms Foundation, 306
Freeman, Douglas Southall, 296, 309
Freese, Paul, 322, 325
Freethought Press Association, 162
Friends of Poland, 300
From the Ground Up (RH film), 118
Front Page, The (film), 216
Funk & Wagnalls Company, 197, 202
Furness, Betty, 236

Gable, Clark, 241
Gale, Zona, 165
Gallery, Tom, 122
Gano, Richard, 323
Garbo, Greta, 185, 235
Garden City Publishing Co., Inc., 262, 294, 316
Gardner, Erle Stanley, 299, 304
Garland, Hamlin, 83, 228
Garson, Harry, 93
Gaynor, Janet, 67, 206
George, Grace, 42, 46
George H. Doran & Co., 58, 116
George Washington: (biography by Hughes); *Human Being and the Hero, 1732-1762, The*, 175-178; *Rebel and the Patriot, 1762-1777, The*, 186-189; *Savior of the States, 1777-1781, The*, 210-211
Geraghty, Carmelita, 122
Get-Rich-Quick Wallingford (film), 157
Ghosts of Yesterday (RH film), 81
Giant Wakes, The (RH novel), 301
Gibson, Charles Dana, 59
Giddings, Frank Henry, 84
Gift Wife, The (RH novel), 49, 253
Gilbert, John, 185
Gillingwater, Claude, 122
Gimme (RH film), 129, 132-133
Girl on the Barge, The (RH film), 203
Gish, Lillian, 66
Glass, Montague, 108
Globe Theater, 75-76
Gloria's Romance (RH film serial), 75-76
Godey's Magazine, 19, 29
Goldbeck, Willis, 128
Golden, Grace, 20

Golden Ladder, The (RH novel), 203, 222, 152-153
Goldwyn, Samuel; Eminent Authors formed by, 4, 94-95; films Hughes stories, 96, 111, 112, 118-119, 123, 125; friendship with Hughes, 125, 137-139, 141-142, 336; praises Hughes, 103-104, 114, 120, 134, 299
Goldwyn Pictures Corporation, 94, 111, 139, 153
Gompers, Samuel, 301-302
Good Housekeeping, 222, 232, 235, 303
Goose Creek Oil Field, 43
Gordon, Huntley, 153
Gordon, Leon, 184
Gottschalk, Ferdinand, 42
Goulding, Alf, 162-163
Graham, Sheila, 246
Grant, Cary, 224
Grauman, Sid, 242-242, 299
Grauman's Chinese Theater, 205
Graves, Ralph, 150, 166
Great Biographers, The (Britt), 245
Great Gangster Pictures, II, 308
Green, Alfred E., 120
Greenleaf, Raymond, 308
Gregory, Judge Pat, 324-327
"Greta" (RH poem), 74, 295
Grey, Zane, 224
Griffith, David W., 66-67, 113, 119
Grosset & Dunlap, 193, 206
Grozier, Edwin A., 105
G. Schirmer, 116-117
Guest, Edgar A., 243
Guide to the Best Fiction, 153
Guide to the Best Historical Novels and Tales, 153, 202
Gwenn, Edmund, 299
"Gyges' Ring" (RH poem), 18, 33, 259
Gyges' Ring and Other Verse (RH book of poetry), 295

Haggin, Ben Ali, 184
Haiphong, Indo-China, 144-145
Haldeman-Julius Monthly, 196
Hale, Alan, 233
Hall, Alexander, 233
Hall, James, 204
Hall, Bishop Joseph, 16
Hall, Mordaunt, 234
Halliday, John, 224

Hambidge, Gove, 86, 221
Hammerstein, Oscar, 249
Hammett, Dashiell, 213
Hampton's Magazine, 60
Hansen, Armin, 184
Harding, Warren G., 107
Harlow, Jean, 204
Harper & Brothers, 61, 64-65, 72, 77, 79, 90, 99, 104-106, 125, 137, 152, 163, 167, 186, 201, 212-213, 222, 232, 236
Harper's Bookshelf, 65
Harper's (magazine), 33, 104, 107
Harriman, Karl Edwin, 59
Hart, Albert Bushnell, 179, 188, 211
Hart, William S., 242
Harvard University, 16, 17, 32
Hawks, Captain Frank, 242
Hays, Will H., 135, 242
Hearing Is Believing (Heiner), 296
Hearst's Cosmopolitan, 203
Hearst's International and Cosmopolitan, 202, 295
Hearst's Magazine, 78, 81
Hecht, Ben, 207
Hedge, Charles L. and Julia (Agnes's parents), 17
Heiner, Marie (Hays), 296
Heir Not Apparent (Finstad), 326
Hell's Angels (film), 194, 204, 205, 216
Hepburn, Katharine, 257
Herbert, Hugh, 299
Herbert, Joseph, 38
Hersholt, Jean, 124, 203, 298, 299
His Fabulous Fortune (RH book), 274
Historians' History of the World, 30, 32, 42, 174
History of the New York Stage, A, 21
His Wife and His Work (RH film), 67
Hitler, Adolf, 249
H. K. Fly Company, 52
H. Livermore, Inc., 215
Hoffman, Arthur, 37
Hold Your Horses (RH film), 111
Holland, John, 205
Hollywood; Anti-Nazi League, 249: Morality of, 125, 126; Roosevelt Hotel in, 206: Ten, 291

Hollywood Citizen-News, 315, 320
Hollywood Plays (book), 212
Hollywood Reporter, 290
Hollywood Writers' Wars, The (Schwartz), 247
Holmes, Burton, 312
Hoover, Herbert, 225, 227, 241, 241, 242, 312
Hope, Bob, 299
Hope, Gloria, 124
Hopkins, Arthur, 109
Hopper, E. Mason, 111, 115, 118
Hopper, Hedda, 140, 289, 199
Home Book of Modern Verse, The (Stevenson), 316
Houghton Mifflin, 263
House Un-American Activities Committee, 289-292
House-Warven, Publishers, 296, 305, 308, 313
Houston, Texas, 2, 42-43, 83, 103, 121, 146, 149, 165, 205, 258, 322, 324
Houstoun, Mrs. James P., 165
Howard, John Tasker, 294
Howard R. Hughes Medical Research Laboratories, 165
Howard, Roy, 246
Howe, E. W., 180
Howell, Greta Hughes (sister), 5, 17, 31 *See also* Hughes, Greta; Witherspoon, Greta
Howell, James Frederick (Greta's husband), 17, 31
Howells, William Dean, 41
Howey, Walter, 216
Hubinger, John C., 48
Hudson, Ohio, 13, 14
Hughes, Adelaide Manola Bissell (second wife), 46, 68; acting career, 45-47; co-author of screenplays, 75-76, 129, 139; illness and death, 143-145; marriage to Rupert, 46; poems of, 103-104, 132, 154-155; social life of, 53, 104, 112, 132-133, 142; voyages to Orient by, 133, 143
Hughes, Adella Prentiss (Felix's first wife), 43, 132, 142
Hughes, Agnes Wheeler Hedge (first wife), 17-18, 25, 30, 38-40
Hughes, Allene Gano (Mrs. Howard, Sr.), 43, 121

Hughes, Avis Bissell (step-daughter), 46, 53, 103, 142, 161, 194, 205, 217, 323-324, 327
Hughes, Baby (brother), 8, 218
Hughes, Charles Evans, 145
Hughes, Elizabeth Patterson Dial (third wife); background and description of, 157-159, 161, 196-197, 209, 235; illness and death, 278, 299-300, 344; married life with Rupert, 161-162, 181-185; named in estate battle, 350; reaction of Jean and Avis to, 161; writing by, 275, 277-278
Hughes, Ella Rice (first wife of Howard, Jr.), 165-166, 205
Hughes, Elspeth Hedge (daughter); birth of, 25; childhood, 30, 39, 40, 46, 103; *See also* Lapp, Elspeth Hughes
Hughes, Felix Turner (father); assisting family, 9, 17-19, 26; background and marriage, 2, 4; career of, 4-6, 8-9, 42-43, 153; civic leadership, 9, 32-33, 169; death and burial, 170, 218; disappointment with grand-son, 147-149; moves to Los Angeles, 151; Rupert's affection for, 154
Hughes, Felix (brother); background, 5, 8; career in music, 31-32, 43, 109, 142-143, 212, 232; education in Europe, 17, 31; marriages and divorce, 142, 229, 275, 295; in Los Angeles, 169, 198-199; nephew's treatment of, 1, 158, 159-160, 161; relationship with Rupert, 142-143, 216, 275, 301, 313, 317-319
Hughes, Greta (sister), 5, 17 *See also* Howell, Greta; Witherspoon, Greta
Hughes, Howard Robard, Sr. (brother); at Rupert's brunches, 133; birth of, 5; death of, 146; early life, 11-12, 17, 32; in oil business, 32, 322; inventions, 43-44, 82-83; marriage, 43; son disregards terms of will, 2, 147-148; wife's death, 121

Hughes, Howard Robard, Jr. (nephew); birth and early life of, 5, 32, 43, 83, 103, 121, 134; aviation records, 252-253, 257-258; control of Hughes Tool by, 2, 43, 148, 151-152; death of, 322; estate battle, 40, 322-327; marriages and divorces, 165, 207, 321; motion picture career, 166-167, 194, 204-207, 216, 217; parents' deaths, 133, 146; and Rupert, 1-4, 122-123, 133-150, 252-253, 257, 321; strange life of, 321-327

Hughes, Jean (baby sister), 6, 218

Hughes, Jean Amelia Summerlin (mother), 175; encourage-ment of offspring, 5-8; and grandson Howard, 2, 43, 158-159; grief expressed, 146-147; illness and death, 198, 217-218; marriage, 4, 154; move to Los Angeles, 151; Rupert's letters to, 112-114, 120, 132, 141, 148-149, 158, 198; tributes from Rupert, 154, 295

Hughes, Lloyd, 124

Hughes, Marion Harris (Mrs. Rush), 142, 200

Hughes, Reginald (brother), 5, 6, 218

Hughes, Robert C., 325

Hughes, Ruby Helen (McCoy) Parrott (Felix's third wife), 276, 280, 292, 299, 301, 307, 312-315, 317-319

Hughes, Rupert; and Adelaide's suicide, 144-145; biographies, writing of, 174-175, 187, 200; birth of, 5; books by. See individual listings; capital punishment, opposition to, 194-195 ; censorship, opposition to, 85-86, 108-109, 125, 221; Communism, opposition to, 248, 249, 264-265, 292-293, 330-331; charities supported by, 68, 99, 69, 300; deafness, 88, 109, 229-230, 296, 314; descriptions of, 7, 13, 36, 80, 96, 128, 135, 186, 190, 219, 222, 228, 236, 251, 314-315; divorce, from Agnes, 38-40; views on, 79-80, 139-140, 226-227; early career; as reporter,

17, 18, 19; editor, 18, 21, 30, 44; with Storiettes, 18; with world history, 30, 32, 34, 42; earnings, 45, 65, 96, 102, 104, 117, 119, 121, 136, 142, 210, 229, 236, 339, 344; highest paid story writer, 78; highest paid screen-writer, 128; education of, 9, 11-14; Adelbert College, 14-16, 19; St. Charles College, 11-13; Western Reserve Academy, 13-14; Yale University, 13-16, 28; Elspeth, affection for, 40, 278, 281, 293; Eminent Authors and, 94-95, 98, 110, 114; films associated with. See individual listings; George Washington, biography and articles about, 174-175, 179, 186-188, 215, 220-222, 226, 231, 286, 296, 307-309, 316-320, 330, 331; correspondence about, 173, 179, 307, 319; speeches about, 172, 185, 201-202, 209, 210, 179; plans for fourth volume, 225, 253, 306-307,; Hollywood, defense of, 185; honors and recognition, 111-112, 149, 215, 219-220, 223, 243, 326, 330, 335-336, 353; honorary degree, 212, 243-244; testimonial dinner, 297-298; illness and death of, 315, 317-319; international affairs, views on, 107-108, 263-264; marriage, views on, 76, 226-227; marriages, 17-18, 46, 159; military career, 71, 76-77, 80, 89, 93, 94, 169-180; with California State Guard, 269, 271, 298; as military censor, 85-93; with National Guard, 25, 26, 27, 47, 71, 76-81; music; books and articles about, 29-30, 36-37, 48, 116-119; compositions by, 14, 17, 116, 119, 295; education in, 15, 27, 31; as musician, 13, 14, 290-291; Nazis, opposition to, 239-54; patriotism of, 292, 319; Patterson's death and, 279-280; plays by. See individual listings; poetry by, 16, 26, 27, 33, 74, 94, 122-124, 317-318, 327; public

speaking, 13-14, 15, 16, 65-67, 75, 81, 96, 111, 128, 171, 201-202, 209, 220, 226-227, 242, 245, 250, 265, radio and television, 227, 255, 258, 266-268, 317, 331; Camel Caravan emcee, 249-251; as commentator, 291-292, 297, 298, 301, 302-303, 305; religion, 9, 12, 13, 18-19, 33, 173-174, 208-209, 337-338; controversy over, 166-168, 171-174, 178, 238-239, 331-332; residences, 5, 6, 325; Bedford Hills, 57, 59, 67-68; Los Feliz Boulevard (Arabian Nights home), 193-197, 325, 327, 353-354; Western Avenue, 115, 131; sleep and work habits, 43, 134, 219; smoking, views on, 18, 41, 215; success of Excuse Me, 555-56; success of The Old Nest, 60-61; and Will Rogers, 202, 255, 257-259; women's rights and abilities, views on, 29, 61, 72, 79, 215, 245, 273-274, 292; writers, assistance to, 101, 189, 207-208, 226-227, 241; writers, controversies with, 97, 261-265, 309-311; writers' organizations, 73, 213, 228-229, 237-238, 248, 306

Hughes, Rush Bissell (stepson); career in films and radio, 122, 126, 213, 276; childhood of, 46, 53, 103; personal life, 142, 200, 213; question of adoption, 53, 130, 327; role in estate battle, 323, 327

Hughes, Ruth Stonehouse (Felix's second wife), 216, 276

Hughes Tool Company, 2, 43, 146, 148, 165

Humanist (magazine), 307, 313

Humphrey, Marmaduke (pseudonym), 27

Huneker, James G., 27, 28, 64, 79, 82

Huntington, Henry E., 164

Hurst, Fannie, 137

Hussay, George, 312

Huston, Walter, 299

Hutchinson & Co., Ltd., 178

Illinois School for the Blind, 268

In a Blaze of Glory (RH novel), 274, 284
In a Little Town (RH stories), 77
Independent (magazine), 54, 58
Ingersoll, Robert G., 156
Inspiration Pictures, 205
In the Midst of Life (RH play), 38
Institution for the Blind, 28
International News Bureau, 49
International Press Bureau, 233, 253
Inquisition in Hollywood, The (Ceplair and Englund), 247
Iowa; Homecoming of Iowa Authors, 69; Press and Authors' Club, 69; State University of, 32; University of, Iowa Authors Collection, 202, 302, 330
Irwin, Will, 59

Jablonski, Edward, 30
James, Louis, 38
Jarrolds, 233, 253, 274, 284
Jeanne Greta, 31, 74. *See also* Hughes, Greta
Jessel, George, 299
Jessup, Alexander, 223
Job, The (Lewis), 84
Johanna Enlists (RH film), 81, 125
John C. Winston Company, 311
John Muth (RH novel), 18
Johnson, Eric, 299
Johnson, R. U., 25
Jolson, Al, 199
Joplin, Mo., 32
Judge, Arline, 251

Kabah-Adventures in the Jungles of Yucatan (RH foreword), 308
Karloff, Boris, 243
Kaufman, Albert, 93
Keble School, 17
Kelland, Clarence Budington, 287, 299
Kelley, Edgar Stilman, 28
Kemper, Collin, 38
Kennedy, Madge, 96
Keokuk, Iowa, 5-8, 11, 13, 17, 32, 42-43, 49, 55-56, 136, 151, 168, 170
Keokuk and Western Division, Burlington System, 8, 42
Keokuk & Western Railroad, 7, 42
Kern, Jerome, 76, 89

Kerr, Russell, 261, 294, 303, 316
Kerr, Sophie, 165
Kid, The (Chaplin film), 97
Kindel & Anderson, 322
King, Basil, 95
King, Henry, 205
King, Marian, 195
Kipling, Rudyard, 22
Kirby, A. M., 145
Kleine, George, 67, 75
Knickerbocker Theater, 69
Knollenberg, Bernhard, 271
Koontz, Louis Knott, 226
Krohn, Ernst C., 155

Ladies' Man (RH novel, film), 212, 213, 214
Lady Who Smoked Cigars, The (RH novel), 61, 301
Laemmle, Carl, 249
Lakerim Athletic Club, The (RH book for boys), 7, 22-23
Lakerim Cruise, The (RH book for boys), 49
Lakerim stories, 284, 303, 311
Lakewood, Ohio, 220
La Marr, Barbara, 126
Lamb, The (film), 69
Lambs, The, 322, 332
Lancaster, Mo., 4, 5, 6, 56, 214, 329
Landau, Richard, 308
Landis, Cullen, 124
Lang, Fritz, 249
La Plante, Laura, 122
Lapp, Edward John (son-in-law), 141, 151, 220, 278, 280, 283-284
Lapp, Elspeth Hedge Hughes (daughter); illness and death of, 278, 283, 304; letters and visits from father, 220, 227, 275, 278, 281-283; marriage and family, 141-142, 151, 158, 169, 207; named in estate battle, 318-320, 325-326; *See also* Hughes, Elspeth Hedge
La Rue, Jack, 224, 233
La Shelle, Kirke, 38
Lasky, Jesse L., 89, 235, 298, 312
Lasky, Jesse, Jr., 271
Last Rose of Summer, The (RH novel), 61, 316
Lauria, Lew, 298
Lauria, Mrs. Lew, 299
Lavery, Emmet, 288, 290
Lawler, Emmett (Tully), 135

Lawrence, Edmund, 203
Lawrence, Walter N., 42
Lawson, John Howard, 248-249, 290, 292
L. C. Page & Company, 29, 36, 49
Ledwidge, Frances, 116
LeRoy, Baby, 224, 225, 233
LeRoy, Mervyn, 167
Lester, Kate, 124, 129
Leutner, W. G., 244
Levien, Sonya, 224
Levine, Nat, 237
Lewis, Rev. John, Jr., 17
Lewis, Sinclair, 68, 84, 215, 307
Liberty (magazine), 155; lists greatest authors, 224; RH articles in, 252, 255, 264, 270; RH co-author of novels in, 237, 263, 265; RH stories in, 155
Library of Congress, 34, 210, 225
Lichtig, Harry (agent), 296, 308
Life (magazine), 15, 21, 52
Lindbergh, Charles A., 189, 233
Lioness, The (RH play), 71
Lippert, Robert L., 308
Lippincott's (magazine), 214
Literary Digest, 49
Literary Digest International Book Review, 138, 152
Little Rock Public Library, 180
Living Authors, 214
Lombard, Carole, 217, 223
London, Jack, 69
London, England, 30-31, 38, 44, 52
London Times, 168
Long, Ray, 64, 73, 223, 224, 230
Long Ever Ago (RH book, stories), 87, 88, 120, 169
Look Your Best (RH film), 120, 129, 130
Lorimer, George Horace, 68, 164
Los Angeles Chamber of Commerce, 261
Los Angeles Evening Herald & Express, 312
Los Angeles Examiner, 226, 298, 320, 330
Los Angeles Times, 77, 84, 142, 154, 182, 238, 279, 297, 298, 299, 302, 320, 329
Los Feliz Improvement Association, 185, 329
Lothrop Publishing Company, 36

367

Love Affairs of Great Musicians (RH book), 36
Lovely Ducklings, The (RH novel), 197
Love Song (RH novel), 232-233
Lowe, E. T., 110
Lowell, Amy, 117
Loy, Myrna, 243
Lubin, Sigmund, 81
Lugosi, Bela, 243
Lummis, Annette Gano (aunt of Howard Hughes, Jr.), 121, 146, 165, 322, 324
Lummis, Frederick Rice (Annette's husband), 146
Lummis, William Rice (cousin of Howard Hughes, Jr.), 320, 322
Lyon, Ben, 204

McCarey, Leo, 289
McCarthy, Joseph, 291
McClure, Phillips & Company, 35
McCormick, John, 130
McCormick, Virginia, 117
McCutcheon, George Barr, 59
McFarren of the FBI (RH novel), 308
McGuinness, James Kevin, 248, 289
McIntyre, Avis Hughes. *See* Hughes, Avis
McIntyre, O. O., 229
McNaught Syndicate, 189, 232
McOmie, Margaret, 182, 235
Macy, John Albert, 214
M'lle New York (magazine), 27-28
Madison, Cleo, 153
Maltin, Leonard, 224, 225, 251
Maltz, Alfred, 314
Man Between, The (RH play), 48, 49, 59
Man That Might Have Been, The (RH film and story), 60, 77
Mantle, Burns, 21
Manuscripters of Los Angeles, 306
Man Without a Home, The (RH novel), 236
March, Fredric, 243, 249
Marion, Frances, 299
Marion, George F., 68
Mark Twain Society, 197, 253, 294
Marlowe, Julia, 45
Marquand, John P., 259
Marsh, Mae, 66

Masquers, The, 298
Masson, T. L., 138
Maugham, W. Somerset, 97, 215
Maurice, Arthur B., 114, 138
Mayer, Louis B., 186, 189, 298
Mayo, Archie, 167
Melville, Herman, 167
Memphis, Mo., 4
Mencken, H. L., 37, 245, 288
Mendes, Catulle, 116
Mendes, Lothar, 217
Menjou, Adolphe, 289, 290
Men Who Make Our Novels, The, 106
Meredith, Charles, 110
Mermaid and Centaur (RH novel), 201
Merwin, Samuel, 108
Methodist Episcopal Church, 108, 196
Metro-Goldwyn-Mayer, 157, 162, 162, 167, 216, 246
Metro Pictures Corporation, 65, 68
Metropolitan (magazine), 61, 88
Metropolitan Opera, 31, 78, 143
Meyer, C. F., 145
"Michaeleen! Michaelawn!" (RH story), 89, 169, 189
Middleditch, E. T., 127
Milestone, Lewis, 204, 207, 216
Military Intelligence Branch, General Staff, U. S. A., 85
Miller, Patsy Ruth, 123
Milton H. Berry Institute, 222, 239
Minter, Mary Miles, 125
Miss Fane's Baby Is Stolen (RH film), 233-234
Mississippi River, 6, 8, 11, 18, 32, 77, 105, 168
Missouri, a Guide to the "Show Me" State, 272
Missouri, Iowa & Nebraska Railway Company, 6, 8
Missouri Writers Guild, 137
Miss 318, (RH book, story), 53-57
Miss 318 (RH vaudeville sketch), 59
Miss 318 and Mr. 37 (RH book, story), 57-58
Mix, Tom, 189, 243
"Mobilizing of Johanna, The" (RH story), 85
Moffat, Yard and Company, 49
Moffitt, John Charles, 290

Momma, and Other Unimportant People (RH book of stories), 105
Money Talks (RH film), 167
Montgomery, Robert, 299
Mooney, Tom, 216
Moore, Colleen, 119-120, 122-123, 128-130, 134, 166, 216, 292, 327
Moore, Owen, 167
Moore, Tom, 111, 118
Moore, Victor, 299
Moreno, Antonio, 129
Morgan, Ralph, 299
Morris, Chester, 223
Morris, Gouverneur, 63, 95
Morris, William, 42
Morrow, William, 174
Motion Picture Magazine, 128, 206
Motion Picture Producers and Distributors Association, 135, 291
Mould, Henry Scrivener and Marion, 45
Mount Kisco, N.Y., 60
"Mouth of the Gift Horse, The" (RH story), 48-49, 77
Moving Picture World, 95
Motion Picture Alliance for the Preservation of American Ideals, 289
Mowbray, Alan, 299
Mrs. Budlong's Christmas Presents (RH story, book), 56
Mrs. Osborne's Playhouse, 38
Munsey's Magazine, 19, 72
Murray & Gee, Inc., 295
Museum of Modern Art, 330
Musical America (magazine), 116
Musical Courier (magazine), 27, 117
Musical Guide, The (RH book), 35, 36, 58
Musical Record (magazine), 29
Music Lovers' Cyclopedia (RH book), 58, 261
Music Lovers' Encyclopedia (RH, Taylor, Kerr), 261, 267, 294, 303, 316
My Boy (RH play), 47

Nagel, Conrad, 162, 240
Nation (magazine), 57, 58, 72, 187, 244
National Association of the Motion Picture Industry, 108
National Cathedral School, 278

National Conference of Christians and Jews, 222
National Cyclopedia of American Biography, 33
National Genealogical Society Quarterly, 324
National Institute of Arts and Letters, 83-84
National Recovery Administration (NRA), 228-229, 247
National Republican Club, 109
NEA Service, 304
Negri, Pola, 235, 299
Neilan, Marshall,93, 96, 119, 126, 204
Nelson, Donald M., 298-299
Nevins, Allan, 180
New McClure's (magazine), 197
New Orleans, 8, 42, 46
New Republic, 72, 90
New Willard Hotel, 171
New Yorker, 264, 304
New York Herald, 44, 114, 138
New York Herald Tribune, 54, 86, 97, 180, 187, 201, 220, 221, 224
New York Journal, 17-18, 217, 234
New York News, 297
New York Post, 72, 106, 225
New York Public Library, 87
New York Times; Adelaide Hughes, review of book by, 104; articles and essays by RH, 98, 100, 107, 106, 114, 164; editorials about RH, 93, 182; features about RH, 63-68, 80, 118, 238; letter from RH to, 183-104; news about RH, 38-39, 63, 154-155, 181-182, 191, 212, 213, 221, 266, 300, 312, 344; RH books reviewed, 36, 37, 49, 54, 56, 73, 77, 86, 88, 90, 96-97, 149, 166, 173-174, 187-188, 199-200, 222, 225, 237, 251, 277, 282, 286, 326, 330; RH films reviewed, 75, 112, 113, 122, 131, 132, 150, 164, 173, 206, 216, 219, 236, 248, 252; RH plays reviewed, 20, 42, 46, 47, 59
New York Tribune, 145, 164
New York World, 138, 187, 198
Nissen, Greta, 204
Non-Sense of Censorship (film), 108, 118

No One Man (RH novel, film), 213, 223
Normand, Mabel, 97, 125
Nugent, Frank S., 238

Oakie, Jack, 250-251
O'Brien, Edward J., 88, 105, 155, 169
O'Brien, Pat, 298-300
O'Day, Molly, 194
O. Henry, 28
O. Henry Memorial Award Prize Stories of 1929, 202
Olcott, Sidney, 110
Old Folks at Home, The (RH film), 81, 11, 118
Old Home Town, The (RH novel), 168
Old Ironsides (film), 167
Old Nest, The (RH book, film), 55-56, 111-115, 124, 162
Olerich, W. F., 181
Oliver Ditson Company, 34
One Hundred Best Novels Condensed, 105
O'Neil, Sally, 167, 194, 203
On the Razor Edge (RH play), 214
On the Road to Yorktown (RH play, book), 222
Ornitz, Sam, 249
Osborn, E. W., 138
Our American Music (Howard), 294, 316
Oursler, Fulton, 237, 259, 263
Outlook (magazine), 37
Out of the Ruins (RH film), 68
Overton, Grant, 197, 202

Pacific Historical Review, 226
Paderewski, Ignace, 69, 111, 138
Page, Anita, 199
Page, Gale, 295
Palmer, Jaime, 312
Palmer Institute of Authorship, 228
Paramount, 89, 168, 203, 213, 217, 224, 233
Paramount-Artcraft, 110
Paramount Publix, 223
Paramount Theater, 217, 223
Paris, France, 30, 56, 63, 152, 211, 257
Parker, Dorothy, 249
Parker, Sir Gilbert, 97
Parris, Albion, 171
Parsons, Louella, 45, 299

Patent Leather Kid, The (RH film), 193-194, 206
Patent Leather Kid, The (RH story, book), 193-194, 296, 308
Paterson, N. J., 53
Patrick, John, 167
Payne, John Howard, 236
Pearson's (magazine), 48
Pelswick, Rose, 217, 234
Peoria, Ill., 5
Perch of the Devil (RH play), 77
Perkins, Maxwell E.,257-260, 263, 267, 268, 273-274, 277-278
Pershing, General John J., 76, 91
Peters, Jean (second wife of Howard Hughes, Jr.), 321
Petrova, Olga, 65
Phelps, William Lyon, 73, 83, 84, 85, 90
Phi Beta Kappa, 16
Phillips, Lew, 224
Photoplay Authors' League, 247
Photoplay Plot Encyclopedia, 98
Pickford, Mary, 67, 68, 81, 113, 124, 186, 189, 224, 240, 299
Pitts, ZaSu, 126
"Plea for Frankness in Writing History" (RH essay), 188
Poe, Edgar Allan, 19
Poems of Adelaide Manola, 154
Poems of Today, 155
Poetry Society, 104
Poland, 108, 138
Pollock, Channing, 68, 101
Pond, James B. (agent), 105, 110
Porter, Edwin S., 67
Post, Guy Bates, 47
Post, Wiley, 239-240
Powell, Dick, 243
Powell, William, 217-218
President's Mystery, The (RH film, novel), 237, 251
Preston, John Hyde, 236
Pringle, Aileen, 153, 312
Progress (magazine), 260
Progressive Party, 293
Propaganda, analysis of, 89
Prussing, Eugene E., 201, 226
Publishers' Weekly, 211
Puck (magazine), 62
Pullman cars, 51-52
Puritans, 29
Raft, George, 251
Raleigh, Henry, 90
Ralston, Esther, 124, 168
Rascoe, Burton, 90, 245-246, 260

Ray Long and Richard R. Smith, Inc., 224
Reagan, Ronald, 289
Real New York, The (RH novel), 37
Red Book (magazine), 44, 64-65, 73, 76, 83, 100, 197, 206, 223
Reed, Luther, 204
Relyea, C. M., 23, 28
Remembrance (RH film), 123-124, 234
Reno (RH film), 139-140, 157
"Rented Body, The" (RH story), 202, 223
Representative Modern Short Stories, 223
Republicans, 190, 229
Republic Pictures, 237
Reserve, The (yearbook), 15
Reserve Record, 227
Reynolds, Agnes Hedge. *See* Hughes, Agnes Hedge
Reynolds, William Herbert (second husband of Agnes), 38, 40, 141
Rice, Grantland, 116
Richest Girl in the World, The (RH play), 42
Rickenbacker, Eddie, 242
Ricksen, Lucille (Ericksen), 112, 162
Ricksen, Marshall (Ericksen), 112, 162
A Riley Album (RH song book), 34
Riley, James Whitcomb, 34
Rinehart, Mary Roberts, 95
RKO Studios, 321
Robbins Music Corporation, 265
Roberts, Agnes Christine Lapp (granddaughter), 151, 275, 278, 324
Roberts, George W. (husband of Agnes Christine), 275
Roberts, Ilka, 185, 219, 223, 227
Robertson, John S., 124
Robeson, Paul, 243
Robinson, Bill, 243
Robson, May, 243
Rogers, Betty Blake (Mrs. Will Rogers), 240
Rogers, Charles (Buddy), 194, 299
Rogers, Ginger, 257
Rogers, Howard Emmett, 248, 289
Rogers, Will, 178, 189-191, 231-232, 238-243, 306

Romero, Cesar, 243, 308
Rooney, Mickey, 243
Roosevelt, Franklin Delano, 225-228, 237, 273, 281, 292
Roosevelt, Theodore, 87, 101
Rotarian (magazine), 294
Rothapfel, S. L., 110
"Roustabout, The" (RH song), 116
Royal Vistas (RH, Van Royhl), 308
Russell, Rosalind, 250
Russell, R. H., 33

Sadie (RH play), 59
St. Charles, Mo.: College at; 11-13, 254; *Cosmos-Monitor*, 254; Opera House, 12, 20; Proposal to honor Hughes at, 329
St. George's Episcopal Church, 17
St. Johns, Adela Rogers, 194, 233
St. Louis Life (magazine), 21
St. Nicholas (magazine), 22-23, 28, 303
Samuel French, Inc., 214, 233
Sandburg, Carl, 116, 117, 138, 147
Saturday Evening Post; Hollywood, articles about, 234; stories by RH, 48, 54-56, 60, 67, 68, 77, 164, 167, 234, 307
Saturday Review of Literature, 180, 213, 259
Saunders, Avis Hughes. *See* Hughes, Avis
Saunders, John Monk (Avis's first husband), 104, 142, 194, 205, 207, 216, 217
Savage, Henry W., 51, 52, 59, 68
Saved by Parcel Post (film), 59
Schenck, Joseph M., 81, 164, 299, 300
Schindler, Raymond, 299, 303, 304, 312
Scholastic (magazine), 275
Schuberth, Edward, & Company, 34
Schumann-Heink, Ernestine, 31, 242
Schwab, Arnold T., 28
Schwartz, Nancy Lynn, 247
Schweitzer, Albert, 307
Scott, Leroy, 101
Scratch My Back (RH film), 110-111

Screen Playwrights, 263, 264
Screen Writers Guild, 2646-248, 287-291
Scribner's (magazine), 18, 22, 28, 55, 201
Sea Beast, The (film), 167
Second St. Nicholas Anthology, 303
Seitz, Don C., 187
Serao, Mathilde, 38
Shakespeare, William, 7, 15
Sharp-Hughes Tool Company, 43
Sharp, Walter, 43
Shearer, Norma, 162, 186, 235
She Borrowed Her Own Husband (RH play), 44
She Goes to War (RH film), 205-206
She Goes to War, and Other Stories (RH book), 206
Sheldon, Edward, 84
Shelley, Mary Godwin, 236
Sheridan House, 304
Shippey, Lee, 238, 260, 297, 299
Shipton, Clifford K., 256, 257
Short Plays for Modern Players, 214
"Show of Shows," 241-243
Sigma Tau Sigma, 306
Sixty-Ninth Regiment, 26, 71, 76, 77
Skipworth, Alison, 224
Skull and Bones, 19
Sloane, Paul, 224
Smart Set Publishing Company, 36
Smart Set (magazine), 36, 37
Smith, Adele, 198
Smith, Alfred E., 227, 241
Smith, Edward J., 311
Smith, Wilson G., 15
Smith's (magazine), 48
Smoke of Battle (Chambers), 260
Sobel, Robert, 291
Sojin, 203
Songs by Thirty Americans (RH song book), 34-35
Sons of the Revolution, 171, 173, 174
Souls for Sale (RH book, film), 125, 126, 127, 128, 129, 138, 312
Spaeth, Sigmund, 272
Spalding, Lyman, 39
Spanish-American War, 27
Sparks, Rev. Jared, 174
Spencer, Shirley, 236
Spindletop oil discovery, 32

Spiritualism, 105
Sprague, Chandler, 164
Springfield Republican, 57, 90, 304
Standard Index of Short Stories, 60
Stanwyck, Barbara, 243
Stash (Waldo), 101
State Historical Society of Missouri, 137
Stately Timber (RH novel), 256-257, 259-260
Static (RH novel), 222, 295
Statish Language, 107
Steele, James B., 128
Stephenson, Nathaniel W., 187, 226
Steuben Society, 264
Stevenson, Burton, 316
Stevenson, Robert L., 22
Stewart, Donald Ogden, 249
"Stick-in-the Muds, The" (RH story), 105, 197
Stockbridge, Fanny, 122
Stone, Fred, 242, 298
Storiettes (magazine), 18-19
Story of Holly Sloan, The (RH, soap opera), 295
Stotesbury, General Louis W., 78
Street, Julian, 60, 101, 236
Sturges, Preston, 299
Subscription Books Bulletin, 262
Summa Corporation, 322
Sunday brunch, 131, 133, 134
Swanson, Gloria, 299
Sweatnam, Willis P., 52
Sweeney (Hughes's secretary), 55
Sweet, Blanche, 93, 126
Swell Hogan (film), 166
Syracuse, N.Y., 47, 49

Taeusch, H. W., 244
Talmadge, Norma, 81, 164
Tamiment Social and Economic Institute, 302
Taylor, Deems, 261, 294, 303, 316
Taylor, Robert, 250, 289
Taylor, William Desmond, 125
Teachers Are People (RH foreword), 285
Teasdale, Sara, 116
Temple, Shirley, 242-243
Tess of the Storm Country (films), 53, 67, 223-224
Tess of the Storm Country (RH play), 53, 65
Tewson, W. Orton, 168

Thalberg, Irving, 186
There Were Giants in the Land, 272
Thief of Bagdad, The (film), 182
Thirteenth Commandment, The (RH novel, film), 72-72, 81, 110
This Week (magazine), 236, 275
Thomas, Augustus, 68
Thomas, J. Parnell, 289, 291
Thompson, Dorothy, 288
Thompson, Vance, 27
Thompson, William Hale, 188
Thousandth Girl, The (RH novel), 253
Three Stooges, 243
Thwing, Charles F., 53, 115, 211-212, 220, 243-244
Tibbett, Lawrence, 142-143, 215, 299
Tillie and Gus (RH film), 224
Tol'able David (film), 157
Tommy Rot (RH play), 38
Toohey, John P., 100
Toot-Toot! (musical based on RH *Excuse Me*), 89
Torrence, Ridgely, 116
Totter, Audrey, 308
Towne, Charles Hanson, 60, 99
Tracy, Spencer, 243
Transformation, The (RH play), 47, 49
Trans World Airlines, 321
Tree, Sir Herbert Beerbohm, 81, 111
Triangle, The (RH play), 42, 64
Triangle Film Corporation, 81
Trinity Pictures, 203
Triumphant Clay, The (RH novel), 304-306
True as Steel (RH film), 146, 153
True Lover's Knot (RH), 253
Truman, Harry S., 281, 282, 293
Trumbo, Dalton, 292
Truth Seeker Company, 156, 162
Tucker, Sophie, 243
Tully, Jim, 135, 152, 195
Twain, Mark, 8, 18, 22, 41, 175, 197, 235, 253, 277, 294, 312
20 Best Short Stories in Ray Long's 20 Years as Editor, 223
Twentieth Century-Fox, 224, 242, 251
Two Women (RH play), 49-50, 59, 81
Tyler, George D., 77

Uncle Zeb (RH play), 59
United Artists, 113, 206
Universal Pictures, 203
University of Southern California, 228, 234, 260, 306, 330
Unpardonable Sin, The (RH book, film), 83, 86-87, 90, 93-94
Uphill Road, The (RH novel), 222

Valentino, Rudolph, 235
Vallee, Rudy, 242
Van Dine, S. S., 237
Van Doren, Carl, 136-137
Van Loan, Charles E., 101
Van Wormer, Grace, 302
Variety, 110, 113, 120, 122-123, 127, 139-140, 224, 250, 306
Veiller, Bayard, 224
Vein of Gold, The (RH play), 71
Verier, Edward, 307
Vidor, Florence, 126
Vidor, King, 126, 134, 185, 186, 289
Viereck, George Sylvester, 164
Vignola, Roger G., 110
Villa, Pancho, 76
Vitagraph, 60, 67
von Stroheim, Erich, 126

Waite, Frederick, 14, 227
Wagner, Rob, 97
Waldo, Harold, 100
Walker, Charlotte, 42, 100
Walker, Danton, 297
Wallace, Henry, 293
Wallace, Margaret, 217, 233, 236, 259, 268
Waller, Dr. Lorenz M. (doctor), 319
Wall Flower, The (RH film), 119-123
Walsh, George, 139
Wanger, Walter, 217, 289
Warde, Frederick, 38
Warner Brothers, 167, 229, 290
Warner, Jack, 167, 229, 249, 289, 298, 299, 312
War of the Mayan King, The (RH juvenile book), 311
Warren, Earl, 288, 298-300
Washington, George. *See* Hughes, Rupert
Washington, John, 172
Washington, D. C.,34, 46, 84-87, 89-90, 139, 141, 151, 169, 171
Washington Herald, 194
Waters, Safford, 38

Watson, Brig. Gen. LeRoy H., 298
Wayne, John, 289
Webb, Millard, 167
We Can't Have Everything (RH book, film), 76, 78, 79, 89
Weems, Parson (Mason L.), 176, 188
We Live but Once (RH novel), 186
Wellman, Paul, 299
West, Mae, 243
West, Nathaniel, 238
West, Paul, 38
Westchester County, N. Y., 53, 136-137, 154
Western Reserve Academy, 13, 227
Western Reserve University, 13, 55, 58, 80, 115,198, 212, 220, 243-345
What Ails You? (RH play), 59
Whatever Happened to Hollywood? (Lasky, Jr.), 271
What's the World Coming To? (RH novel), 105
What Will People Say? (RH novel, film), 63-64
"When Badger Meets Con" (RH story), 27
When Crossroads Cross Again (RH story and book), 196
"When Pan Moves to Harlem" (RH story), 28-29

Whirlwind, The (RH novel), 36-38
White, Betty, 199
White, Grace Miller, 53, 67
White, Trumbull, 44
Whitewood (Hughes home), 63
Whitney, F. C., 20
Whittier, John Greenleaf, 117
Why I Quit Going to Church (RH essay, book), 155-157
Wieck, Dorothea, 233
Wilcoxon, Henry, 237
William Morrow & Company, 174, 175, 178, 186, 187, 210, 214
Williams, Jesse Lynch, 83
Will Rogers Memorial Commission, 241
Wilson, President Woodrow, 78, 83, 85, 93, 132
Winchell, Walter, 299
Windsor, Claire, 97, 126, 167
Wings (film), 194
Wisconsin Federation of Women's Clubs, 177
"With a First Reader" (RH poem), 44, 316
Witherspoon, Greta Hughes (sister), 32, 45, 78-79, 158, 246. *See also* Hughes, Greta; Howell, Greta
Witherspoon, Herbert (Greta's husband), 31, 39, 74
Within These Walls (RH novel), 137-138
Woman Accused, The (RH novel, film), 224, 237

Woman's Day (magazine), 296
Wood, Sam, 289
Wooden Wedding, The (RH play), 38, 44
Woodward, W. E., 177, 178, 180
Woolf, Edgar Allan, 89
Woollcott, Alexander, 109
World's Best Books, Homer to Hemingway, The, (Dickinson), 316
World's 50 Best Short Novels, The (Overton), 202
World's 100 Best Short Stories, The (Overton), 197
World War I, 68, 71, 78, 79, 80, 81, 83, 106, 107, 139
Wray, Fay, 142, 184
Writers, The, 203-204, 219, 221, 228, 308. *See also* Authors, The
Writers' Club, 203-204, 218, 222, 228, 238, 250. *See also* Authors' Club
Writers Round Table, The, 302
Wynn, Ed, 288
Wynne, Annette, 117
Wynne, G. W., 164

Yale Review, 134
Yale University, 13-14, 16, 18, 19 28-29, 31, 49
Young, Gordon Ray, 77, 78, 84

Zal (RH novel), 37-38, 138
Ziegfeld, Florenz, 75